Poetry of Light
Richard Pousette-Dart

MUSEUM FRIEDER BURDA

HIRMER

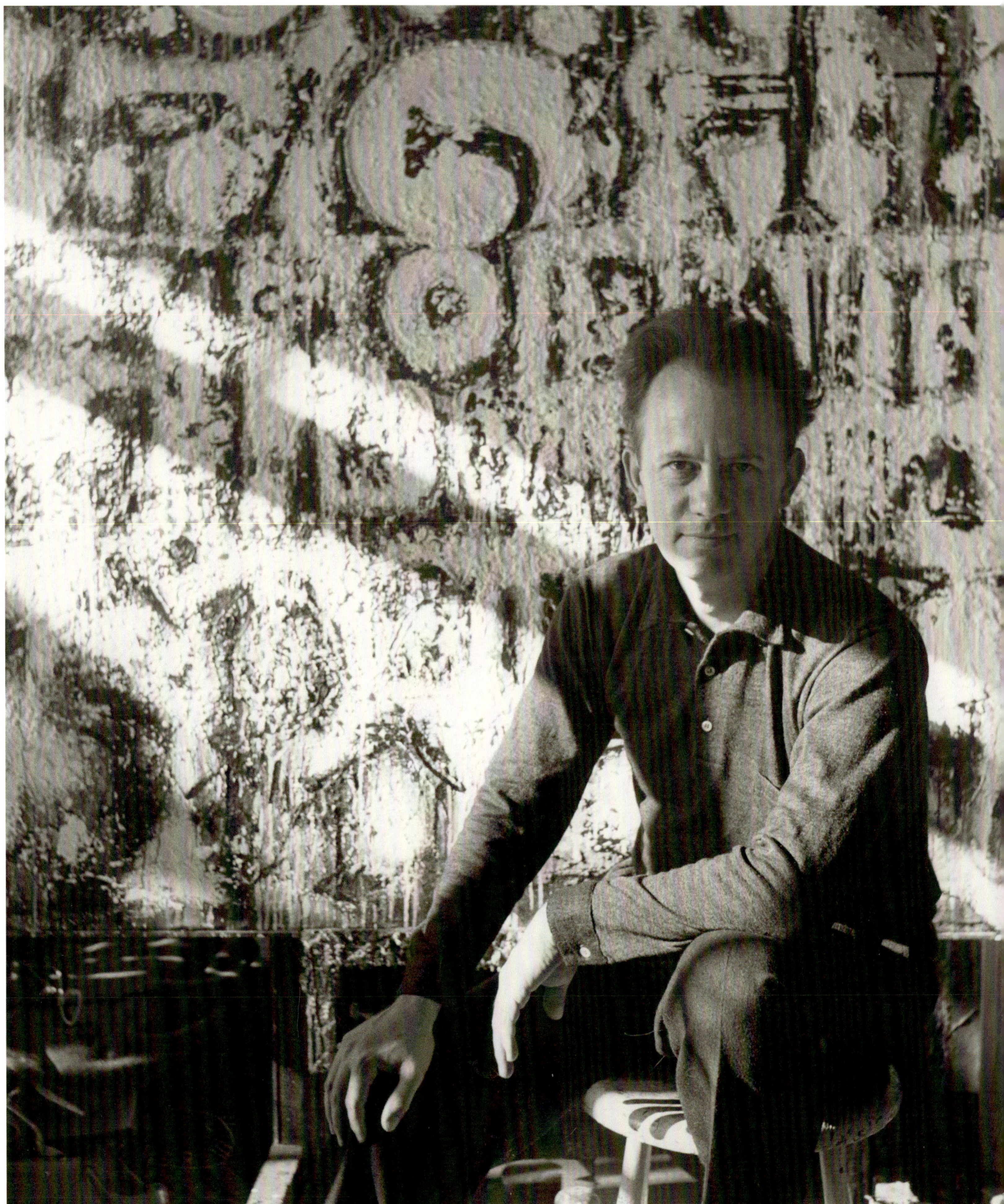

Contents

Foreword

Daniel Zamani

I strive to express the spiritual nature of the universe. Painting for me is a dynamic balance and wholeness of life; it is mysterious and transcending, yet solid and real.
– Richard Pousette-Dart, 1951

American postwar painting plays an important role in the world-class collection that our museum's founder, Frieder Burda (1936–2019), assembled with great passion and an unfailing eye for quality. A movement he was particularly fascinated by was Abstract Expressionism, which is represented in our holdings with significant works by Adolph Gottlieb, Willem de Kooning, Jackson Pollock, and Mark Rothko. Given this wider context of the collection, it seems fitting that our museum is now dedicating a major exhibition to one of the great pioneers of Abstract Expressionism, Richard Pousette-Dart (1916–1992)—a largely self-trained artist who worked in such different media as painting, sculpture, and photography and who played a significant role in the formation of the New York School in the critical juncture that the 1940s and 1950s marked in the global rise of the American avant-garde.

A key influence on Pousette-Dart's early development was the progressive cultural and intellectual environment facilitated by his parents. His mother, Flora, was a poet and writer who was a vociferous champion of feminism and whose political activism ranged from fierce advocacy for equality of the sexes to engagement for welfare and socialism. Meanwhile, Pousette-Dart's father, Nathaniel, was himself an artist and encouraged his son's experimentation with drawing and painting at an early age. As editor of the journal *Art and Artists of Today*, Nathaniel was a staunch champion of the freedom of artistic expression at a time when totalitarian systems in Germany, Italy, and the Soviet Union increasingly sought to relegate the role of art to that of a propagandist instrument. This pluralistic stance is brilliantly reflected by a drawing he published in 1938, titled *A Gestaltian Chart of Contemporary American Art* (fig. 1)—a diagram showing diverse strands of modern American painting, in which "abstract" art is given center stage, flanked by other types including "Surrealism" and "Realism" as well as "Primitive and Naive" forms of expression.

Nathaniel's insistence on the artistic need for self-expression chimed with the cultural climate of late 1930s and early 1940s New York—a hub of modern experimentation, in which avant-garde painters increasingly turned toward abstract tendencies in an effort to forge new pictorial paths. Key to this process was the engagement with progressive European painting of the interwar period, including Surrealist automatism as well as semiabstract or abstract works by artists including Henri Matisse, Pablo Picasso, and Vasily Kandinsky. Such vanguard positions were exhibited at prominent venues such as the Museum of Modern Art, which had been established in 1929 with Alfred H. Barr Jr. as its dynamic first director—and one decade later also at the Museum of Non-Objective Painting, which showcased the impressive collection of Solomon R. Guggenheim under the stewardship of art historian Hilla von Rebay. The increasing influence of European artists on the American vanguard scene was soon after dramatically heightened by the presence of numerous émigré painters, for whom New York proved a haven from Fascist persecution throughout the years of World War II. Peggy Guggenheim's gallery Art of This Century was among the many spaces in which European and American artists were exhibited side by side in a dialogue that proved to be highly fruitful for the gradual triumph of international abstraction. In addition to young protégés such as Jackson Pollock and Mark Rothko, Guggenheim was also an important early champion of Pousette-Dart, whose works she honored with a solo show in 1947.

Compositions such as Pousette-Dart's *Beneath the Sea* of 1939 (cat. 1) show close stylistic affinities with the work of Surrealist artists including André Masson and suggest an interest in European easel painting shared by many colleagues, who would soon be perceived as part of the Abstract Expressionist movement. Pousette-Dart's association with this direction in American postwar painting was fostered by his participation in the groundbreaking *9th Street Exhibition of Paintings and Sculpture*, which took place in New York in 1951, as well as his inclusion in Nina Leen's iconic portrait photograph *The Irascibles* (p. 35, fig. 1), which was featured that same year in *Life* magazine and publicly cemented the vision of the Abstract Expressionists as a radical and cohesive new force to be reckoned with. Although Pousette-Dart's contribution to postwar painting is often seen as intimately linked to his formative role within Abstract Expressionism, the artist himself was outspokenly opposed to labels and self-confidently sought to maintain the position of an outsider, forging an artistic path that was predominantly guided by intuition and a relentless joy in experimentation. Pousette-Dart's ideas about art were regularly jotted down in a myriad of small notebooks and conveyed in a more systematic manner in a speech given at the School of the Museum of Fine Arts, Boston, in 1951. There, he foregrounded the role of artistic independence and spoke of painting as a domain linked to an exploration of the invisible and the unknown. "The artist must beware of all schools, isms, creeds, or entanglements which would tend to make him other than himself," he maintained, further noting, "He must stand alone, free and open in all directions for exits and entrances, and yet with all freedom, he must be solid and real in the substance of his form."

While many of Pousette-Dart's colleagues became known for immediately recognizable signature styles—Barnett Newman for his "zip" paintings or Jackson Pollock for his "drippings"—Pousette-Dart's career was marked by constant experimentation with diverse modes of pictorial expression and spilled from painting toward media including sculpture, drawing, printmaking, and photography. Even with compositions that are chronologically not far removed from one another, it is at times hard to believe that these were crafted by one and the same hand—say if we compare works such as *Illumination Vertical* of 1958 (cat. 20), with its rigorous sense of rhythm and spatial order to a composition such as *Presence Number 3, Black* of 1969 (cat. 43), in which numerous tiny dots cover the square picture field in a brilliant example of explosive allover abstrac-

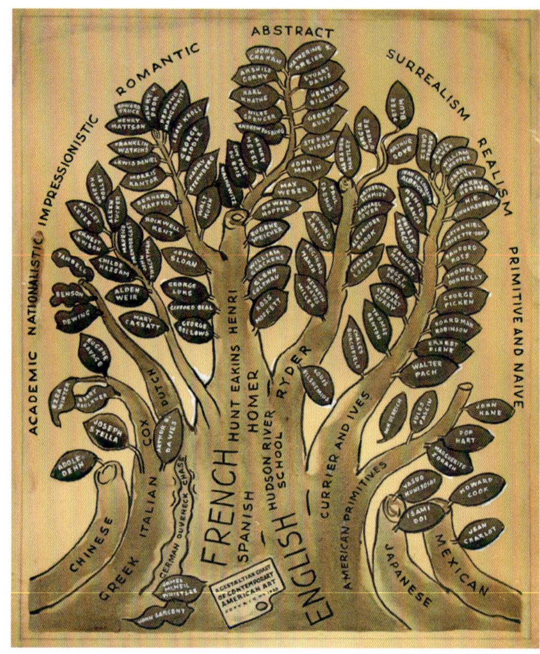

Fig. 1

Nathaniel Pousette-Dart, *A Gestaltian Chart of Contemporary American Art*, 1938, Richard Pousette-Dart Foundation

tion. A constancy in Pousette-Dart's oeuvre was his life-long fascination with the expressive qualities of light—light as glimmer and sheen, light as iridescent reflection, or light as a cosmic force related to the release of unbounded energy and the power of illumination. Such an interest particularly comes to the fore in late canvases such as a *Celebration Birth* (cat. 53) or *Lost in the Beginning of Infinity* (cat. 41), which seem to mirror celestial landscapes and which powerfully evoke the sublime beauty of the night sky. But it also already underpins earlier works such as *Window, Cathedral* (cat. 22) or *Amaranth* (cat. 23), which evidence an interest in medieval metalwork and stained glass windows, whose visual appeal strongly relies on their reflective jewel-like surfaces.

To date, the exhibition *Poetry of Light* is the largest show to be dedicated to Richard Pousette-Dart at a museum outside the United States. With over 130 loans from seventeen international collections—among them paintings, sculptures, objects, drawings, notebooks, and photographs—it offers a rich and multifaceted overview of the artist's long and productive career, spanning a chronological arch from the late 1930s through to the early 1990s. Bringing to life such a complex and opulent exhibition would have not been possible without the unwavering support of the Richard Pousette-Dart Foundation, which has helped in innumerable ways and whose director, Charles Duncan, has been key in shaping the exhibition's content, structure, and narrative from the very beginning. As co-curator of the show, I would like to thank him for both his impeccable scholarship and his great pragmatism with regard to all of the logistical and organizational challenges related to mounting an international loan exhibition of such wide-ranging scope. At the foundation in New York, my thanks are also due to Dana Martin as well as all of the members of its board. I also wish to express my heartfelt gratitude to the many members of the artist's family, who have steadfastly supported our project, among them Joanna Pousette-Dart, Jonathan Pousette-Dart, Chris Pousette-Dart, and Jason Novros.

At the Museum Frieder Burda, my sincere thanks are due to my colleagues on the executive board, Elke Burda, Dominic Kamp, and Florian Trott—and to all external members of our advisory board, Klaus-Albrecht Gerstenmaier, Bert Antonius Kaufmann, Christine Macel, Florian Schulte, and Gražina Subelytė. I would also like to thank each and every member of our museum team for their hard and diligent work behind the scenes, first and foremost the exhibition's enthusiastic and highly organized project manager, Judith Irrgang. Last but not least, I want to express my immense gratitude to all of our esteemed international lenders—both private and institutional—for parting with their beloved treasures for the duration of our show, among them the Brooklyn Museum, the Museum of Modern Art, and the Whitney Museum of American Art in New York.

In his aforementioned 1951 address in Boston, Pousette-Dart spoke of painting in staunchly poetic terms, highlighting that "Art for me is the heavens forever opening up, like asymmetrical, unpredictable, spontaneous kaleidoscopes. It is magic; it is joy; it is gardens of surprise and miracle. It is energy, impulse. It is question and answer. It is transcendental reason. It is total in its spirit." The exhibition at the Museum Frieder Burda is an invitation to embark on just such a journey through "gardens of surprise and miracle"—a joyful and fascinating dive into the artistic universe of one of the most important representatives of American postwar abstraction.

Acknowledgments

For their kind help and support in organizing the exhibition, our heartfelt thanks are due to the following people:

Amy Black, Alex Brown, Kim Conaty, Beatriz Cordero Martín, Samantha Cortez, Frank del Deo and Ben Barzune, Ursula Dix, Lucy Economakis, Stacey Epstein, Joya Erickson, Kimberli Gant, Marc Glimcher, Lily Goldberg, Otto and Kirstin Hübner, Megan Kincaid, Marissa Klein, Dustin Knittler, Amanda Kopp, Elizabeth Larghi, Jared Ledesma, Glenn D. Lowry, Dana Martin, Jennifer Mittica, Jason Novros, Anne Pasternak, Clarissa Post, Christopher Pousette-Dart, Joanna Pousette-Dart, Jonathan Pousette-Dart, Scott Rothkopf, Elayne Rush, Jillian Russo, Anna Sido, Lowery Sims, Susan Song, Barbi Spieler, Peter Stevens, Gražina Subelytė, Michele Tayler, Ann Temkin, Richard Lee Wilding, and Lucy Winokur.

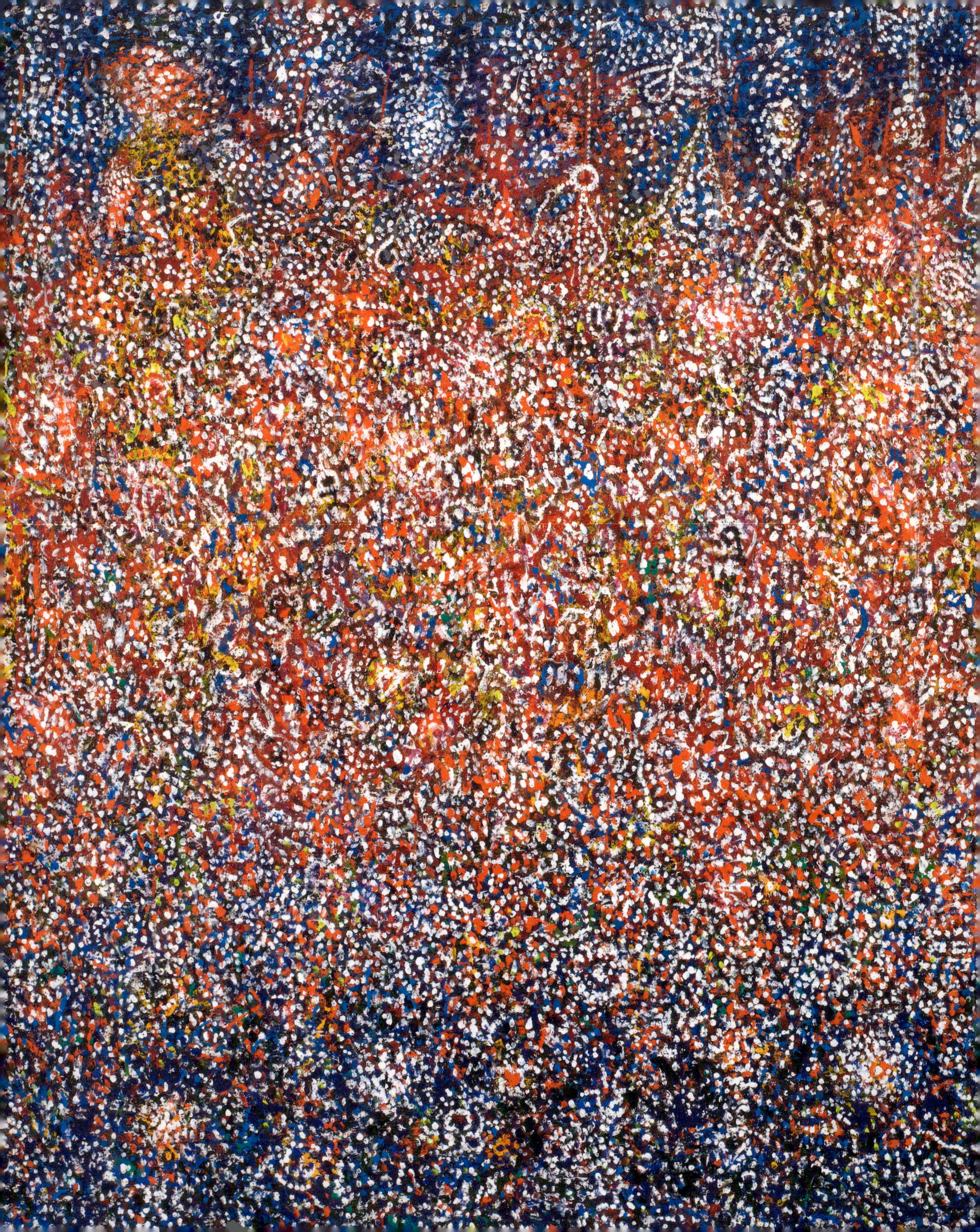

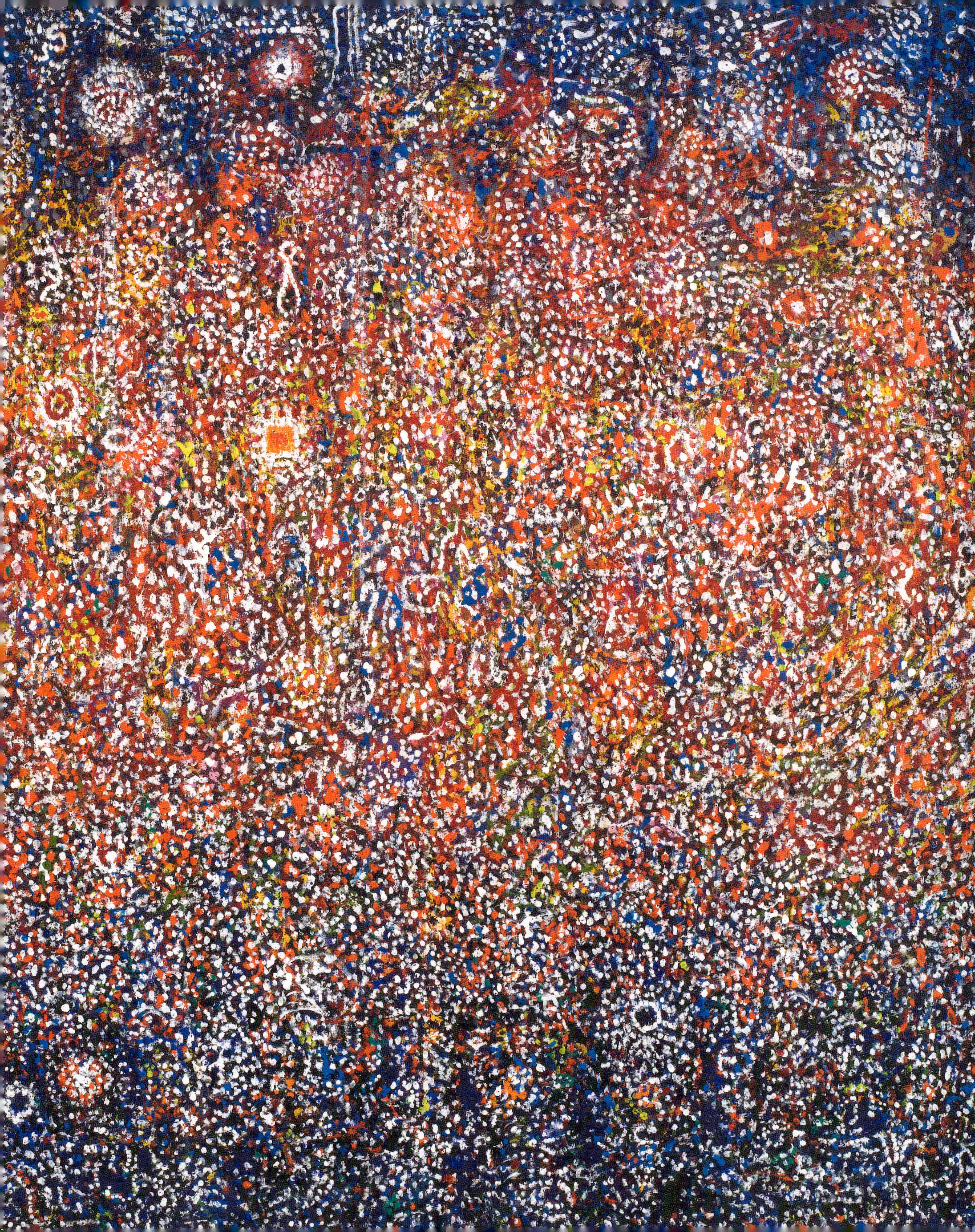

Richard Pousette-Dart
The Abstract Transcendentalist

Charles H. Duncan

In January 1951, at the age of thirty-five, Richard Pousette-Dart enjoyed widespread recognition as one of the "Irascibles," an informal group of avant-garde New York painters who advocated for the inclusion of advanced strains of art in the Metropolitan Museum of Art's exhibition *American Painting Today, 1950*. Standing at the far left in Nina Leen's now-iconic photograph published in the popular magazine *Life*, Pousette-Dart's presence within this assembly of leading American painters has done much to cement his identity as a first-generation Abstract Expressionist artist. That same month, Pousette-Dart delivered an address to students at the School of the Museum of Fine Arts, Boston, as a participant in the exhibition *American Abstractionists, Loaned by the Betty Parsons Gallery*. This lecture encapsulated observations and personal philosophies he had recorded in his private studio notebooks during the previous decades, and the text came to serve as Pousette-Dart's defining art statement (see pp. 205–11 for the complete text). Speaking to an audience of young artists, he celebrates a universal conception of form, advocates for the transformative qualities of the creative process, and situates his own artistic orientation and working methods within a universe that invites intuitive, individual freedom. His excitement for works of art in the Boston exhibition is palpable as he lauds the progressive spirits of his fellow creators: "There is a vitality and beauty in art today as penetrating and as all-embracing as has ever existed."[1]

Readily evident in this address is the influence of nineteenth-century American Transcendentalist writers including Ralph Waldo Emerson and Henry David Thoreau, as well as John Keats's Romantic-era axiom, "Beauty is truth, truth beauty,—that is all / Ye know on earth, and all ye need to know."[2] The core values of Transcendentalism—self-reliance, intuition over reason, the divinity of nature and the human actor, and the corrupting tendencies of society (especially upon "true art")—are central to Pousette-Dart's worldview, and no less than ten of his paintings bear *Transcendental* in their titles. These ideas are passionately articulated in his Boston text and underlie his advocacy for educational self-discovery and pacifism. Importantly, they were well formed prior to his serious activities as a painter, and considerations of Pousette-Dart solely within the context of twentieth-century criticism overlook this deeper foundation.

Although Richard Pousette-Dart is widely identified as a leading first-generation Abstract Expressionist, by nature he was a fiercely independent artist who embodied Emerson's principle of self-reliance.[3] In the same address he cautioned, "The artist must beware of all schools, isms, creeds, or entanglements which would tend to make him other than himself." He recommended, "We must learn to look past titles and labels and names and reputations." He often invoked the phrase "asymmetrical balance" when referring to his own artistic output, and the term is useful for characterizing his highly unique artmaking program. The imprint of sculpture and photography enters and exits his painting; the sheer physicality of work is offset by spiritual dimensions; the intuitive interplay of line, form, color, and especially the sensations of light are refashioned and revisited through a unique visual vocabulary charted over the course of six decades. In the larger view, Pousette-Dart's art draws from an indeterminant dialogue between interior and observable worlds, and its creative energy rests on the cusp between the conscious and unconscious—what the artist referred to as "the living edge." His unfixed position within the critical cannon mirrors this notion of asymmetrical balance.[4] It is through such a spirit of nonlinear continuity that we may best consider the exhibition *Poetry of Light*.

Richard Warren Pousette-Dart was born in Saint Paul, Minnesota, in 1916 and moved with his family to Valhalla, New York, a suburb of New York City, at the age of two. His grandfather, Algot Pousette, was a silversmith and painter of French Huguenot origin who emigrated to Minnesota during the nineteenth century. His parents, originally Nathaniel Pousette and Flora Dart, were highly progressive thinkers who, in 1913, hyphenated their names at marriage in an "act of mutual esteem"—a radical gesture at the time. Nathaniel was trained as a fine artist at the Pennsylvania Academy of the Fine Arts and at the time of Richard's birth was an instructor at the College of St. Catherine and the St. Paul Institute. Flora was active as a suffragette and published poems and essays in local Minnesota newspapers on socialism, ethics, and gender equality.

Pousette-Dart was raised within a culturally engaged household that supported his diverse range of youthful explorations. Mechanically inclined, he built pinhole cameras and sophisticated electronic contrivances, and routinely dissembled clocks and cameras to understand their inner workings. By his teens he was a licensed ham radio operator. Pousette-Dart maintained an extremely close relationship with his mother, who was active within an intimate community of poets and musicians, instilling in her son a deep appreciation for the poetry of Keats, Ezra Pound, and the Transcendentalists, as well as contrapuntal music, especially fugues by Bach.[5] In 1935 Flora published her first book of poetry, prompting Richard to populate his own notebooks with poems, sketches, and personal philosophies. These notebooks became central to his artistic practice, and he kept one within reach in his studio for the remainder of his career. When Richard eventually left home to live in New York City, he initiated a robust written correspondence with Flora through which he developed the language of his own philosophical views.

Deeply interested in art pedagogy, Nathaniel Pousette-Dart maintained an attic studio within the family home, where he introduced Richard to the rudiments of drawing and painting. A touching record of the close, early artistic relationship between father and son endures in a photograph of Nathaniel and twelve-year-old Richard drawing each other's portraits that appeared in *The New York Times* and other newspapers in 1928 (fig. 1).[6] Professionally, Nathaniel balanced a career as a commercial art director at the J. Walter Thompson Company with fine art pursuits that included

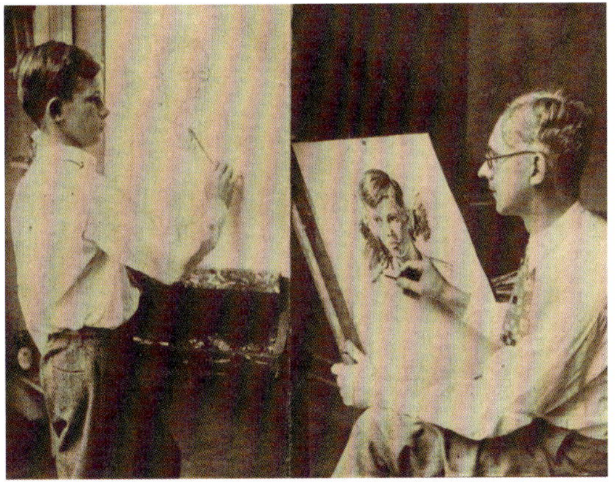

Fig. 1

Richard Pousette-Dart and his father, Nathaniel, drawing each other's portraits, 1928

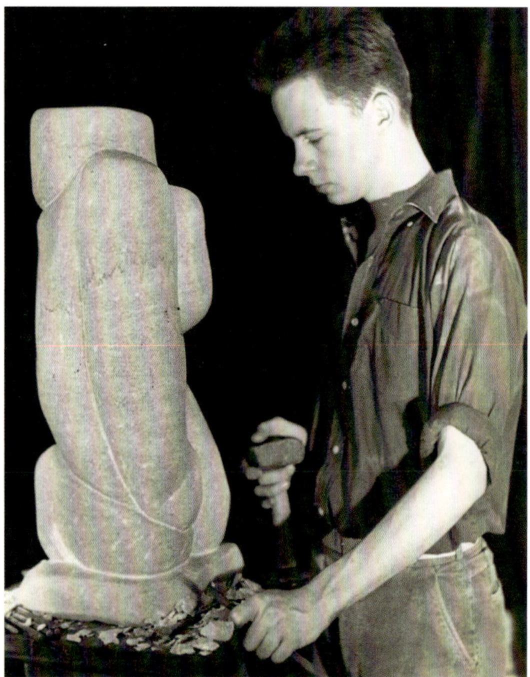

Fig. 2

Richard Pousette-Dart with *Tennessee Marble*, ca. 1937, photographer unknown

editing volumes on prominent American painters; publishing the art periodicals *Art of Today* and *Art and Artists of Today*; and founding the Art Adventure League, a correspondence course in art instruction—all as he advanced his own career as a painter. Nathaniel's publications explored topical conversations concerning realism and abstract modernism, as well as European versus American trends in art. Philosophically, he embraced John Dewey's influential *Art as Experience* of 1934 as he dedicated issues of his magazines to groundbreaking American collectors such as Albert C. Barnes and Duncan Phillips. Nathaniel collected non-Western art and engaged in educational projects with artists of the 1930s ranging from Berenice Abbott to William Zorach, further expanding his son's early artistic awareness.

For his own education, Richard Pousette-Dart enrolled at Bard College in Annandale-on-Hudson, New York, in 1935, but withdrew before the completion of his first semester to pursue an independent program of education in New York City. As he noted in 1937, "It was at this time that I first began to become seriously interested in sculpture. I spent all my time drawing, reading, writing, listening to music . . . I dreamed sculpture."[7] The main body of Pousette-Dart's 1930s stone sculpture demonstrates his intense, early interest in dynamic human figures, heads, and animal forms. Around this time, he became acquainted with the charismatic Russian-born John D. Graham, whose interests in so-called primitive art, as well as psychoanalytic theory and European modernism, elevated Graham to a role of considerable influence with many emerging Abstract Expressionist painters, including Jackson Pollock, Willem de Kooning, and Adolph Gottlieb. To support himself, Pousette-Dart worked in the photographic retouching studio of Lynn T. Morgan, an associate of his father, where the precise work of altering negatives by hand came to influence his later painting technique. Concurrently he began to pursue photography as a serious artistic practice, evident in accomplished portraits of John Graham and his mother, Flora, from this period (see cats. 100, 104).

Around 1937 Pousette-Dart's aesthetic passions were ignited by carved works in stone and wood by French-born British sculptor Henri Gaudier-Brzeska, a leading figure within the Vorticist movement.[8] Like Graham, Gaudier championed the unmediated expression of emotive forces exemplified by so-called primitive art and favored

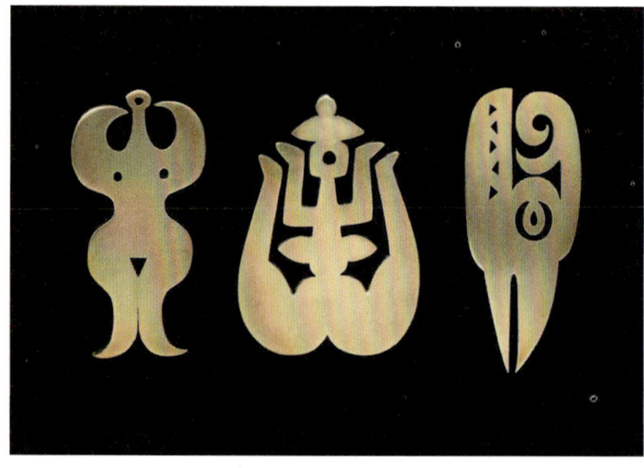

Fig. 3

Richard Pousette-Dart, three untitled *Brasses*, ca. 1939–79 (see cats. 54–96)

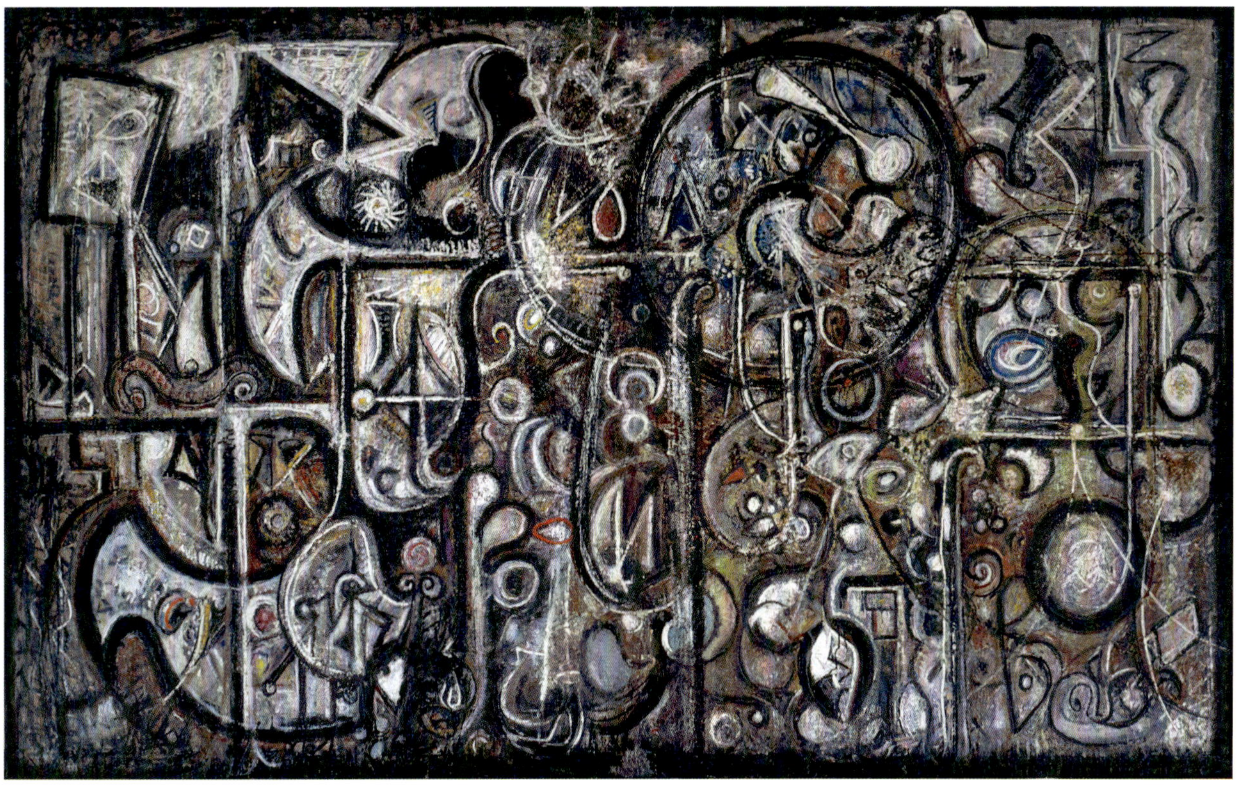

Fig. 4

Richard Pousette-Dart, *Symphony No. 1, The Transcendental*, 1941–42, Metropolitan Museum of Art, New York, Purchase, Lila Acheson Wallace Gift, inv. 1996.367

non-Western approaches to figuration. Inspired by Gaudier's practice, Pousette-Dart began to design and craft small, flat, hand-cut brass sculptures in geometric and reduced organic forms (see cats. 54–96). Citing the British art theorist Clive Bell's term "significant form," Pousette-Dart became deeply interested in why elemental shapes—crosses, spirals, circles—appear ubiquitously throughout world cultures and are imbued with spiritual, transcendent meanings.[9] The demands of cutting, smoothing, and burnishing brasses by hand—each required approximately two weeks to complete—led the artist to comprehend elemental forms as tactile entities that could be transliterated into paintings, especially through dense, sculptural accretions of pigment. Pousette-Dart would create more than two hundred pocket-sized "brasses" during his lifetime, and they came to serve as the fundamental visual vocabulary for his painting and other two-dimensional work.

By 1940 Pousette-Dart turned his focus to painting, and early works are energetic, allover compositions of line and interlocking shapes stabilized by underlying grids and contained within conceptual frames. *Beneath the Sea* (cat. 1), for instance, organizes a fantastic array of organic imagery including scallop shells, amoebic and cellular shapes, plant forms, and stylized birds through the painstaking use of oil and ink on stretched parchment in a manner similar to medieval manuscript illumination. Painted in 1941–42, *Undulation* (cat. 3) demonstrates that Pousette-Dart rapidly matured toward masterful, large-scale easel painting, a format he significantly advanced within the New York School. Living and working in a small first-floor railroad apartment on East Fifty-Sixth Street in Manhattan, it was during this period that he completed the epic and influential *Symphony No. 1, The Transcendental* (fig. 4), which at nearly twelve feet (355.6 cm) proved too large to enter the Marian Willard Gallery when he first attempted to exhibit it. Together with Pollock's *Mural* of 1943 (University of Iowa Museum of Art) and Arshile Gorky's *The Liver Is the Cock's Comb* of 1944 (Buffalo AKG Art Museum), this work is now regarded as a breakthrough for the adoption of heroic-sized easel painting by Abstract Expressionist artists.

Pousette-Dart often studied non-Western objects at the American Museum of Natural History and held a deep interest in primordial imagery, as can be observed in *Animal Forms* (cat. 2). Here, a dense arrangement of cellular and elemental shapes is achieved via heavy applications of pigment, as well as the reductive process of incising or scraping, techniques employed by the artist to great effect throughout his career. Pousette-Dart did not rely on preliminary studies for his paintings but drew intuitively from his repertoire of shapes and linear themes first conceived within his notebooks and brasses. Later paintings such as *Chavade* (cat. 13), *Fountains of Penelope* (cat. 26), *Wall of Signs* (cat. 32), and *Naples Fugue* (cat. 25) demonstrate that he deployed these forms via widely divergent treatments of pigment and surface density during later decades. A number of Pousette-Dart's early complex drawn and painted compositions, including *Blue Transition/Convolutions of Music* (cat. 9), additionally display strong affinities to the diagrammatic schemes of circuit boards and glowing vacuum tubes that he was deeply familiar with as an electronics hobbyist.

During the first half of the 1940s, Pousette-Dart held solo shows at the nonprofit Artists' Gallery and at Willard, who also showed David Smith and Mark Tobey, yet his exchanges during the formative years of Abstract Expressionism appear to be limited to a close circle of personal friends and family (his wife during that period, Lydia Modi, was a painter) as well as nonartist Quakers with whom he engaged in pacifist activities. There are indications that he studied firsthand the work of Europeans exhibited in New York during the 1930s and 1940s—*Forestness* (cat. 8), for example, incorporates sand intermixed with oil paint in the manner of Jean Dubuffet.[10] Among the Americans, there are strong affinities between Pollock's painting of the mid-1940s and Pousette-Dart's *Eagle's Nest* (cat. 7): both artists were close to John Graham, had exhibited at Peggy Guggenheim's groundbreaking gallery Art of This Century, and Pollock positively acknowledged Pousette-Dart's work in 1946.[11]

From the outset, Richard Pousette-Dart's work has been widely regarded for its spiritual overtones. Critic Henry McBride in January 1945 wrote that he "builds his canvases with intense feeling, believing in the material awareness of spirit."[12] Recently, scholar Lucy Kent has introduced the term "spiritual aestheticism" to describe Pousette-Dart's wide-ranging familiarity with mystical literature by Jakob Böhme, George Santayana, Lao-tzu, D. T. Suzuki, and P. D. Ouspensky, in addition to his principal alignment with Transcendentalism.[13] While a painting such as *Crucifixion, Comprehension of the Atom* (cat. 6) ostensibly depicts a crucifix or atomic plume, suggesting organized religion as well as anxiety surrounding the historical crisis of World War II, caution should be applied to such literal readings.[14] Pousette-Dart was fundamentally opposed to war, yet more broadly he was fascinated by the atomic nature of the universe, and embraced the role of artist as seer who assimilates and reinvents the miraculous harmony of his observable surroundings: "The truly integrated creating mind sees in art the beauty of universal meaning everywhere."[15] Ultimately the artist maintained that "the spiritual nature of art is not a category or any representation, but is an expression of wholeness, a revelation and affirmation, of the substance, the meaning, and the forever evolving, growing and transforming nature of life."[16]

In 1948 Pousette-Dart joined the Betty Parsons Gallery, which was inextricably linked with the Abstract Expressionists and progressive postwar American art. That year *Brasses and Photographs* featured portraits of fellow artists as well as nature studies. The exhibition was groundbreaking considering the paucity of photographic exhibitions in New York galleries prior to mid-century, and it served as an important milestone in forwarding the aesthetic possibilities of this medium to New York School artists. A review by Rosalind Browne noted, "In his ethereal photographs, at times textured to look like fine painting, he often uses double exposure to invest special meaning to his subjects."[17] In *Barnett Newman* (cat. 107), for example, he employed superimposition to combine a tightly cropped view of the painter's head with a pre-Columbian figurative stone carving. The overall effect is disquieting, as the contours of the sculpture,

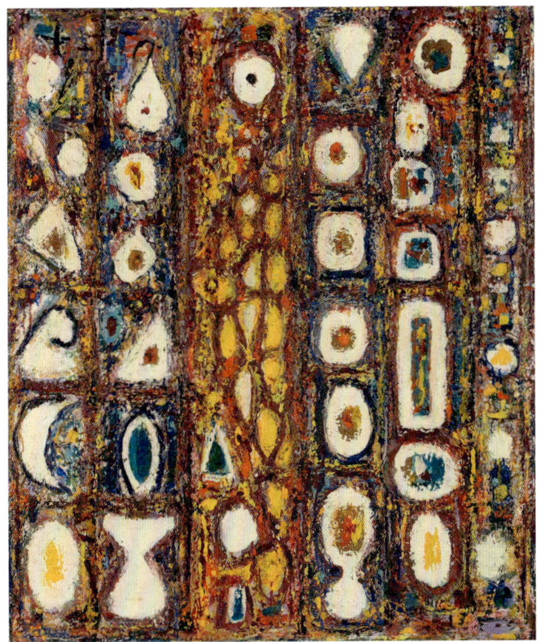

Fig. 5

Richard Pousette-Dart, *Le Bijou*, 1957, private collection

which emerge largely out of shadow regions, distort the likeness of Newman, especially where his eye is encircled by the large ear of the sculpture and his skin and mustache appear fused with its stone surface. Signifying Newman's devotion to art of this strain, the photograph juxtaposes opposites—ancient and contemporary, animate and inert, creator and work of art—within a unified image that recalls the layering and interlocking forms of Pousette-Dart's paintings. Ultimately, for the artist, the miracle of photography was its ability to harness and refashion the qualities of light, and the lens was analogous to Emerson's "transparent eye-ball," which captures nature rather than simply reflects it.[18] As Pousette-Dart noted, "I am really fascinated, and always have been, with the magic of the lens. But the lens can lie. It's the eye, it's the mind behind the lens that has the ability to see and perceive."[19]

By the end of the decade, Richard Pousette-Dart' s work had been exhibited in solo shows in New York and abroad at the twenty-fourth Venice Biennale; the Museum of Modern Art acquired his painting *Number 11: Presence* (1949); and he was a perennial exhibitor at the Whitney Museum of American Art's *Annual Exhibition of Contemporary Art*. In December 1950, facing the impending demolition of his New York City apartment building, he relocated to a farmhouse in the rural community of Sloatsburg, New York. The following spring he was awarded a prestigious Guggenheim Fellowship, allowing him to focus on the body of work now referred to as White Paintings. Examples such as *Chavade* (cat. 13), *Descending Bird Forms* (cat. 16), and *White Etude* (cat. 14) employ graphite on subtly variegated titanium white grounds to create diaphanous, light-filled compositions that accentuate calligraphic impulses. Throughout his career, Pousette-Dart intermittently reduced his use of color, introducing and then diffusing highly saturated hues through scraping and layering to arrive at overall neutral effects. Present are the traces of organic forms derived from his brasses, but emphasis is placed, instead, on the accumulation of interwoven line. Concurrently, Pousette-Dart crafted a series of freestanding sculptures from steel and found objects including *Apparition* (cat. 28) and *Creature of Clouds* (cat. 12), whose striations of wire suggest a three-dimensional mode of drawing related to the White Paintings.

Following this period of intense graphic investigation, Pousette-Dart returned to colorfully saturated canvases referred to as Gothic Paintings, in reference to the magnificent stained-glass windows of fourteenth-century cathedrals and jewel-encrusted reliquaries (see fig. 5). Painted in 1955, *Illumination Gothic* (cat. 18) offers a kaleidoscopic celebration of color, light, and vertical form, realized through a panoply of painterly approaches that include linear outline defined by brush, dense precincts of palette-knife work, and drips and runs of pigment commonly associated with the aleatory practices of Abstract Expressionism. The label *Byzantine* additionally identifies works such as his 1958 paintings *Amaranth* (cat. 23) and *Blood Wedding* (fig. 6), linking effects achieved on

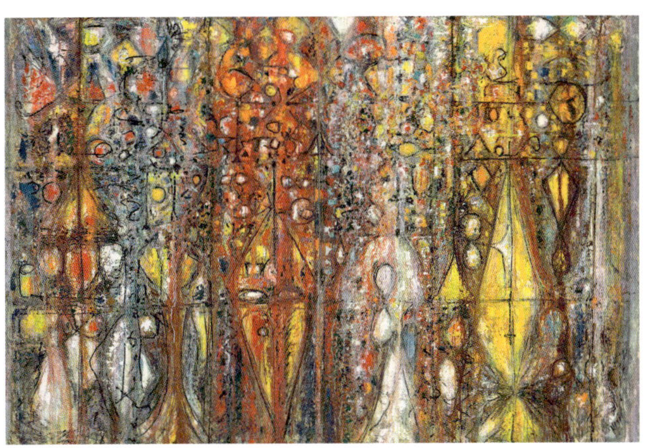

Fig. 6

Richard Pousette-Dart, *Blood Wedding*, 1958, private collection

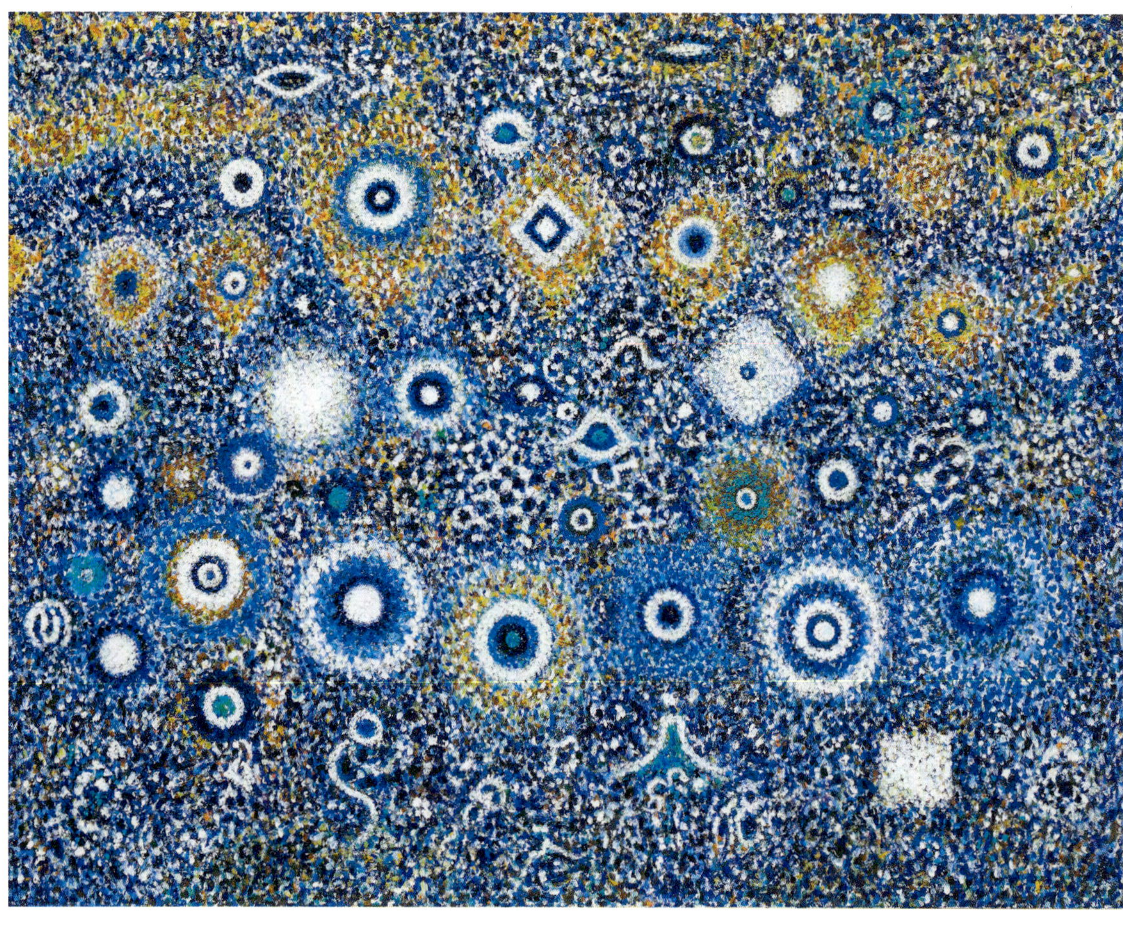

Fig. 7
Richard Pousette-Dart, *Night Landscape*, 1969–71, private collection

canvas through the application of small accretions of paint to the shimmering qualities of mosaics. Harnessing the effects of light was an overarching concern of Pousette-Dart's visual poetry—one that he understood comprehensively though his practice of photography—and the conceit of the picture plane as an illuminated window subdivided by tracery was explored with great success, extending earlier uses in *Window, Cathedral* (cat. 22) to *Window Number 4* (cat. 21). Metaphorically, the brilliant Gothic and Byzantine Paintings offer a harmonious mediation between disparate forces. In the artist's words, "I want to keep a balance just on the edge of awareness, the narrow rim between the conscious and sub-conscious, a balance between expanding and contracting, between silence and sound."[20]

In 1960 Pousette-Dart purchased a large, stone carriage house in Suffern, New York, thirty miles north of New York City, where a spacious, sun-filled second-floor studio afforded views to the nearby Ramapo Mountains upon which the effects of natural light modulated during the day. Almost immediately, his painting and drawing technique gravitated toward the application of multitudinous, small touches of paint and minute lines of ink, layered and combined to yield luminous, allover image fields. Often erroneously associated with the rigorous, color theory–based nineteenth-century movement Pointillism, Pousette-Dart's technique instead was entirely intuitive, and ultimately derived from his experience retouching photographs, where scrutiny of the granular structure of film revealed to the artist that "all form is made up of so many points of light and that everything has a molecular structure."[21] Works such as his 1967 painting *Hieroglyph Number 7* (cat. 42) pulsate optically, conveying expanding and converging recessional depth in the service of an integrated, transcendent statement. Within it, traces of a blue orb provide an underlying structure for atomized particulars that fluctuate as the viewer's eye travels over the expanse of the painting, invoking a durational viewing experience akin to listening to music. Accordingly, the artist referred to the cumulative process of adding and flattening layered touches of pigment as "tuning," and as he had noted in his Boston address, "the order of a work is due to its harmony and integration, not to its complex number of parts or superficial simplicity."[22]

Following his first museum retrospective, held in 1963 at the Whitney Museum of American Art, Pousette-Dart continued to explore a wide variety of themes and approaches within his painting. *Meditation on the Drifting Stars* (cat. 51), *Lost in the Beginning of Infinity* (cat. 41), *Within the Moon* (cat. 52), and *Night Landscape* (fig. 7) suggest infinite, heavenly landscapes devoid of human referents or horizon lines, yet the artist in 1987 affirmed that "he has never been consciously painting celestial bodies in space; in fact, it is through his paintings that he has now become interested in astronomy."[23] He also continued to reimagine elemental forms first embodied within his brasses through a series of black-and-white canvases and works on paper from between 1978 and 1980 that include *The Square of Light* (cat. 34), *Black and White Fugue* (cat. 29), and *Wall of Signs* (cat. 32). Ostensibly a dramatic departure from his allover color fields of vibrating light, the artist stated in one of his notebooks that "Black and white is the guts of color," fully aware that the dualities of the two chromatic extremes encompass the totality of all hues.[24] As evident by two black-and-white arches that reimagine the latticed structures of his earliest compositions (cats. 30, 31), Pousette-Dart's concern for the properties of light, captured through vibrating tonalities of pigment and dense surfaces that affect the perception of viewing, remained a lifelong pursuit.

During the closing decades of his life, Pousette-Dart developed a passion for teaching, initially conducting classes at his home and then accepting academic positions at Columbia University, Sarah Lawrence College, and the Art Students League of New York. In a teaching statement from the 1970s he expressed his aversion to structured, formalized lesson plans, insisting that "mandatory skills are destructive to the inspiration of true, original, creative thinking and feeling."[25] Advancing Emerson's credo "To be yourself in a world that is constantly trying to make you something else is the greatest accomplishment," Pousette-Dart asserted, "I am not interested in teaching painting, I am interested in teaching people how to be themselves."[26] His oft-repeated entreaty to his students was "you must strive to get on the thread of your own being."[27]

Ultimately, Pousette-Dart viewed artistic creation as a mirror to the wonderous, all-encompassing mechanics of the universe. Image-rich accomplishments such as *Celebration Birth* (cat. 53) need to be approached, first and foremost, through a totality of experience; one feels their "presence" without having to comprehend the smaller worlds from which they are composed. His creative output opens a door to a different level of awareness; a sensory mode that is experiential, intuitive and transcendental by its very essence. In the artist's own words, "Paintings are a presence, they are best known by the spirit they leave with us after we have left them."[28]

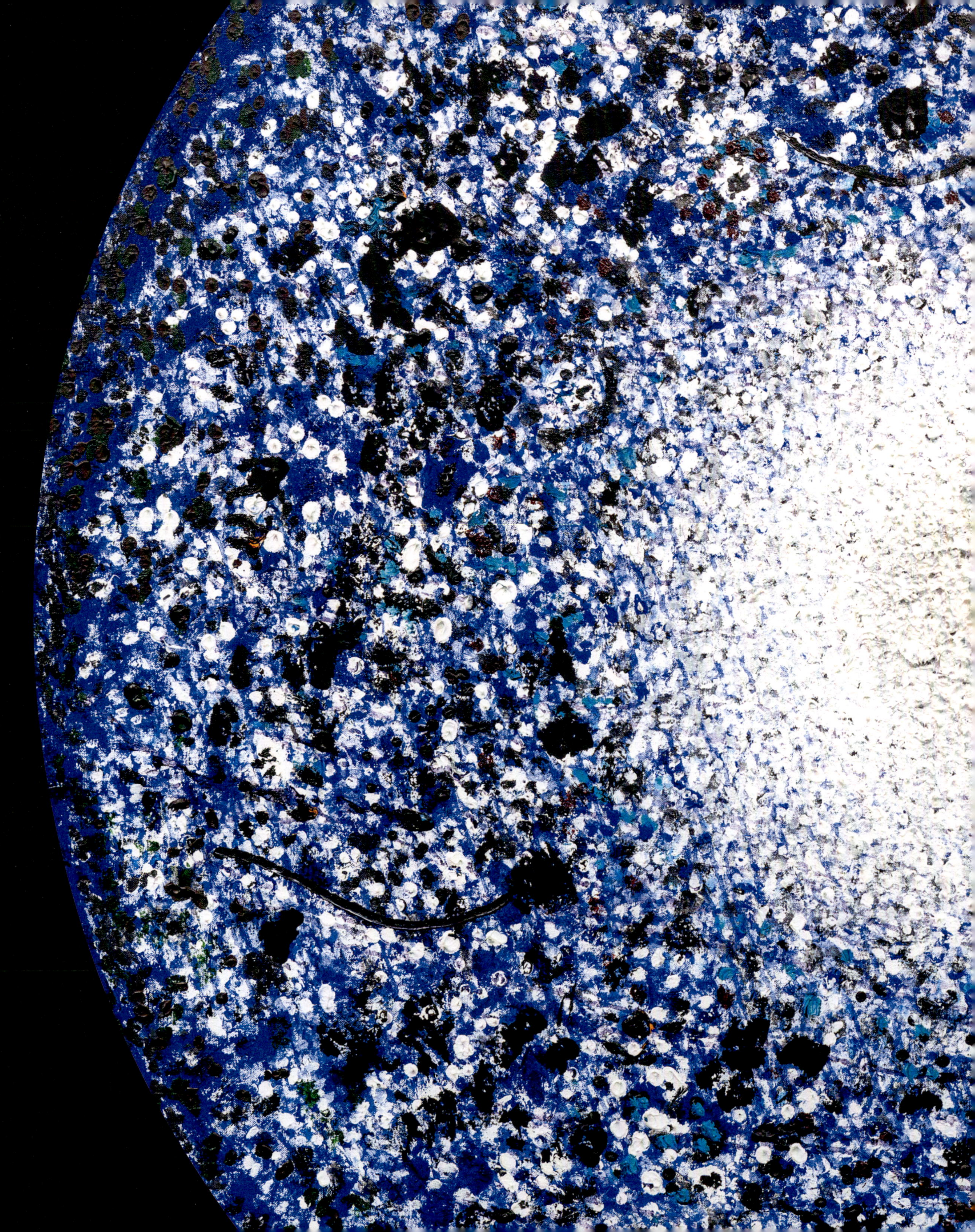

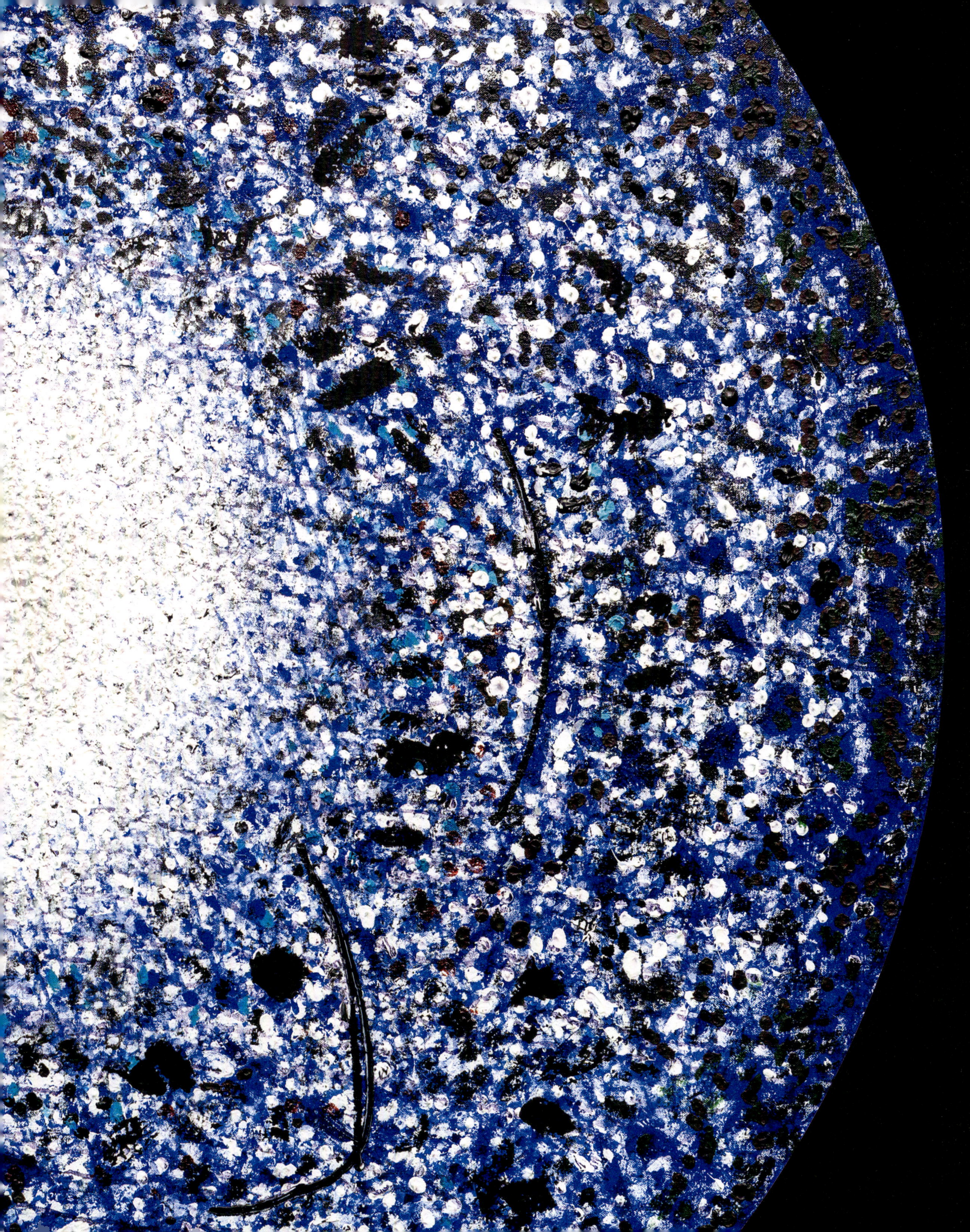

“A Garden of Forms” The Art of Richard Pousette-Dart

Megan Kincaid

With seemingly constant motion of hand and intellect, Richard Pousette-Dart cut across media without boundary, shifting from one discipline to another. Though best known as a painter, his unbridled creative expression stretched into sculpture, watercolor, sketches, hand-held brasses, experimental and commercial photography, and mixed-media collage incorporating found objects. From his family, he nurtured passions for literature, poetry, and music. Wide-ranging influences, an egalitarian spirit, and a nonhierarchical outlook facilitated this nonlinearity and genre-bending.

The artist’s final studio in Suffern, New York, where he worked from 1960 until his death in 1992, still hums with his polyphonic process. A workman’s desk, tucked in the corner of the light-soaked space, testifies to the numerous handicraft projects he undertook alongside his large-scale paintings and sculptures, housing the various tools, materials, and devices that served those projects. A metal organizing cupboard still atop the desk recollects an attempt to rein in the overflow. Small, handwritten identificatory labels on each drawer provide a roadmap for where to find the sundry instruments that comprised Pousette-Dart’s lesser-known artistic arenas and convey his eclectic intermediality: “colored drawing inks,” “undeveloped negatives,” “nails tacks,” “glass aluminum plate gold leaf,” “scissors small files duco cement,” “little watercolors little watercolor papers little watercolor sets,” and “ink remover lighter fuel oil.”

Despite the seeming impossibility of coalescing these broad-spanning pursuits, a cohering force can be detected from within Pousette-Dart’s artistic output. Across his career, distinctive, if not signature, forms traverse media and decades. Most recurrent are vital symbols including pulsating circles, undulating biomorphs, glyphs, spirals, and whorls that appear either as freestanding entities or as part of collective assemblies. Ranging in their complexity from elemental geometries to animistic shapes resembling fish and birds or coiling baroque aggregates, they attest to the diverse visual cultures he consumed. In addition to the mythopoetic symbology sourced from archaic cultures by his modernist peers questing for purportedly “universal” content, Pousette-Dart also grasped distinctive forms found in nature, the built environment, domestic furnishings, technologies, and his own inventions.[1] Though akin to fellow members of the New York School, who maintained that their imagery aspired to the “tragic and timeless,” he wielded a differentiating desire to plot diverse forms, from the quotidian to the cosmic, amid an interconnected and intwined web.[2]

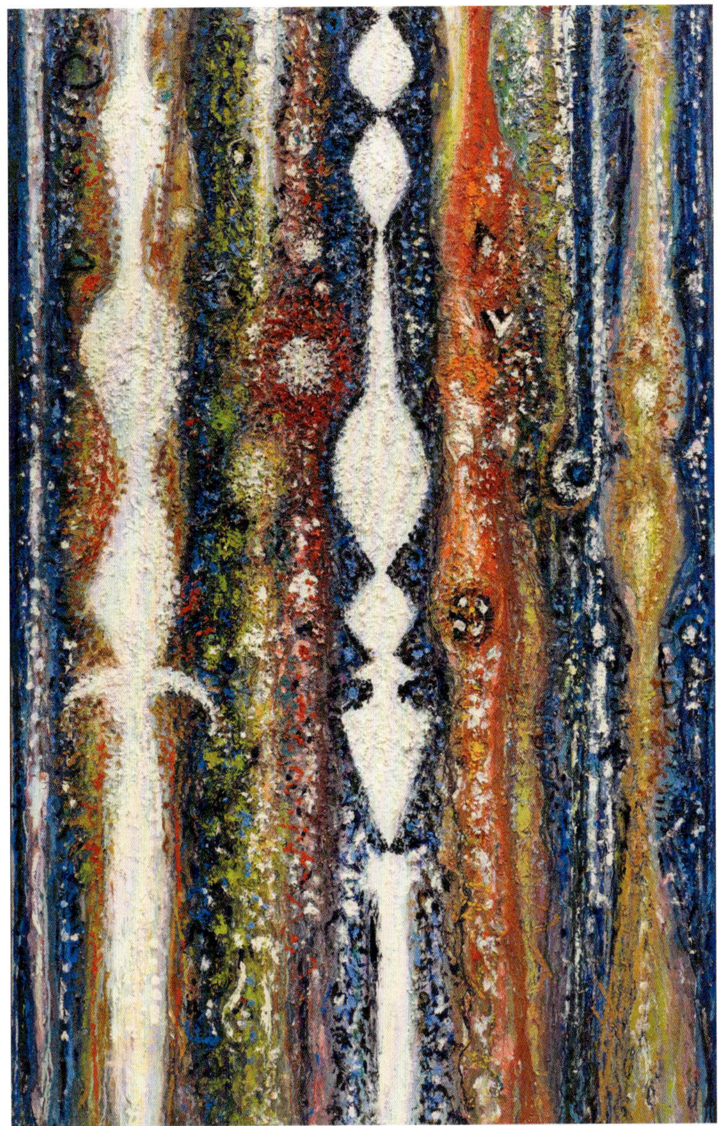

Fig. 1

Richard Pousette-Dart, *Illumination Vertical,* 1958 (cat. 20)

The centrality of form to Pousette-Dart's conceptual framework is revealed by his statements and supported by the formative literature, which frequently notes the impact of British art critic Clive Bell's definition of "significant form" on the young artist in the 1930s and 1940s.[3] Set out in his influential 1914 publication *Art*, this concept posited that form could strike emotional chords through its precise visual configurations—something Pousette-Dart would amplify in his singular modification of forms. In seemingly endless pages of studio notebooks (spanning quixotic mantras, poetic fragments, elongated theoretical exegeses, diagrams, sketches, watercolors, and even built-up miniature paintings), the word *form* crops up on nearly every page. However, in his slanted, cursive script and spinning, convulsive thinking, form does not serve as a delimiting force nor a prompt to reduce painting to its essential elements. On the contrary, form here signals opportunities for growth and communality.

Pousette-Dart's recurrent yet evolving lexicon of symbols and structures activates what he, in the last years of his life, termed "a garden of forms"—signaling to his abiding conception of these visuals as abundant, organic, yet decidedly cultivated, or the product of effortful and tender tilling. In this way, his effacement of traditional media and genre boundaries indicates not only a progressive intermediality, but moreover announces a countermodel to modernist formalism. This phrase, though scrawled on but one of thousands of notebook entries, precisely enlivens the artist's enduring aesthetic philosophy, a system of beliefs and guideposts under development from a precociously early age.[4] As he expounded in a notebook of the 1990s:

> *a garden of forms which are neither old nor new but arise from the inner excitement of passion & dream & vision to see & to care & to be / does it have the struggle & the marks of your hands upon it.*[5]

While it is possible to extract resonant philosophic provisos from nearly any page of Pousette-Dart's studio notebooks, this entry highlights the distinguishing features of his indelible notions of form and formalism. In strides, he posits form as a moral action and locates an ethical humanist mode of artmaking through invention, conviction, and imagination—as part of the "vision to see & to care." Here, the artist's historical context, particularly the critical discourse surrounding American abstraction, emerges as a constructive foil. If generations of critics and art historians have asserted that the foundational texts and subsequent institutionalization of Abstract Expressionism produced a mythic "modernist subject"—a rigorously rational yet inward and solipsistic creature born from Clement Greenberg's precepts of pure opticality and nonobjectivity—then Pousette-Dart concertedly refused to model the disinterested and disembodied artist augured by conventional formalism.

Merging visuality with affective benevolence, he proposed that artmaking could facilitate empathetic connectivity and embodied knowledge (note that for this artist, "to care" is connected to the existential infinitive "to be" and that the artwork should bear the "marks of your hands upon it"). Whereas vacated, nonobjective form aligned with what Robert Storr has diagnosed as Greenberg's "absolute pessimism" and withdrawal, Pousette-Dart's opposing framework animates a "revolutionary optimism."[6] Resuscitating the existential malaise that purportedly plagued his generation, this artist seriously regarded the aesthetic and relational possibilities of "inner excitement." Thus, framed within the discourse about art's agency to enact positive social change, "a garden of forms" tenders a powerful invective to claim art's conscientious action, creation of worlds, convection of energy, emotional vibrancy, and empathic connectivity.

When Pousette-Dart entered the vanguard scene in New York as a sculptor at the tail of the 1930s, intellectually advanced but without formal artistic training, he had already evolved firm convictions about art's vibrational communicability and its faceted interconnection to a greater cosmology. The son of a painter and a poet, he tended to express his ideas on art through poetic verse—aiding a reconstruction of the nascent theoretical premises upon which he built his enduring aesthetic credo. The February–March 1938 issue of *Art and Artists of Today* included a poem by Pousette-Dart entitled "Vortex." Signed R. W. P.-D. and scrunched beneath a mired essay on the allures of Mexico by his friend and mentor John D. Graham (riddled with period stereotypes of the "humble primitive," unflinching condemnations of Mexican muralism, and proclamations of pre-Columbian sculpture as "the greatest sculpture the human race has ever produced"), Pousette-Dart's poem provides a welcome palate cleanser. In it, he ruminates on the structural arrangement of the universe, what he envisions as an "opulent convexity." Form takes on both dimensionality and an organizing role, giving visual semblance to the mysteries of the spirit, to elusive and unseen forces which nonetheless radiate energy and forge relationships between seemingly discrete objects:

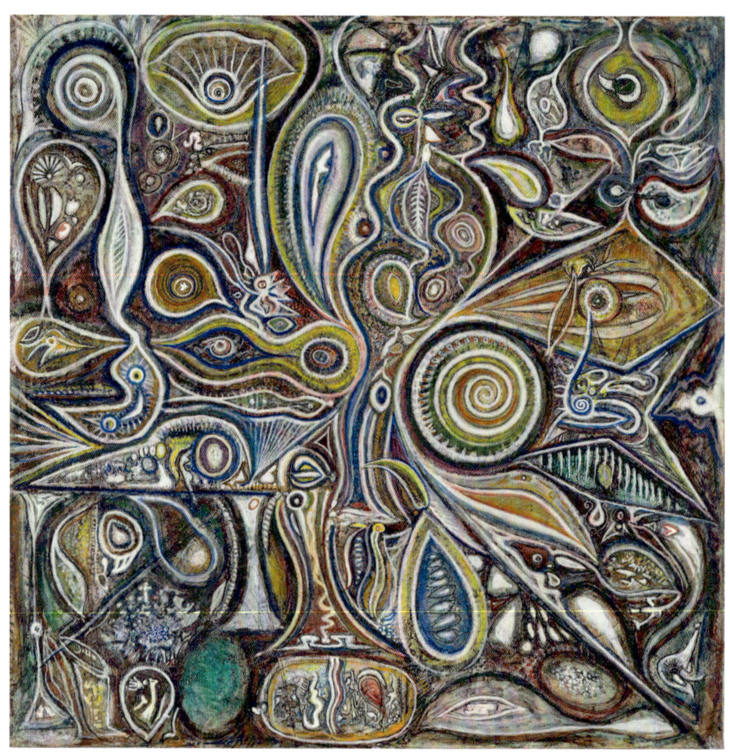

Fig. 2 Richard Pousette-Dart, *Beneath the Sea*, 1939 (cat. 1)

Form is many planes
Plane is many lines
Line is many points

Planes are not always visible
Lines are not always visible
They are part of form
Which is always visible
And is ever power.[7]

Transitioning to painting around 1940, Pousette-Dart bridged his theoretical postulates on form with pictorial statements. An early work entitled *Beneath the Sea* and executed in 1939 (cat. 1) might even be seen as an exemplar of "a garden of forms"—an expressly subaqueous landscape in which a variety of evocative organisms pulsate and gather. With organic shapes that suggest a fluidity of substance, dozens of forms slither about the surface in discreet compartments. Resembling water droplets, dashing microbes, nesting embryos, growing cells, waves, zigzags, prisms, roving eyes,

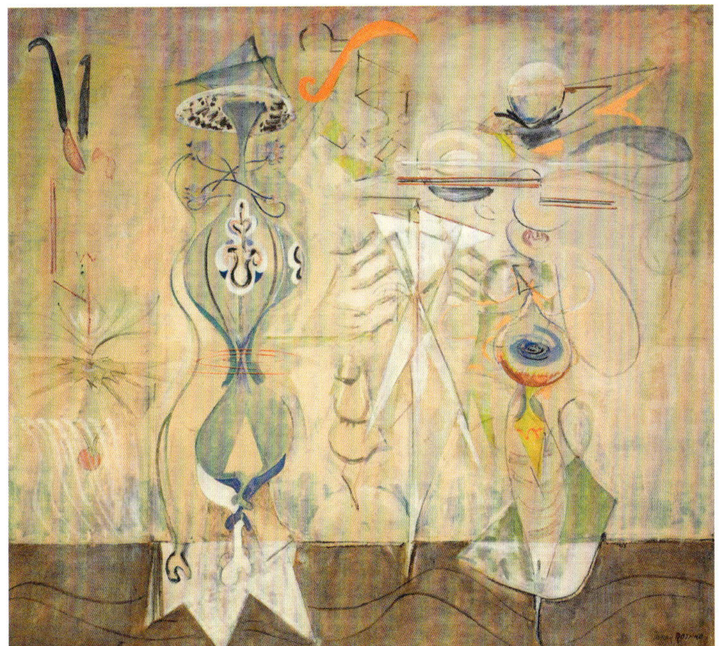

Fig. 3

Mark Rothko, *Slow Swirl at the Edge of the Sea*, 1944, Museum of Modern Art, New York, Bequest of Mrs. Mark Rothko through the Mark Rothko Foundation, Inc., inv. 429.1981

and feathers, these entities imbue the composition with an animacy and affective vitality. Along the bottom edge of the canvas, a small capsule contains a microcosmic universe in which the foment of form itself appears the principal subject. Note the multicolored vertical wave that splits the shell, yellow bolt, cyclones, and dispersed dots.

As we watch this world awaken, Pousette-Dart's theory that the artistic process "entails really the creation of the world" rings out.[8] Rather than represent the observable, an artist endeavors to disentangle the underlying structures and intwining forces to apprehend the universe as a potentially intelligible system (or, to borrow from Lucy Lippard, "to penetrate the world's disguises").[9] In an interview given in 1974, Pousette-Dart elaborated that world creation involves meditative demystification and self-orientation: "I think with every work of art in a sense, you are retraining the world in miniature. You are redefining your total comprehension or total love or total awareness. I mean I think an artist is one who endlessly enjoys a contemplation of the universe."[10] In essence, formalism as sense-making—as he elsewhere averred: "The true artist continuously calculates the nature of the universe. He makes visible what cannot be seen."[11] The aesthetics of revelation vary across this artist's creative output, from worked-over and dense surfaces that carry the struggle of their making or the alternative levity and luminosity of his White Paintings, in which forms emanate from the white ground as if shadows from beyond (see cats. 13–16).[12]

In this way, the amorphic ambiguity of the vaguely allusive forms in *Beneath the Sea* might be conceived of as organisms amid one phase of their evolutionary development as they settle and plot their place within an overarching cosmic totality. Visually and thematically, the painting intersects with Mark Rothko's large-scale 1944 tableau *Slow Swirl at the Edge of the Sea* (fig. 3), another scene of ecstatic creation featuring a biomorphic couple that spins and rotates—jointly constituting their being through motion. Christopher Rothko has observed that this composition might have signified his father's recent uplift and joy upon meeting his soon-to-be-wife. To this point, the work is subtitled *Mel Ecstatic*.[13]

Similarly, Pousette-Dart's model of formalist engagement stipulates that form derives from passion and conviction—what he described as "inner excitement." In this context, excitement exceeds eagerness and enthusiasm, instead connoting stimulation and arousal, the kind of activating energy visualized by *Beneath the Sea*. That is to say, the painter's own excitability, passion, and conviction can likewise invest pictorial imagery with energy and vitality. Look, for instance, at the dense orb in *The Center* (cat. 5)—encircled with emphatic black lines and coated with thick campaigns of encrusted paint. The anchoring structure is connected to its surroundings through a series of dynamic lines, brisk black and undulating white. These wirelike tendrils either extend from or inversely act upon the sentient sphere, as if repeatedly jolted by electromagnetic bolts. Form, in turn, figured as a conductive force, bathes the canvas in prismatic light in which overlaid planes and smaller orbs simmer and glow.

A pendant painting, entitled *Crucifixion, Comprehension of the Atom* (cat. 6), further concretizes the way this body of work constellated form *within* and *as* circuits of energy. A vertically oriented crucifix, delineated in white and black and capped by an ovoid head, anchors the composition. Beneath, a latticed assembly of multicolored geometries recedes into a black background. The order imposed by the structured grid contrasts with a vaporous cloud bursting atop the cross hilt of the crucifix.

Given the title and date of the painting (made just one year before the atom bomb was dropped), this combustion might suggest a reflection on the detonation of atomic energy. Its conflation with religious iconography intimates the apocalyptic dread roused by the threat of nuclear technologies, which Pousette-Dart, a conscientious objector, likely perceived with acute admonishment. Beyond the narrow coordinates of wartime existentialism, these works nestle into the "all-pervasive zeitgeist" of the period's discourse of energy and machinic power. David Anfam's discussion of this biomechanic nexus vis-à-vis Jackson Pollock's iconic *Mural* of 1943 (University of Iowa Art Museum) helps clarify how Pousette-Dart's energized and energizing forms map onto a cache of artworks that "joined the buzzing 'energy and motion' out there in the modern civilization of the airplane, the atom bomb, the radio,' and so forth to a model of the self as akin to a container or battery that introjected and stored these roiling forces."[14]

Pousette-Dart's apprehension of form through the rhetoric and logic of energy conduction also stemmed from more intimate coordinates: his hobby of amateur "tinkerer." Throughout his life, the artist studied, deconstructed, and assembled gadgets such as radios, clocks, and cameras—all of which folded into his artistry. As a teenager, he built his own handheld radios, which he used for daily communications with amicable strangers. In 1934 the first of several letters of complaint from the Federal Communications Commission Engineering Department regarding a ham radio he was licensed to operate arrived at his parent's home. Two years later, in June 1936, another complaint was issued after his sister had caused a stir jumping into some neighboring radio lines. The anonymous complaint detailed, "There is a radio amateur station operated by one Pousette Dart [*sic*] at Valhalla, New York which is disturbing to listeners there. A girl seems to use the station."[15] Further to his imbrication in electrical circuitry and manually operated communication systems, when enrolled at Bard College for one semester in 1935, Pousette-Dart took a job manning a telephone switchboard. When he moved to New York to pursue a career as an artist, he, like many of the Abstract Expressionists, supplemented his income with a commercial art gig. His was in a photography retouching atelier, where he learned the technical side of the production process.

These preoccupations grew alongside and fortified his artmaking, as biomechanic forms and symbols permeate his oeuvre. For all its cosmic overtones, the remarkable *Blue Transition/Convolutions of Music* (cat. 9), a riot of faceted forms in jewel tones tempered by a gridded armature, resembles circuitry boards and preamplifier diagrams found in the Heathkit instruction manuals Pousette-Dart consulted to put together assorted electronics.[16] Here, one considers the sprinkle of tiny white orbs in *Blue Transition/Convolutions of Music*—stardust, electric lamps, camera flashes, spark plugs? Further down this allusive network, his recurrent circle might recollect the aperture of a camera and the knobs of a radio. Plotted alongside his theories about form's energetic potential, the visual transposition of the circle-as-knob also supposes that, when rotated, the switch could unleash frequencies and "turn on" the device. In his composition *Sky Presence, Circle* (cat. 50), a luminous orb suspended amid an allover surround of vibrational dots and staccato lines may flexibly signify a transcendental realm, the diaphanous glow of the sun, the dispersal of light from a powerful bulb, an electromagnetic field, or molecular energy. Indeed, as the artist applied daubs of paint to the canvas, assiduously harmonizing the saturation of pigments to adjust values of light and dark, his iterative gestures paralleled the way one attentively calibrates electronics by dialing the knob, doubling back to reduce static, and finally resolving into a unified hum.

On an easel in the artist's Suffern studio, there hangs a reproduction of Giovanni di Paolo's *Creation and Expulsion of the Souls from Paradise* (1445, Metropolitan Museum of Art, New York), a masterpiece of Sienese painting in which concentric circles enclose a primordial landscape, parodically placed beside a red plastic ring on a baby's toy

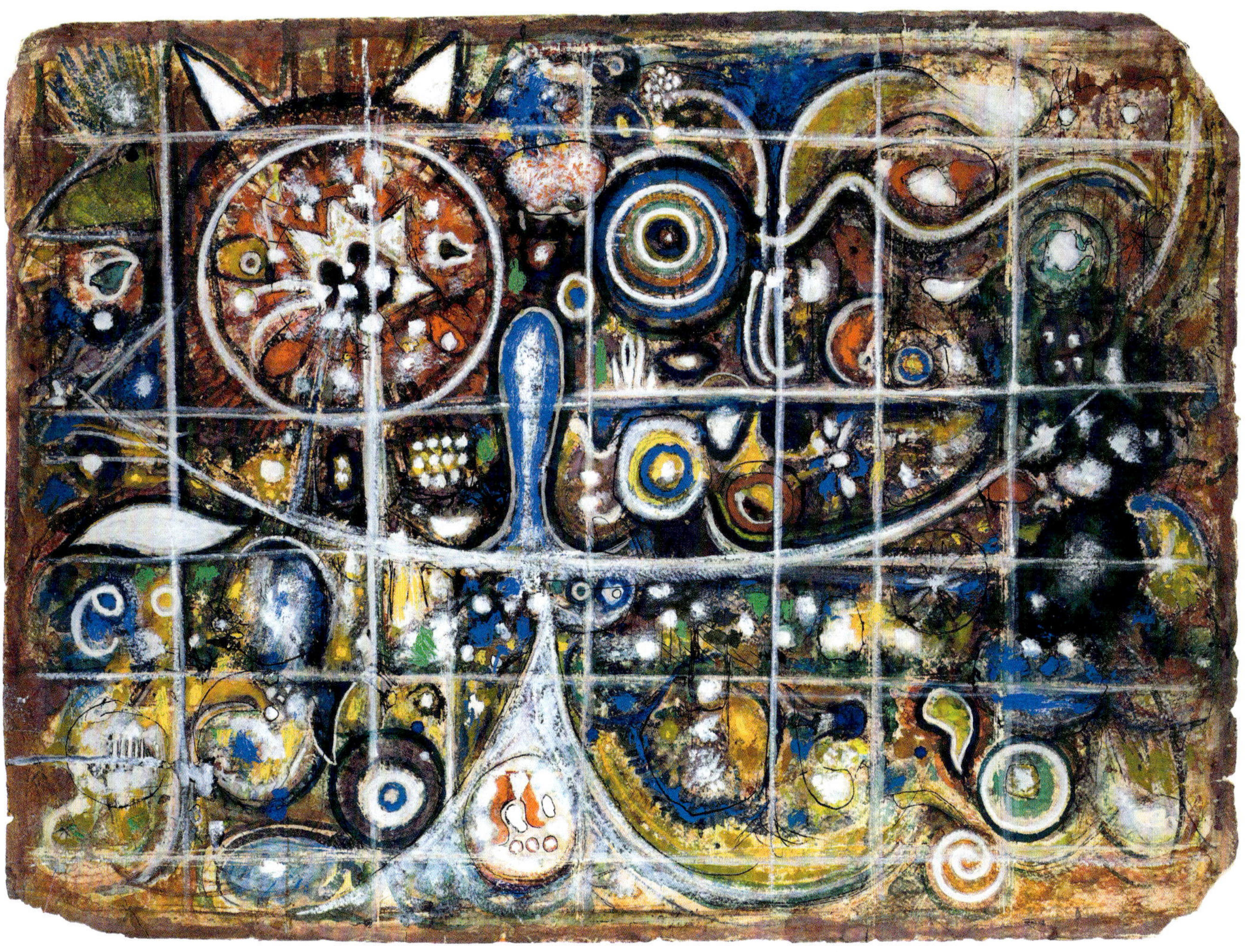

Fig. 4 Richard Pousette-Dart, *Blue Transition/Convolutions of Music*, 1942–43 (cat. 9)

formerly belonging to one of the artist's grandchildren. That the overarching scene, which Pousette-Dart likely saw at the Metropolitan Museum of Art after it had entered the collection in 1975, relays the banishment of Adam and Eve from the Garden of Eden, befits the sacrilegious tenor of the artist's tongue-in-check analogy—in the postlapsarian condition all connotations of the circle are equally valid. Concerning the circle, Pousette-Dart averred, "Our lives are filled with circles, even down to structural cells, circles that live, circles that don't live, or the sun or automobile wheels or pies, or anywhere, everywhere."[17] However, there remains a productive friction between Pousette-Dart's heterogenous references and his desire for form to remain elusive and enigmatic. As Joanne Kuebler rightly determined of this artist, "Ultimately, the forms elude definition, precluding a simple reading of the painting. They are tenuously and ambiguously suggested . . . ."[18]

Pousette-Dart's sophisticated understanding of point-to-point circuitry also lent distinctive contours to his artistic theories, fine-tuning his postulates about how art both assembles and reflects "being." Beyond hazy mysticism or transcendent humanism, his theorizations were grounded in his study of self-contained mechanics that required the precise placement of parts for the device to function. He mapped circuitry logic onto the aesthetic, biologic, and cosmic, analogizing the apparatus of a radio or television with yet more convoluted and complicated systems. Critically, he perceived of these nodal arrangements not as brittle and restrictive but as "magically" pliable and adaptive. Another page from the same studio notebook in which Pousette-Dart rhapsodized on "a garden of forms" corroborates the equivalents he drew between form, machines, humans, and space and his abstraction of electricity as a connective substance:

> *There is a magic in you that can come out*
> *& speak grandly in whatever you wish to do.*
> *A magic in electricity—in light—in photog-*
> *raphy—in darkness—in radio—television—*
> *the transmission of wave frequencies, time—*
> *how mysterious & beautiful time is. Someone*
> *said it is the mind of space & space is the*
> *body of time. (We make music in time as we*
> *make sculpture & painting in space).*
> *To see a picture come out in a photographer's*
> *darkroom is filled with mystery & beauty—*
> *to see forms arise out of a flow of paint or to*
> *watch oil drops spread in water or watercolors*
> *bleed upon a wet page—to mold or turn a*
> *pot upon a wheel or better yet by hand to mold*
> *a shape that moves us greatly, such is like*
> *a grail—to see through a camera's lense [sic]*
> *your own vision to let your eye find its own*
> *picture is sometimes to stop time & see eternal*
> *beauty—in one picture we can sometimes*
> *see more than in many movies—whole vistas*
> *frozen in this eternal moment—*
>
> *To make with boards & saw & hammer a*
> *table your own—to form it out of your feeling—*
> *to find your own way of doing of culling*
> *of forming & rubbing this can be a thing of*
> *beauty & a joy forever.*[19]

Pousette-Dart's vision allies craft as well as the fine arts with the construction of the universe. Forging connections between the way forms emerge through the "flow of paint" and the fabrication of a table through joining and sanding, he broke with the medium specific demands of modernist formalism. For the artist, beauty and joy resided in the activation of one's hands no matter the materials or result. Instead, his evaluative criteria for assessing the work of art are rearticulated in his statement on the "garden of forms": "does it have the struggle & the marks of your hands upon it." His emphasis on artistic process as agonistic and marked helps unite the seemingly disparate corners of his practice from his layered paintings that convey the exertions of continuous revision to the brasses he produced entirely by hand. Once again, the intermediality and physicality of his theory of form comes to the fore.

The brasses, begun in the late 1930s, crystallize this point. The process demanded a high degree of technical proficiency and focus, relying upon the artist's meticulous and handheld manipulation. Several unfinished brasses in the artist's Suffern studio help reconstruct this process. After experimenting with different configurations and making preparatory sketches in his notebooks, Pousette-Dart placed a piece of white adhesive tape onto one side of a brass bar, where he would draw the intended form with graphite pencil. Then, using handheld tools, he would carefully cut, burnish, and polish the metal—a process that took weeks for one small brass. For the artist, the specialness of these objects derived from their tactile manufacture: "Mine is a tactile approach to art. People have mostly lost their tactile sense . . . . The hand is a spiritual thing and is never still."

On the other end of the feedback loop, the brasses, which could be held in the hand, slid into a pocket, or worn as jewelry, were "living things that become radiant" once they adorn the body.[20] Notably, brass possesses especially strong thermal conductivity and, when handled, absorbs the body's heat. When a selection of the brasses was included in D. Kenneth Winebrenner's volume *Jewelry Making: A Guide to Creative Contemporary Work in Jewelry* (1953), the entry specified that Pousette-Dart intentionally devised "shapes which appeal to the sense of touch" referring to "their edges and overtones, contours and surfaces" as conducive to tactile appreciation.[21] In addition to the brasses' sensorial multiplicity, they also tender categorical conflations.

Figs. 5-6

Richard Pousette-Dart, twenty-four untitled *Brasses*, ca. 1939–79 (see cats. 54–96)

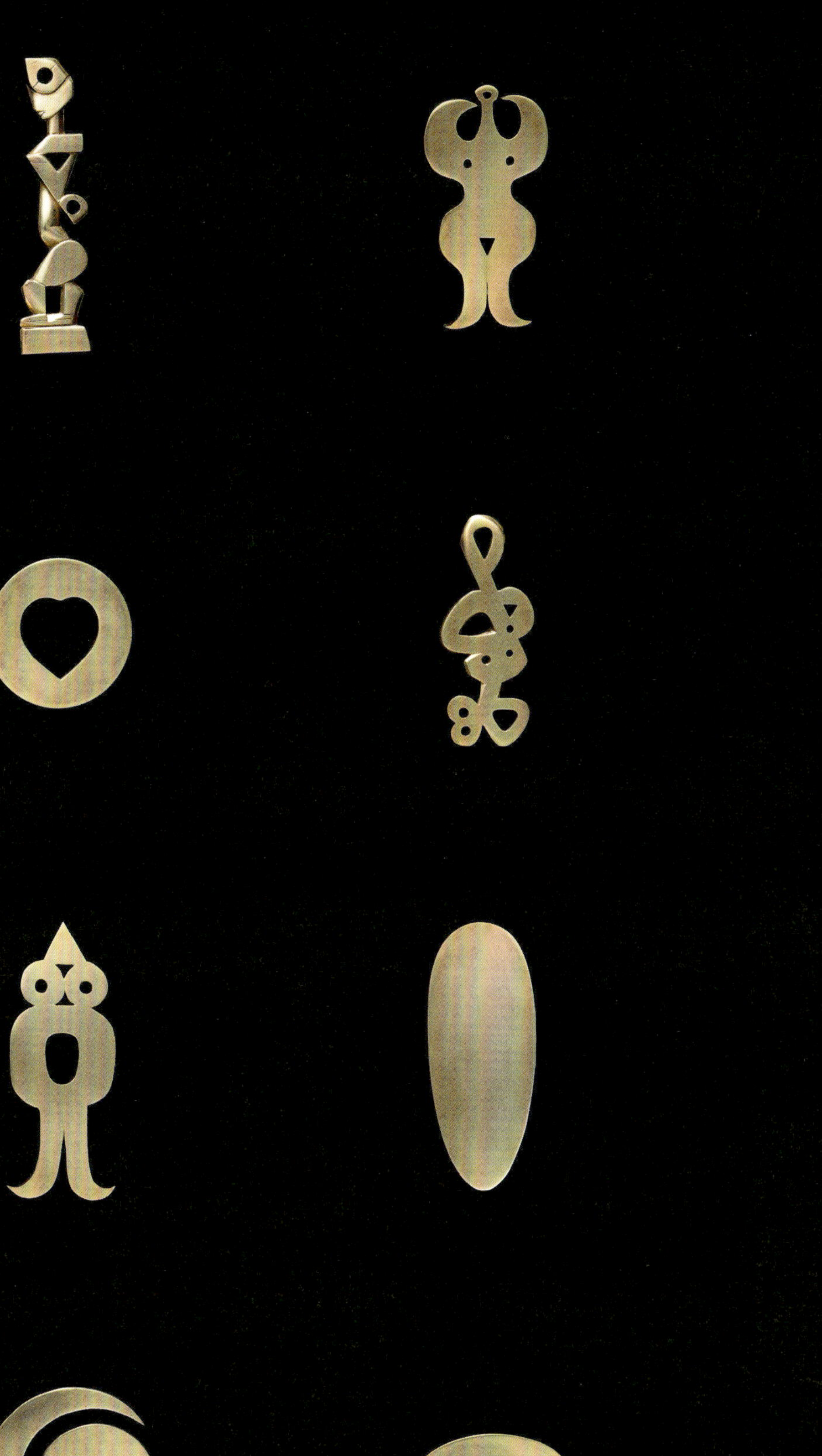

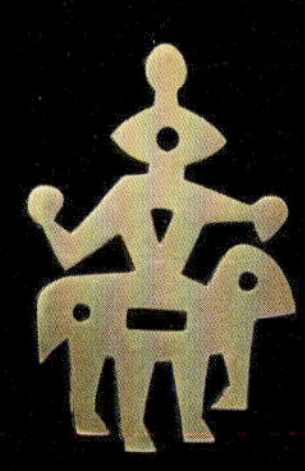
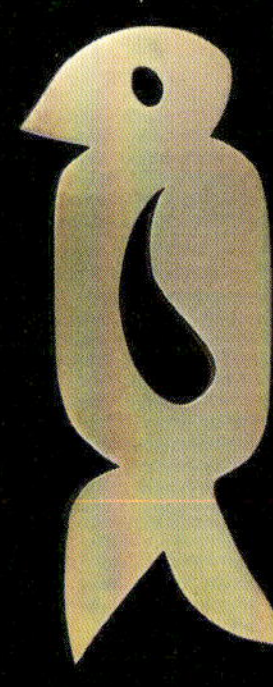
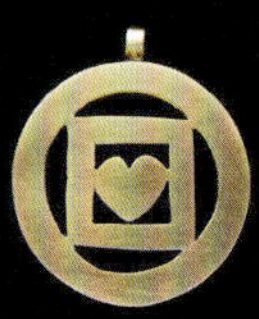
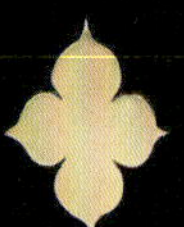
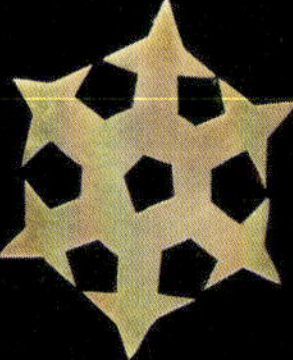
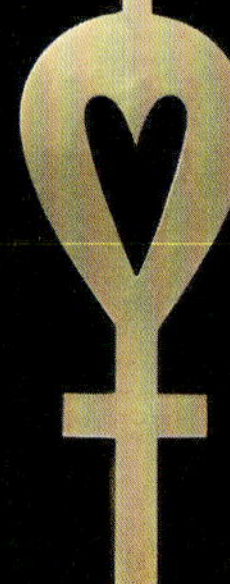
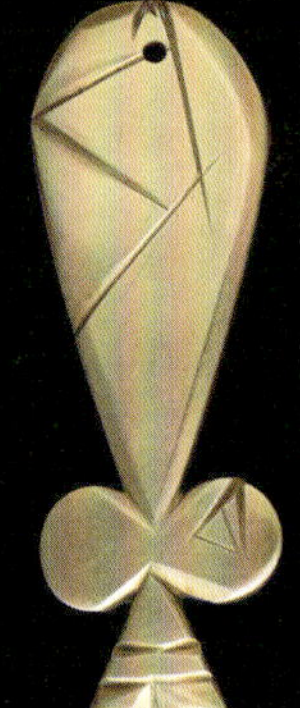
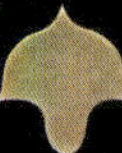
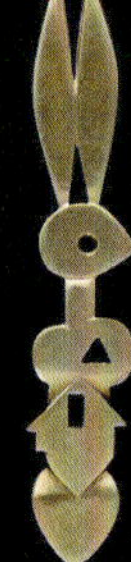
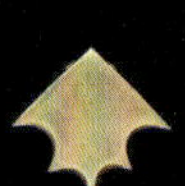
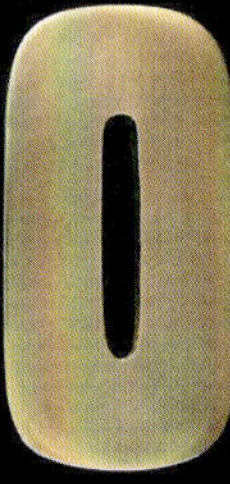
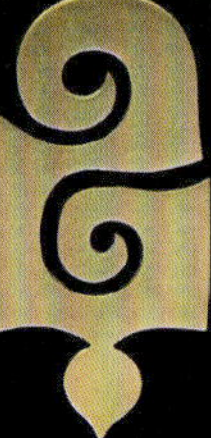

Pousette-Dart considered the brasses to be both fine and applied arts, exhibiting them alongside photographs in his 1948 solo show at the Betty Parsons Gallery, *Richard Pousette-Dart: Brasses and Photographs*, and notating prices for the sale of these works as jewelry or amulets.[22]

The brasses also isolated the panoply of forms found in Pousette-Dart's paintings and sculptures. While the sharp corners and rounded edges of the metal surfaces often dematerialized into amorphous washes of pigment to the point that they are gauzy and unrecognizable, certain paintings stabilize the iconography shared between media. In *Illumination Vertical* (fig. 1), two white verticals stand apart from the surrounding bands where diamonds, bladed spikes, and glyphs form a composite of different forms we also find in the artist's brasses. Taken together, the unitary surfaces of the brass and unmodulated white suggest that these painted totems utilize white to signify a cutout or relief sculpture (or propose some kind of shedding as the brasses morph into pigment). In either case, a host of paintings are endowed with this sculptural dimension, among them *Window, Cathedral* (cat. 22), *Window Number 4* (cat. 21), *Pillars of Odysseus* (cat. 24), *Illumination Gothic* (cat. 18), and *Fountains of Penelope* (cat. 26). In addition to Greek myths, these titles also direct architectural and spatial connotations.[23] These forms, fostered in the three-dimensional world and translated into pictorial terms, slip between opaque opticality and sensuous materiality.

Pousette-Dart's approach to form divulges a spirited humanist frequency—one that uniquely reasserted the place of love and feeling in the process of artistic creation. This valence might follow from formative exchanges with his mother, poet Flora Pousette-Dart. In the preface to her volume of poetry entitled *I Saw Time Open*, she spoke of an "ecstatic revelation" and the moment of greater insight, when "some portion of a familiar landscape, some aspect of daily life, some idea hitherto accepted as commonplace, is suddenly lighted up as though by a giant searchlight." Stumbling upon these forms, she mused, could only "occur in solitude, outside of time" and yet, "they convey an overwhelming brotherhood, and demand expression."[24] In a letter of August 2, 1940, Richard wrote his mother "from the office":

> *Dear Mother,*
>
> *This morning your book of poems came back from the bindery and it is just about perfect, simple and unaffected and sincere and rather poetic looking. It is very satisfying to me and stimulating.*[25]

As he regaled her with the disappointments of his quest to rent a suitable studio in New York and reports about recently completed sculptures, he confided, "I have had a few spurts of poetry but am so disgusted with the results—*I cannot work over my poems*." What he could work over, however, would be his garden of forms. There, he would nurture and tend a visual ecosystem by mining the worlds around him with his own "giant searchlight." In this same letter, Pousette-Dart shared that he had continued "making more Symbols" and that he was "in love with a dozen different ideas," noting his particular interest in the complex form, in which a circle surrounds a square that houses a heart, diagramming it twice in the letter. These emotive symbols would surface in several brass carvings (see, for instance, the object on the top right-hand corner of p. 30), but never directly appear in a painting—nevertheless, their sentiment resounds. Speaking of the shape, he continued, "It is about as pure & full as it can be made. I will make casts of this one & give it to all my friends." For Pousette-Dart, the potential of form evidently moved from aesthetic structure and embodied touch onto empathic kinship.

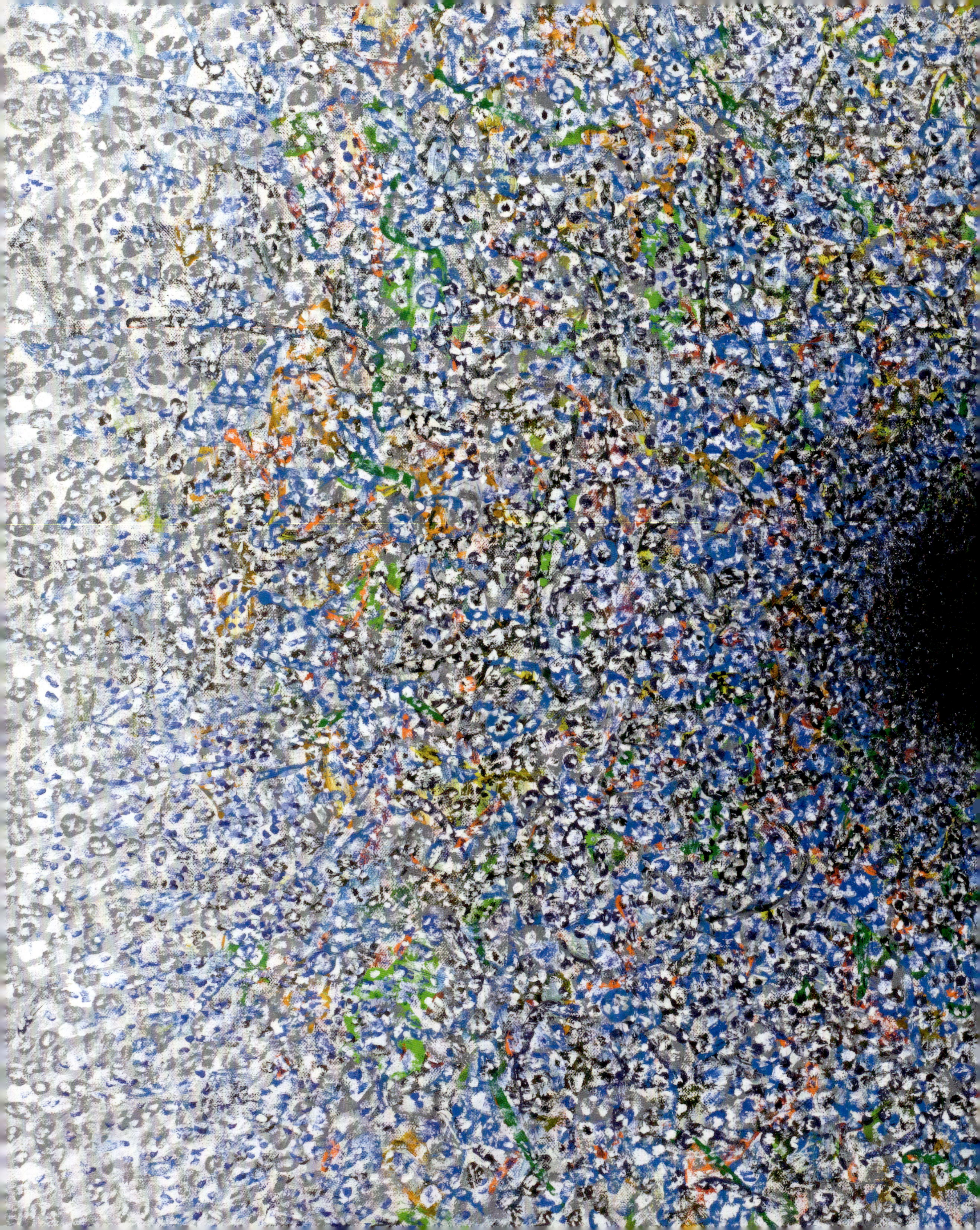

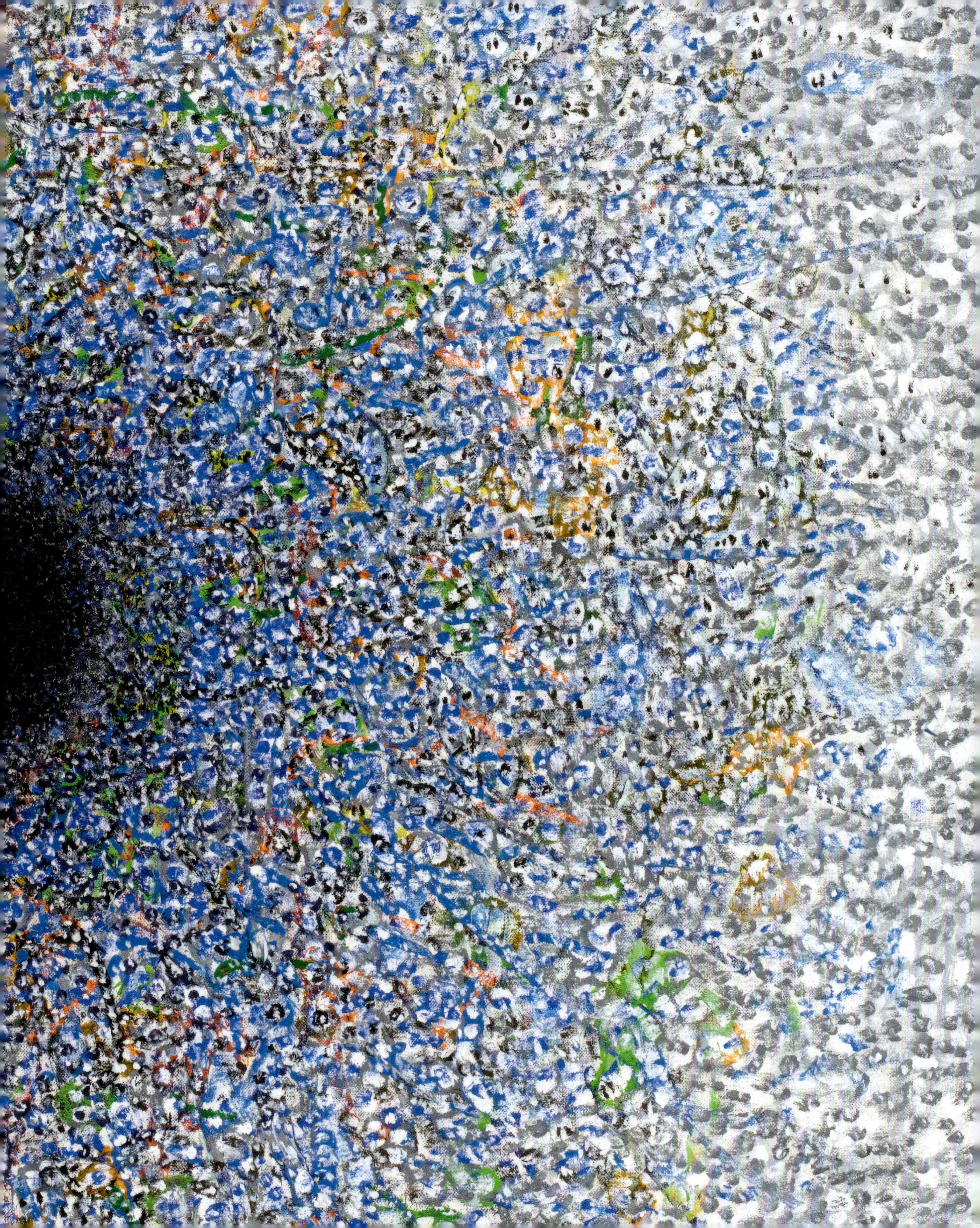

Richard Pousette-Dart The Conscientious Creator

Beatriz Cordero Martín

The artist . . . must stand alone, free and open in all directions for exits and entrances, and yet with all freedom, he must be solid and real in the substance of his own form.[1]
— Richard Pousette-Dart, 1951

As an artist whose work contributed significantly to the aesthetic and theoretical currency of the New York School, Richard Pousette-Dart was a vital figure among first-generation Abstract Expressionists. He was just twenty-five years old when the Artists' Gallery in New York organized his first solo exhibition in 1941, and during the 1940s his canvases were shown alongside works by Willem de Kooning, Mark Rothko (twelve and thirteen years older, respectively), and Jackson Pollock (four years his senior) in foundational group shows organized by Howard Putzel for his 67 Gallery and at Peggy Guggenheim's Art of This Century. By the age of thirty-five Pousette-Dart had received recognition from art critics as well as general-interest magazines, including *Look* and *Life*, and participated in annual exhibitions at the Whitney Museum of American Art, the Art Institute of Chicago, and the Museum of Modern Art (MoMA) in New York, which acquired his canvas *Number 11: A Presence* (1949) in 1950.

In December 1950 Pousette-Dart left New York City for the peaceful town of Sloatsburg in upstate New York and would twice relocate locally, continuing to cherish the natural surrounds near Harriman State Park and the Hudson River. Working within this setting, the artist's output embraced more fully distilled and open compositions realized in large formats, and he afforded particular attention to color and light effects created through the meticulous application of multiple layers of paint. Throughout his career, interests in spirituality, poetry, music, and nature deeply impregnate his oeuvre. As someone who believed in "creating art as a way of being,"[2] Pousette-Dart strove within his work to offer a meaningful visual referent to truth, cosmic balance, and human interconnection. The exhibition *Poetry of Light* provides a unique opportunity to observe the organic growth of Pousette-Dart as an artist and reveals how his artistic and intellectual independence were true catalysts for his unique evolution.

A Loner Among the Abstract Expressionists

Richard Pousette-Dart benefitted from an exceptional upbringing. The son of painter Nathaniel Pousette-Dart and poet Flora Pousette-Dart, he grew up in a household abundant with American

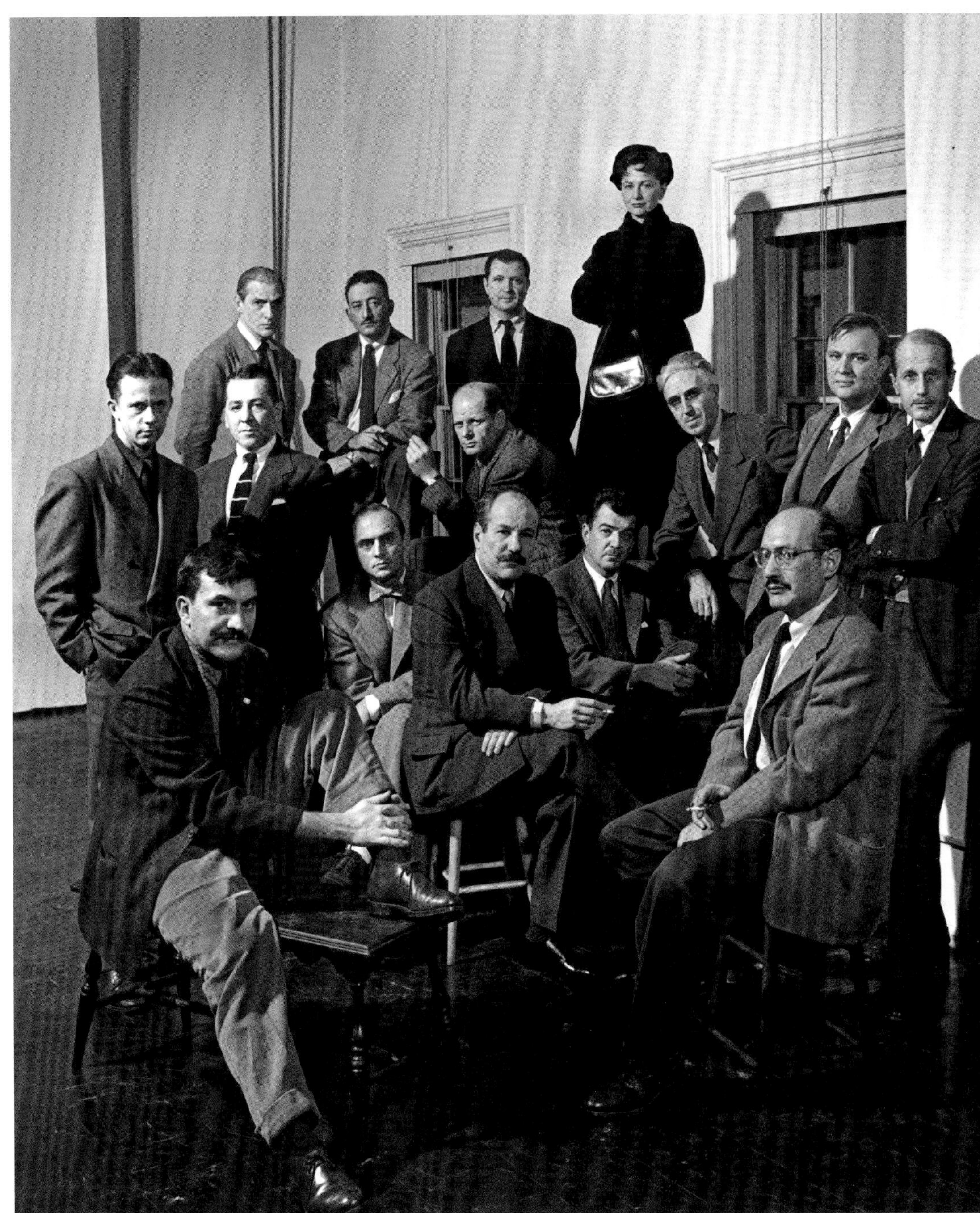

Fig. 1

Nina Leen, *The Irascibles*, 1950

modern art and non-Western cultural objects, and his family engaged in lively exchanges concerning Transcendentalist philosophy, poetry, and music. Debates on the importance of art education and social justice were frequent among his parents and their circle of friends, which included such authoritative figures as John D. Graham and Alfred Stieglitz. Having learned the fundamentals of painting independently in his father's studio, Richard later found higher education trivial and regimented by comparison, and he ultimately abandoned Bard College during his first semester. Beyond his parents' influence, friendship with artist and writer Graham proved constructive, particularly Graham's ideas about the power of art to unlock the subconscious, a subject popularized during the period by the contributions of Carl Jung.

Like many New York artists interested in "advanced art"—a term applied to modernist abstract art during the 1940s—Pousette-Dart gravitated to select midtown galleries and small artists' gatherings, including those held at "The Club" on East Eighth Street. While he claimed to have only "attended the Club once or twice,"[3] his participation in a three-day symposium in April 1950 cemented his fellowship with colleagues in attendance.

At the gathering, a group of artists resolved to send an open letter to Roland L. Redmond, president of the Metropolitan Museum of Art, to protest of the museum's "reactionary" curatorial stance, which the group anticipated would affect the exhibition *American Painting Today*, scheduled for the following year. Eighteen painters signed the letter, and ten sculptors added their names in solidarity. On May 22, 1950, *The New York Times* published the letter on its front page. The following day *The Herald Tribune* defended the museum in an editorial titled "The Irascible Eighteen,"[4] a label subsequently adopted by *Life* magazine in an article about the controversial exhibition. *Life*'s editors detailed the story of the artists who had confronted the museum, and included a photograph by Nina Leen of fifteen of the eighteen "Irascibles" (fig. 1).[5] According to Bradford Collins, the compelling story of the protest letter, the amplification of the controversy in the press, and the subsequent publication of several articles about modern art (and artists) in *Life* created "a paradigmatic instance of . . . [a] larger metanarrative" that contributed to the democratization of modern art in the postwar period.[6]

Although the artists portrayed within Leen's Irascibles portrait today are recognized as the most prominent group of first-generation Abstract Expressionist painters, Pousette-Dart stated in a talk delivered in 1951 at the School of the Museum of Fine Arts, Boston,[7] "These artists do not wish to be labeled, nor should they be, for their true relationship is extremely separate and they relate to one another only as all things do to the universe."[8] The desire to create autonomously was, however, impractical, given that many had exhibited together for years,[9] especially at the Betty Parsons Gallery[10] and Art of This Century.[11] Highly adverse to a commercial orientations toward art, Pousette-Dart believed that appearing in *Life* was a collaboration with "the Establishment."[12] He later downplayed his participation in this mediatic episode, declaring that he remained "at the fringe of it."[13]

Although Richard Pousette-Dart is strongly identified with the New York School, a number of critics have noted that aspects of his oeuvre are divergent from the mainstream of Abstract Expressionism.[14] First and foremost, and regardless of medium or period, his compositions invariably possess a pronounced compositional harmony and absence of existential angst, distancing Pousette-Dart from the majority within his cohort. Although abstraction was championed in postwar America for its associations with "democratic" values, most American artists felt the need to differentiate themselves from their European counterparts, embracing a sense of tragedy and evoking roughness.[15]

Fig. 2
Richard Pousette-Dart, 1940s, photograph by Maggie Meredith

Pousette-Dart, conversely, primarily remained aloof from these tendencies. Described as a "spiritual optimist"[16] and "an incredibly joyful, optimistic person" whose "art resonates with a lucid happiness,"[17] the artist noted that creation for him was a source of joy,[18] and passages in his studio notebooks reflect his lifelong passion for beauty.[19] Ultimately, the lyrical expressiveness of his paintings, his interest in transcendentalism, and his unyielding advocacy for an art that would unify all people through an elevated version of themselves distinguished Pousette-Dart from his contemporaries.[20] The painter himself addressed the nonconformist nature of his work: "I am an artist of concealed power of the spirit, not of the brute physical form."[21] His self-affiliation with the "power of spirit" gave way to an individualistic attitude at a time when self-determination characterized by manly bravura became a symbol of a newly dominant America.[22] Proud of his independent character, Pousette-Dart described himself as a "loner."[23] And as spiritual man who loved nature and poetry, he avoided alcohol, refused to eat animals, and, as will be expanded upon within this essay, passionately resisted war.

Artist and Dreamer

I always felt that my point of view was that of a creator, a conscientious creator rather than a conscientious objector. As a solution to war . . . we have to come to the realization it is not enough to object; we must find ways to create in peaceful terms.[24]

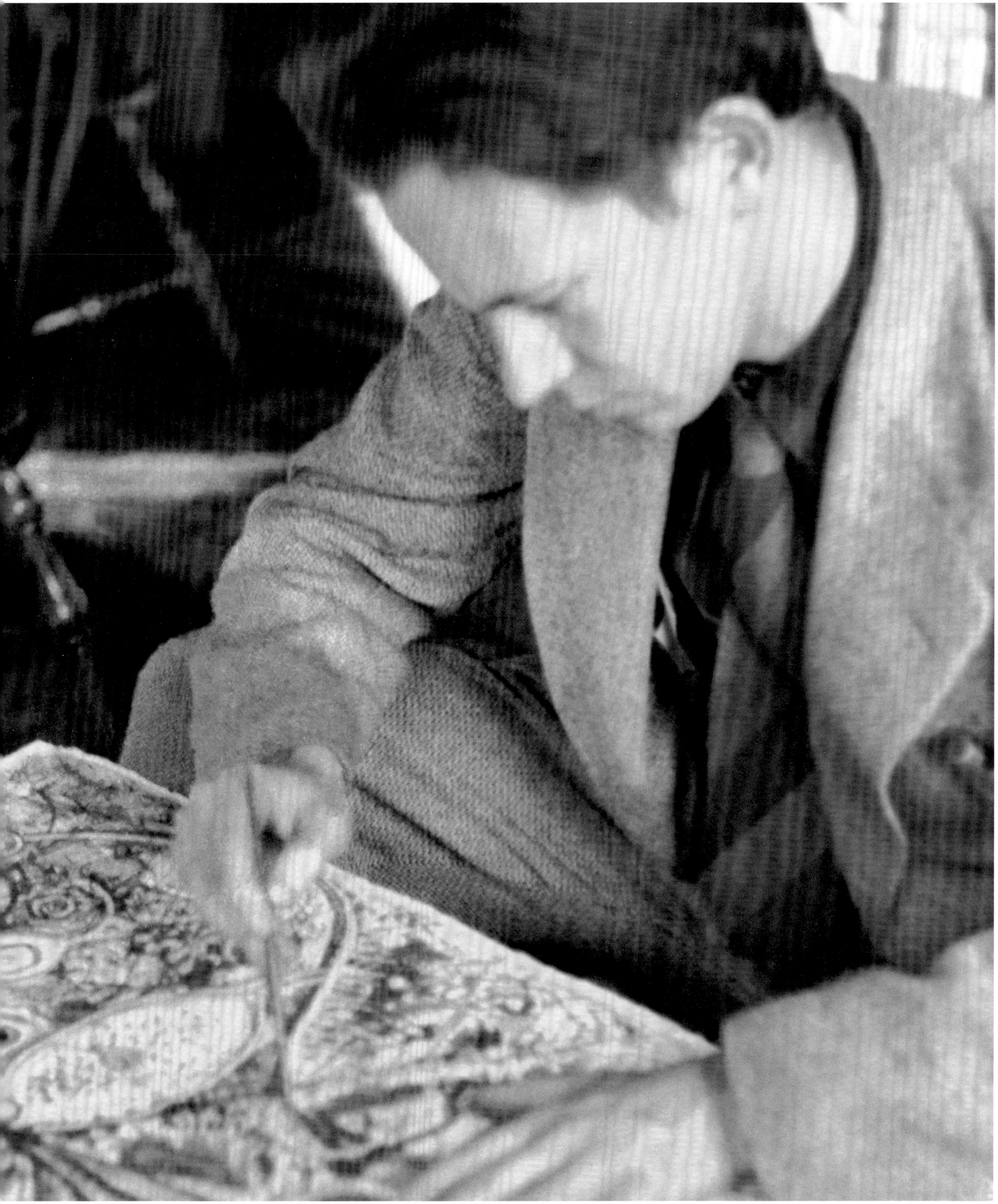

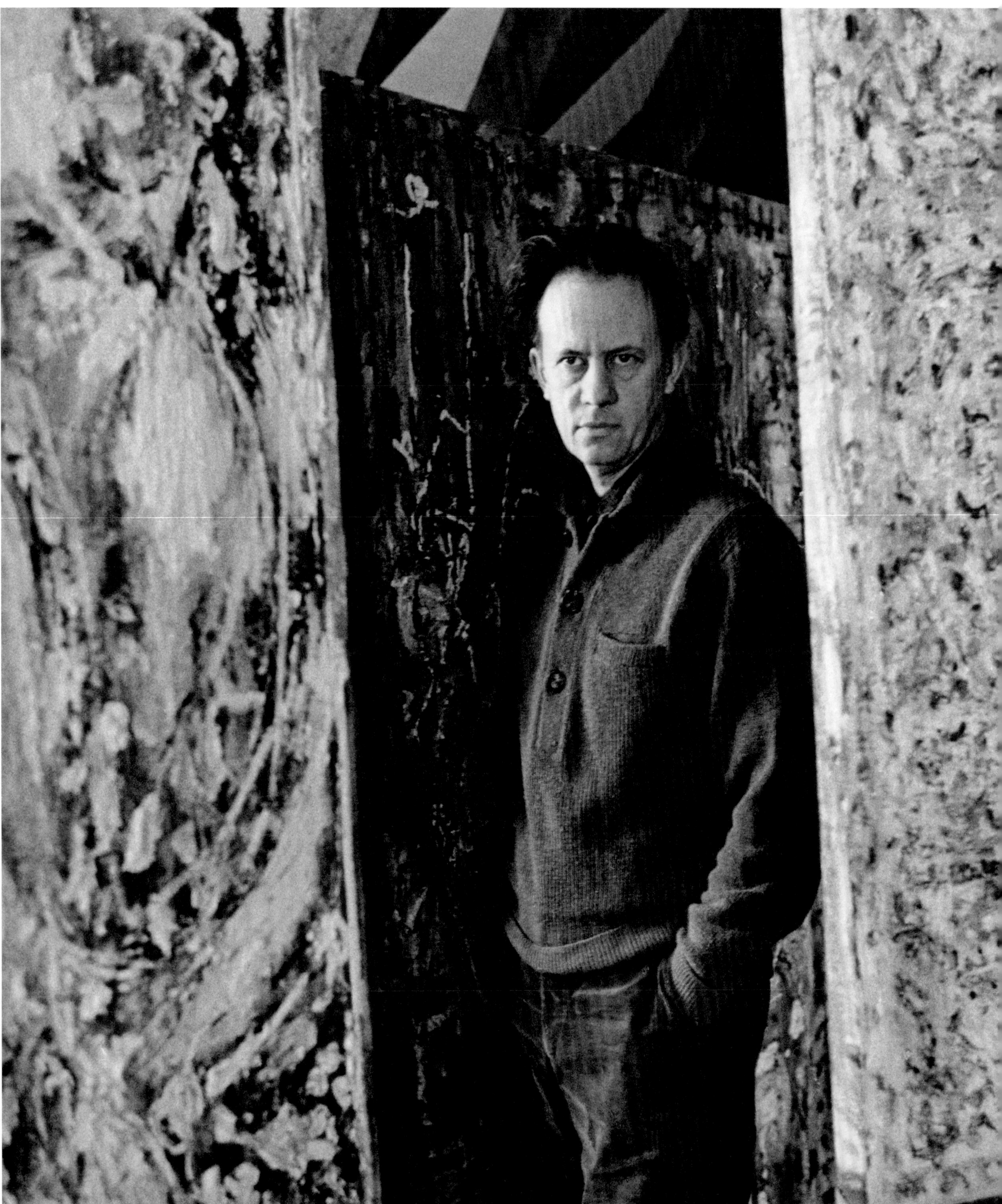

Fig. 3

Richard Pousette-Dart in his Suffern studio, 1962, photograph by Herb Breuer

The first time Pousette-Dart publicly articulated his anti-war views was in February 1935 in an essay for his high school yearbook titled "I Have Been Called a Dreamer." In it, he expresses radical opposition to war and the militaristic profit-making of the United States at a time when most Americans were yet to become concerned with rising authoritarianism in Europe (the invasion of Ethiopia the following October and, more determinately, the outbreak of the Spanish Civil War the following year would bring new preoccupations to the fore). In "I Have Been Called a Dreamer," he professed that in the United States the problem of militarism was systemic, promoting a self-fulfilling prophecy of making young people "war minded." Pousette-Dart confronted "the hypocrisy of having capital punishment in a country . . . where young men are taught the ways of killing [in] institutions of higher education"[25] and denounced the links between the military and American universities. Beyond considering all war immoral, Pousette-Dart stood against the blind obedience required by the military. He claimed that "discipline is of no value unless it is self-imposed," and that "military discipline means instant obedience without intervention of thought."[26] Although these ideas were formed at a young age, Pousette-Dart's arguments regarding the need to discover and defend one's own values persevered throughout his life, especially through his role as a teacher through which he advised students to arrive at their own paths and views.[27]

Adhering to such staunch anti-military beliefs, Pousette-Dart refused the draft in 1940. Upon receiving his draft card, he tore it up and sent it back to local authorities together with a deeply passionate letter, one of many he wrote between 1940 and 1941. These letters reiterated beliefs first expressed in "I Have Been Called a Dreamer," including military training as an "education in hate" and war "the negation of humanity."[28] In the summer of 1941 he elaborated, "in pursuing what I believe to be the goodness of humanity, the truth of God, and a love for my country, I cannot further cooperate with those forces, those laws, or those people whom, according to God, I believe to be corrupt (consciously or unconsciously) and who, I believe, are further and further leading humanity toward degradation, immorality, catastrophe and total chaos."[29] Such declarations suggest that Pousette-Dart's pacifism was rooted within a religious framework, as it was for a great majority of conscientious objectors in the United States prior to the Vietnam War.[30] Ultimately he was relieved of military duty by a sympathetic draft officer, who chose not to have the artist incarcerated nor sent to a public service camp, as many of his fellow war resisters were forced to endure.[31]

Equally influential on Pousette-Dart's early activism was the writing of New England Transcendentalist Henry David Thoreau, which Richard and his mother, Flora, had studied in depth. Thoreau's "Resistance to Civil Government," published in 1849 and later known as "On the Duty of Civil Disobedience," highlighted the immorality of the Mexican-American War, and it became a seminal text for conscientious objectors during the unpopular entry of the United States into World War I.[32] That Thoreau's objection to war on ethical grounds was combined with notions of radical self-reliance—exemplified in his influential book *Walden* (1854)—deeply resonated with the young artist. Ultimately, Pousette-Dart remained a vehement war resister from the mid-1930s to the 1970s, first fighting conscription, then protesting World War II, and during the last decades of his life campaigning against nuclear weapons. Today his archive contains copious materials that reveal his activist interests: pamphlets, newspapers, informational brochures, invitations to lectures, and abundant correspondence with many organizations working toward securing amnesty for men imprisoned for their anti-war convictions,[33] especially after World War II.

Pousette-Dart believed art was "a reflection of being,"[34] thus his thinking was interwoven with his spirituality, and his activism with his artistic creativity. He thought everyone should find their true calling, become whole, and serve others through their own, personal work. In his words: "The person who realizes wholeness in himself is the real soldier. He is fighting on the front lines, of creative imagination, or creativity—he'll die for that. But he won't die killing other people."[35] For Pousette-Dart, art was "the heavens forever opening up . . . magic . . . joy . . . gardens of surprise and miracle,"[36] and he embraced the opportunity of transcending by offering powerful visual references that would serve as a reflection on cosmic equilibrium and human interconnection, the same universal order and human brotherhood he sought to protect with his anti-war activism.

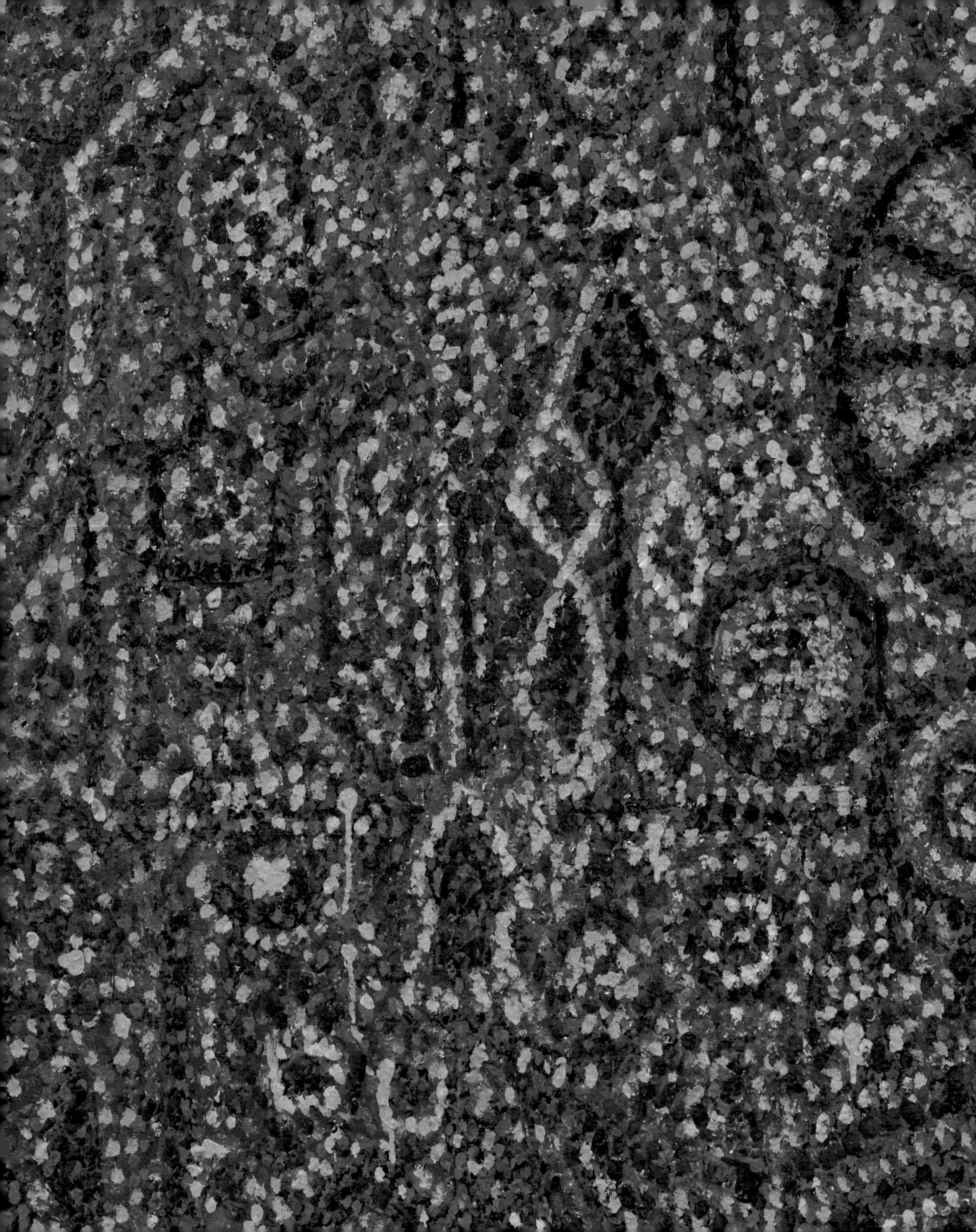

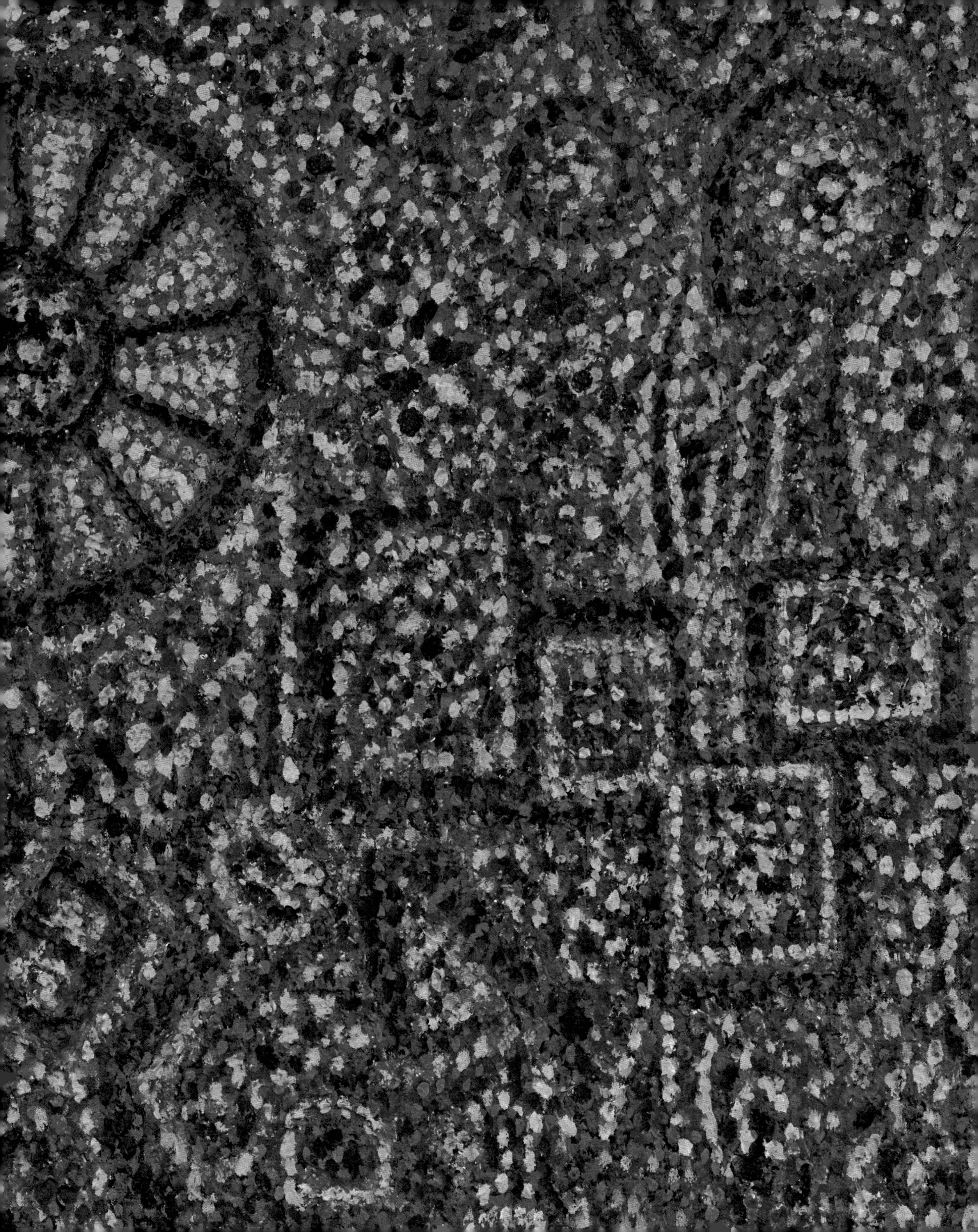

Through the Artist's Lens
Richard Pousette-Dart as a Photographer

Charles H. Duncan

Among the core group of Abstract Expressionists, Richard Pousette-Dart is best described as a nonconformist. A pacifist and vegetarian who rarely indulged in alcohol, his intense philosophical orientation and steady demeanor stood in stark contrast to the bravura of colleagues who inhabited the now-legendary downtown tavern scene. In 1950 he left New York City for Orange and Rockland Counties to the immediate north, where he lived and worked for the remainder of his life. Pousette-Dart's relocation is often misconstrued as a flight from the urban art community: in fact, it was precipitated by the impending demolition of his East Fifty-Sixth Street apartment building, and only after an extensive search for a suitable replacement in Manhattan did he and his wife, Evelyn, settle upon a more spacious and affordable base. During the decades that followed, Pousette-Dart enjoyed a dual orientation, working in a series of studios in the relative quietude of the countryside while continuing to exhibit in New York City at the Betty Parsons Gallery, teach at Columbia University and the Art Students League of New York, and maintain loyalties with peers in both locations.

Today the Richard Pousette-Dart Foundation preserves the artist's extensive personal and professional correspondence, as well as hundreds of studio notebooks containing his philosophies, sketches of elemental forms and human figures, and passing practical notes. Early correspondence gives insight into his activities during his semester at Bard College in 1935, as well as the formative years immediately following. Particularly illuminating are letters from family members and a core group of nonartist fellow conscientious objectors. Surprisingly absent from these sources, however, is a chronicle of the interchanges that one might expect to find between Pousette-Dart and his Abstract Expressionist colleagues. The handful of letters from peers, including Mark Rothko and Hans Hofmann, are brief and practical. Pousette-Dart made a point not to speak about his contemporaries, acquiescing only when pressed for remembrances about recently passed friends, such as Ad Reinhardt, of whom he noted: "Like myself, he stayed on the periphery of the art arena although he enjoyed entering, speaking at the club and any place there was a fray. He had absolute opinions . . . . Although we worked very differently, I felt he had great integrity as an artist and a human being."[1]

A body of fine-art photography by Pousette-Dart helps fill this lacuna by offering a fascinating visual record of the artist's many and varied close personal relationships. A notable component of this photographic work is his daringly modernist portraits that serve as a nexus through which to explore Pousette-Dart's intellectual circle. Combined with a series of accomplished nature studies, likely to have been completed during the mid-1950s, the centrality of photography to the artist's overall artistic practice becomes evident. In fact, when the representational imagery that appeared in Pousette-Dart's early sculpture, drawing, and painting gave way to nonfigurative abstraction during the early 1940s, photography largely filled this role and remained an enduring mode of figurative expression throughout the remainder of the artist's career.

Beginnings

Photography was a lifelong passion for Richard Pousette-Dart, commencing with experiments with pinhole cameras as a child. Among the earliest extant photographic prints by Pousette-Dart are botanical photograms (cat. 97). Created during the mid- to late 1930s, they lay the groundwork for a favored mode of photographic image-making wherein light emerges from darkness. These photograms were realized by placing leaves and stems on light-sensitive paper and exposing the entire assembly to light. The camera is not necessary for this process, which creates silhouetted images with soft transitions where the irregular edges of objects cast shadows.[2] The subjects of these photograms mirror imagery found within Pousette-Dart's early drawings and studio notebooks, and his interest in isolated selections of flora—leaves, buds, stems, and petals—is additionally foregrounded in his letters to close friends and notebooks that contain actual, pressed specimens. Thus, the photograms were formative experiments within his program of nature-based abstraction that was ultimately realized through drawing, painting, sculpture, and, eventually, lens-based photography. Even at this early juncture, Pousette-Dart's prodigious mechanical aptitude advanced his experimental darkroom practice. He also benefitted from a professional position in the Manhattan photographic retouching studio of art director, painter, and printmaker Lynn T. Morgan, a professional colleague of Pousette-Dart's father, Nathaniel.[3]

The form of the human head was similarly a lifelong fixation for Pousette-Dart, populating his loose sketches, notebooks, and etchings of the late 1930s, and the entire trajectory of his photographic oeuvre. An early photograph of the artist gesticulating dramatically is part of a series of four self-portraits in which Pousette-Dart experiments with isolating his face and hands (cat. 101). He employs a similar strategy with great success in a portrait of his mother, *Flora Pousette-Dart* (cat. 100), captured in profile under soft illumination that accents her aquiline nose. In both photographs, the faces of the sitters emerge out of negative voids, downplaying contextual orientation. Flora's visage additionally mimics African or pre-Columbian masks, objects that Pousette-Dart admired in his father's collection of so-called primitive art and studied during his frequent visits to the American Museum of Natural History.

It is impossible to assess Pousette-Dart's artistic development without referencing the formidable imprint of his family. Flora Pousette-Dart was a poet and musician with deep interests in Theosophy and avant-garde literature—the work of Ezra Pound especially—and she served as a sounding board for Richard's nascent spiritual and philosophical explorations. Nathaniel Pousette-Dart was a painter trained at the Pennsylvania Academy of the Fine Arts, a founding member of the Federation of Modern Painters and Sculptors, and a teacher and writer on art who edited a notable series of books on American painters. Nathaniel was, additionally, a prominent art director during the pivotal 1920s when advertising and commercial art transitioned from hand-based illustration to photography. In this role, he interfaced with leading commercial and fine-art photographers such as Alfred Stieglitz, Paul Outerbridge, and Berenice Abbott; the latter compiled a photographic education program for a project spearheaded by Nathaniel called the Art Adventure League. These pursuits further encouraged Richard Pousette-Dart's commitment to his photographic practice.

Developing Networks and Techniques

It is likely that Pousette-Dart first encountered Russian-born émigré artist John D. Graham through his father, who reviewed Graham's artwork and influential volume *System and Dialectics of Art* of 1937 in his magazine *Art and Artists of Today*.[4] In 1938 Richard became friendly with Graham and his wife, Constance, and in 1940 purchased Graham's painting *Blue Abstraction* (1931). In the summer of 1940, Pousette-Dart created the well-known photographic portrait of Graham cradling an oversized wooden shoe in Graham's living room on Sidney Place, Brooklyn Heights (cat. 104). Pousette-Dart later recalled that the eccentric Graham often struck dramatic poses when greeting guests at his home. The photograph presents him, dishabille, clasping the carved prop: a fitting fetish item for the flamboyant provocateur. Pousette-Dart preferred to work under natural illumination, and he noted in regard to the Graham sitting that the exposure "did not have sufficient light—taken indoors without the sun—a foggy day . . . I will take more in sunlight."[5]

The 1940s was a breakthrough decade for Richard Pousette-Dart, commencing with a solo exhibition of his painting and sculpture at the nonprofit Artists' Gallery in 1941. By mid-decade, his paintings, watercolors, and brasses had been shown at the Marian Willard Gallery, Peggy Guggenheim's Art of This Century, the Federation of Modern Painters and Sculptors, and the Museum of Modern Art. Pousette-Dart group of colleagues quickly grew to include Jackson Pollock, Willem de Kooning, Arshile Gorky, Adolph Gottlieb, Hans Hofmann, Lee Krasner, Robert Motherwell, Hedda Sterne, and others. Living and working in a ground-floor railroad flat on East Fifty-Sixth Street, he often socialized at the nearby Fifty-Ninth Street Automat with painters Barnett Newman, Ad Reinhardt, and Mark Rothko, all of whom were active contributors to the early success of the Betty Parsons Gallery.[6] Pousette-Dart joined the gallery in 1948, which by then was the leading venue for progressive postwar American art. In December of that year, his exhibition there, *Brasses and Photographs* (fig. 1), featured portraits of selected gallery artists as well as of Parsons herself.

One champion of the 1948 *Brasses and Photographs* exhibition was Robert Flaherty, the documentary filmmaker famous for *Nanook of the North* (1922), who praised Pousette-Dart as the finest still photographer in America and solicited his involvement in a planned cinematic adaptation of *Around the World in Eighty Days* (this was left unrealized at Flaherty's death in July 1951). Pousette-Dart photographed Flaherty; his wife, Frances; and their daughter, Monica, at their apartment in the Chelsea Hotel on Twenty-Third Street just after completion of Flaherty's 1948 feature film, *Louisiana Story* (cat. 113). A bust-length portrait of Robert from this sitting recalls the Pictorialist sensibilities of Edward Steichen, as well as Alvin Langdon Coburn, whose evolution from Symbolism through Vorticist abstraction presaged Pousette-Dart's own trajectory as a photographer (cat. 116). Here, Flaherty's searching gaze, aging countenance, and downturned mouth are

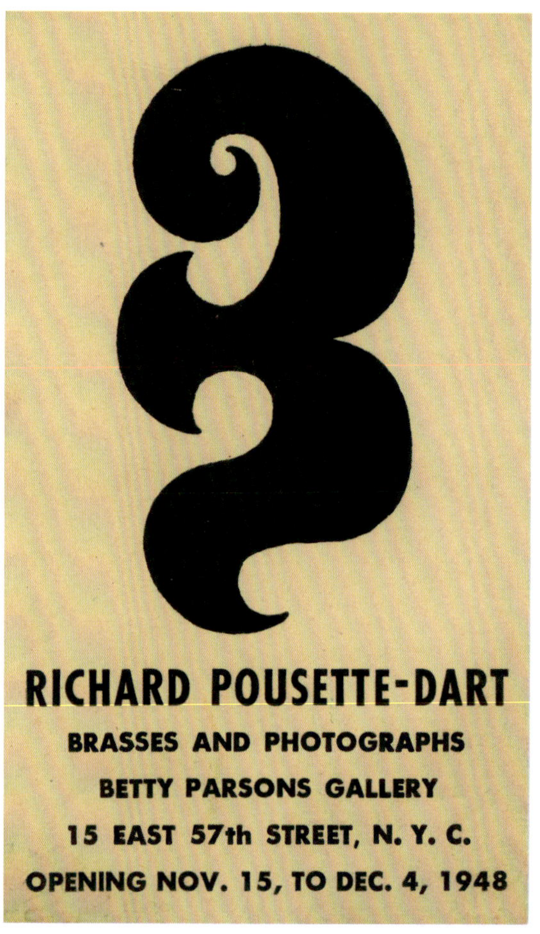

Fig. 1

Exhibition announcement, *Richard Pousette-Dart: Brasses and Photographs*, Betty Parsons Gallery, 1948

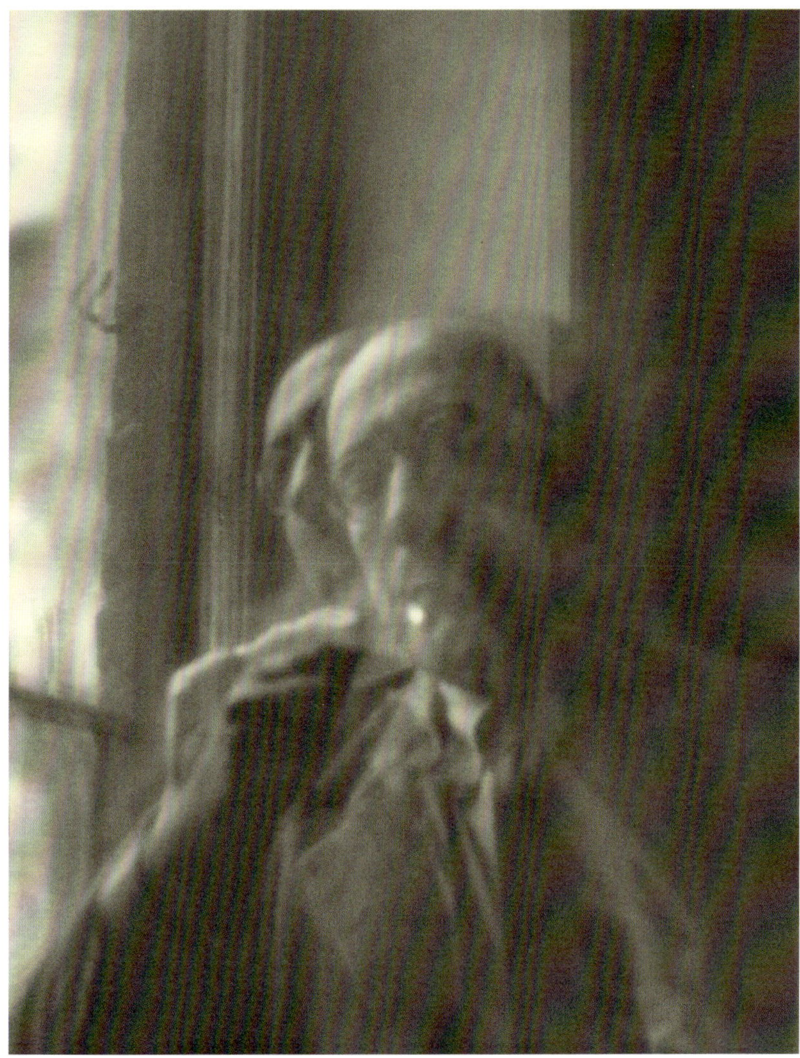

Fig. 2 Richard Pousette-Dart, *Mark Rothko*, 1948 (cat. 105)

expressive of dreamily elegiac authority, and overall his likeness is patently cinematic, invoking Flaherty's renown as a visionary filmmaker.

By the late 1940s Pousette-Dart had begun to experiment with multiple exposures executed in two methods: at the point of capture (two or more images on the same negative) and composited during the enlarging and printing process. In many cases, Pousette-Dart combined multiple views of a sitter into a single hallucinatory image to distort notions of time and spatial orientation. This strategy is employed in a photograph of painter Mark Rothko (fig. 2) that unites two offset likenesses of the painter from the same vantage, recalling Pousette-Dart's paintings of the 1930s that unify interlocking forms within overall compositions. In other compositions, Pousette-Dart pairs likenesses with attributes indicative of his sitters' vocations: painter William Congdon is ingeniously fused with a detail from his striated 1950 painting *Winter Number 1* (cat. 124), while fellow Betty Parsons Gallery artist Theodoros Stamos is captured in natural light in his studio using a Greek textile as a partial backdrop (cat. 109). A distorted patch that floats ambiguously in front of Stamos's face appears first as smoke emanating from the sitter's nose or as a blemish upon the photographic negative; however, this area is in fact a layered, superimposed biomorphic form extracted from the artist's 1949 painting *Road to Sparta*.

In 1946 Saul Leiter moved to New York City to study painting with Richard Pousette-Dart but became enthralled by the elder artist's photography. Pousette-Dart encouraged Leiter's interest in the medium, and the two engaged in numerous sessions discussing the medium and practicing in the darkroom at Pousette-Dart's makeshift kitchen workplace. Soon after, Leiter embarked on a career as a street photographer, for which he is internationally recognized today. In a portrait of Leiter from the late 1940s, Pousette-Dart has applied pigments directly to the surface of the photographic sheet, isolating the sitter's face in the manner of a Russian icon by creating a shroud or surround (cat. 103). Bridging the practices of painting and photography, the trace of the artist's hand in the darkroom process was essential to Pousette-Dart in order to elevate a photographic image beyond simple documentation. As he noted in his journals, "Photographs are reflections through light and mechanics, processes, machines, and if they are to be more they must be altered, distorted, extended, rearranged, transformed and in so doing we may find a work of art."[7]

Highly progressive in his personal outlook, Pousette-Dart's close intellectual circle included numerous women, many of whom he featured prominently within his photographs. During the early 1940s, painter Perle Fine (cat. 114) showed at the Marian Willard Gallery alongside Pousette-Dart, and the two artists similarly were represented by the Betty Parsons Gallery at the end of the decade, although their temperaments were markedly divergent: while Fine was highly active within artists' associations and professional gatherings, Pousette-Dart was fiercely independent by nature. Abstract Expressionist painter Corinne Michelle West exhibited professionally as Michael West (cat. 112) in an attempt to offset bias often faced by women artists. A close associate of influential Armenian-born painter Arshile Gorky, West first visited Pousette-Dart in his painting studio in February of 1945, noting in a letter afterward, "My feelings were those of a person viewing all of life before me as if in a dream on canvas—every emotion, every desire, objectified—so that I was looking in a mirror—a true mirror of the soul."[8] Hope Foye excelled as an opera singer, but due to racism was denied an audition to the Metropolitan Opera. Undeterred, she performed in New York during the late 1940s and in 1950 was awarded a role in the musical *Dance Me a Song*, in which Bob Fosse also performed. It was around this time she was photographed by Richard Pousette-Dart in his Fifty-Sixth Street apartment (cat. 115). Set in front of a mirror, Foye's elegance, optimism, and self-confidence are brilliantly conveyed by the illusion of her looking over her shoulder approvingly at herself. Foye went on to enjoy wide success as an opera singer in Europe, living and performing primarily in Germany and Switzerland.

Later Photographs

By the early 1950s, Pousette-Dart had relocated with his family to Orange County, New York. A 1951 *Self-Portrait* (fig. 3) taken at his home on Eagle Valley Road in Sloatsburg, New York, allows the viewer to peer into his workshop through a circular, lens-like opening and observe the mature artist amidst an array of photographic equipment: 35mm Leicas and large-format cameras, lenses, enlargers, tripods, and development apparatus. Building upon his achievements and recognition as a painter, in 1953 he was awarded third prize in the International Picture Contest staged by *Photography* magazine, a leading journal for professional and amateur enthusiasts, for his compelling portrait of his daughter, *Joanna with Cat* (cat. 120). Such recognition led to commercial commissions from *Vogue*, *Charm*, and other popular magazines for portraits of cultural luminaries, including jazz trumpeters Thad Jones and Roy Eldridge, and choreographer Bob Fosse (cats. 125–27). Pousette-Dart photographed Fosse under natural light on the balcony of the small black-and-white penthouse apartment that Fosse shared with his wife, Joan McCracken. Using a 35mm camera with a wide-angle lens, Pousette-Dart accentuated Fosse's legs, indicating of the sitter's status as one of the leading innovators in popular dance during the period.

Fig. 3
Richard Pousette-Dart, *Self-Portait in Photography Studio*, 1951 (detail of cat. 121)

The quiet beauty of country life reawakened Pousette-Dart's interest in nature. In the masterful *Queen Anne's Lace II* (cat. 98), likely created in Rockland County during the mid-1950s, the tightly cropped emphasis on the flower's radiating

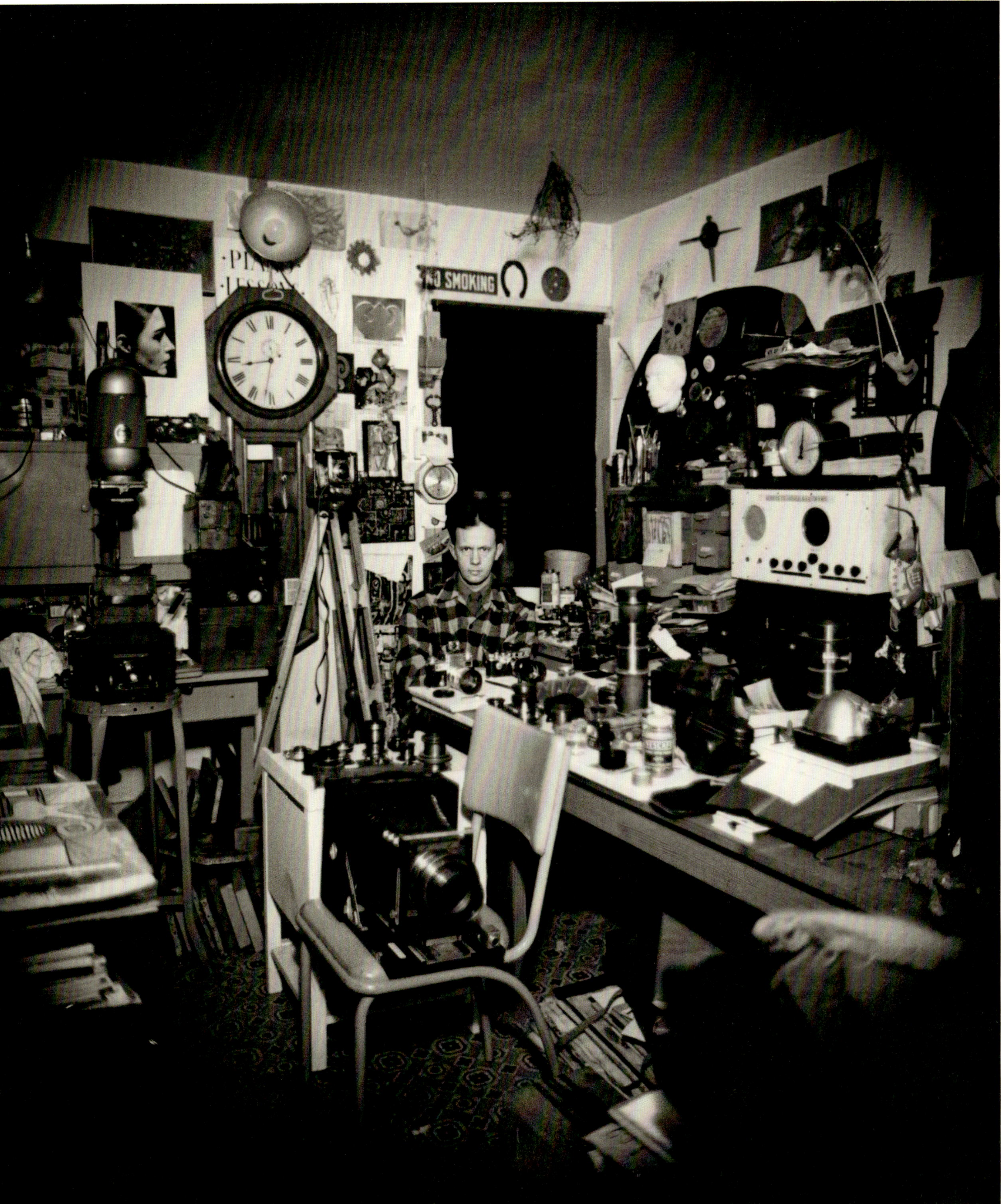
NO SMOKING

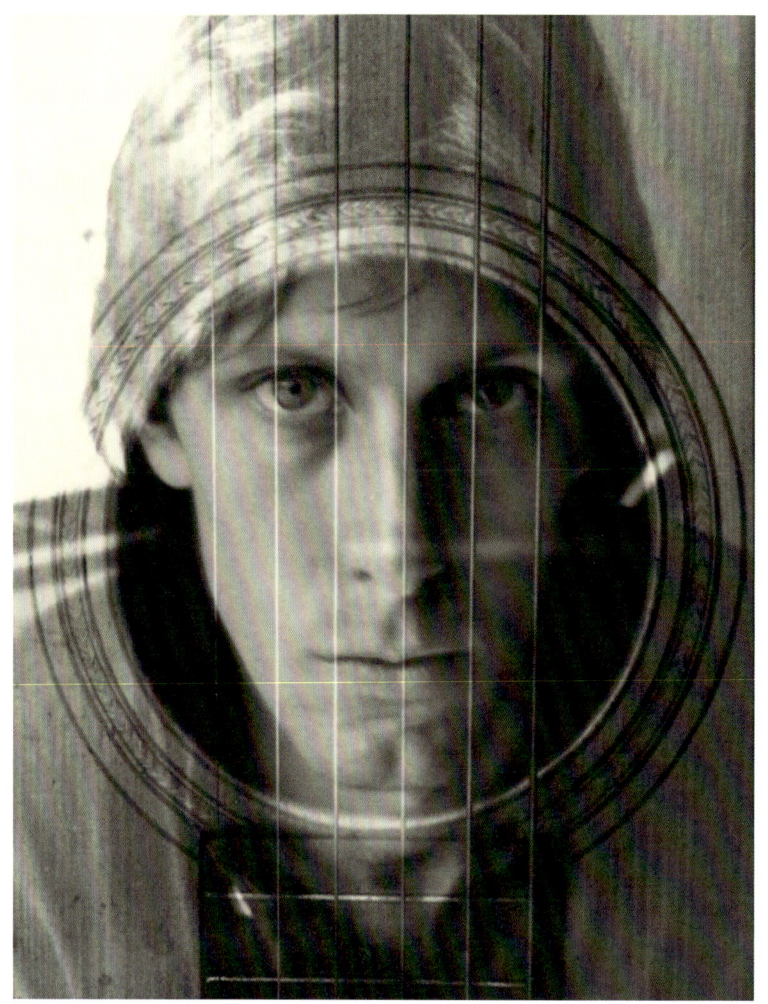

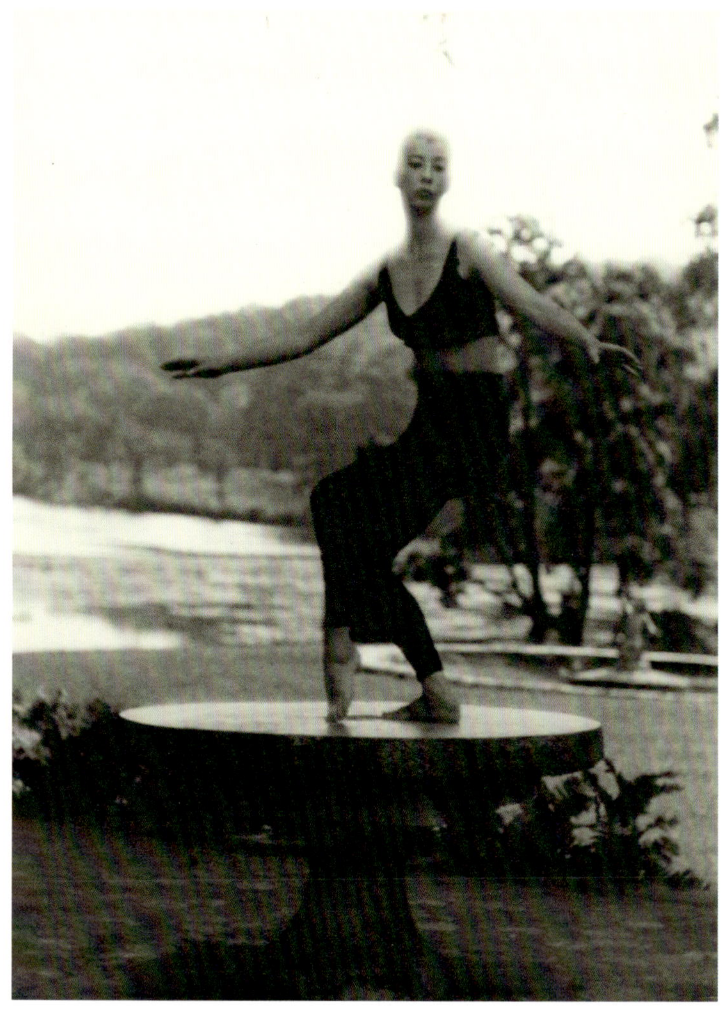

Fig. 4 Richard Pousette-Dart, *Jonathan Pousette-Dart*, 1971 (cat. 110)

Fig. 5 Richard Pousette-Dart, *Sono Osato*, 1960s (cat. 111)

anthers suggests a burst of light captured momentarily and preserved within the picture frame. In this regard, the study shares an affinity with the large canvas, *Presence Number 3, Black* (cat. 43), which features an orb-like, central form built up from multitudinous touches of pigment that dissolve at the edges. Overall, Pousette-Dart's post-1960 painting practice predominantly relies on the accretion of thousands of small dabs of paint. The artist understood this form of facture as analogous to retouching photographic film:

> *All form is made up of so many points of light and . . . everything has a molecular structure. Photography was how I got to the point . . . I'm concerned with form and the nature of light, and I find that I can achieve variations in form through many touches of the brush in a way that I can't with a single stroke of the brush.*[9]

By the late 1950s, Pousette-Dart began a long and personally rewarding role as a teacher of painting at the New School for Social Research, Sarah Lawrence College, Columbia University, and the Art Students League of New York. While prominently regarded as a painter, Pousette-Dart frequently returned to photography during the mature phase of his career to create portraits of close friends, family members, and fellow artists. Two outstanding examples from the 1970s are of his son, Jonathan, a professional musician who is composited with a sound hole from an acoustic guitar (fig. 4), and Sono Osato, a dancer with the Ballet Russe de Monte Carlo and performer in Broadway musicals (fig. 5).

In 1975 Pousette-Dart participated in the exhibition *Artists by Artists—Photographs* at the Zabriskie Gallery, New York, which featured photographs by painters and sculptors, including Constantin Brâncuşi, Ralston Crawford, Alexander Liberman, and Man Ray. Yet, among his close Abstract Expressionist colleagues, only Ad Reinhardt and David Smith displayed more than a passing interest in serious photographic practice. Pousette-Dart's multifaceted approach to media, which additionally included collage and printmaking, is thus largely unique among his New York School peers.

Photography's role in the emergence of modernism during the interwar period is now regarded as self-evident, yet its relationship to American abstract painting in the mid-twentieth century demands further examination. A fruitful approach is not to search for direct or derivative analogues between examples of abstract painting and photography but to consider their shared visual thinking. Speaking of photography's continuing attraction toward the end of his life, Pousette-Dart noted, "I feel everything is a wonderful photographic subject if one has the patience, perseverance and experience to reveal it in its own way . . . . Love is the eye of photography or anything else."[10]

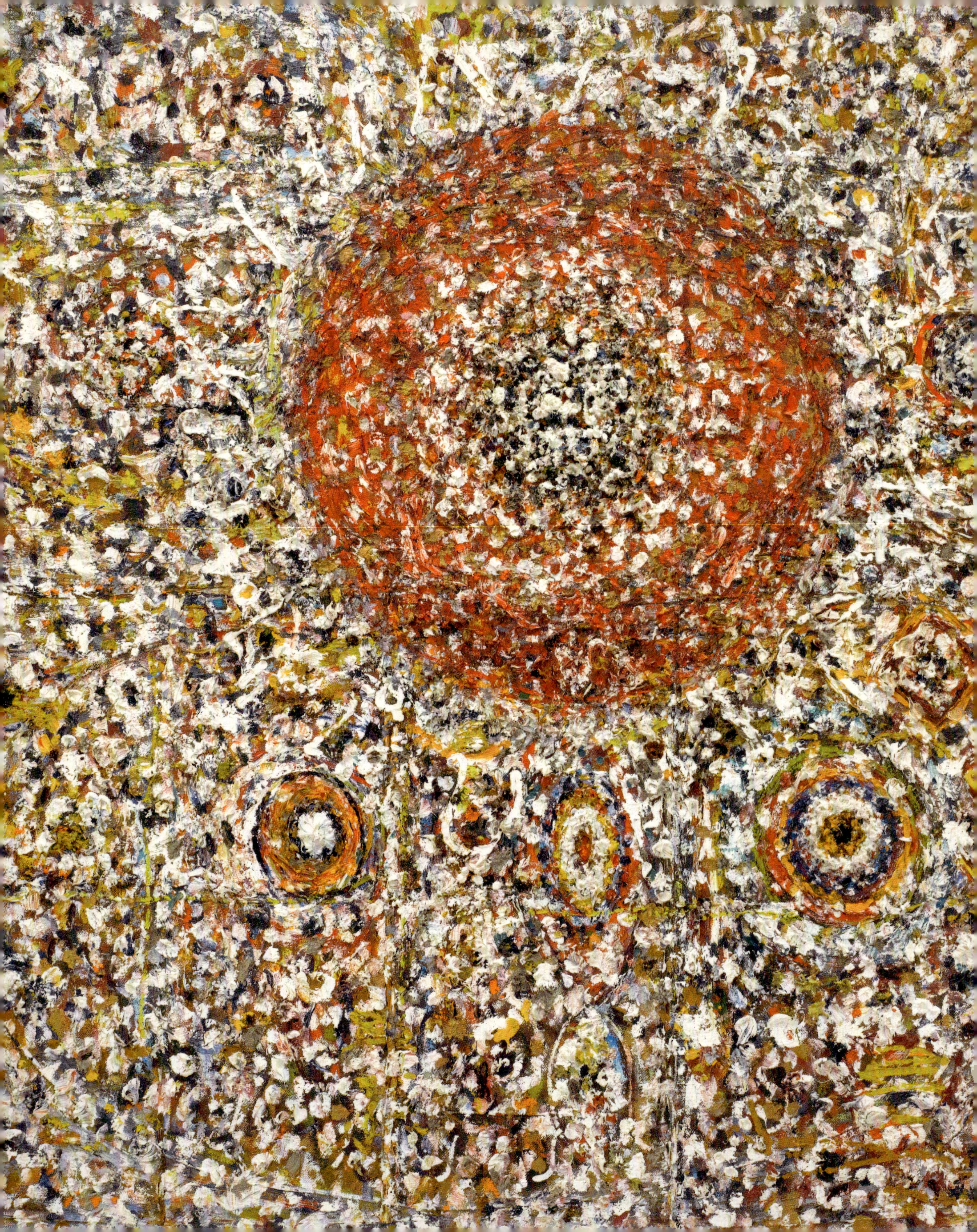

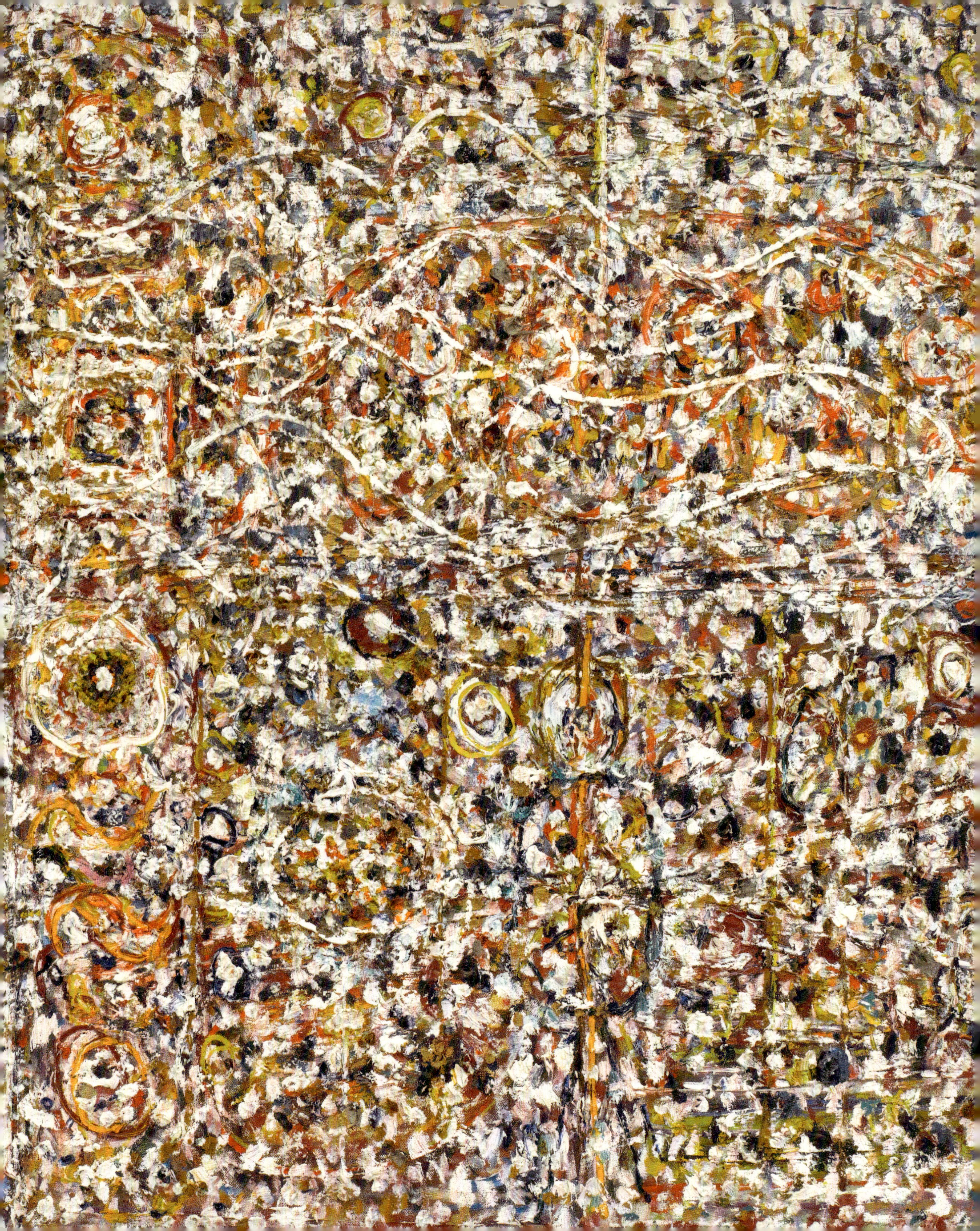

Paintings & Sculptures

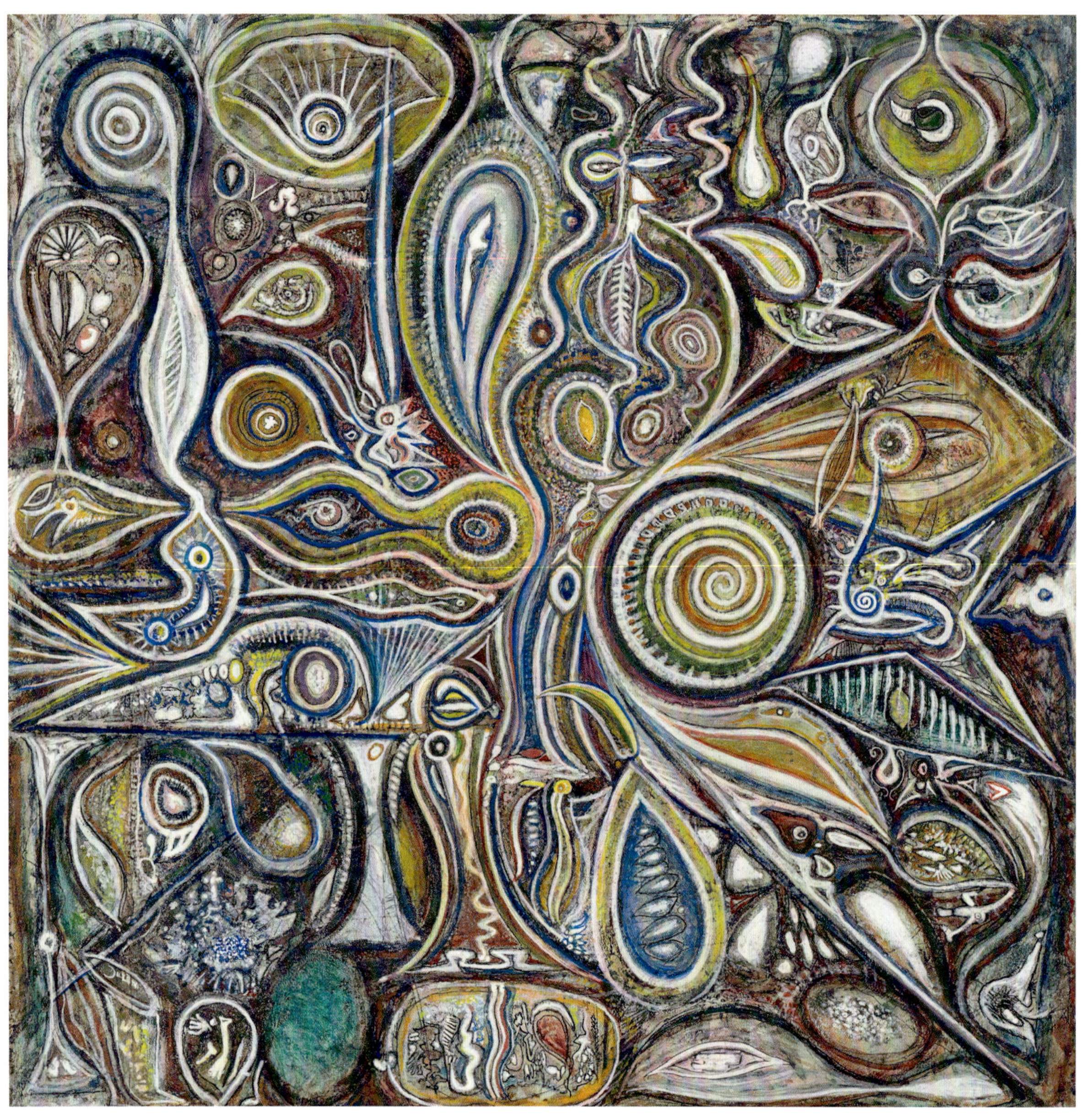

Cat. 1 *Beneath the Sea*, 1939, oil and ink on parchment, 59.7 × 59.7 cm

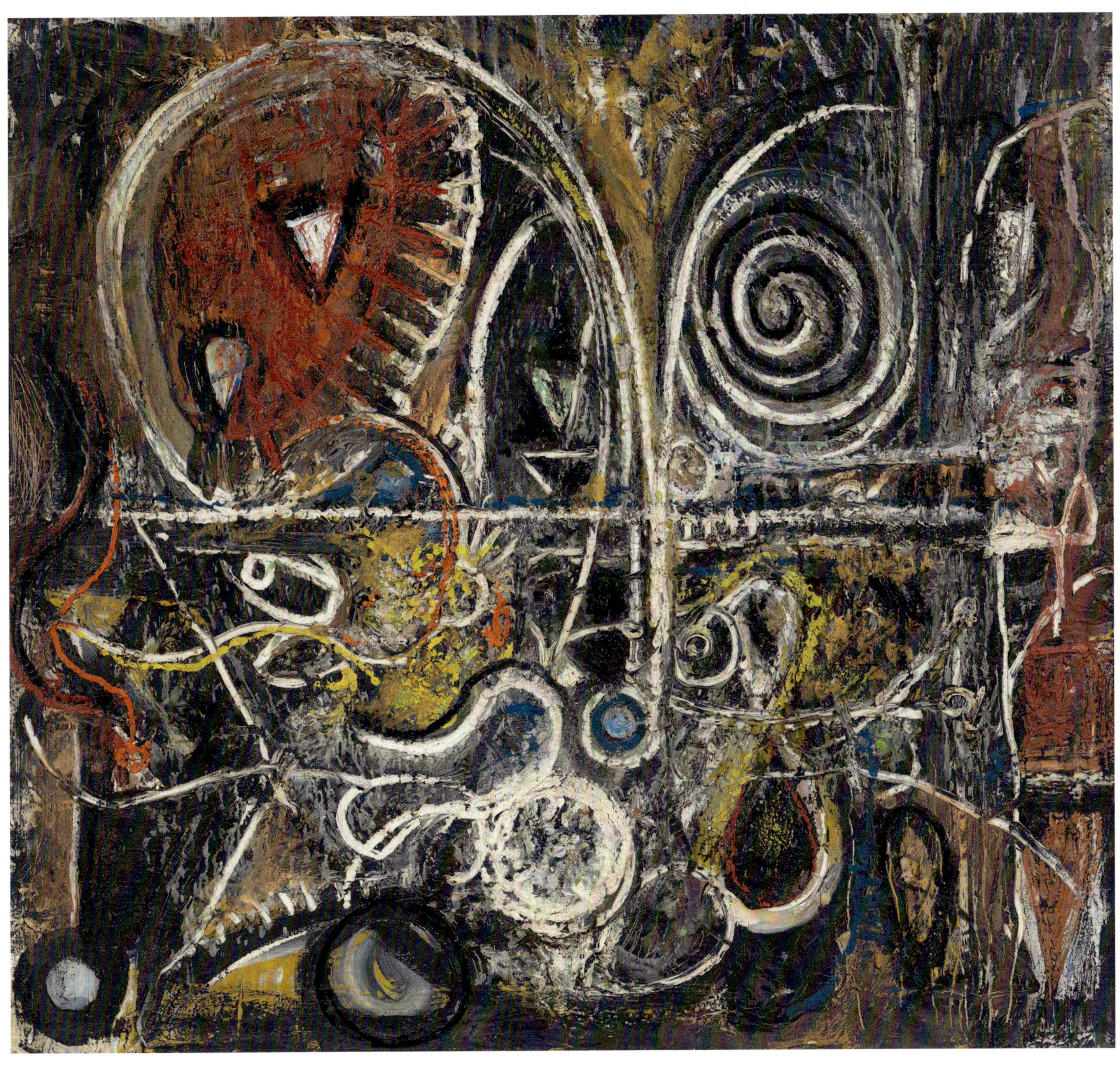

Cat. 2 *Animal Forms*, 1939–43, oil on linen, 97.8 × 106.7 cm

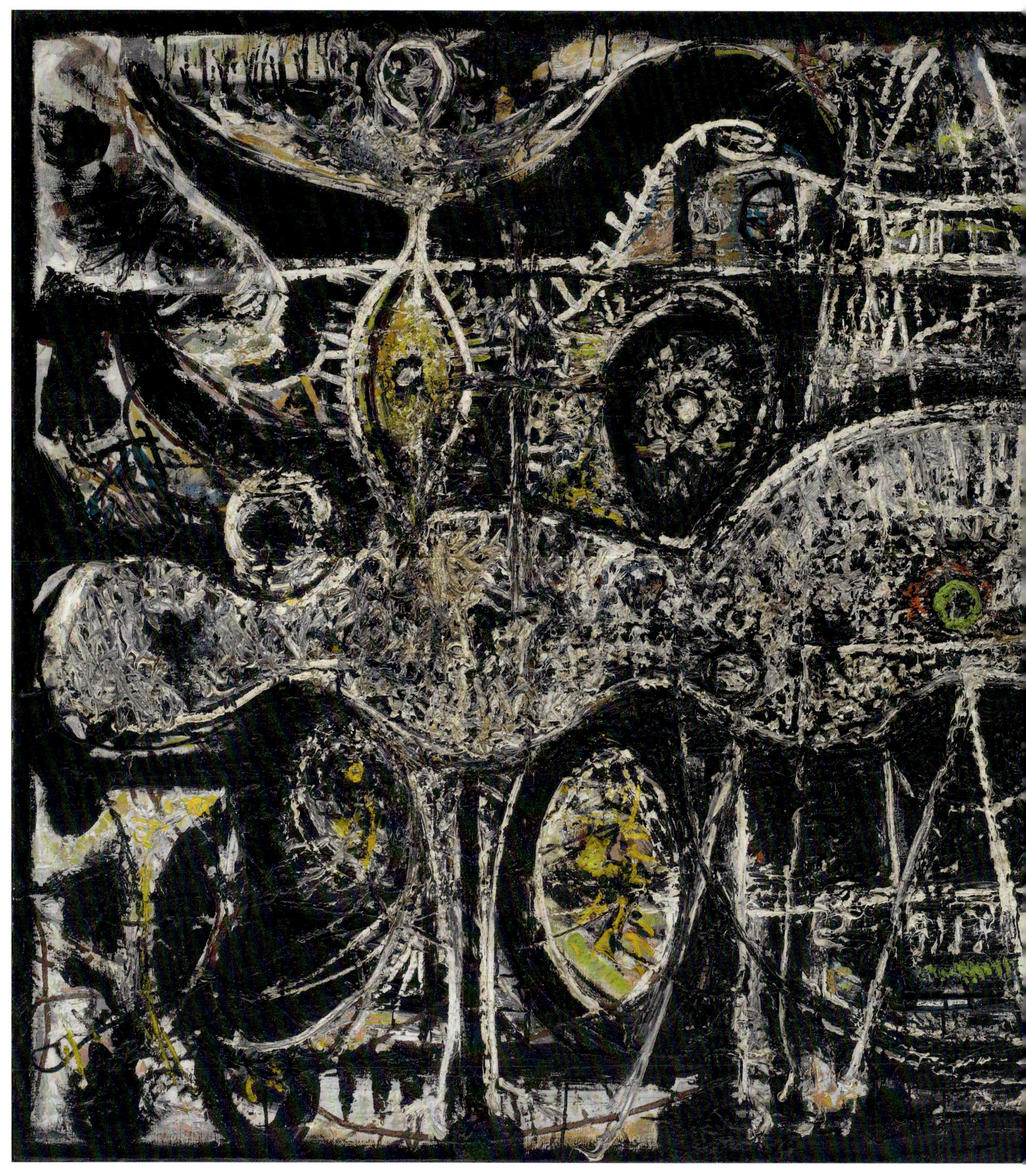

Cat. 3 *Undulation*, 1941–42, oil and sand on linen, 121.9 × 238.8 cm

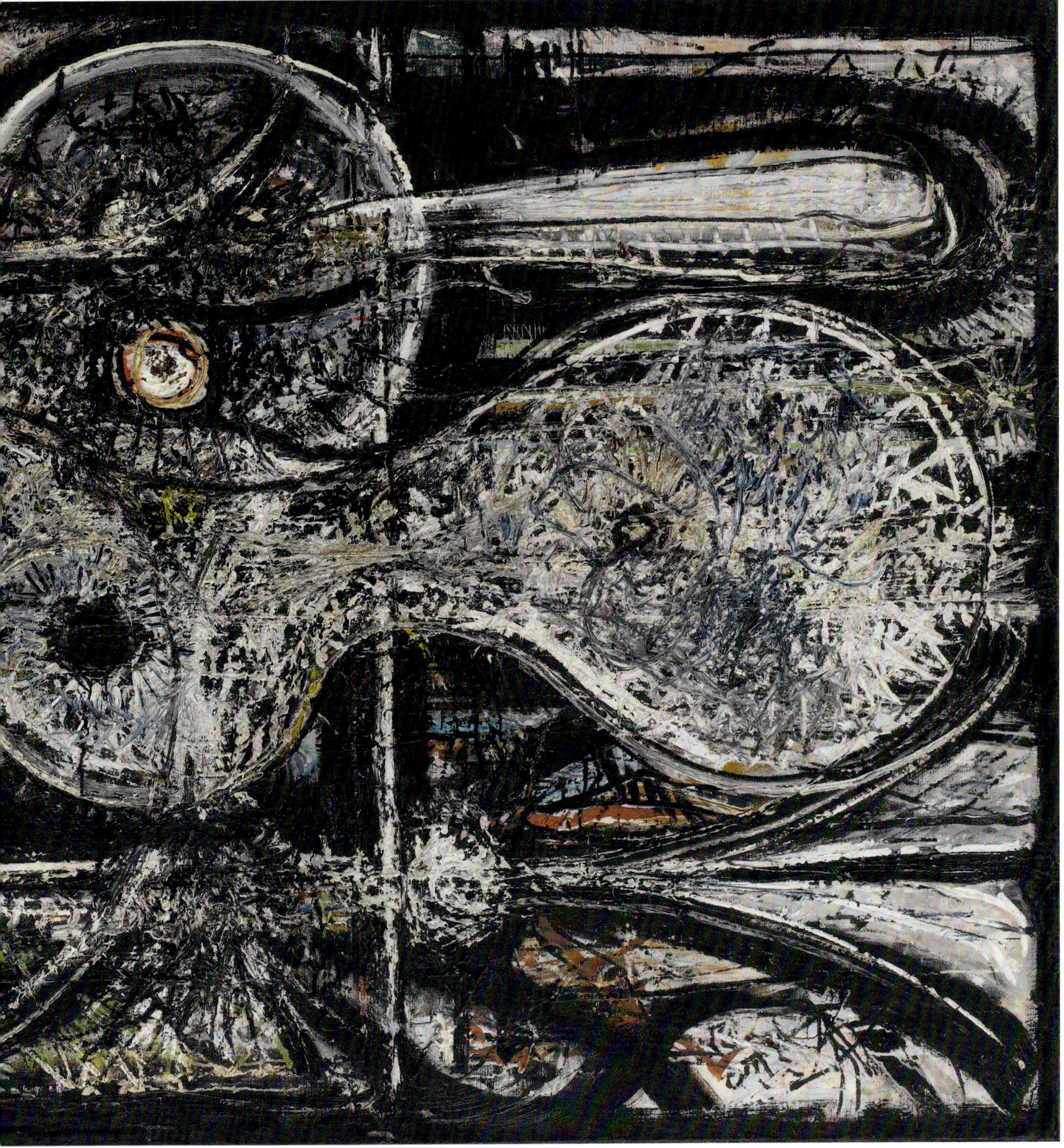

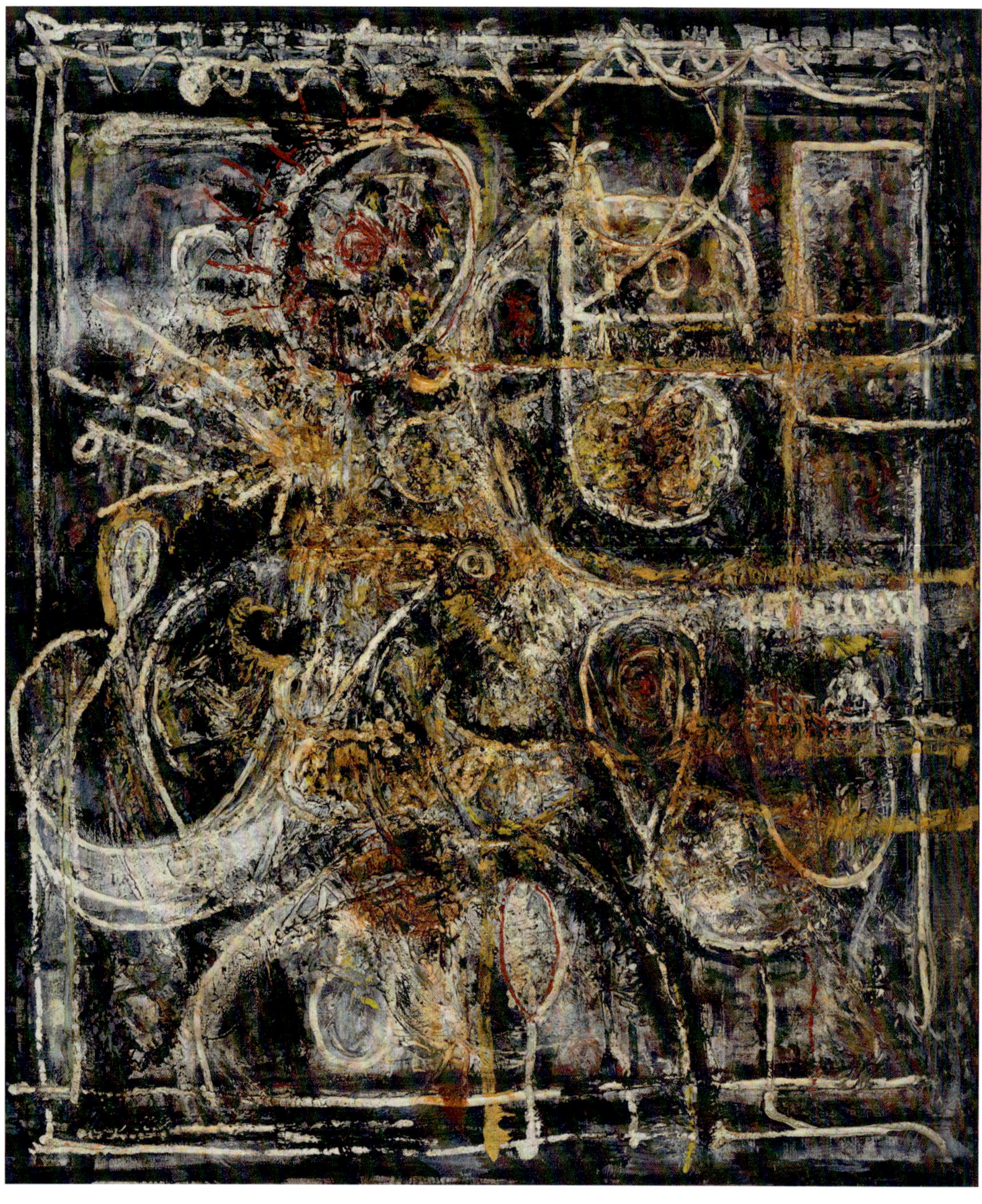

Cat. 4 *Spirit Adagio*, 1943, oil on linen, 124.5 × 109.2 cm

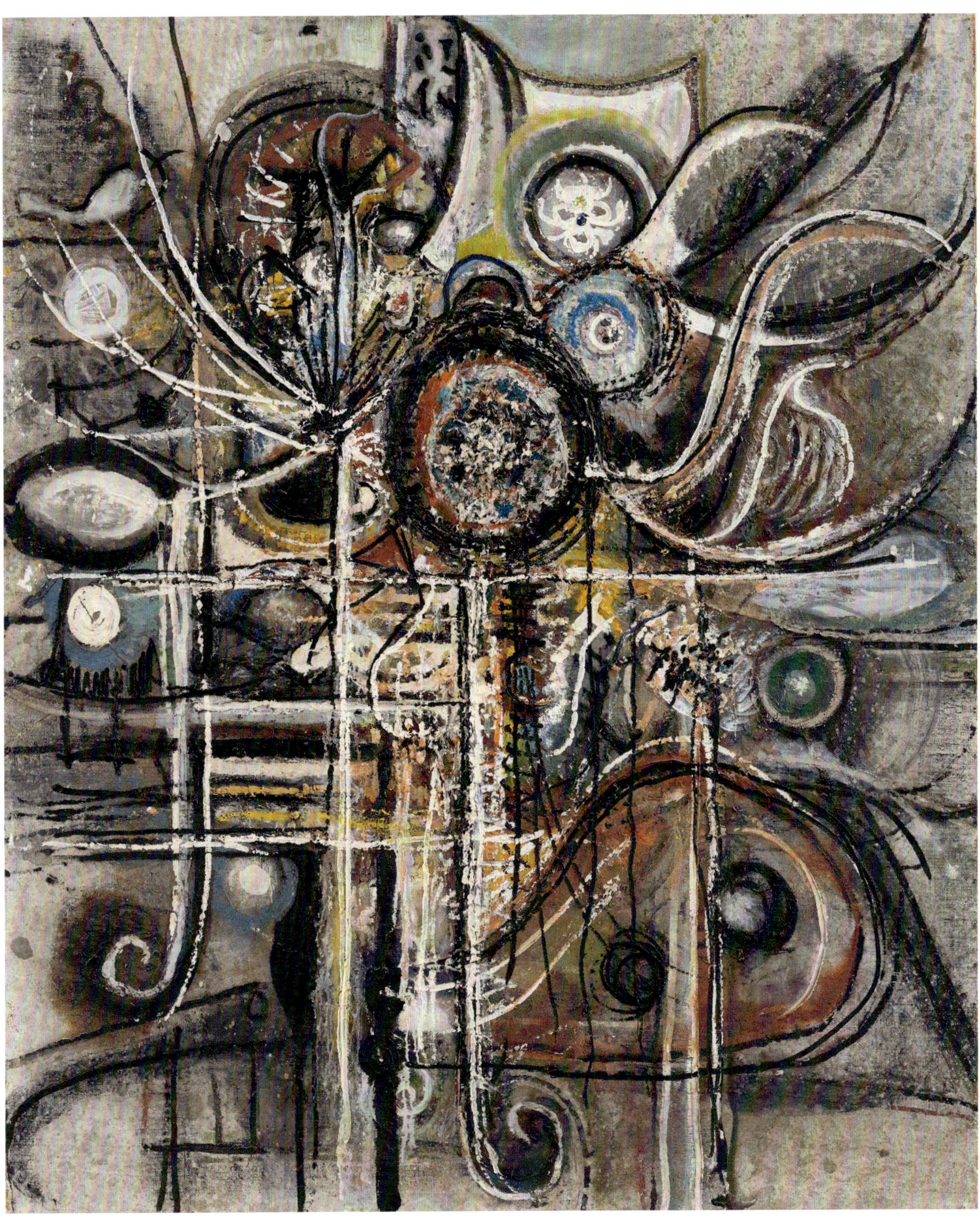

Cat. 5 *The Center*, 1943, oil on linen, 141 × 121 cm

Cat. 6 *Crucifixion, Comprehension of the Atom*, 1944, oil on linen, 197.2 × 124.8 cm

61

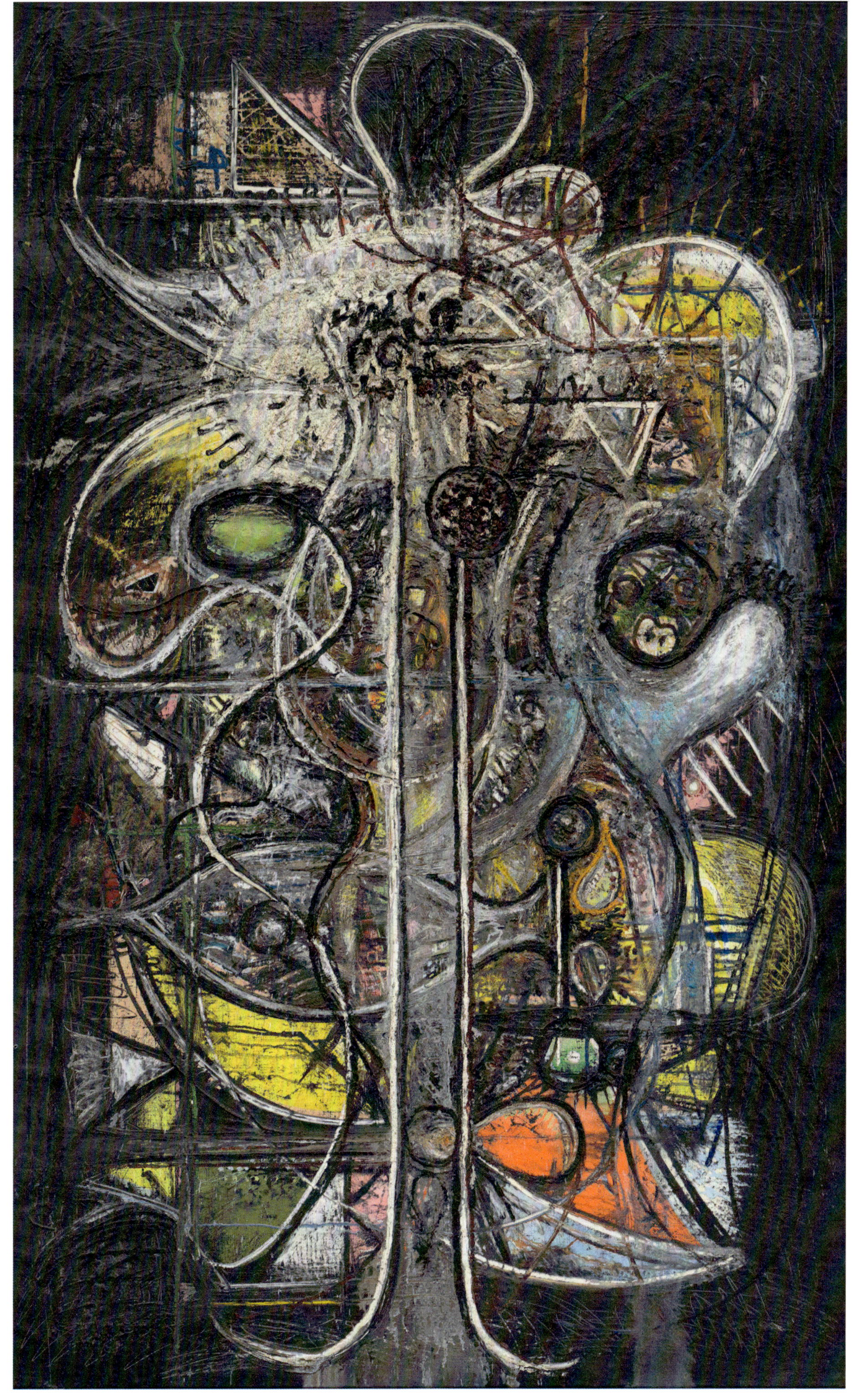

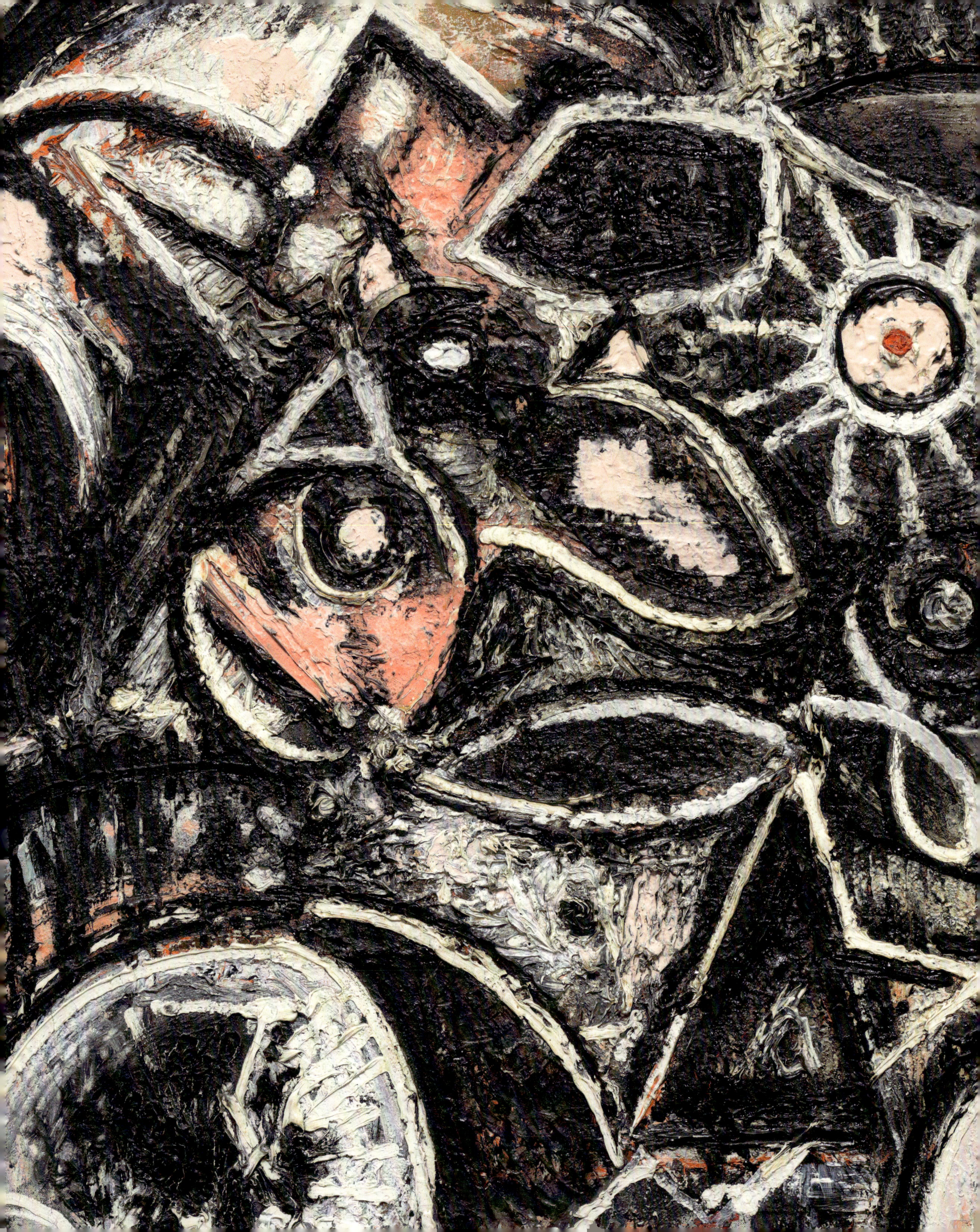

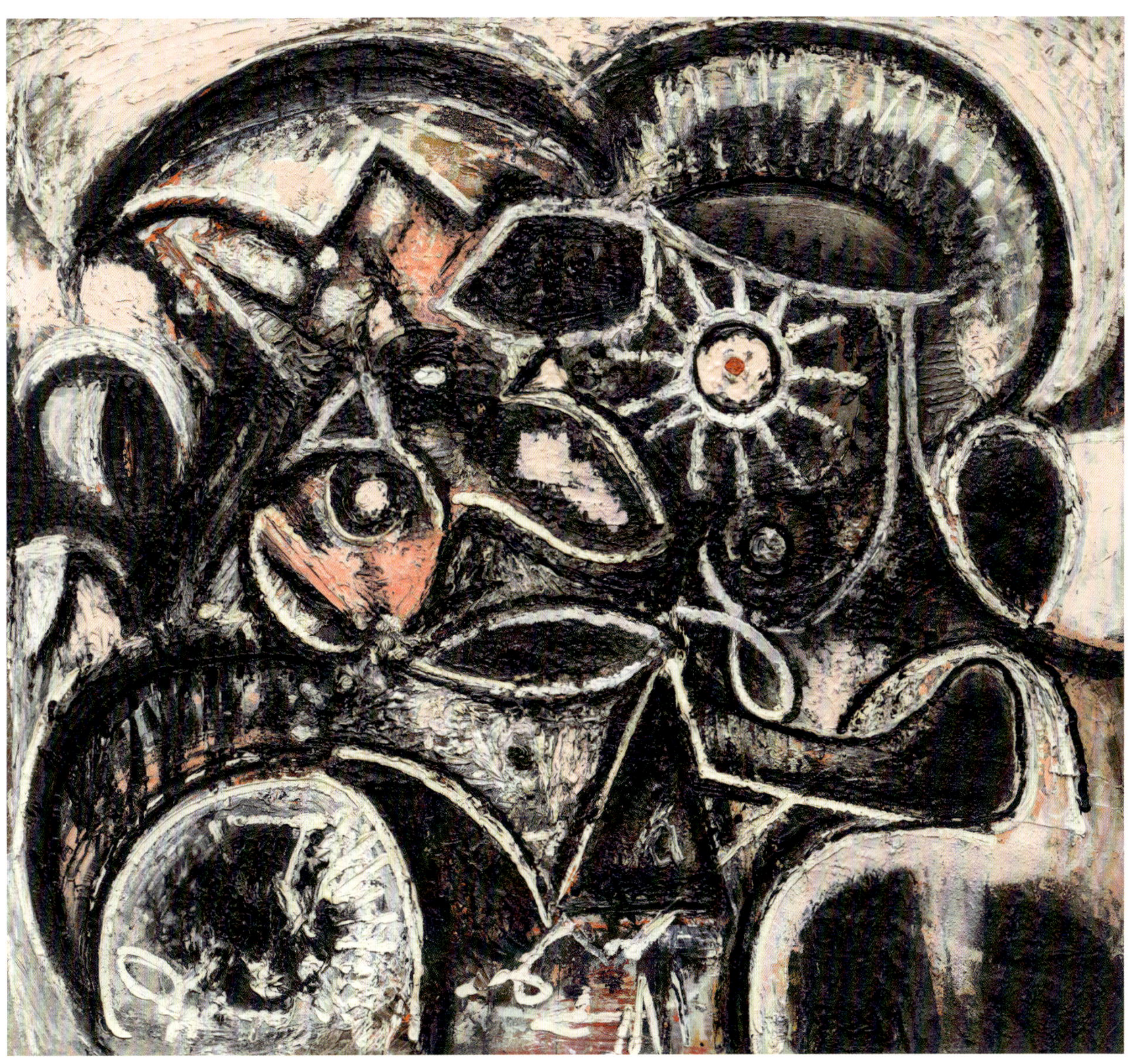

Cat. 7 *Eagle's Nest*, 1946, oil on linen, 91.8 × 101.3 cm

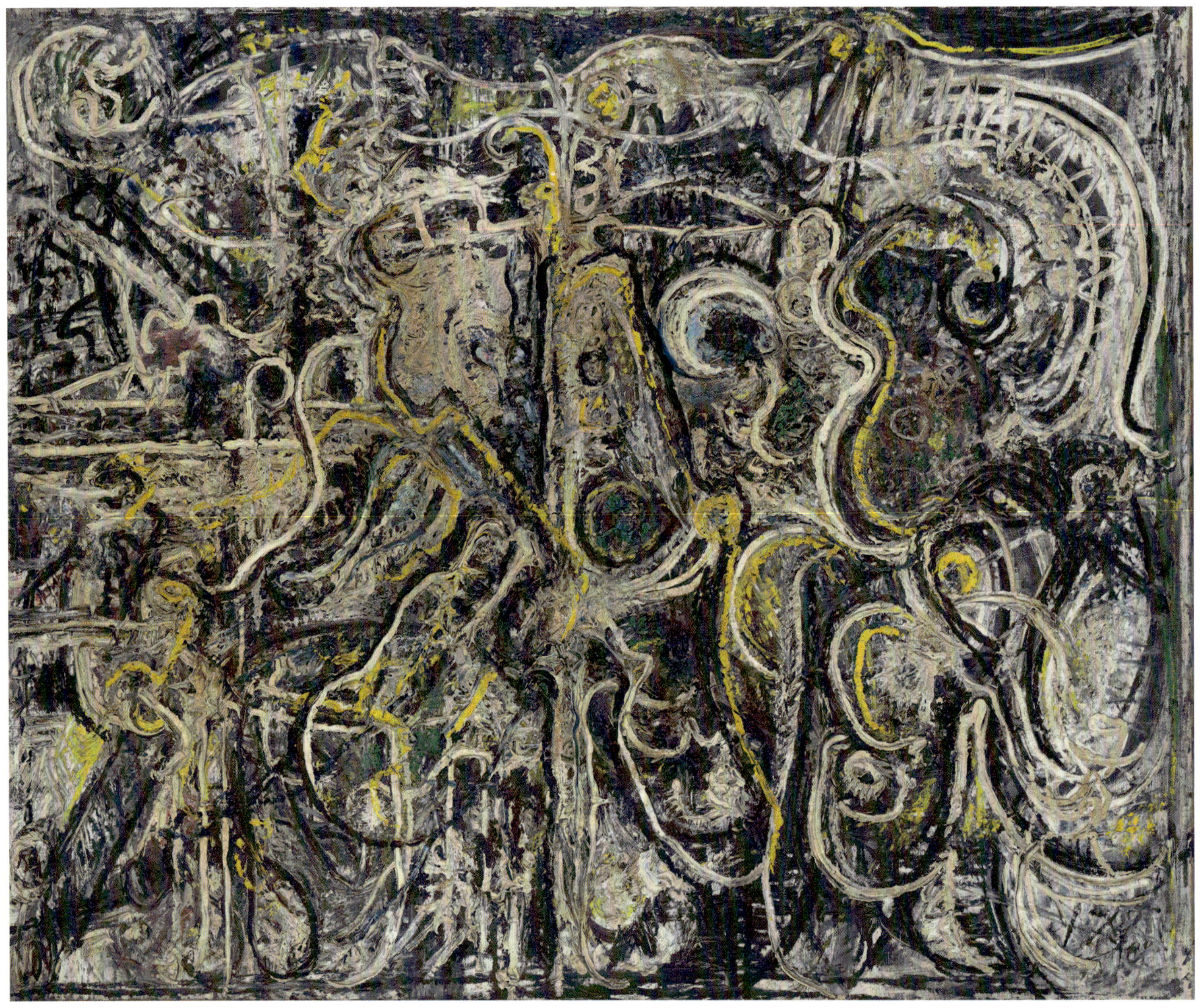

Cat. 8 *Forestness*, 1946, oil and sand on linen, 109.2 × 130.8 cm

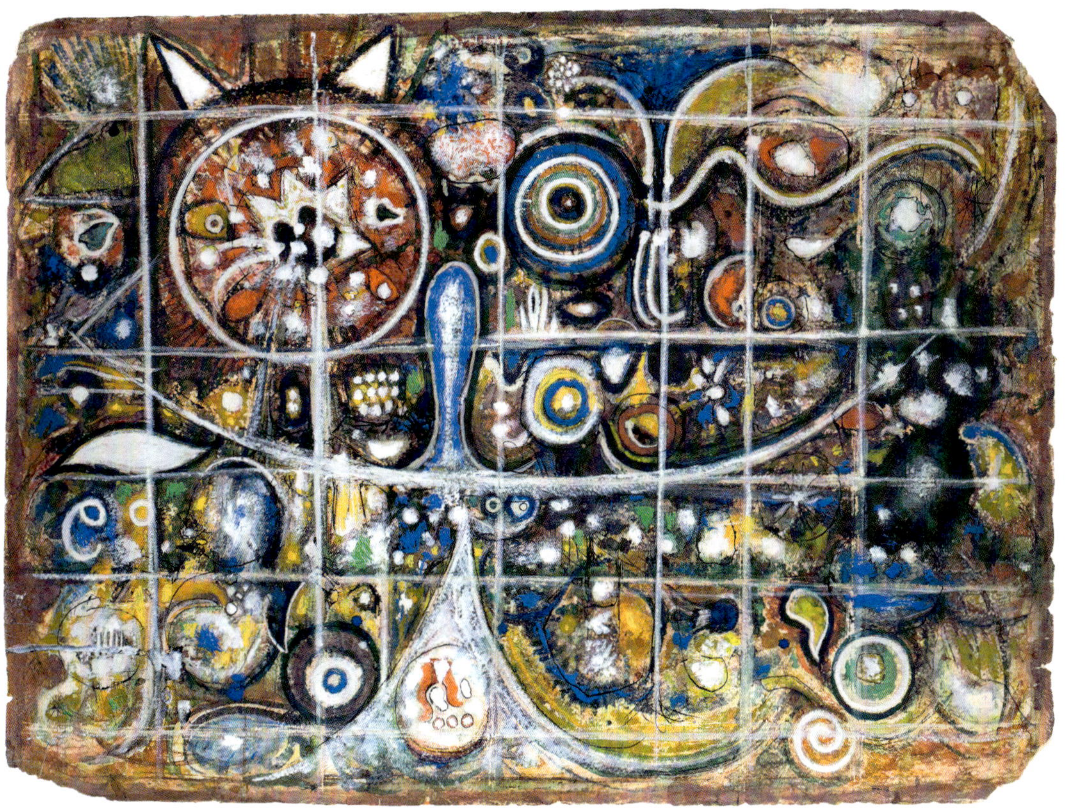

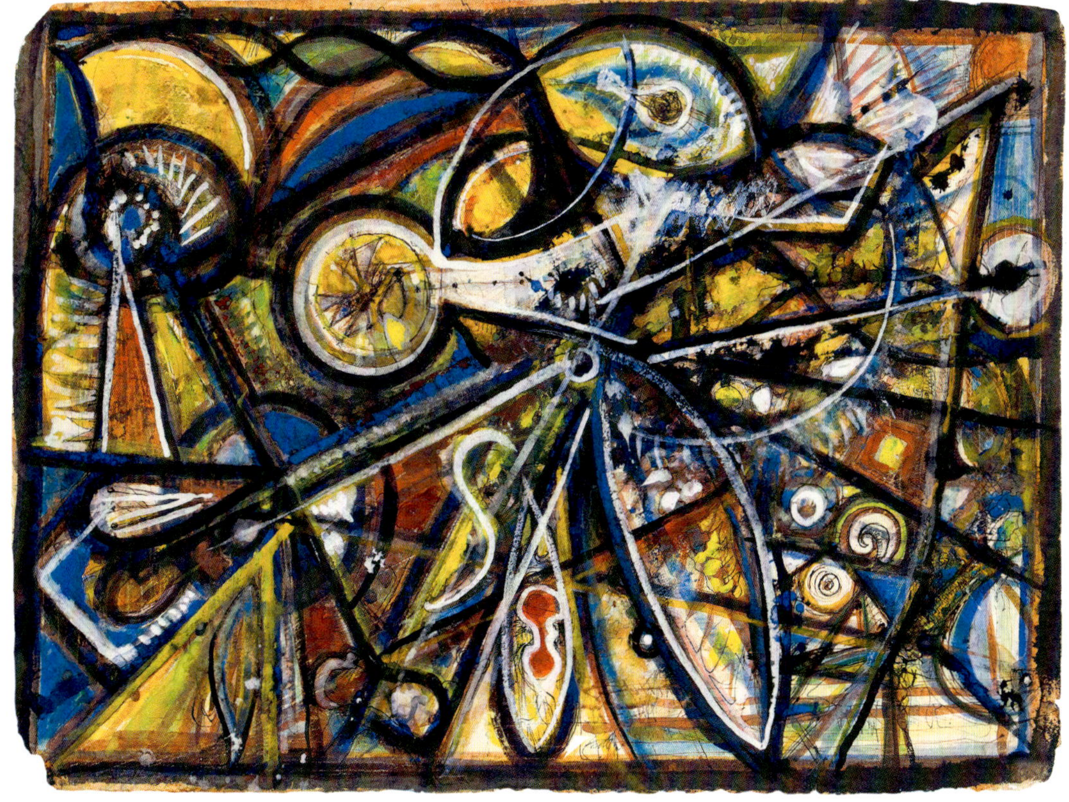

Cat. 9 *Blue Transition / Convolutions of Music*, 1942–43, ink and gouache on paper, 57.8 × 79.4 cm

Cat. 10 *Partitions of Unity*, 1940s, ink and gouache on paper, 57.8 × 79.7 cm

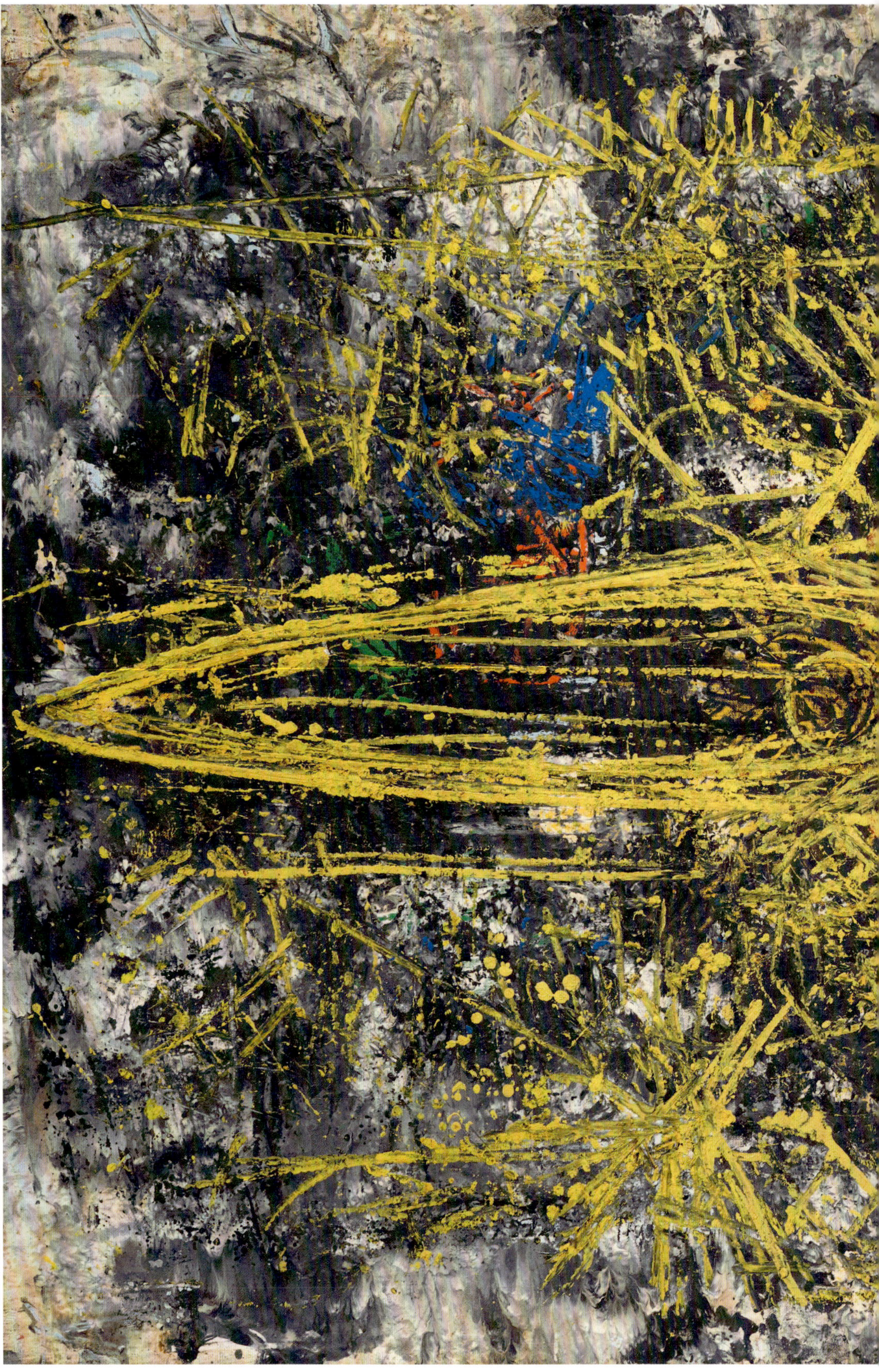

Cat. 11 *Icarus*, 1951, oil on linen, 105.4 × 183.5 cm

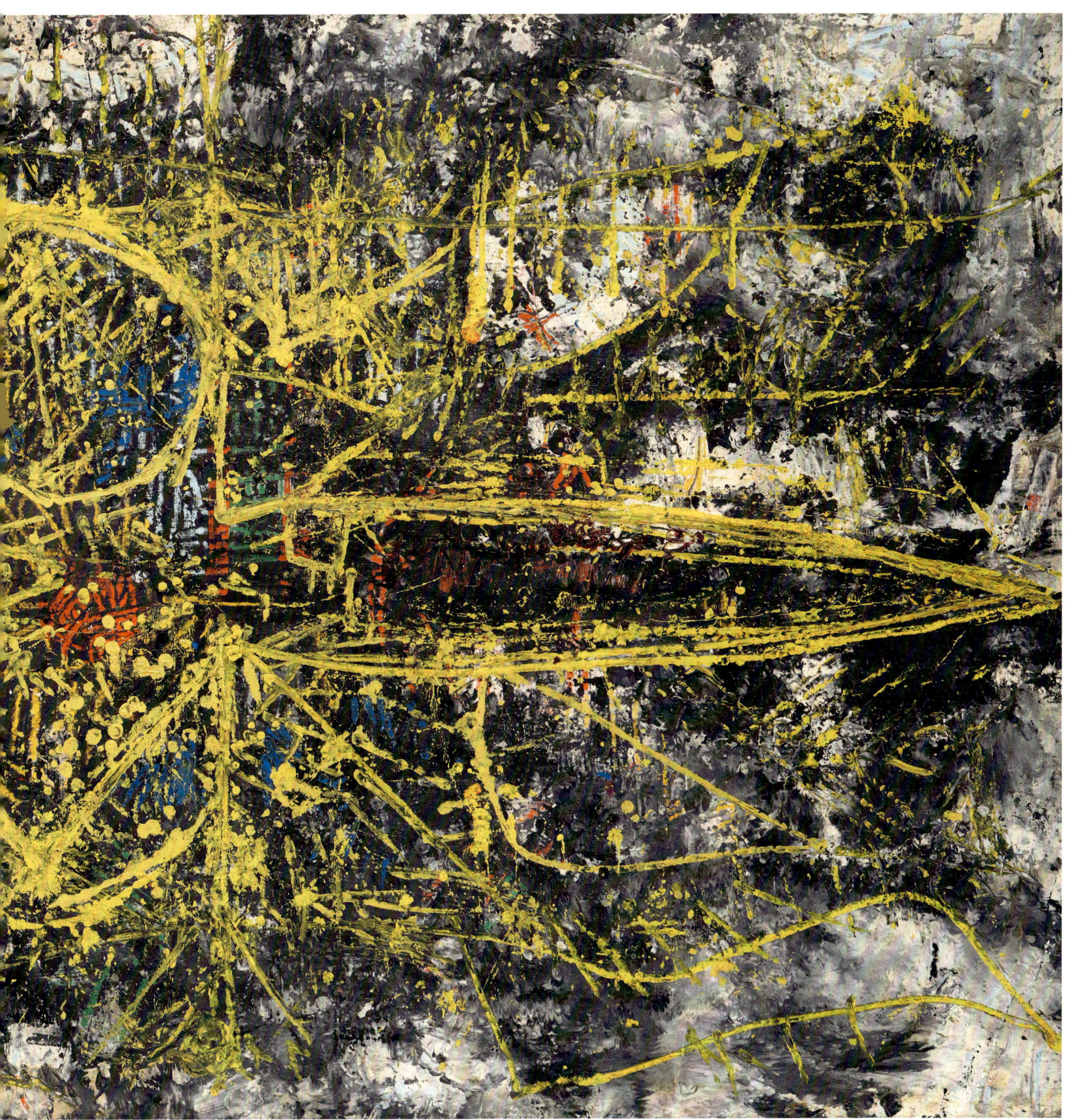

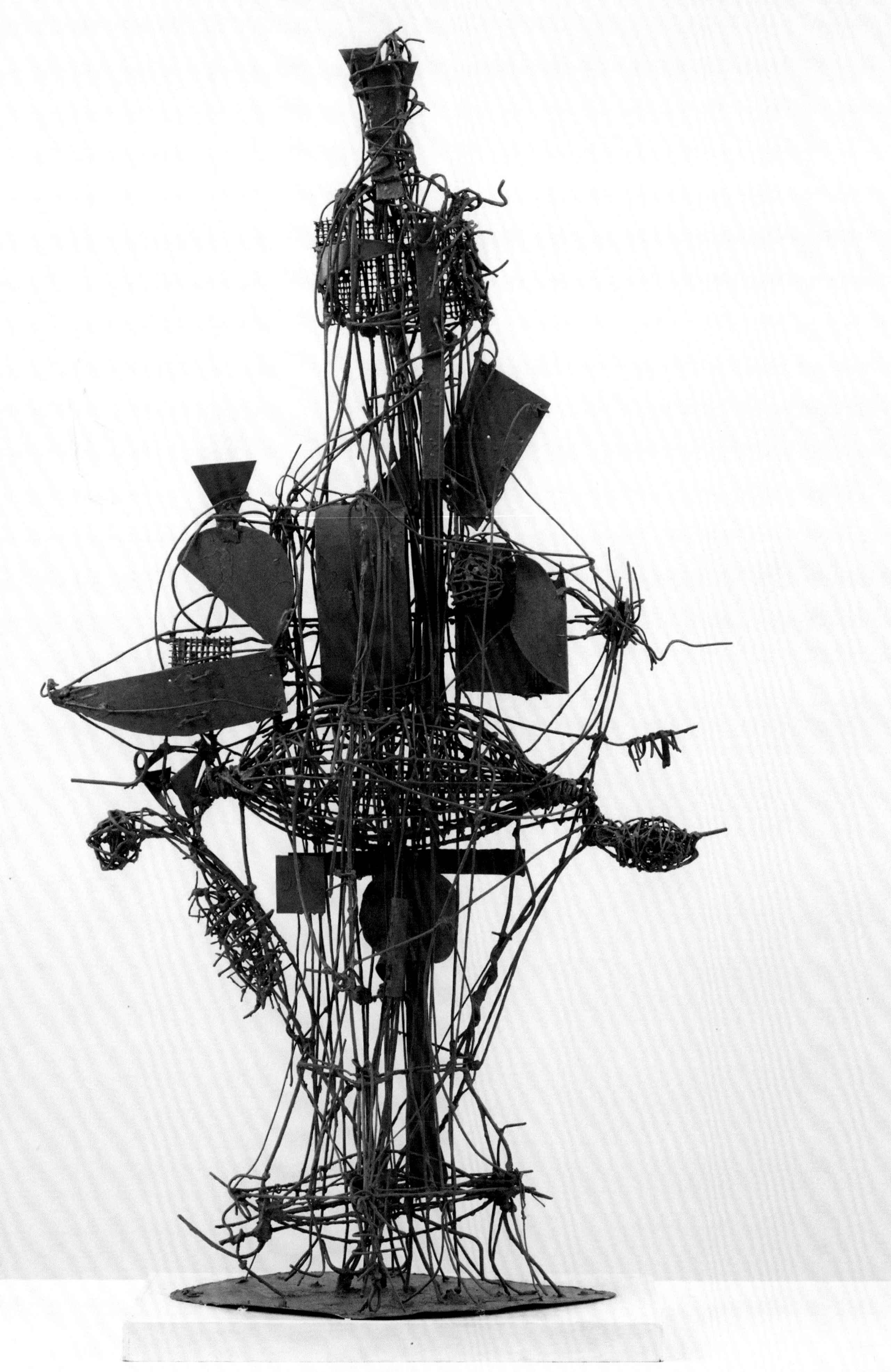

Cat. 12 *Creature of Clouds*, 1951, steel wire and sheet metal, painted gray, 125.7 × 71.1 × 35.6 cm

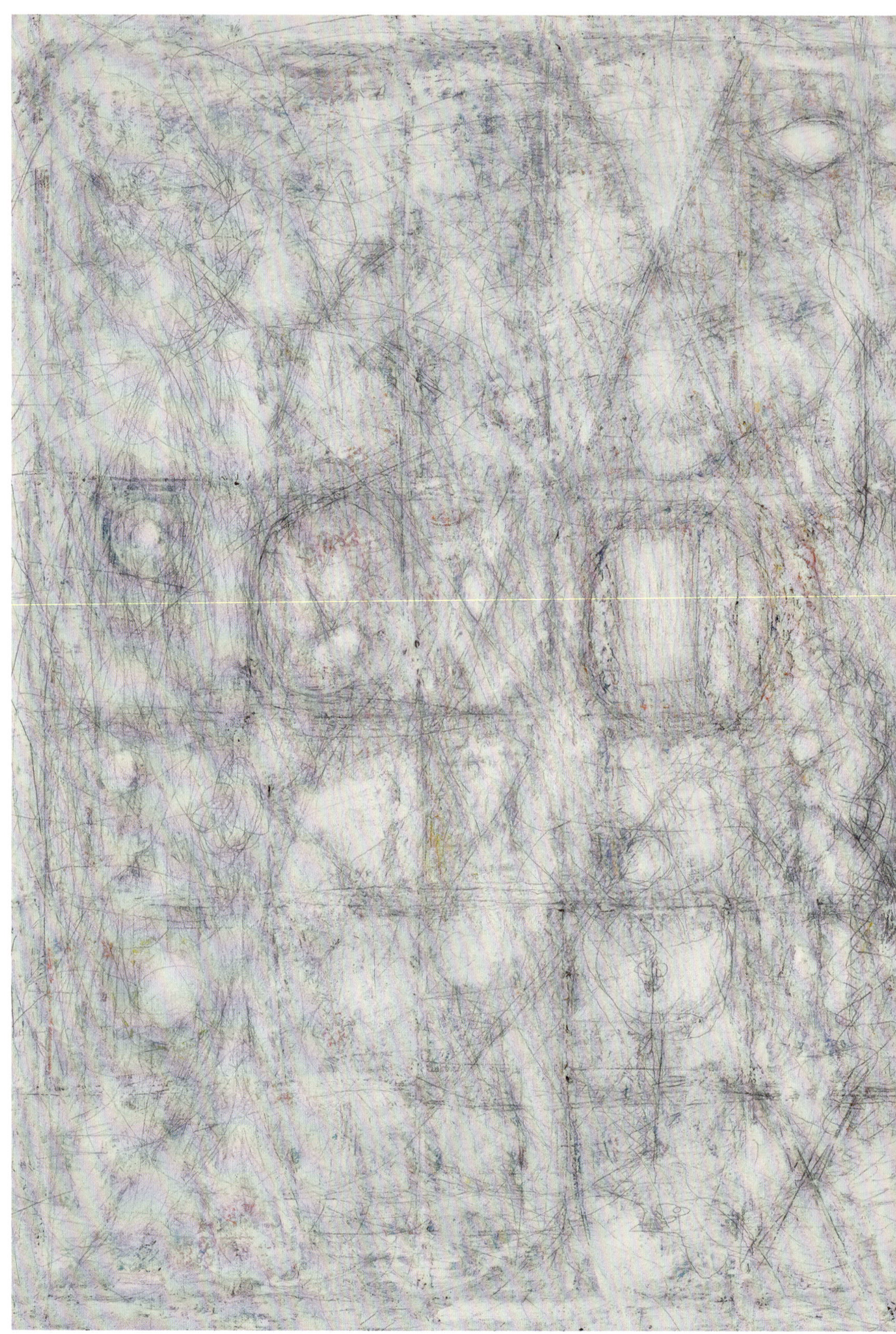

Cat. 13 *Chavade*, 1951, oil and pencil on canvas, 135.6 × 245 cm

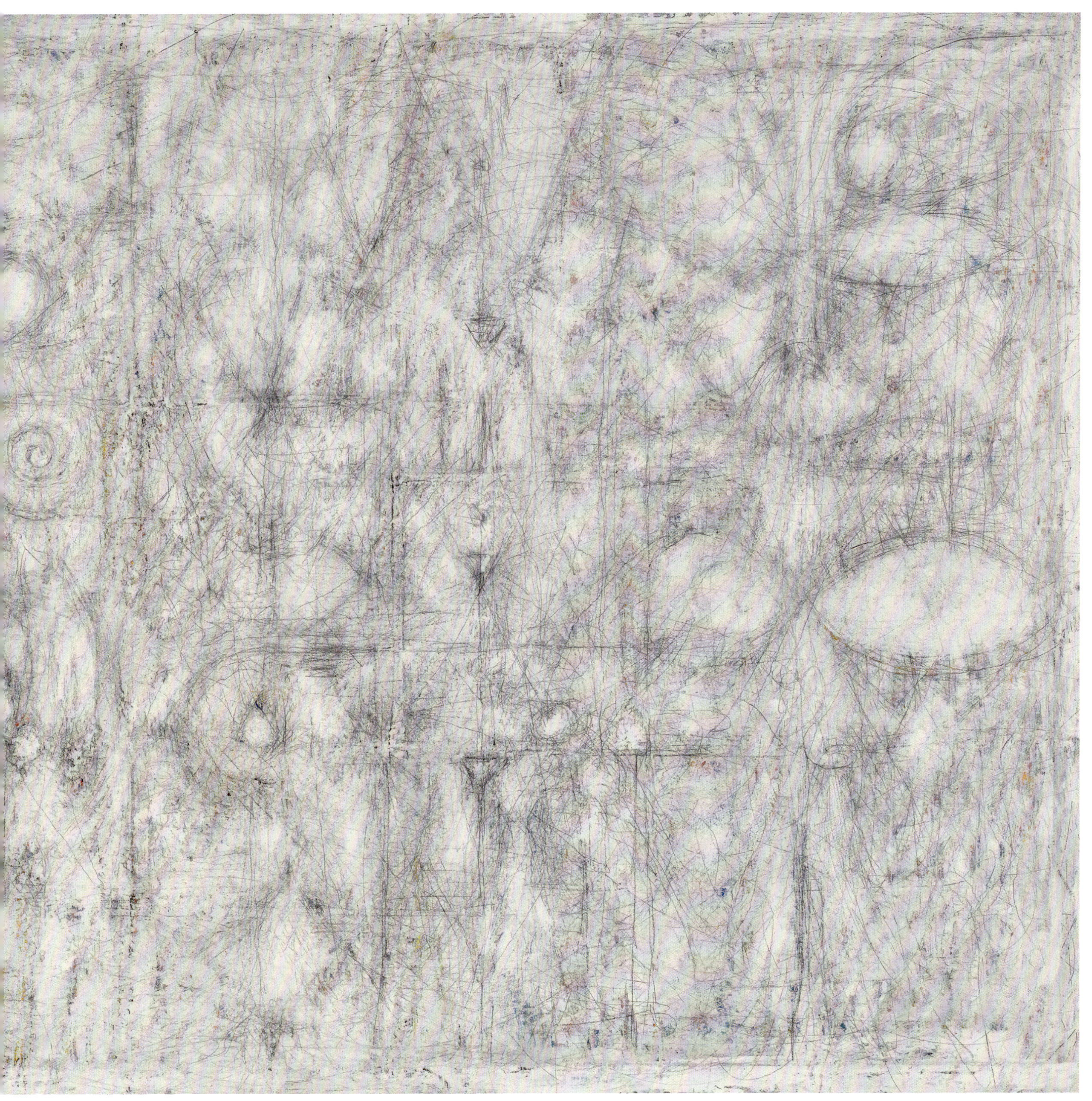

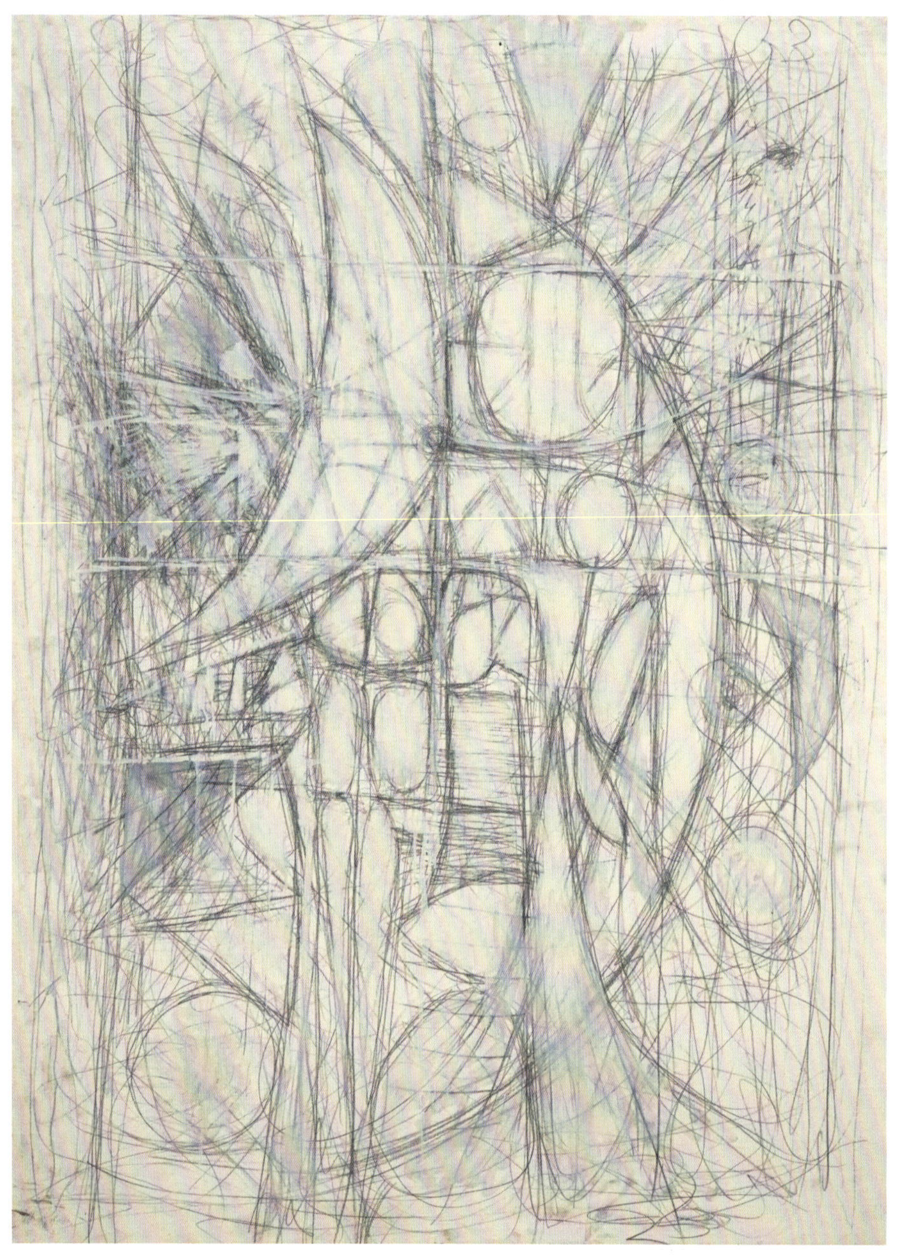

Cat. 14 *White Etude*, 1952, oil and graphite on linen, 125.7 × 93.3 cm

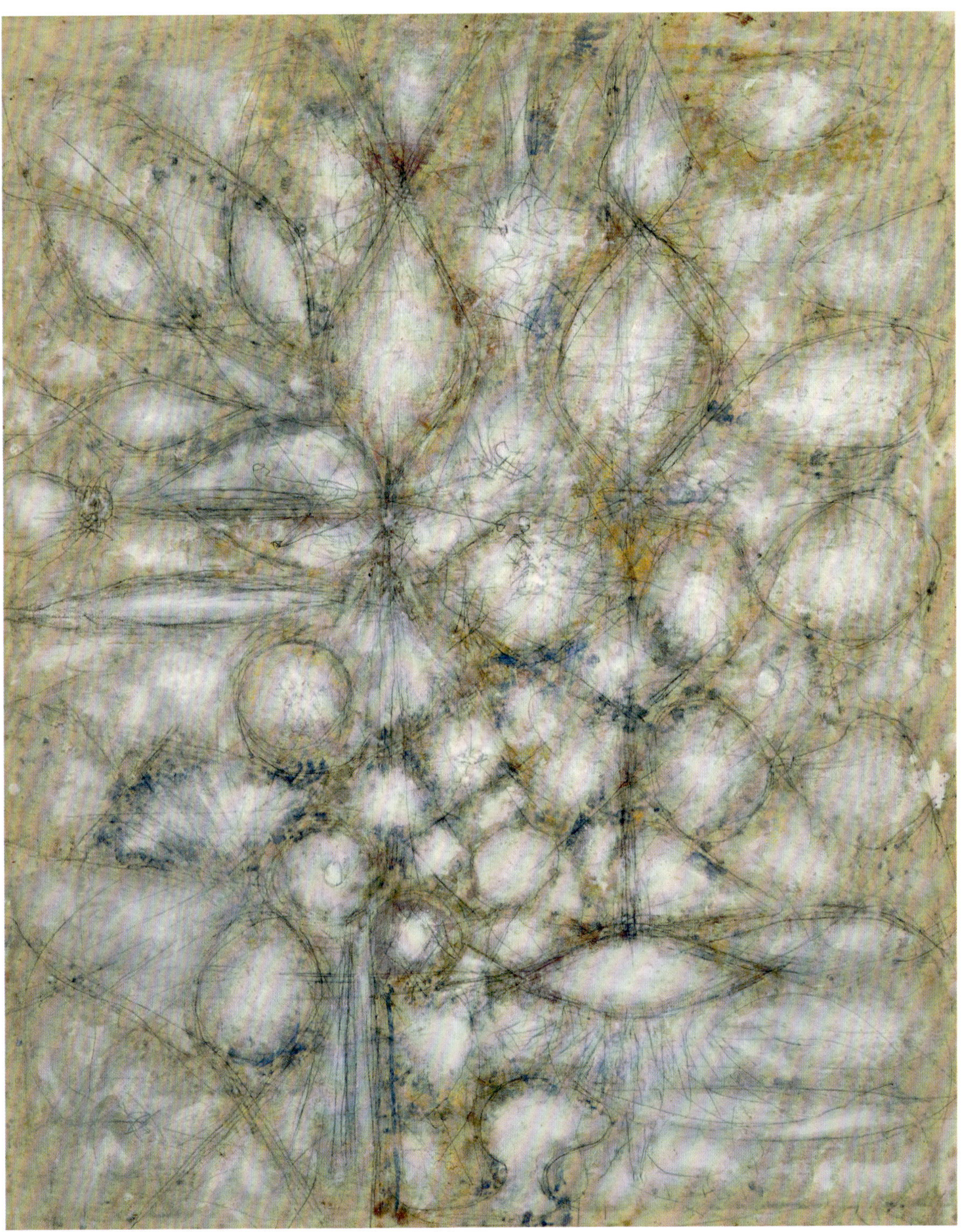

Cat. 15 *Presence Number 5*, 1950-54, oil and graphite on linen, 164.5 × 135.5 cm

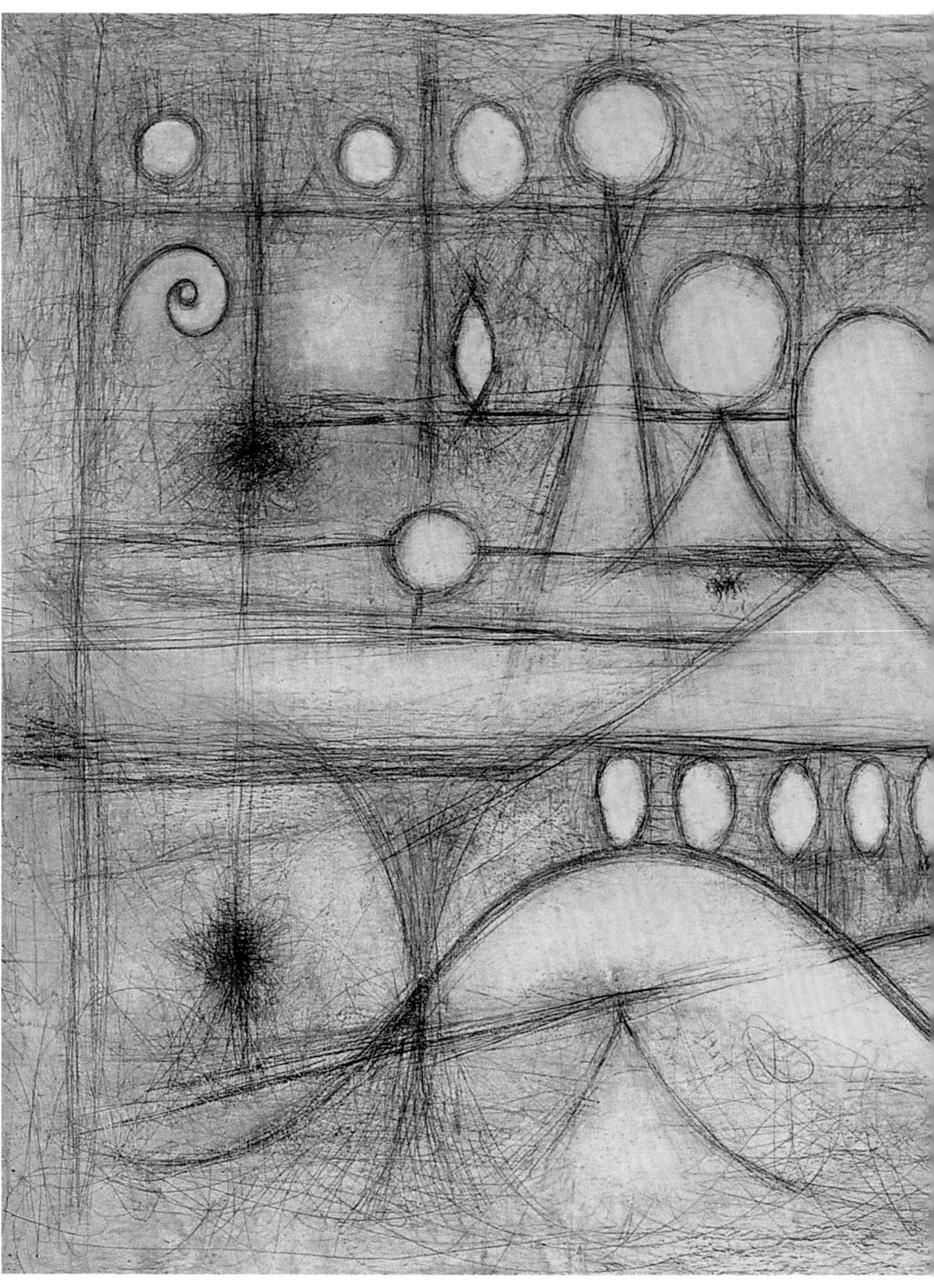

Cat. 16 *Descending Bird Forms*, 1950–51, oil and graphite on panel, 121.9 × 243.8 cm

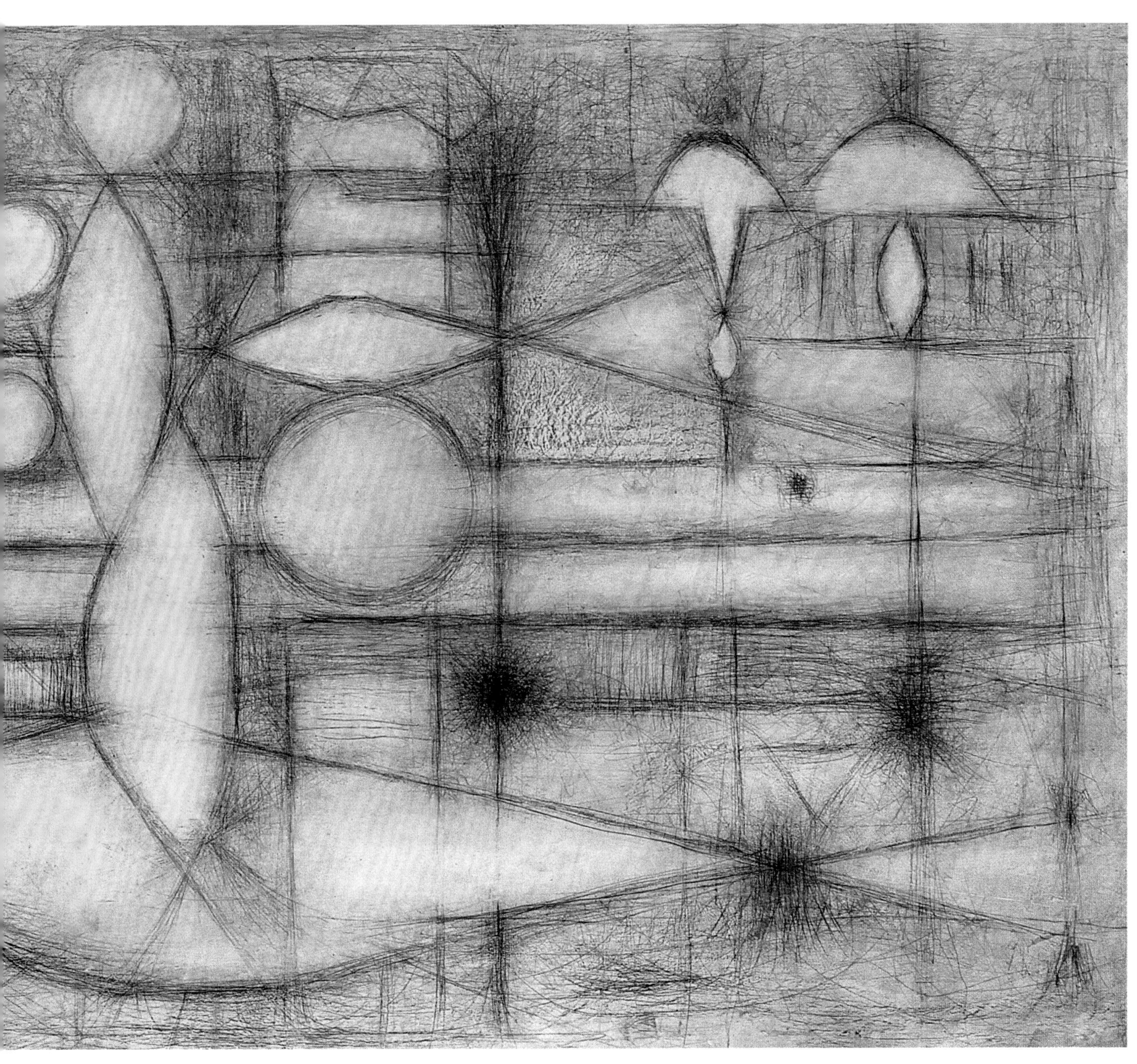

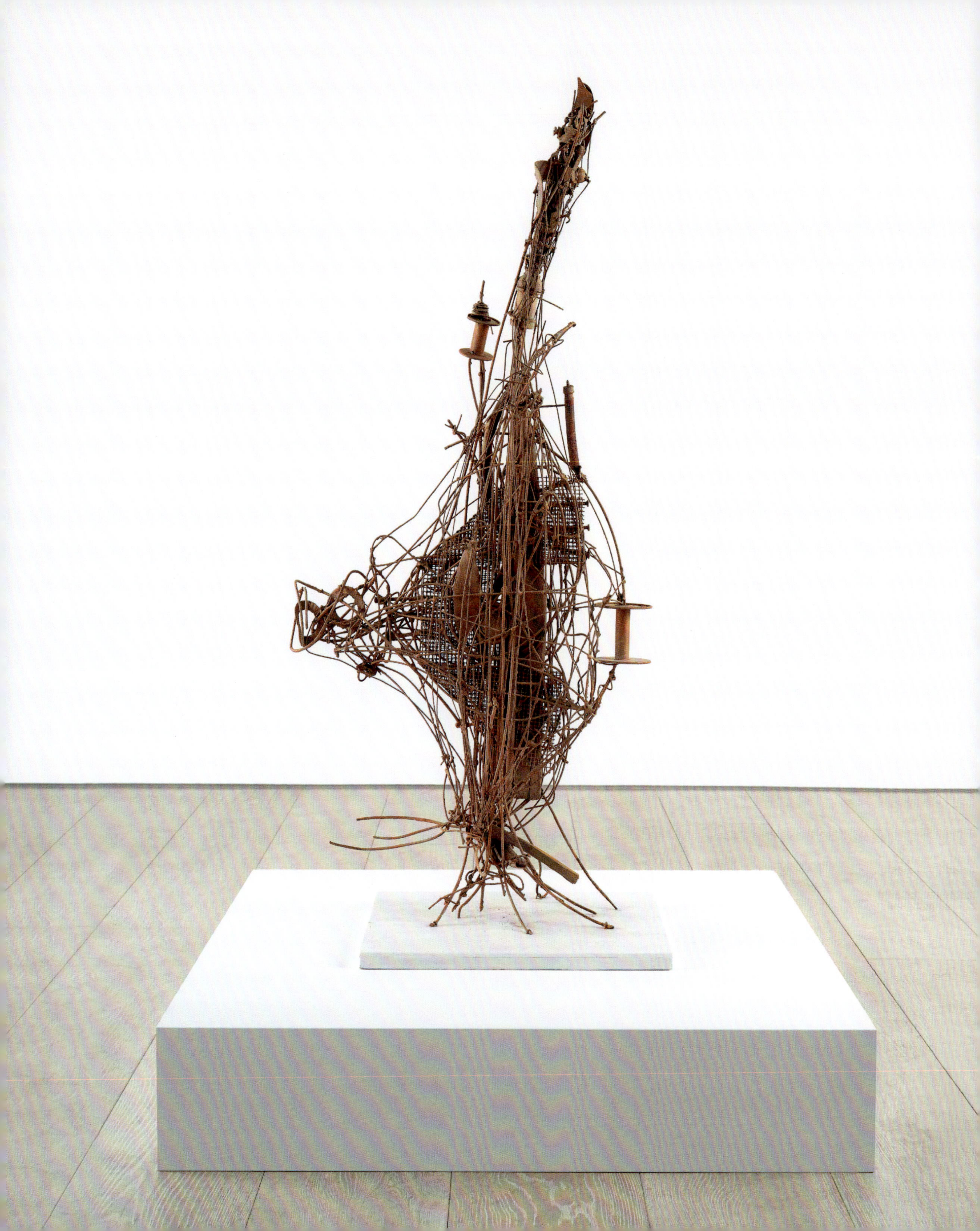

Cat. 17 *Arc of the Bird*, 1951, steel wire and objets trouvés, painted orange, 124.5 × 58.4 × 35.6 cm

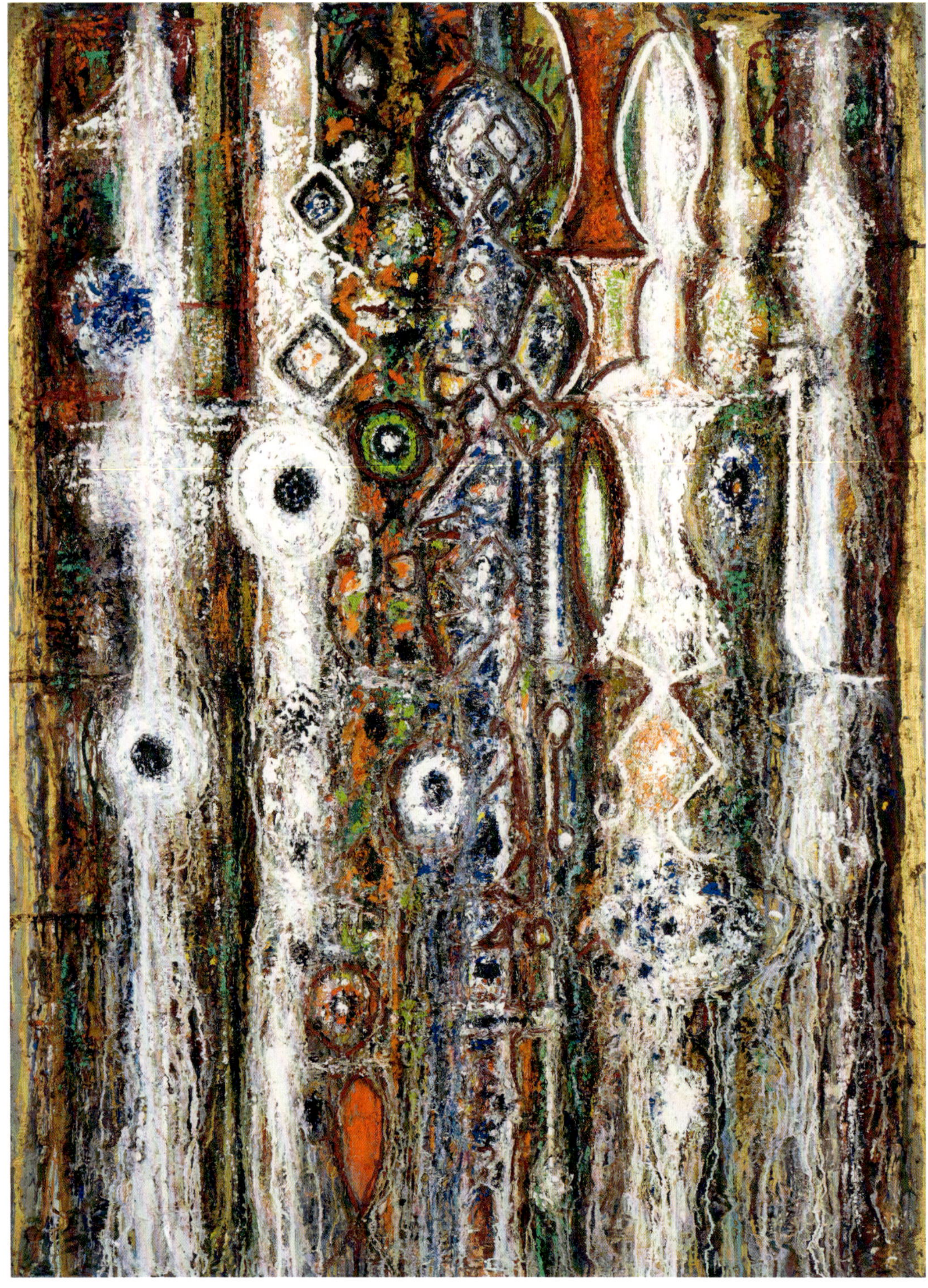

Cat. 18 *Illumination Gothic*, 1955, oil on canvas, 182.9 × 135.9 cm

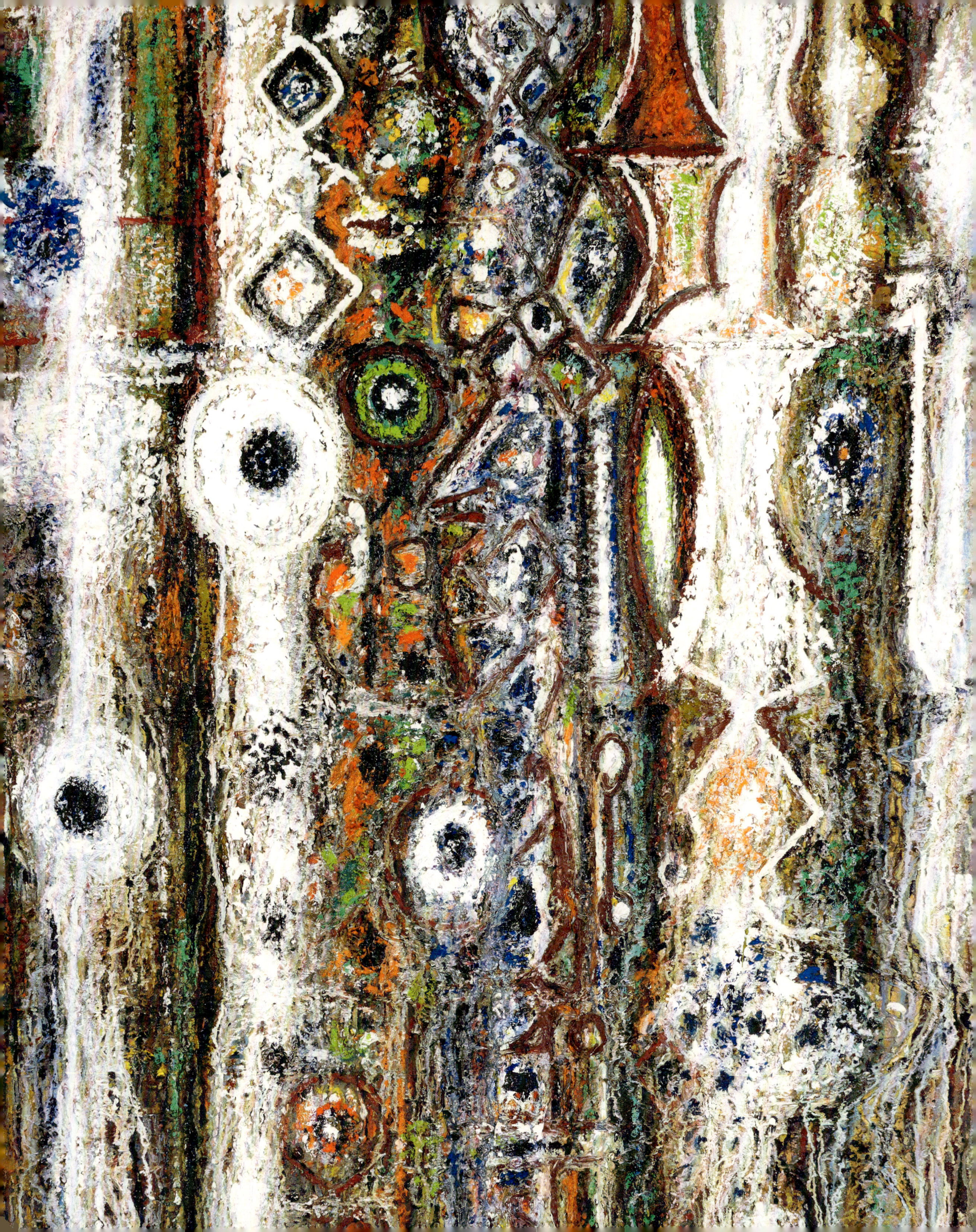

Cat. 19 *The Magnificent*, 1950–51, oil on canvas, 219.2 × 111.8 cm

81

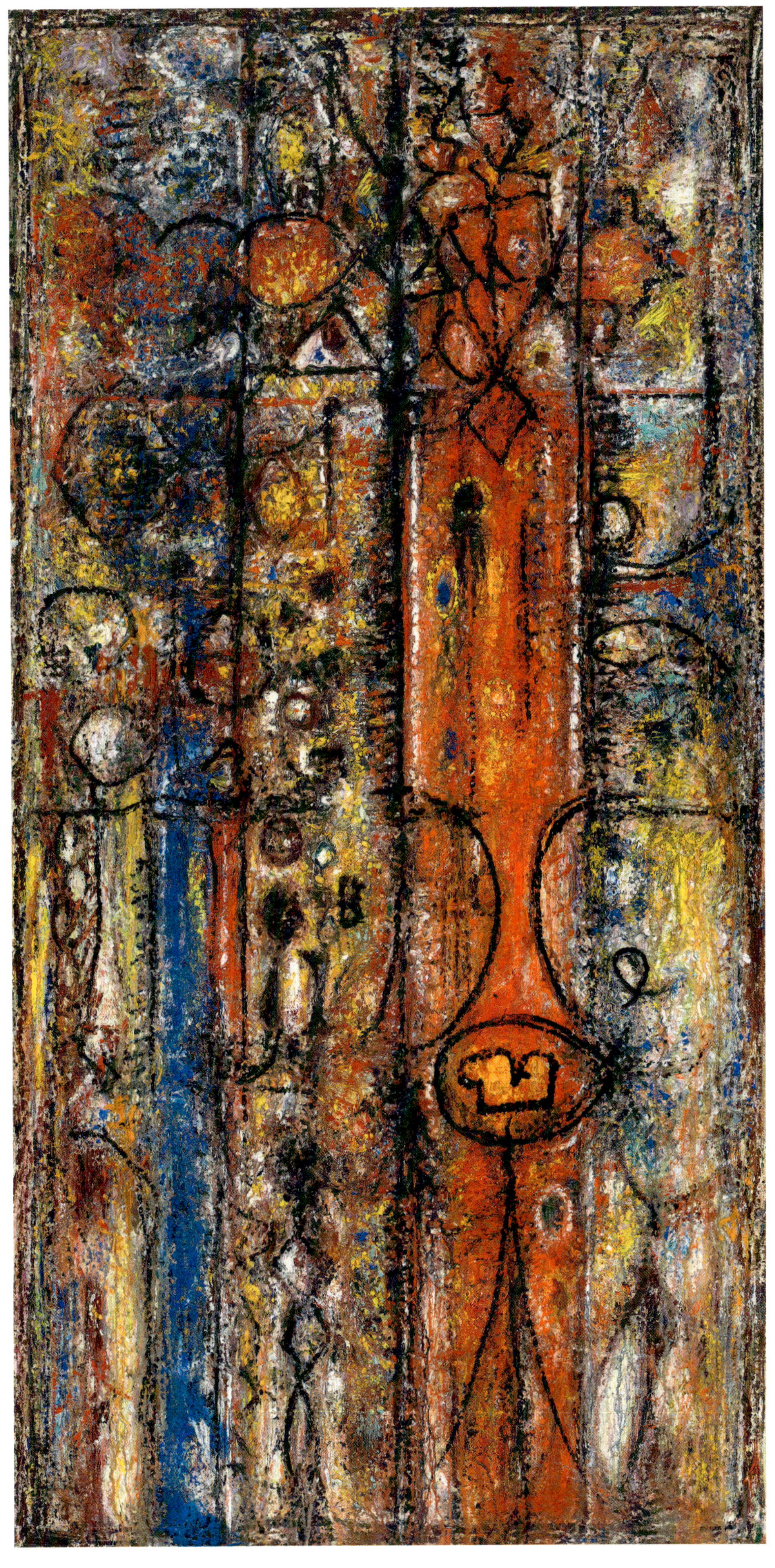

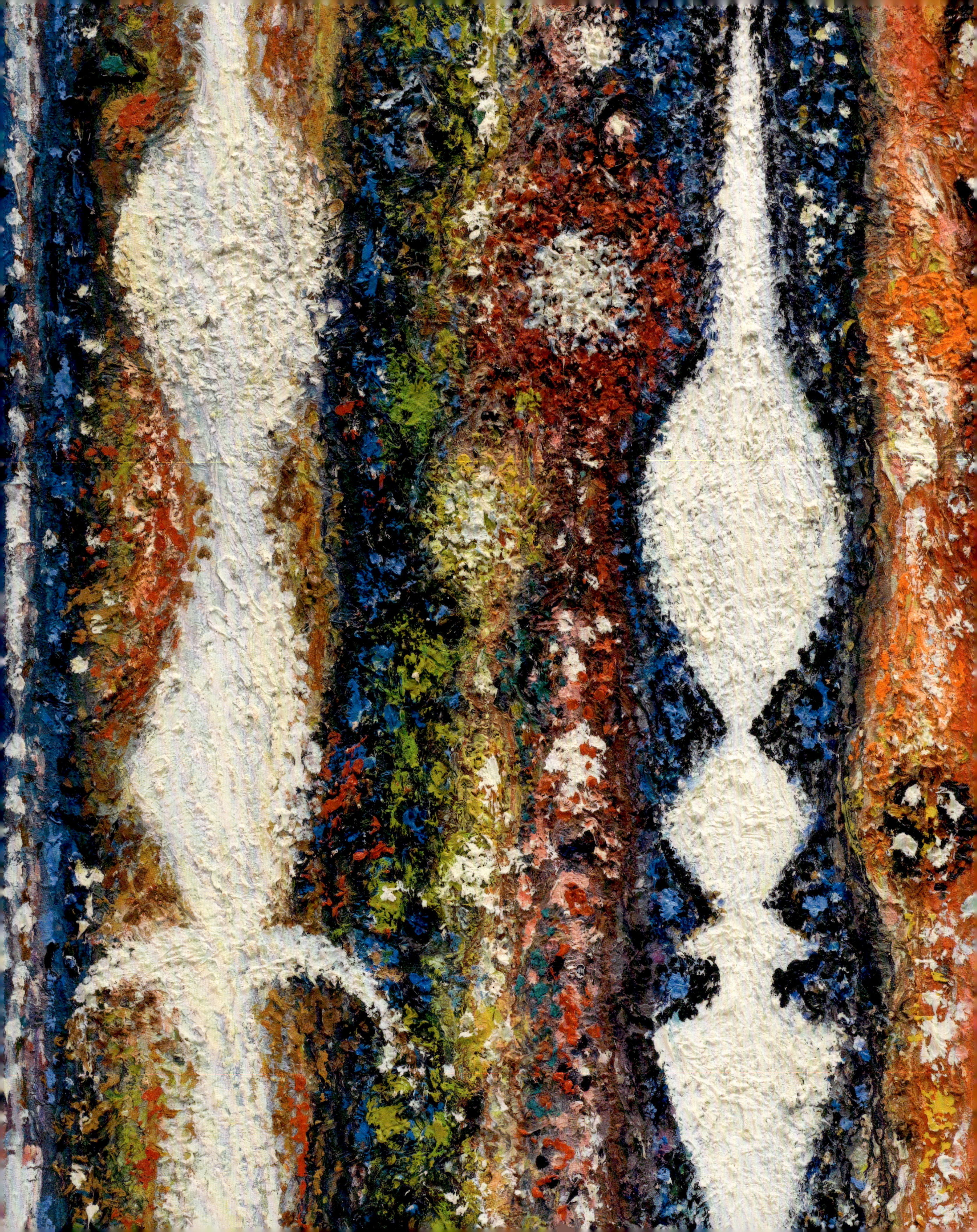

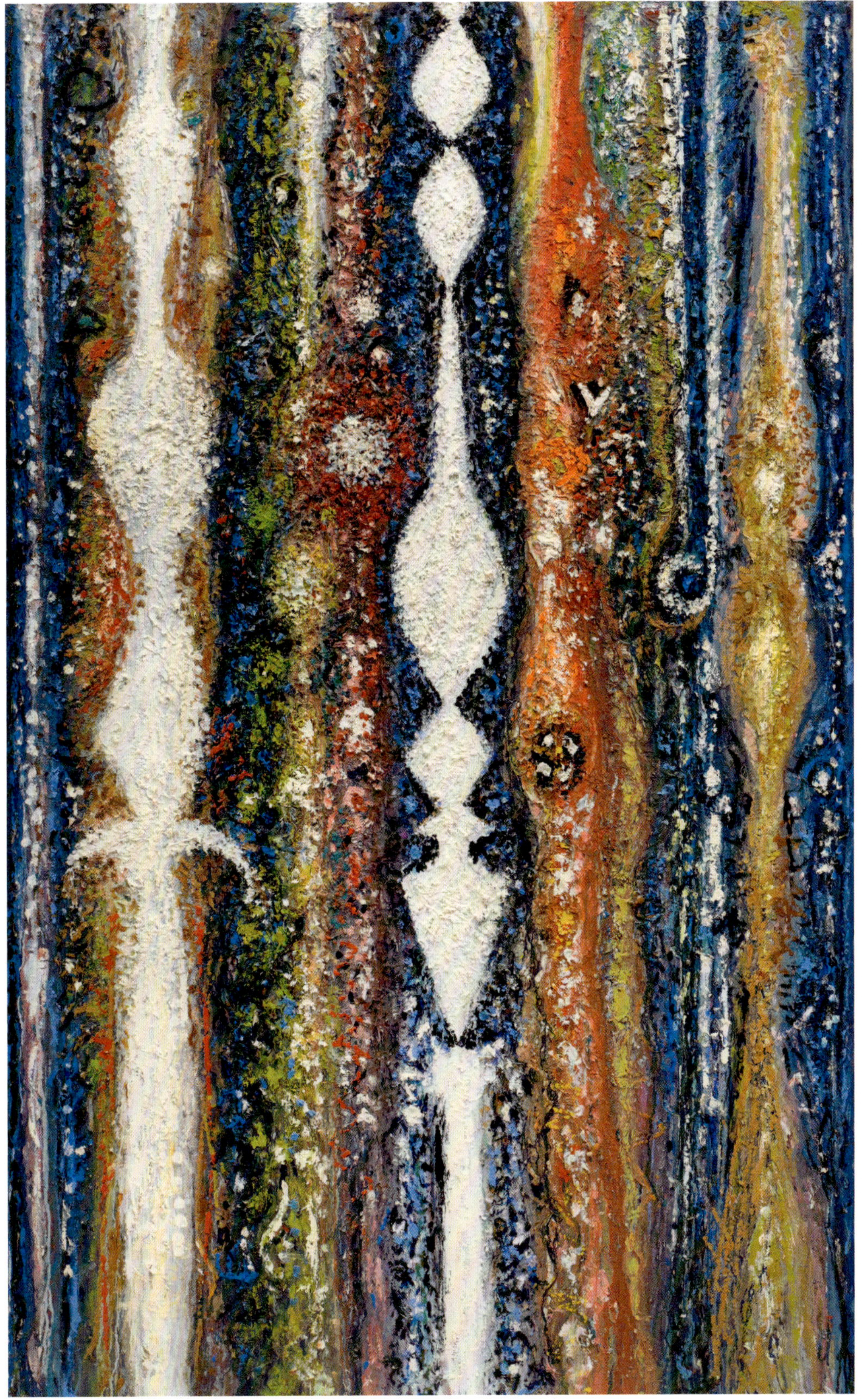

Cat. 20 *Illumination Vertical*, 1958, oil on linen, 199.4 × 123.2 cm

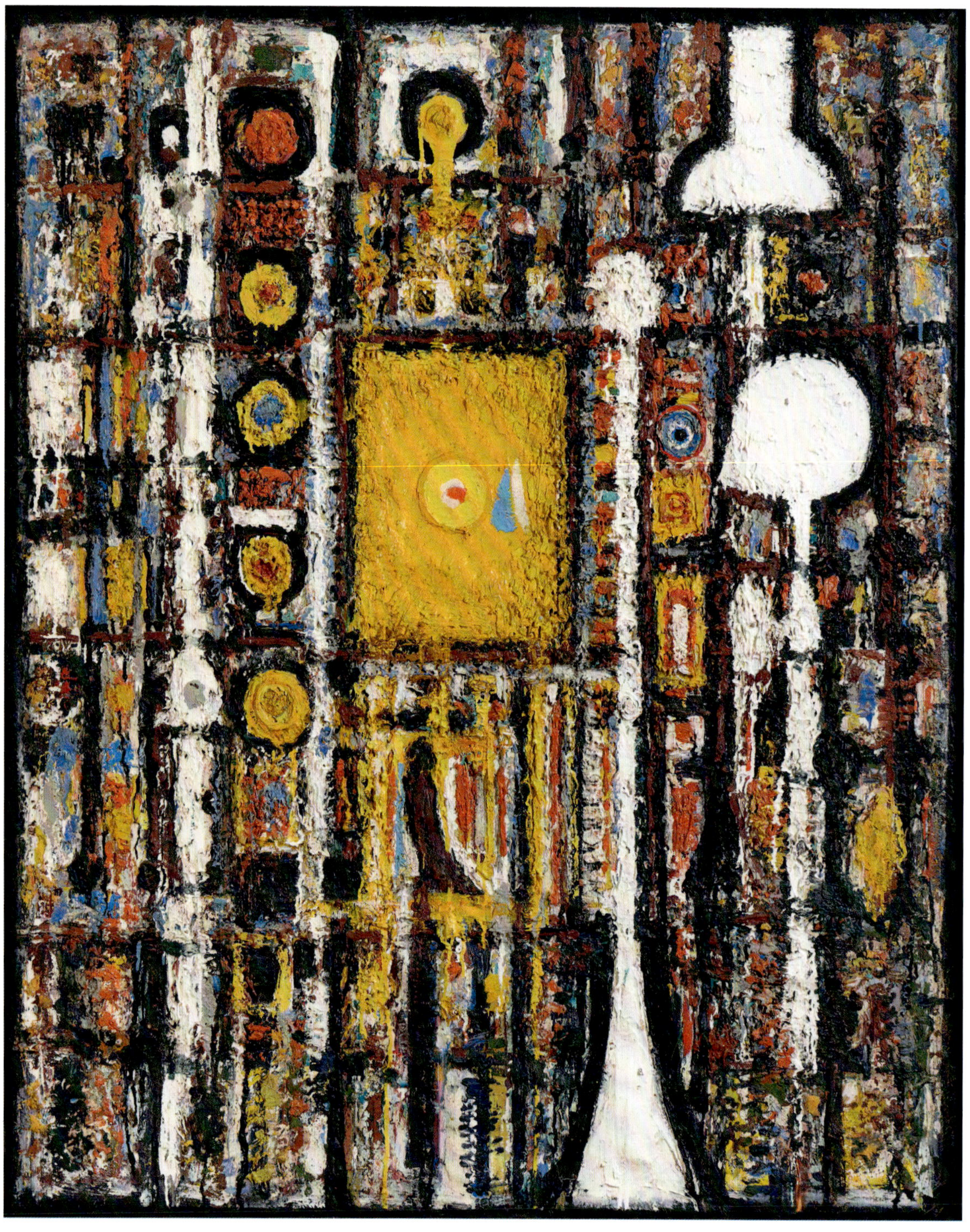

Cat. 21 *Window Number 4*, 1948–50, oil on linen, 134.6 × 111.8 cm

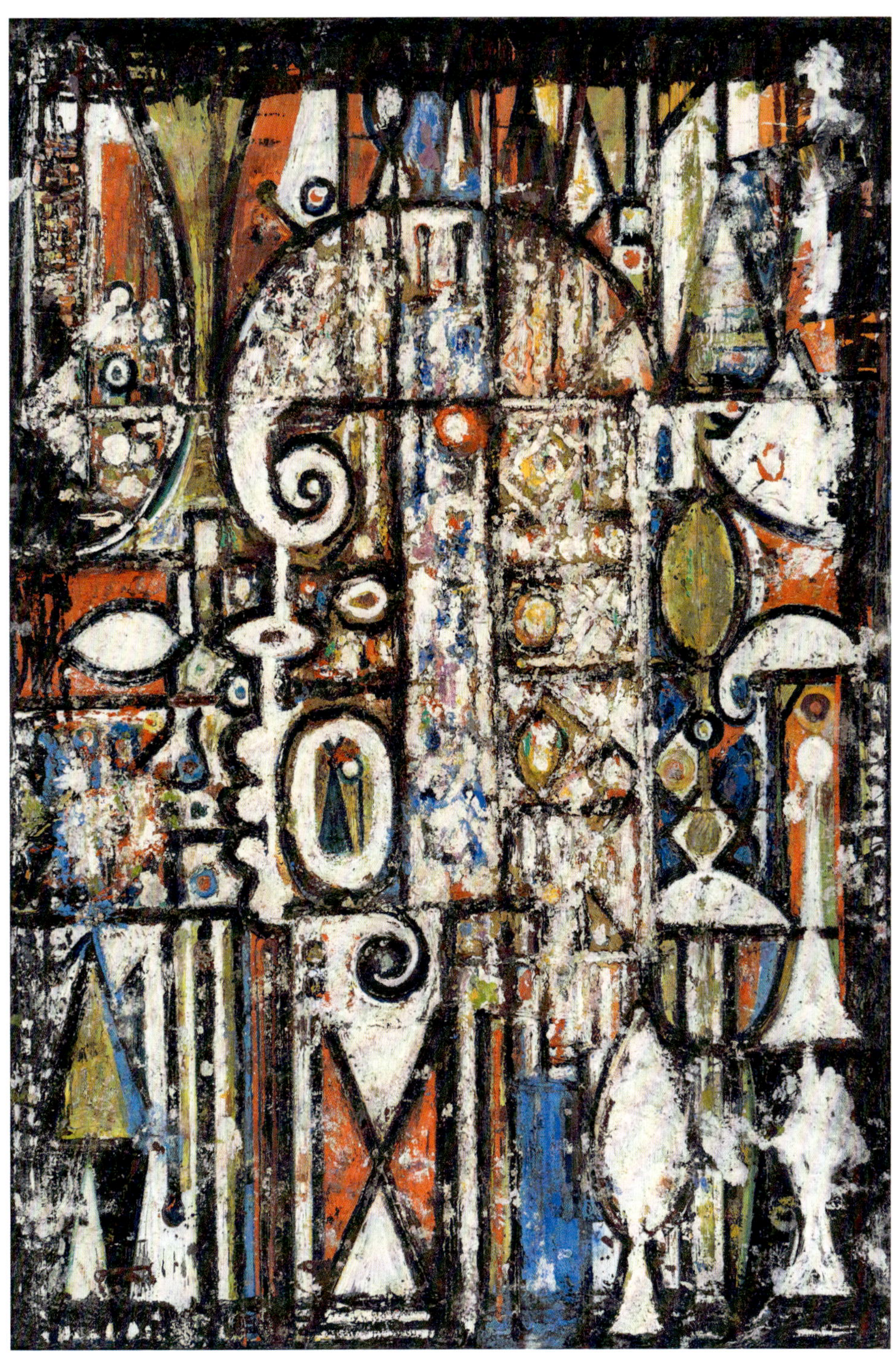

Cat. 22 *Window, Cathedral*, 1941–42, oil on linen, 133.7 × 92.7 cm

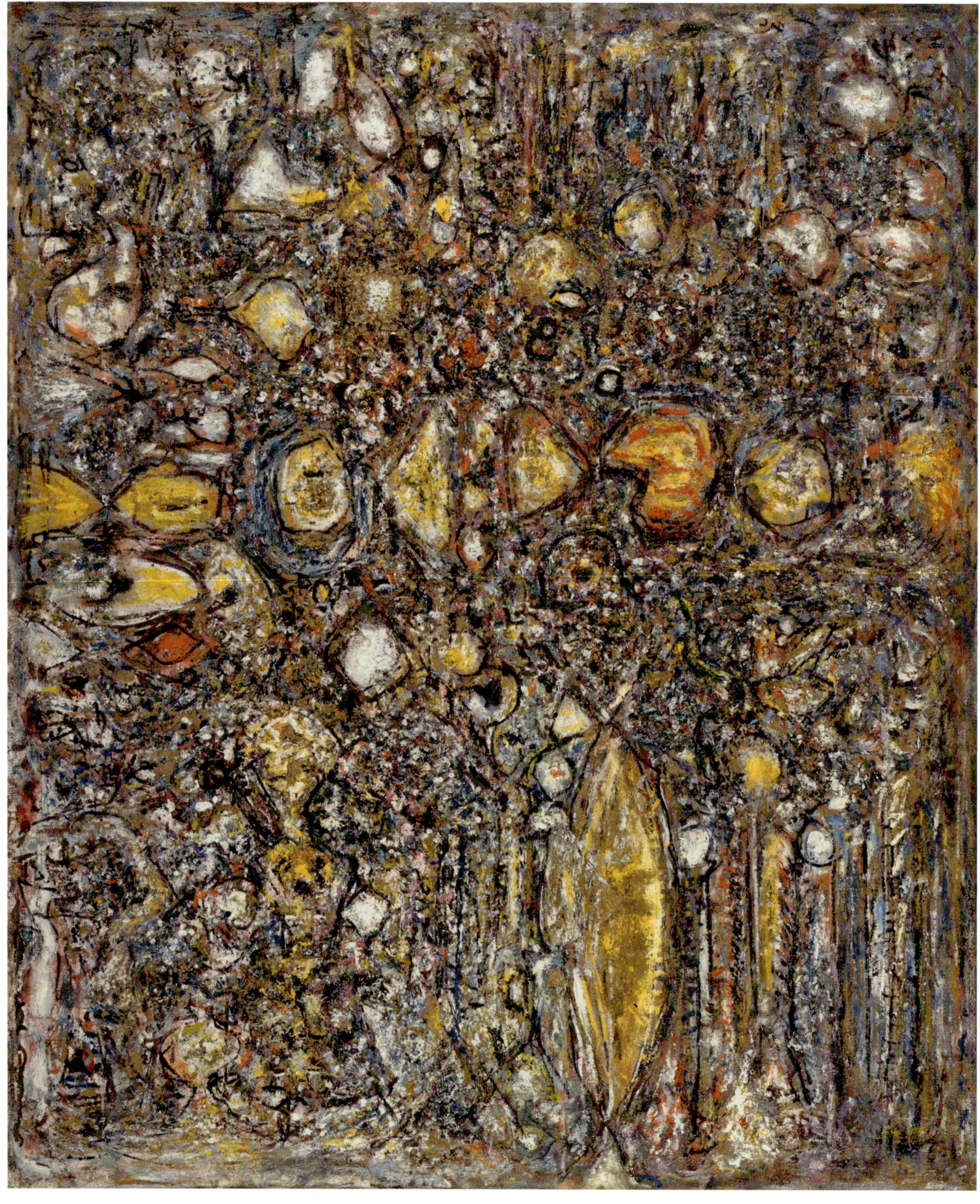

Cat. 23 *Amaranth*, 1958, oil on canvas, 192.4 × 164.5 cm

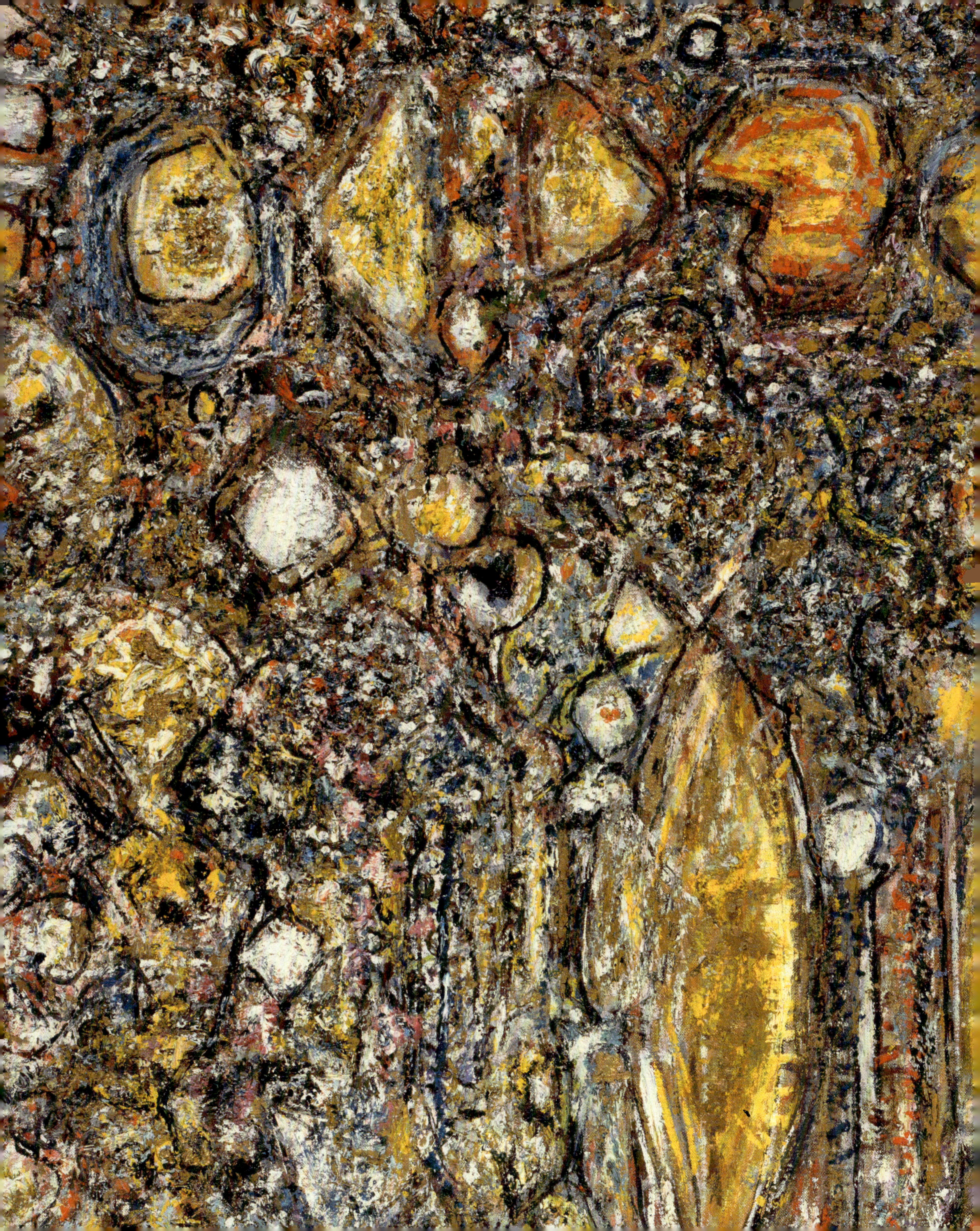

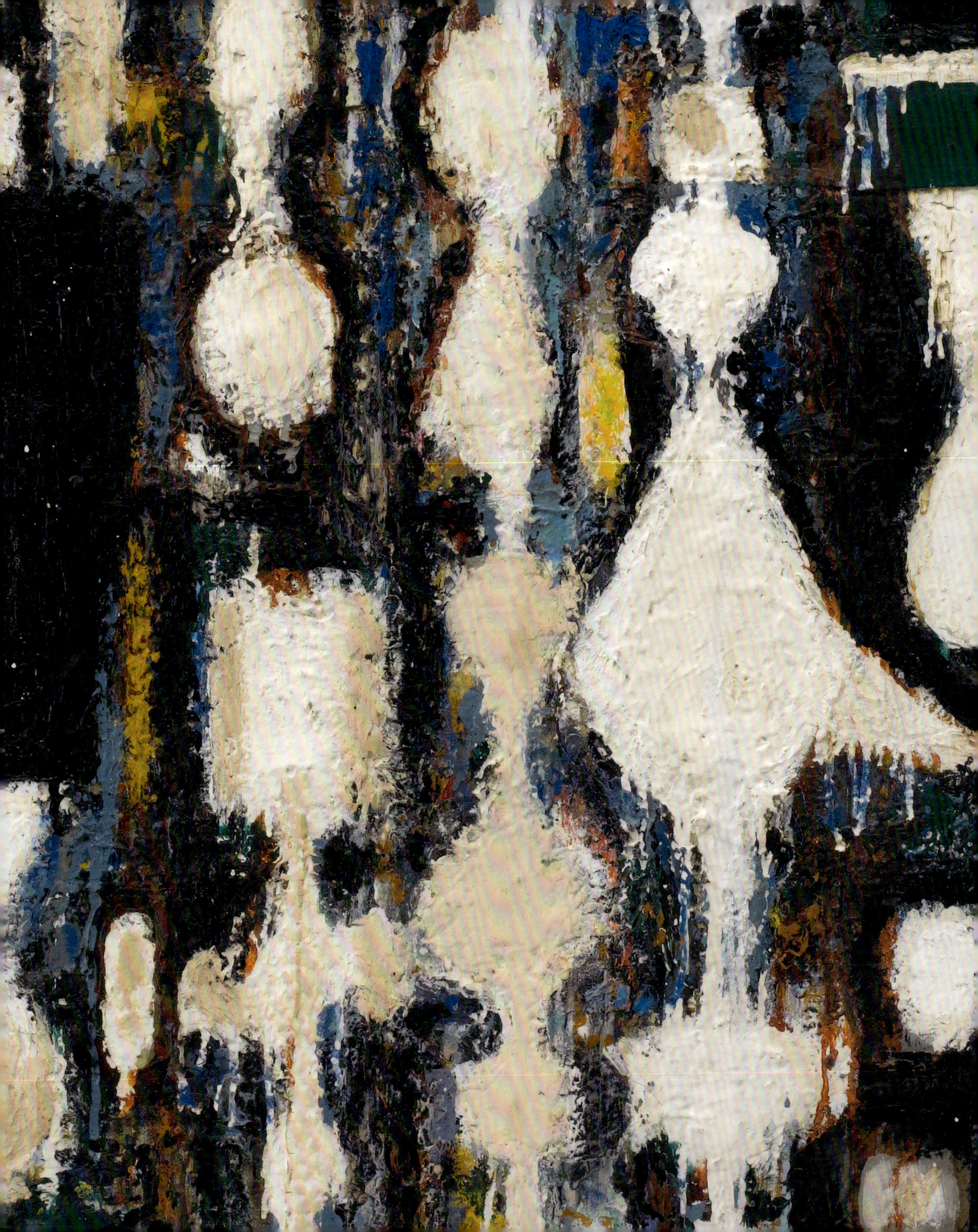

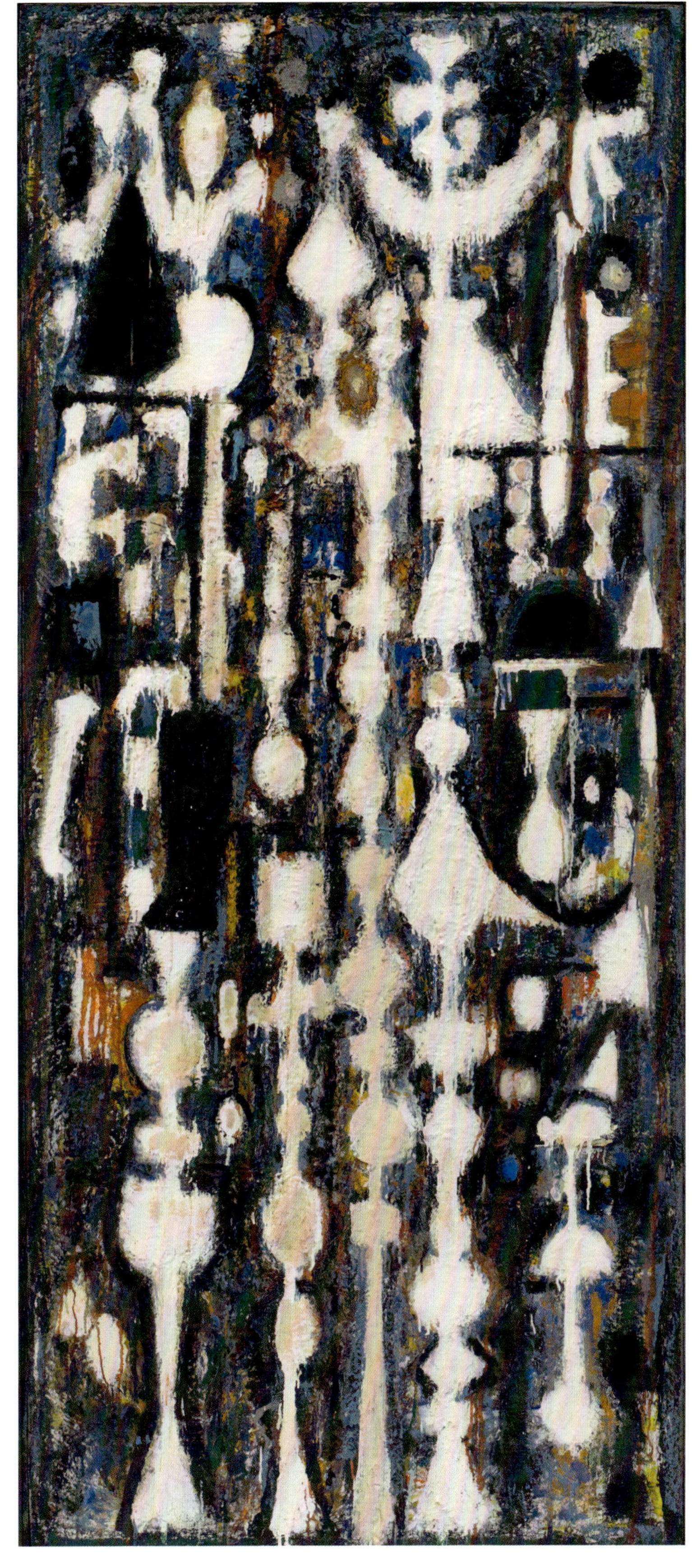

Cat. 24 *Pillars of Odysseus*, 1949, oil enamel and collage on canvas, 203.2 × 88.9 cm

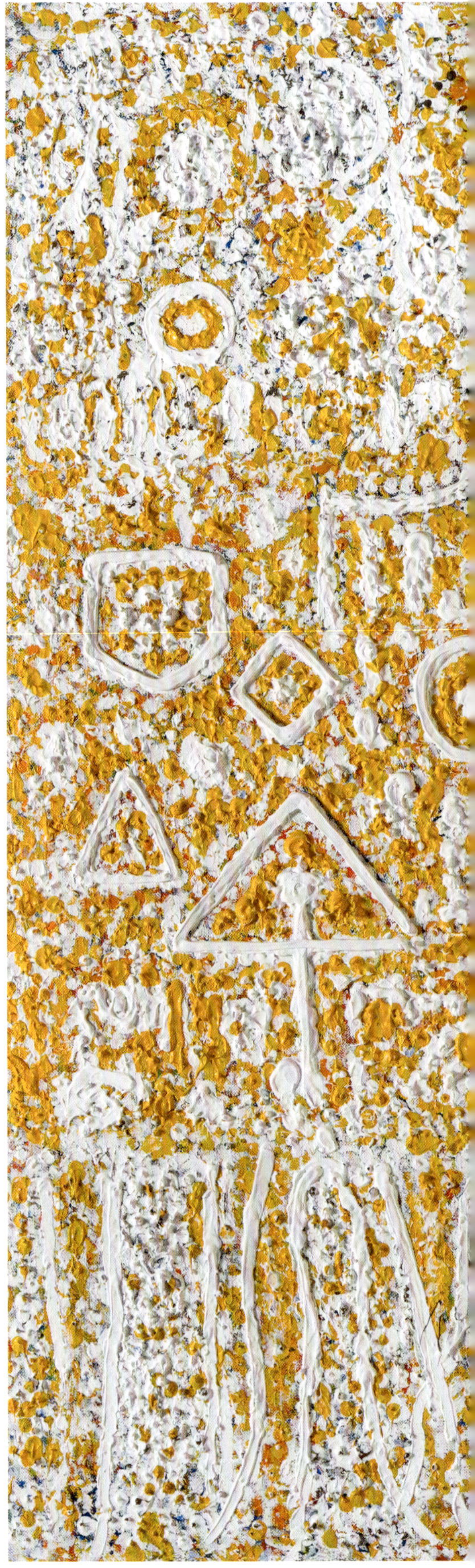

Cat. 25 *Naples Fugue*, 1982, acrylic on canvas, 138 × 183 cm

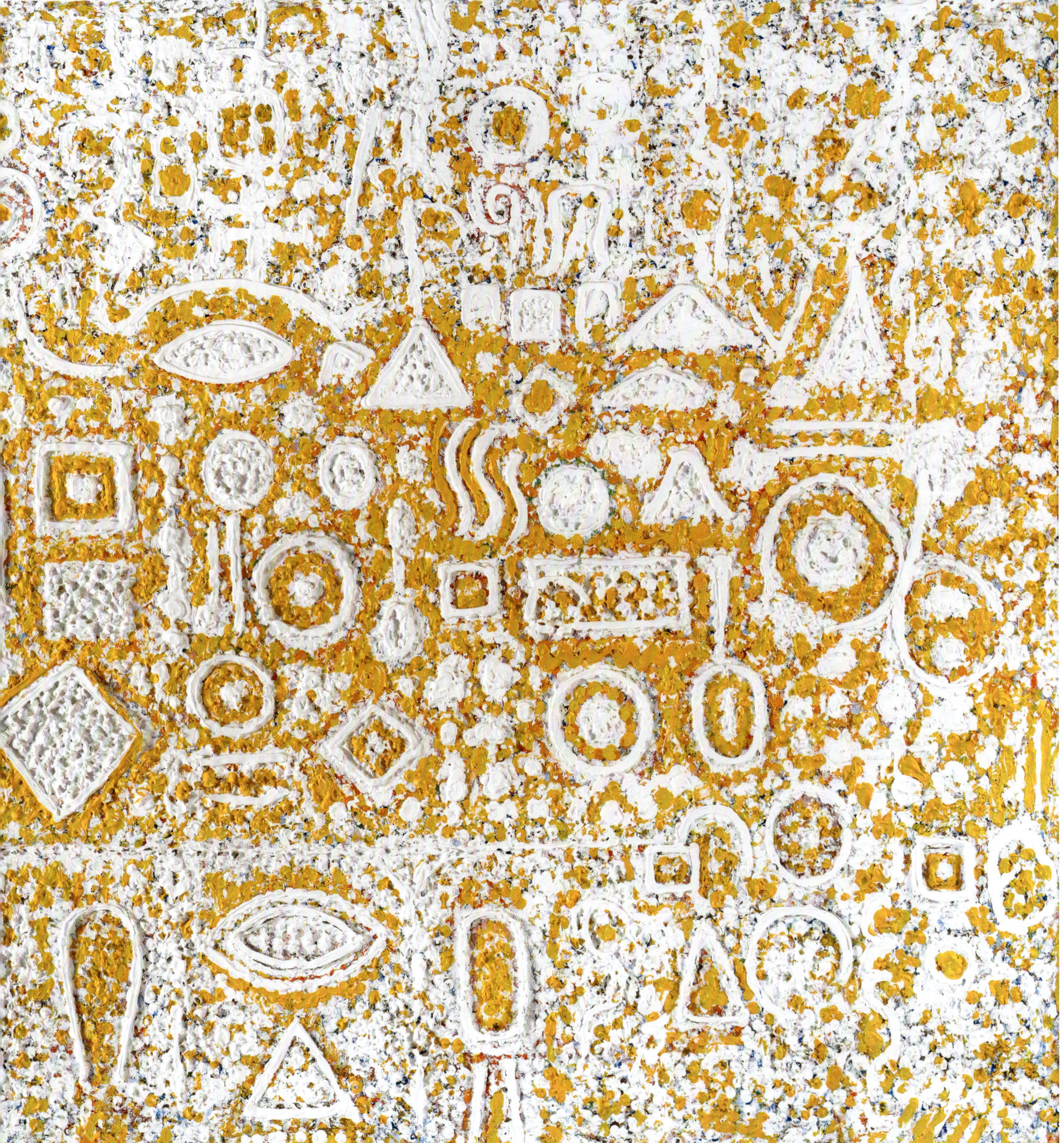

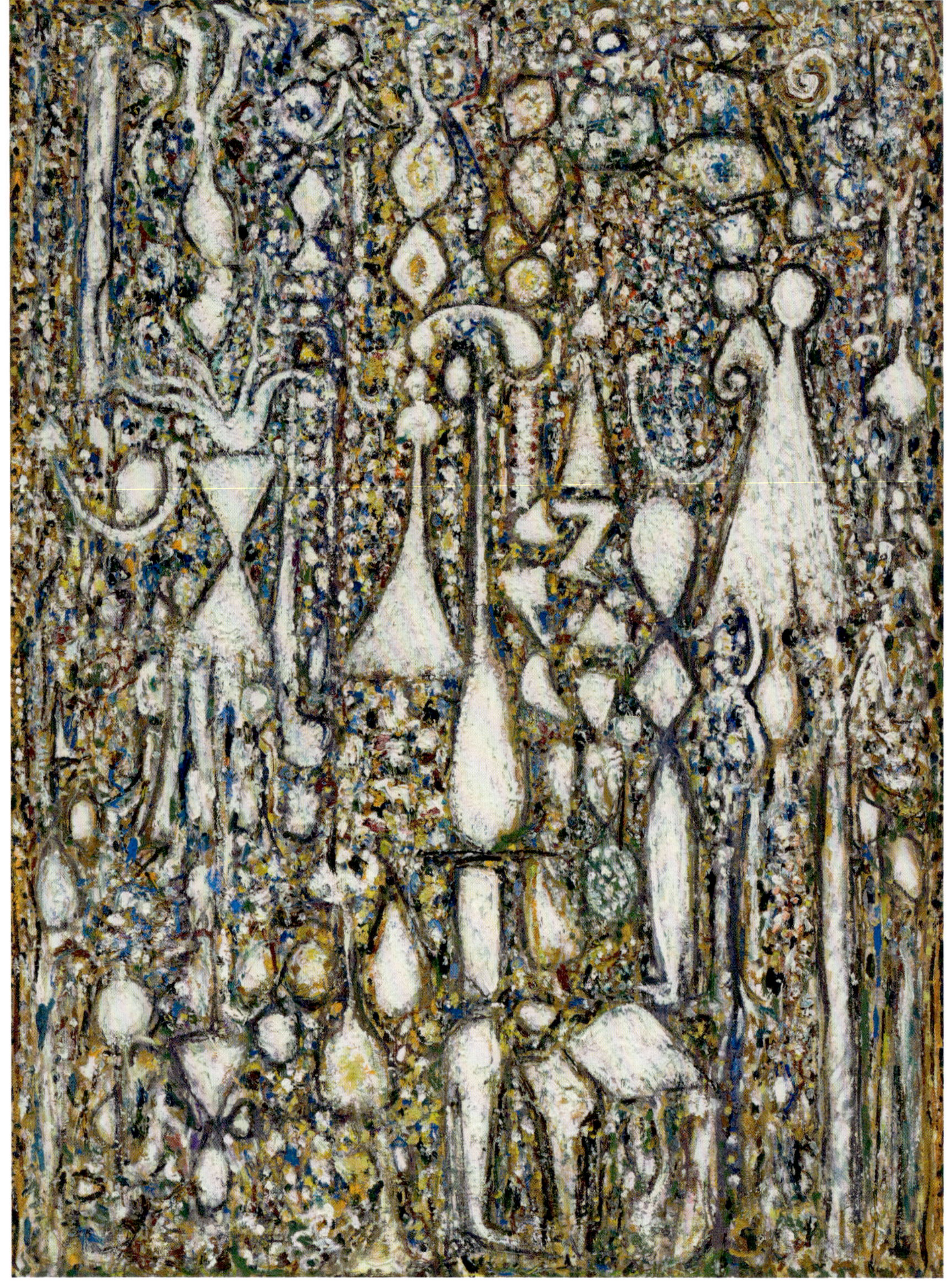

Cat. 26 *Fountains of Penelope*, 1960–62, oil on linen, 189.2 × 144.1 cm

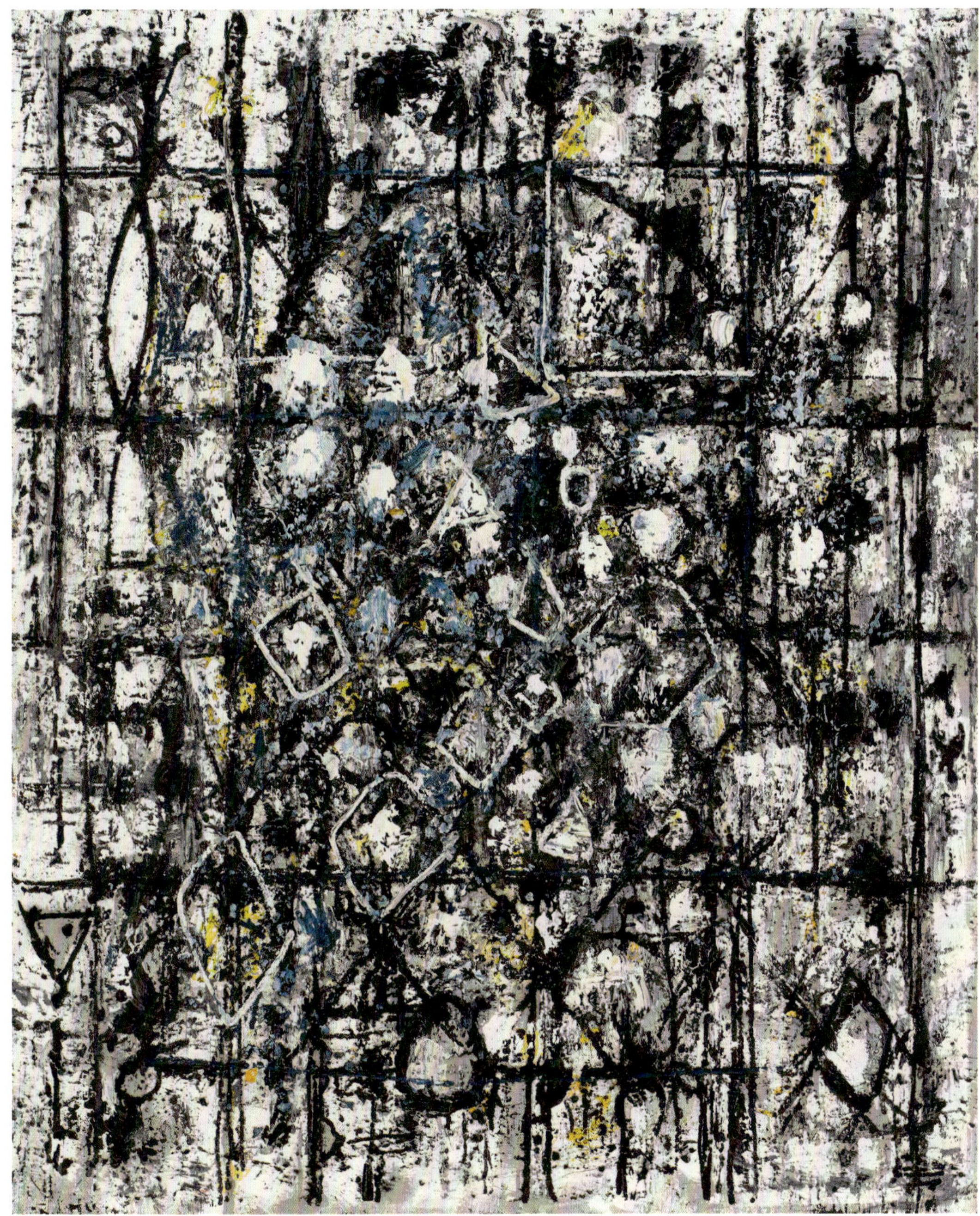

Cat. 27 *Gothic #2*, 1951–52, oil on linen, 152.4 × 127 cm

Cat. 28 *Apparition*, 1951, steel wire and objets trouvés, 223.5 × 55.9 × 53.3 cm

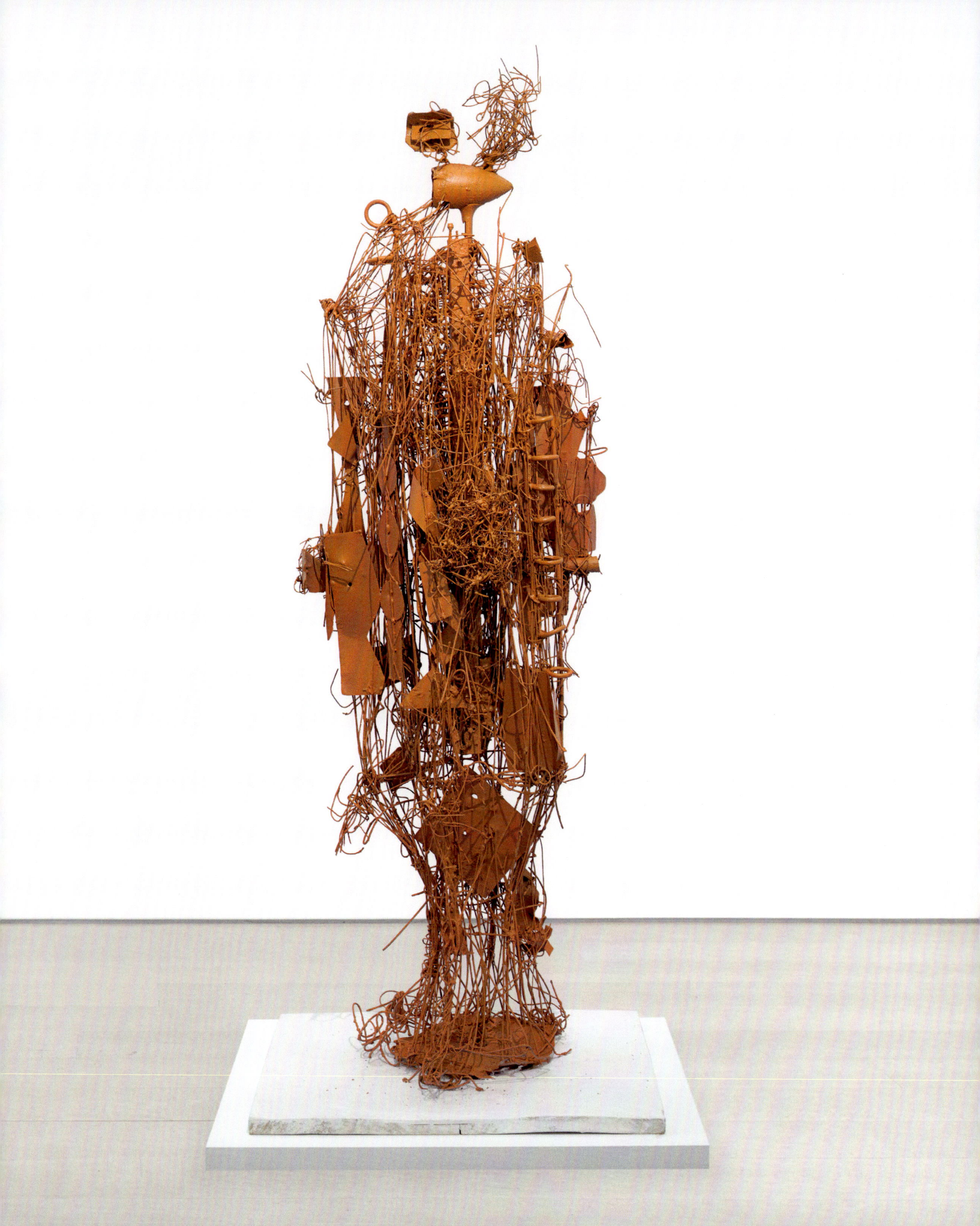

Cat. 29 *Black and White Fugue*, 1979–80, acrylic on canvas, 108 × 217.2 cm

Cat. 30 *Black and White Arch #1*, 1978–80, acrylic on linen, 248.9 × 127 cm

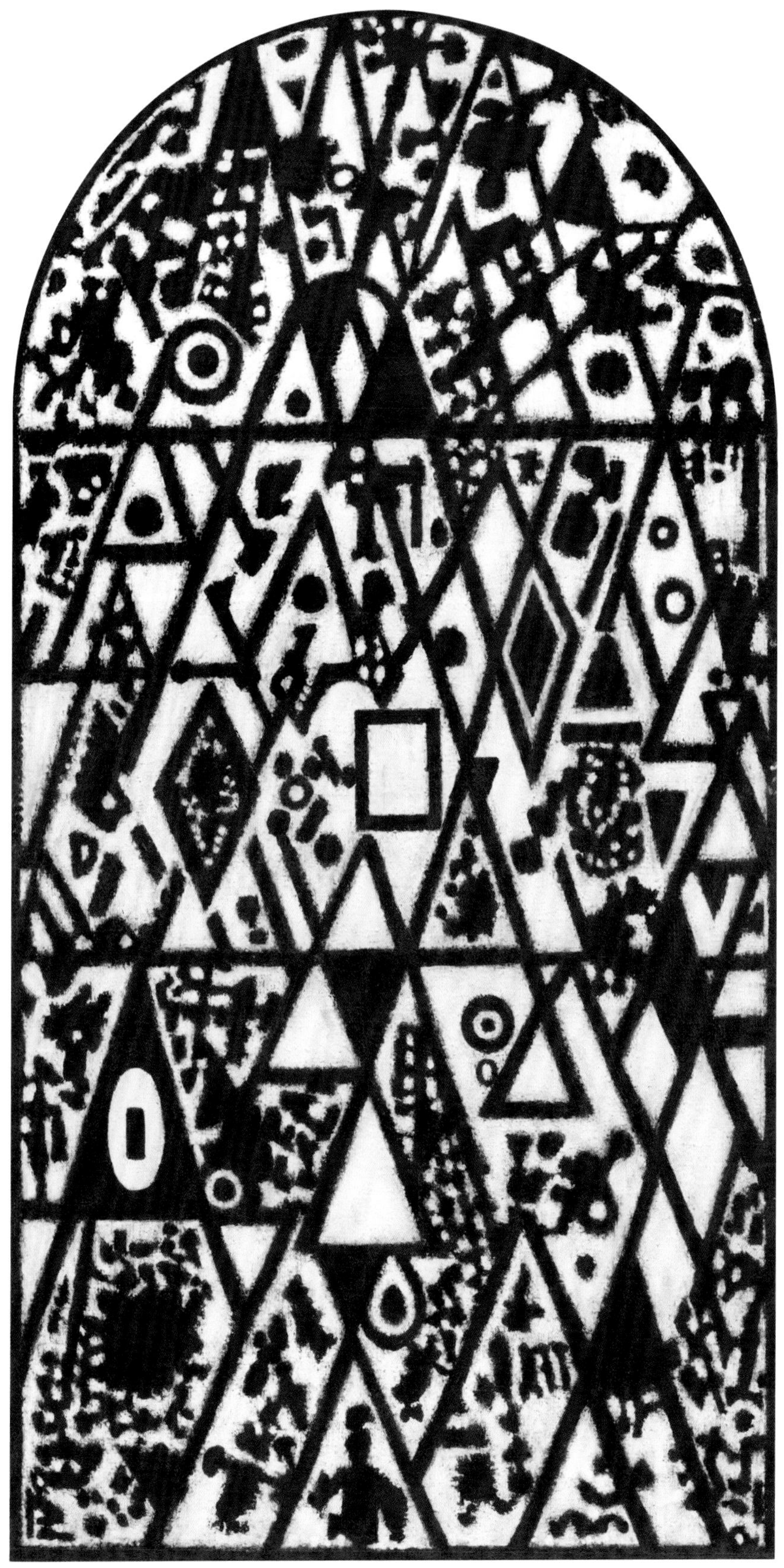

Cat. 31 *Black and White Arch #2*, 1978–80, acrylic on linen, 248.9 × 127 cm

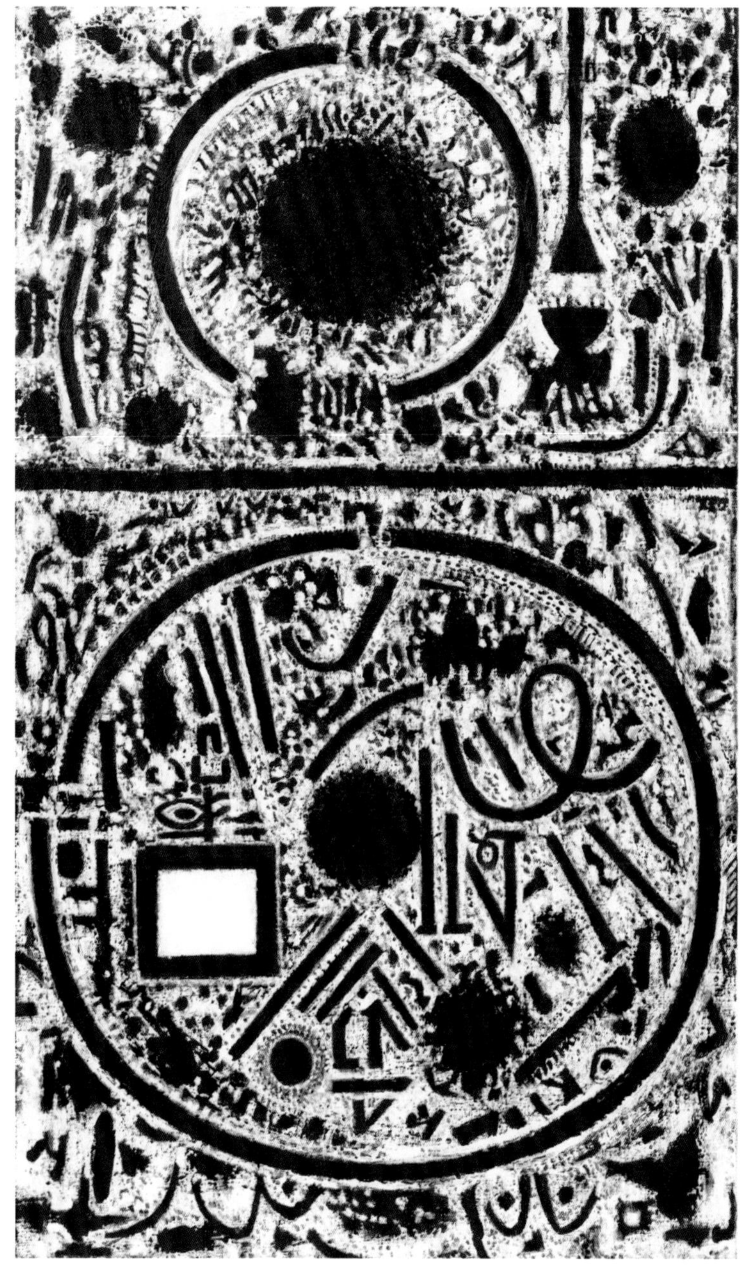

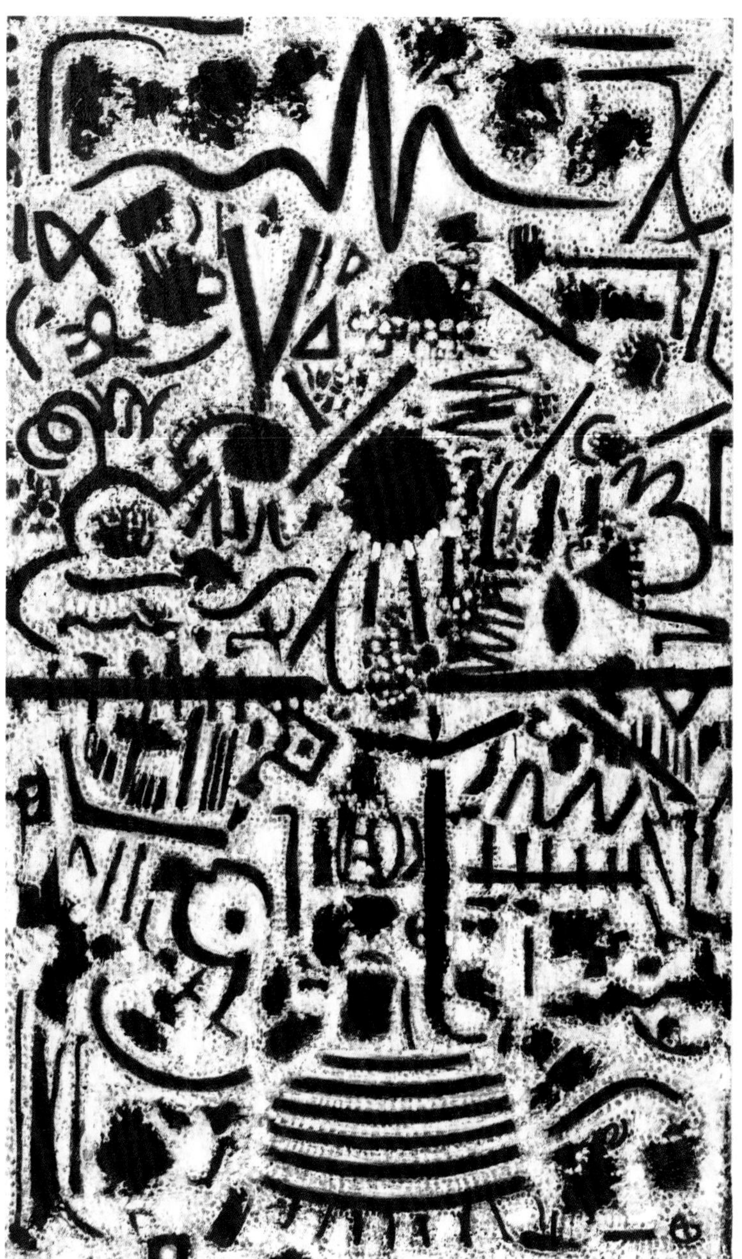

Cat. 32 *Wall of Signs,* 1979–80, acrylic on linen, four panels: each 213 × 128 cm

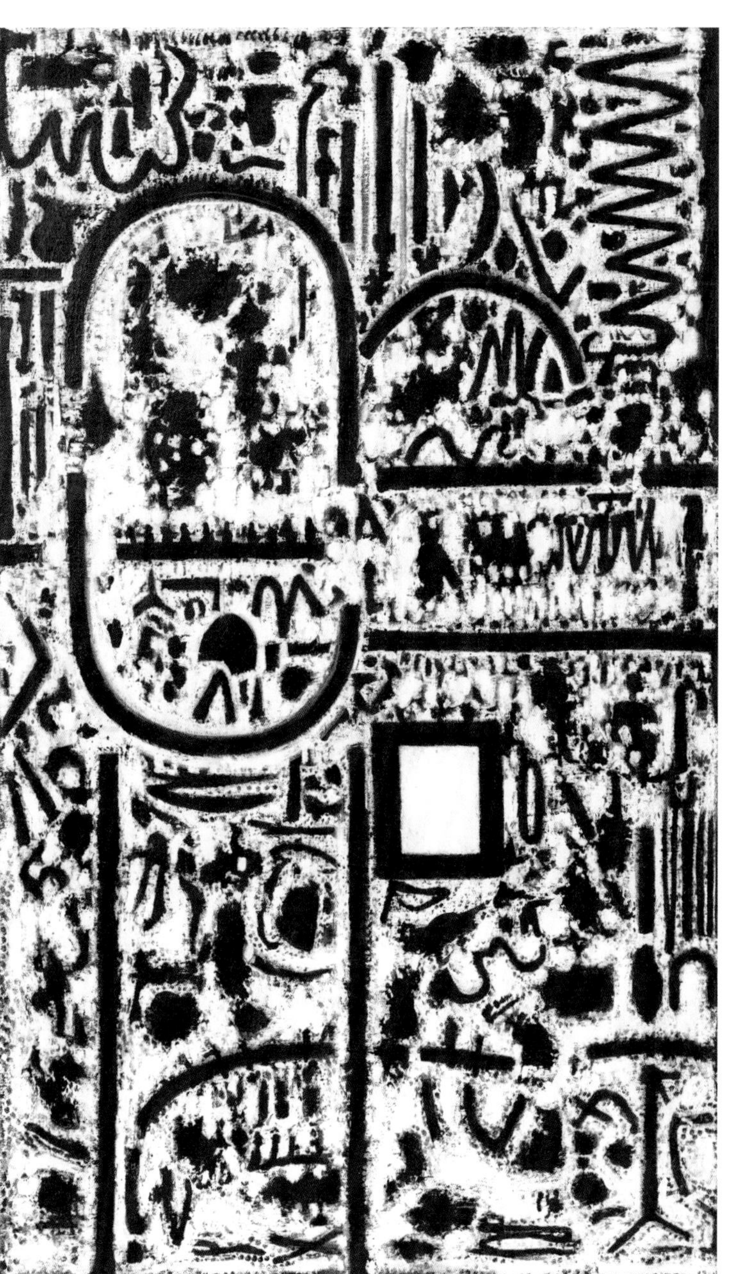

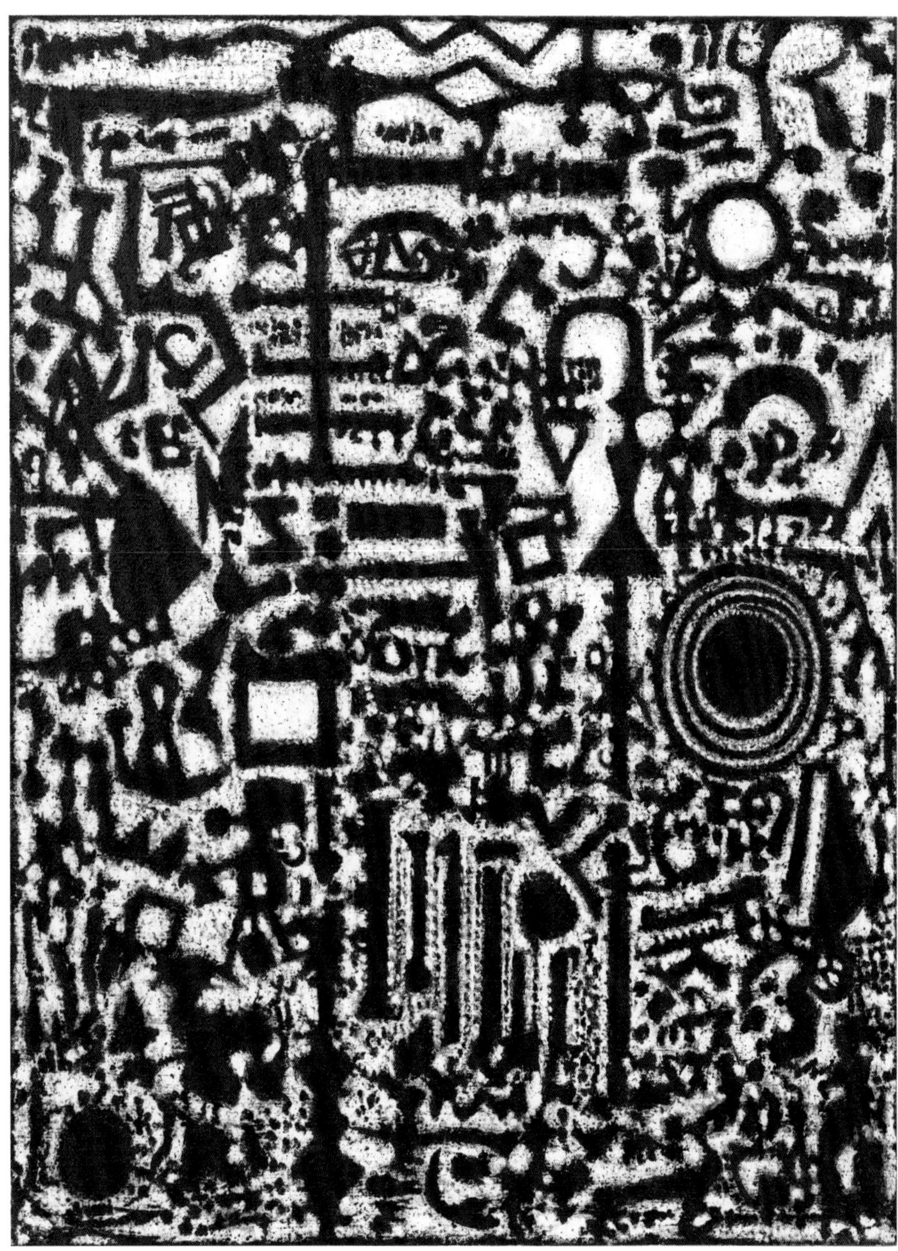

Cat. 33 *Spiral of Darkness*, 1979–80, acrylic on linen, 182.9 × 137.2 cm

Cat. 34 *The Square of Light*, 1979–80, oil on linen, 228.6 × 228.6 cm

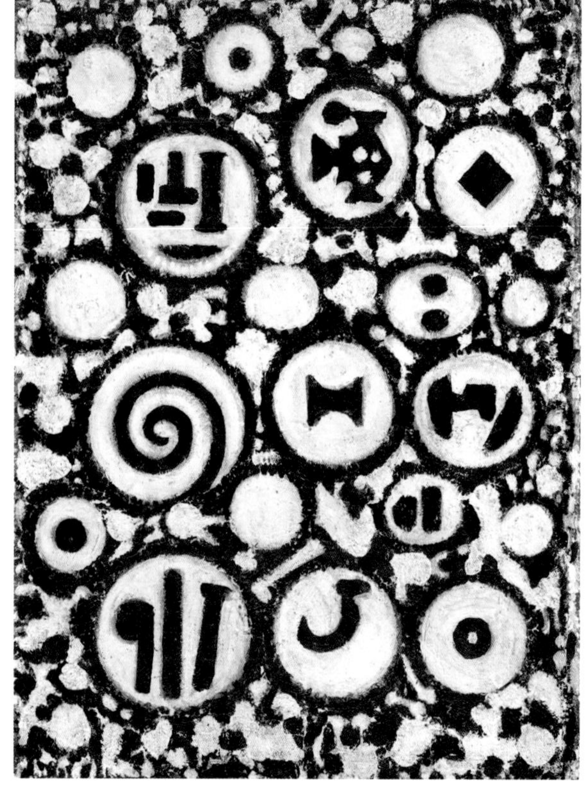

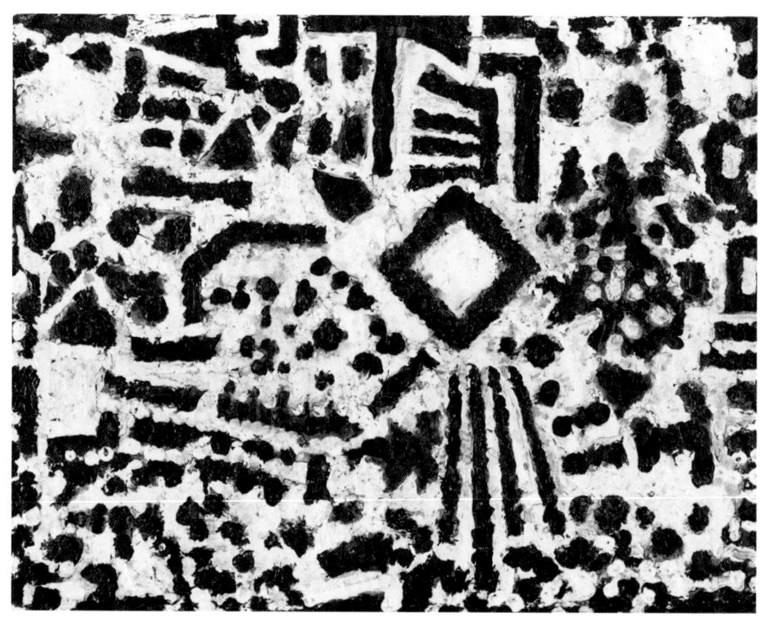

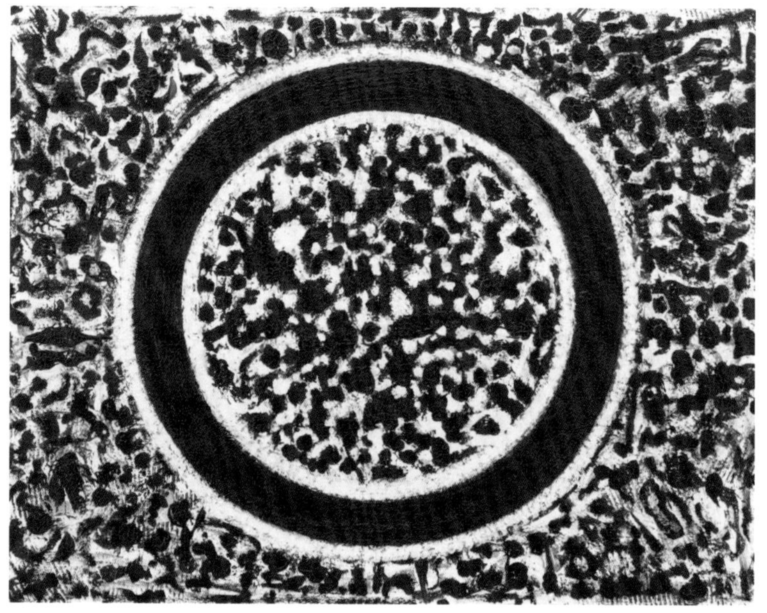

Cat. 35 *Circles, One Spiral*, 1978, acrylic on paper, 76.8 × 57.8 cm

Cat. 36 *Carmine*, 1977–82, acrylic on paper, 57.5 × 76.2 cm

Cat. 37 *Always the Center*, 1978, acrylic on paper, 56.5 × 76.8 cm

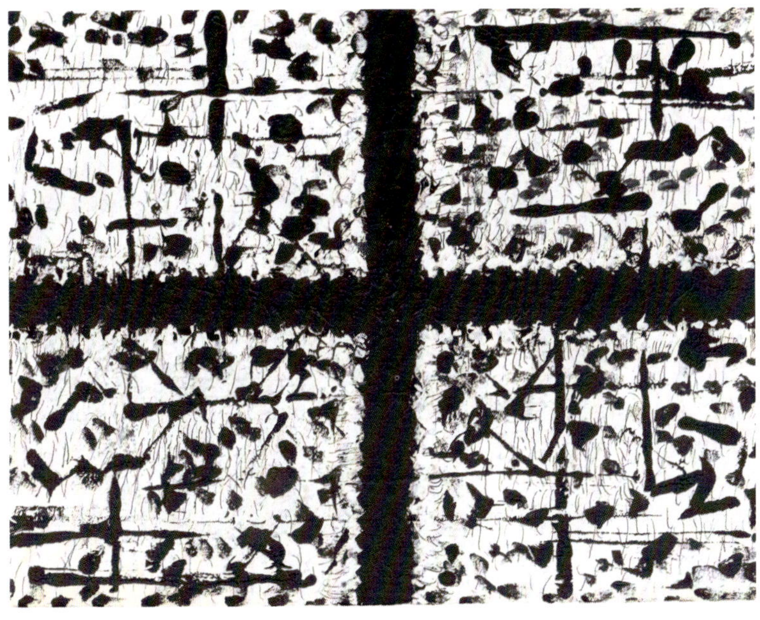

Cat. 38 *Micro Black*, 1978, acrylic on paper, 57.8 × 76.8 cm

Cat. 39 *Inscribed Landscape*, 1979, acrylic on paper, 77.5 × 57.2 cm

Cat. 40 *Four Quarter Harmony*, 1982, acrylic on paper, 57.2 × 76.2 cm

Cat. 41 *Lost in the Beginning of Infinity*, 1991, acrylic on linen, diameter: 182.9 cm

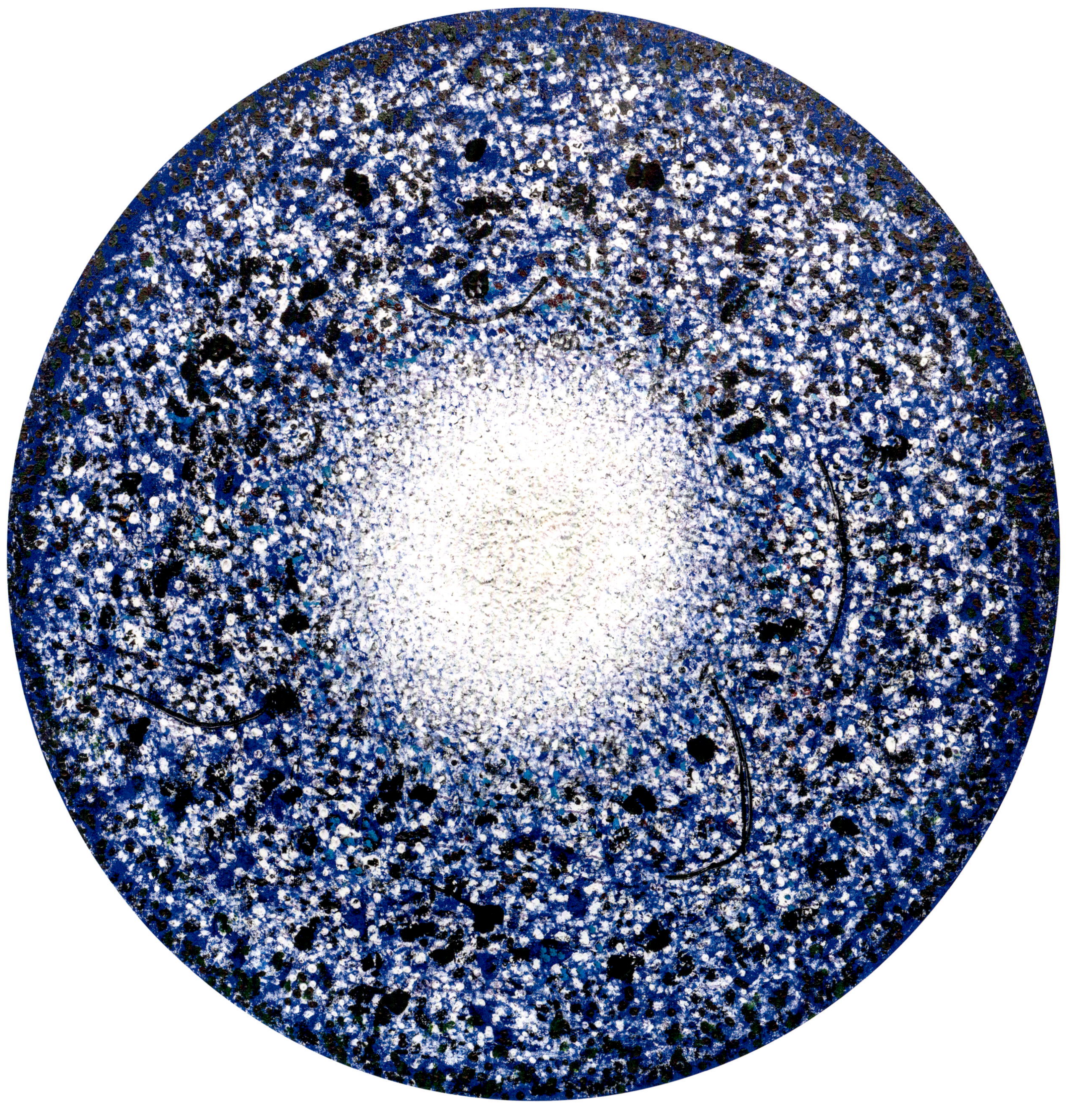

Cat. 42 *Hieroglyph Number 7*, 1968–69, oil on linen, 193 × 129.5 cm

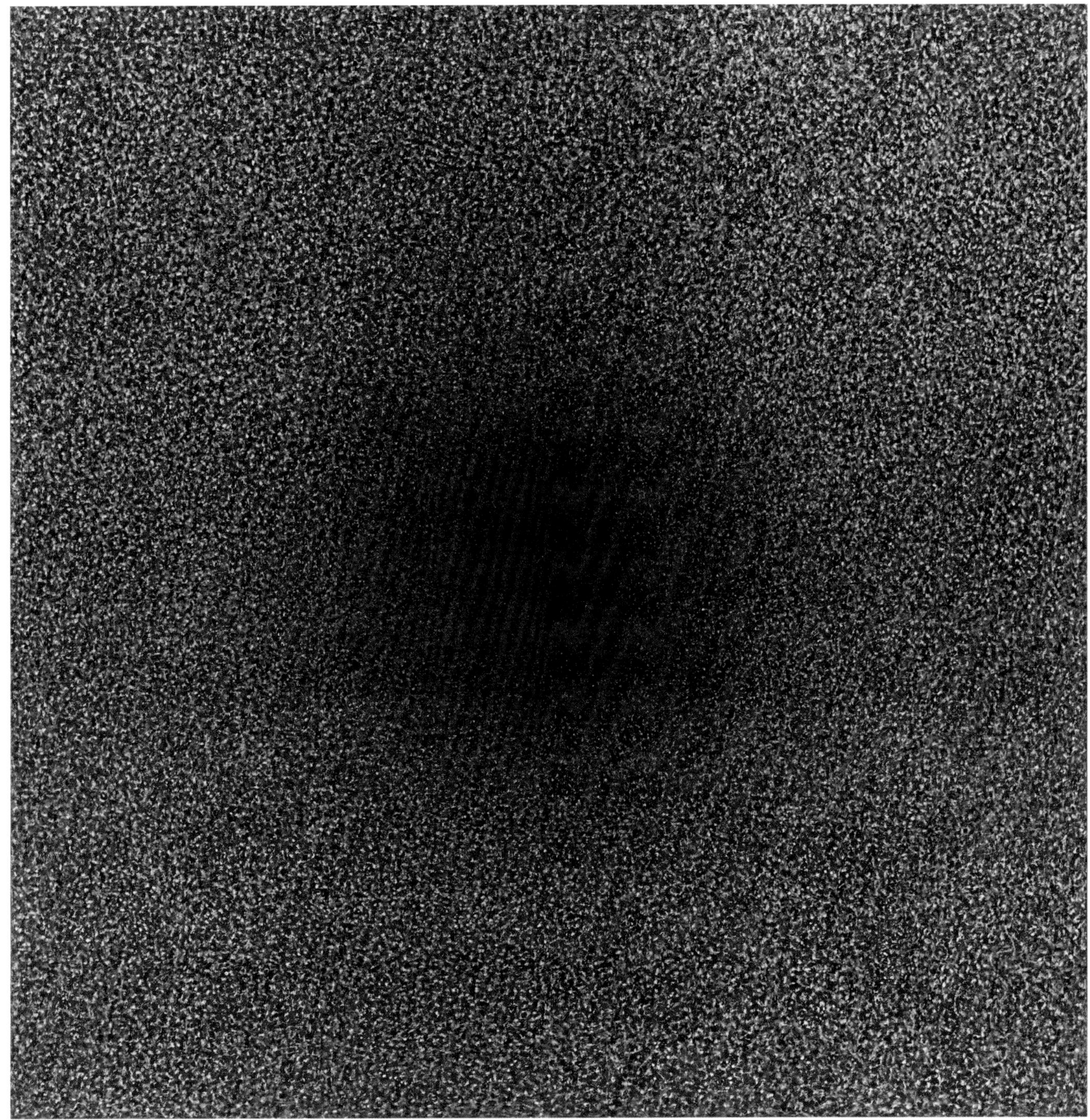

Cat. 43 *Presence Number 3, Black*, 1969, oil on linen, 203.2 × 203.2 cm

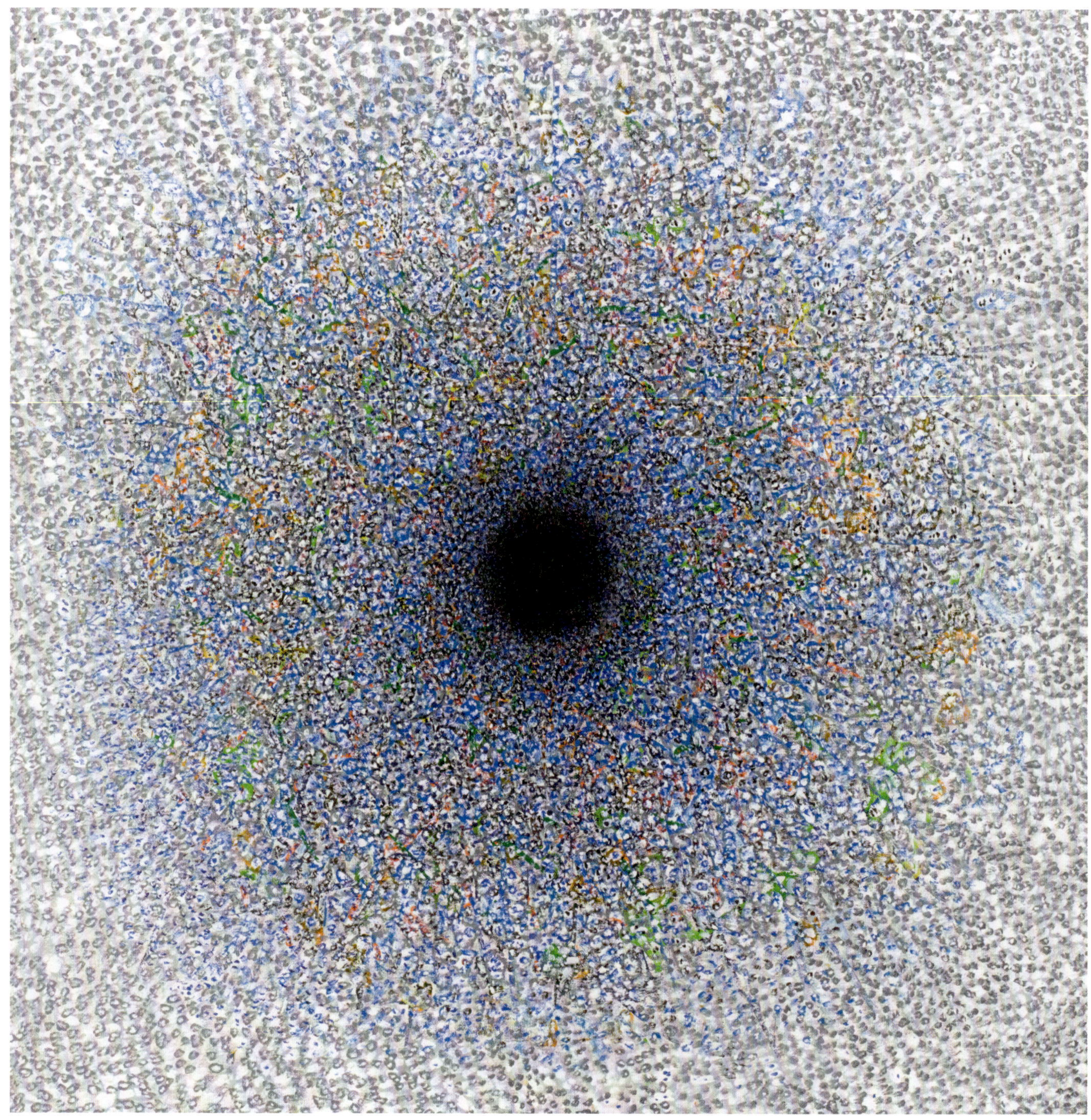

Cat. 44 *Imploding Black*, 1985–86, acrylic on linen, 182.9 × 182.9 cm

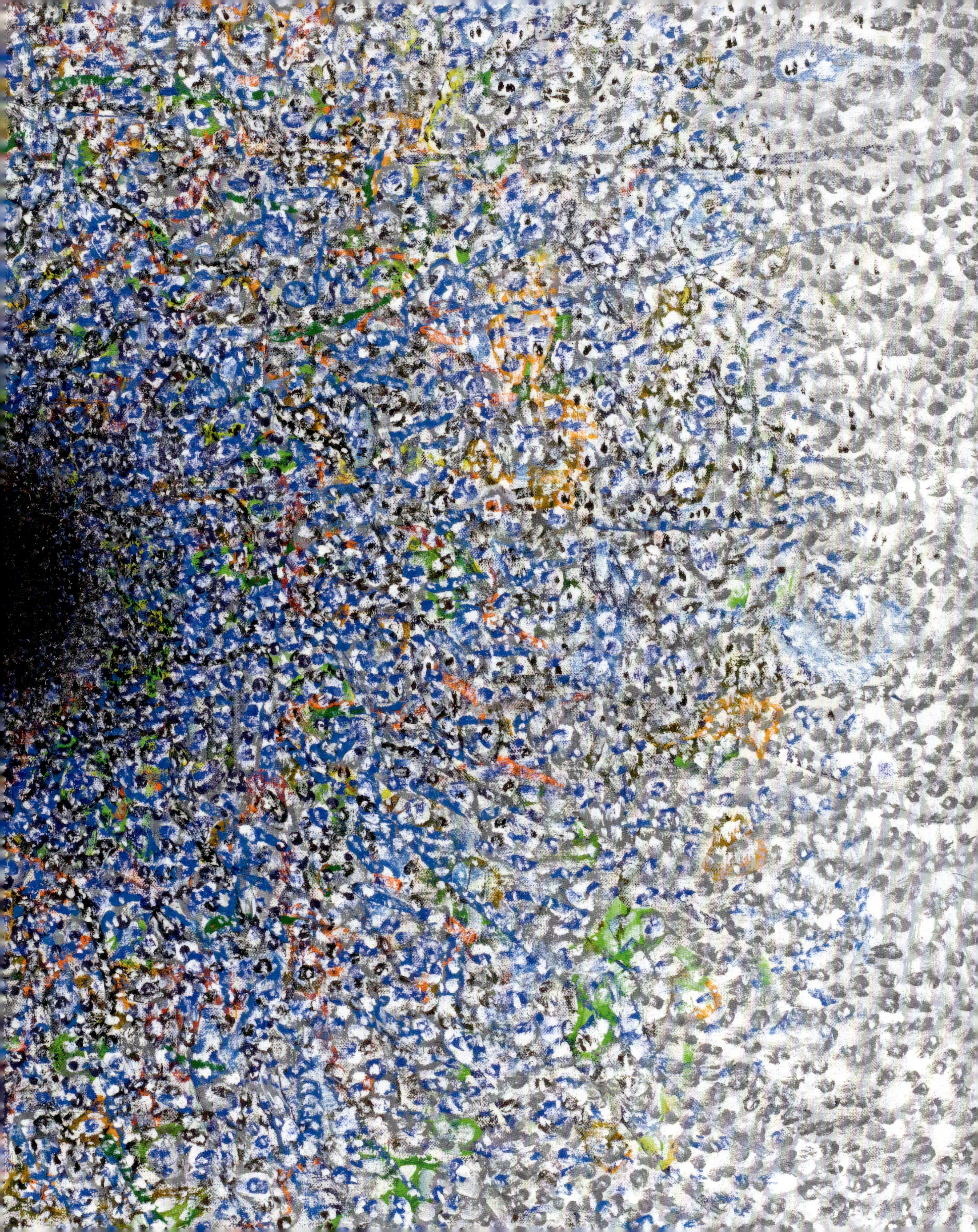

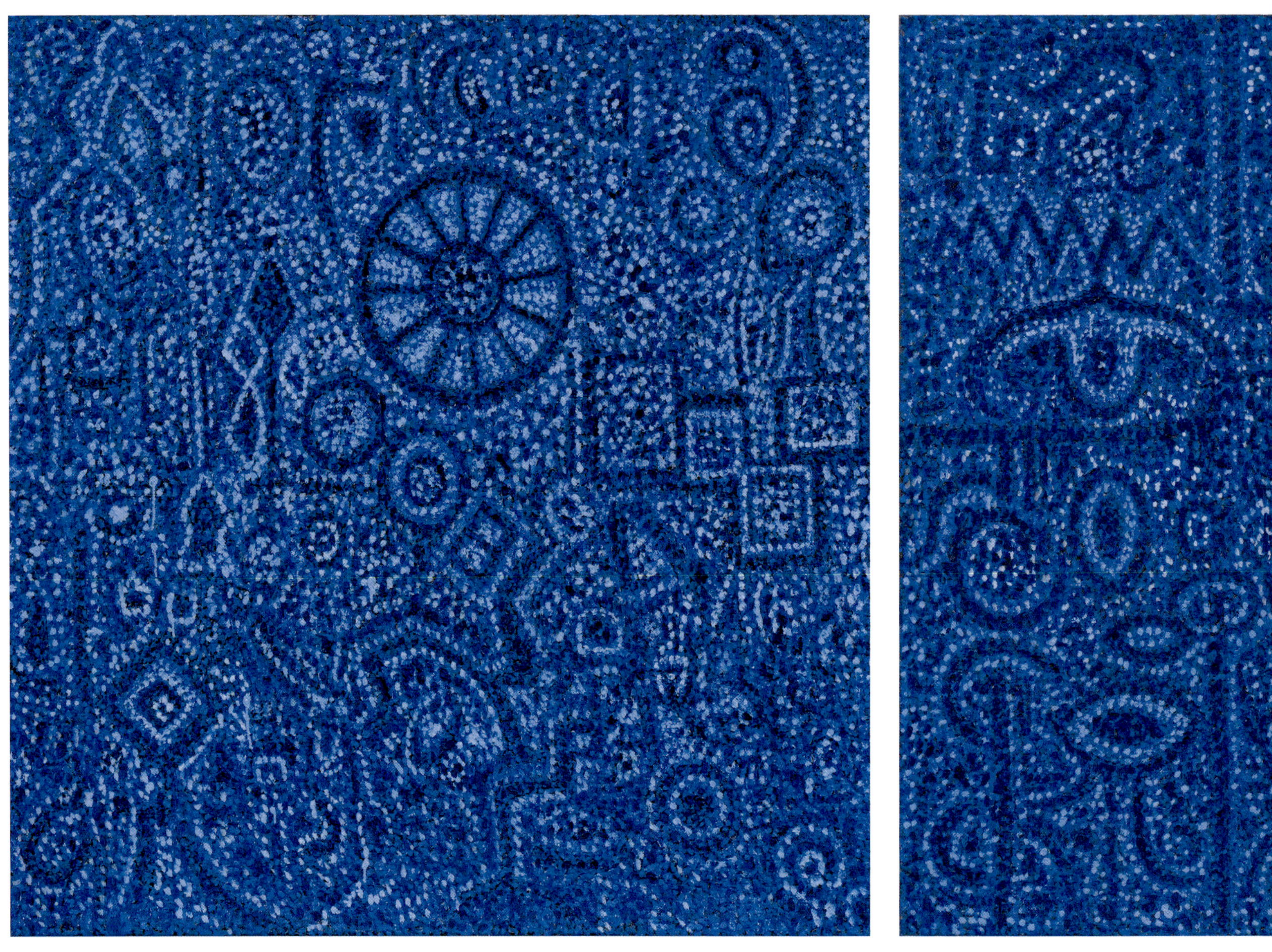

Cat. 45 *Byzantine Cathedral I, II, III,* 1988–90, acrylic on linen, triptych: each panel 183 × 183 cm

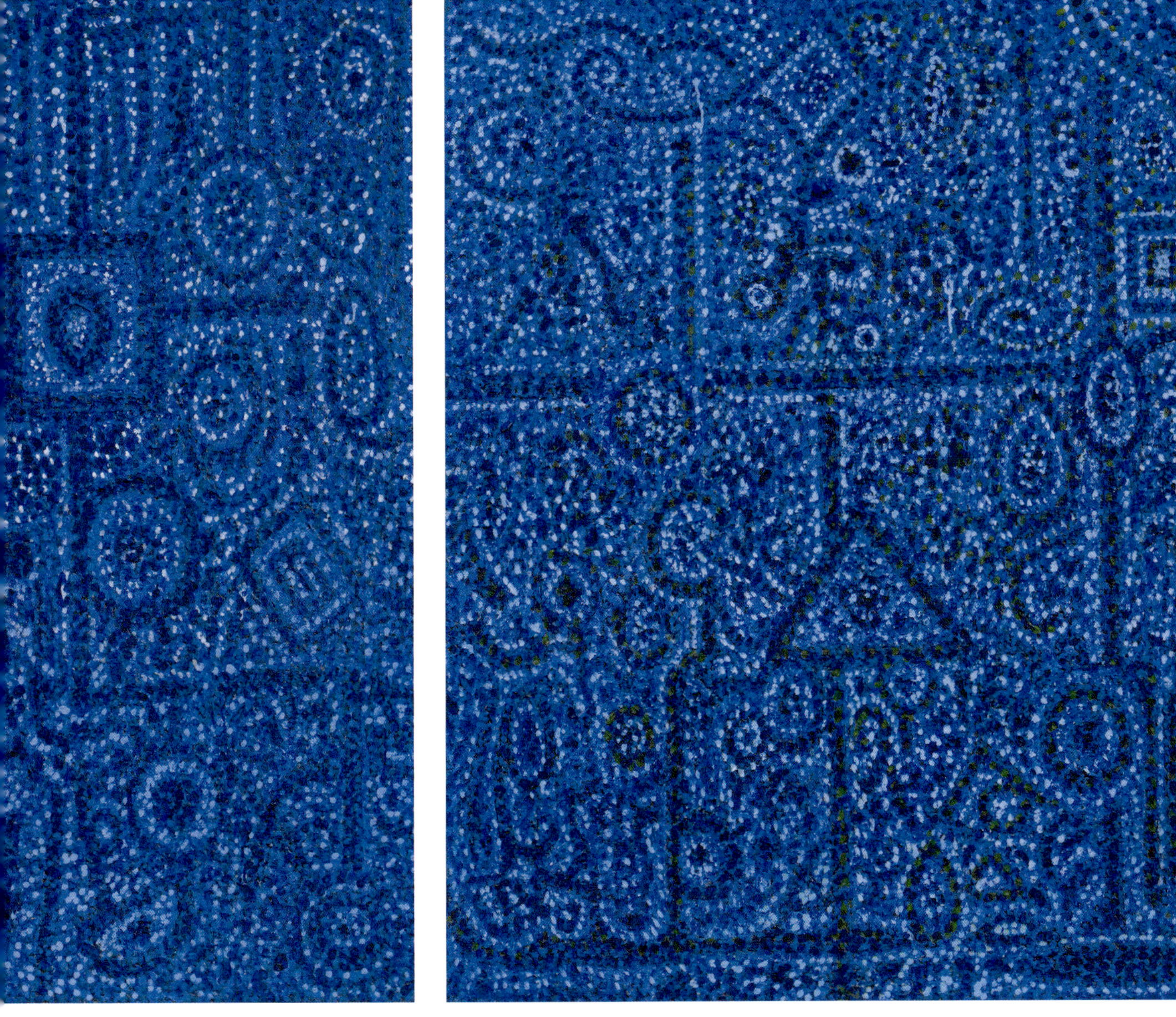

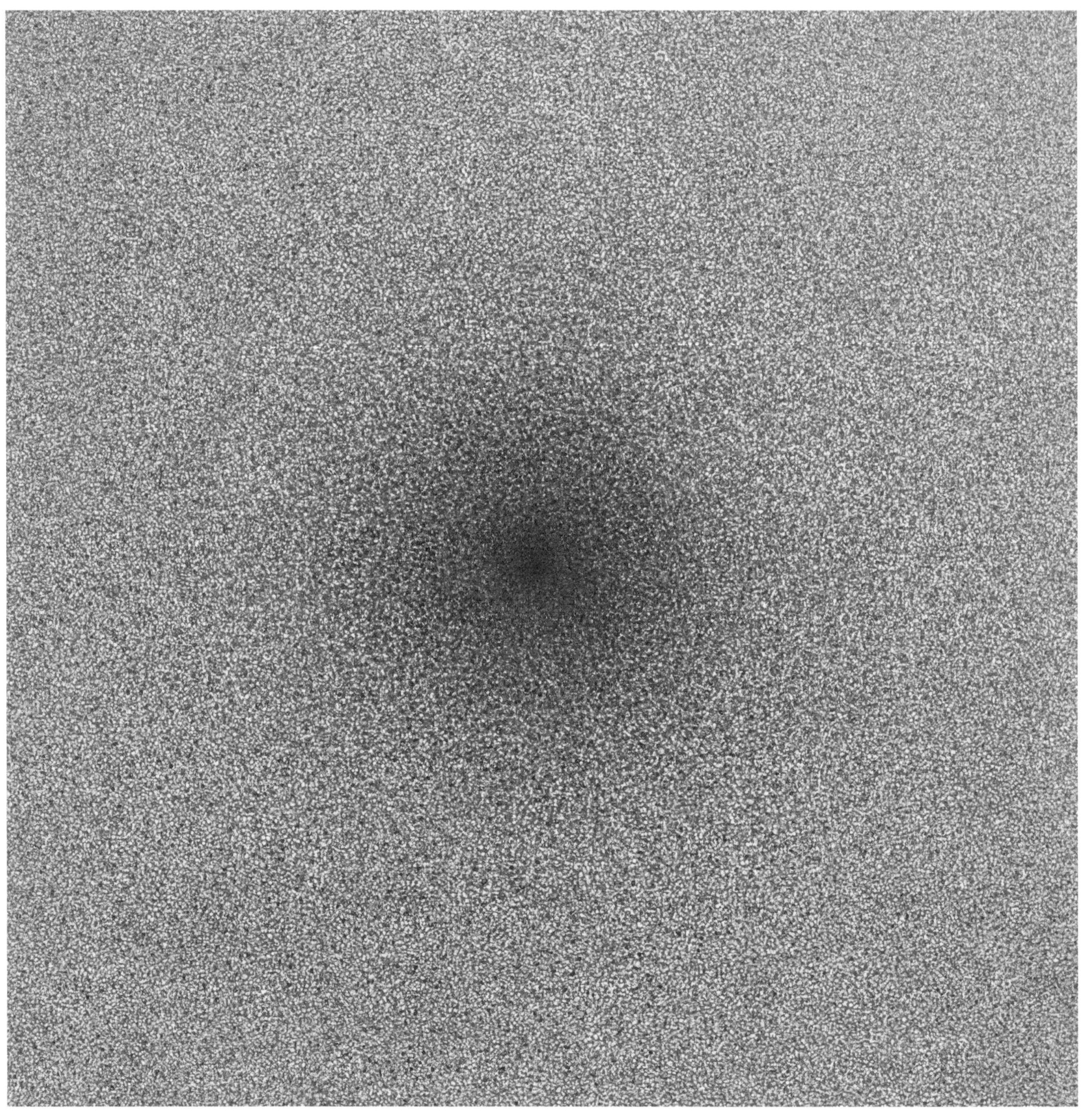

Cat. 46 *Radiance Number 8 (Imploding Red Light)*, 1973–74, acrylic on linen, 228.6 × 228.6 cm

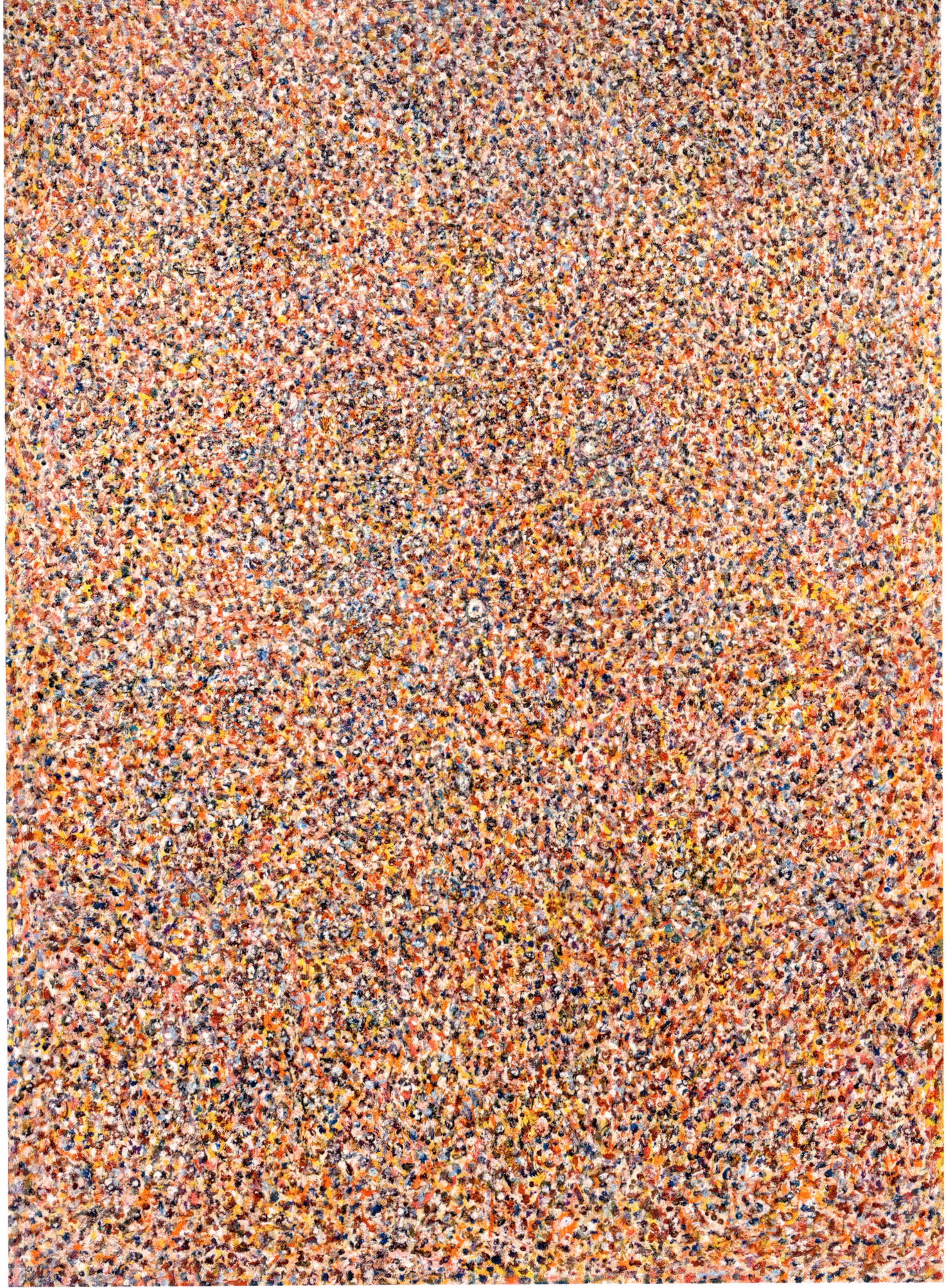

Cat. 47 *Red Presence*, 1960, oil on linen, 188 × 142.9 cm

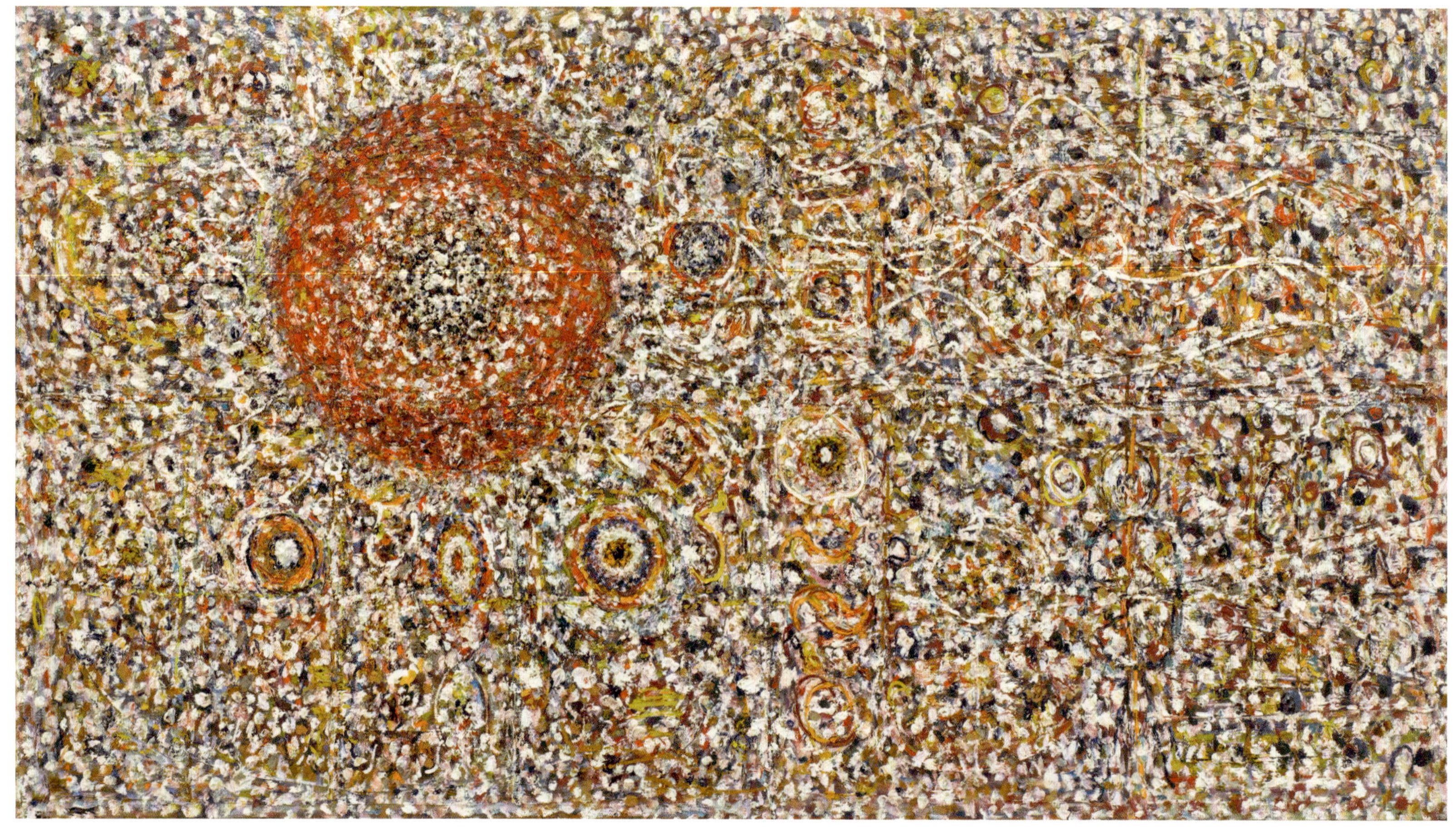

Cat. 48 *From the Flaming Suns*, 1960–64, oil on linen, 133 × 243.8 cm

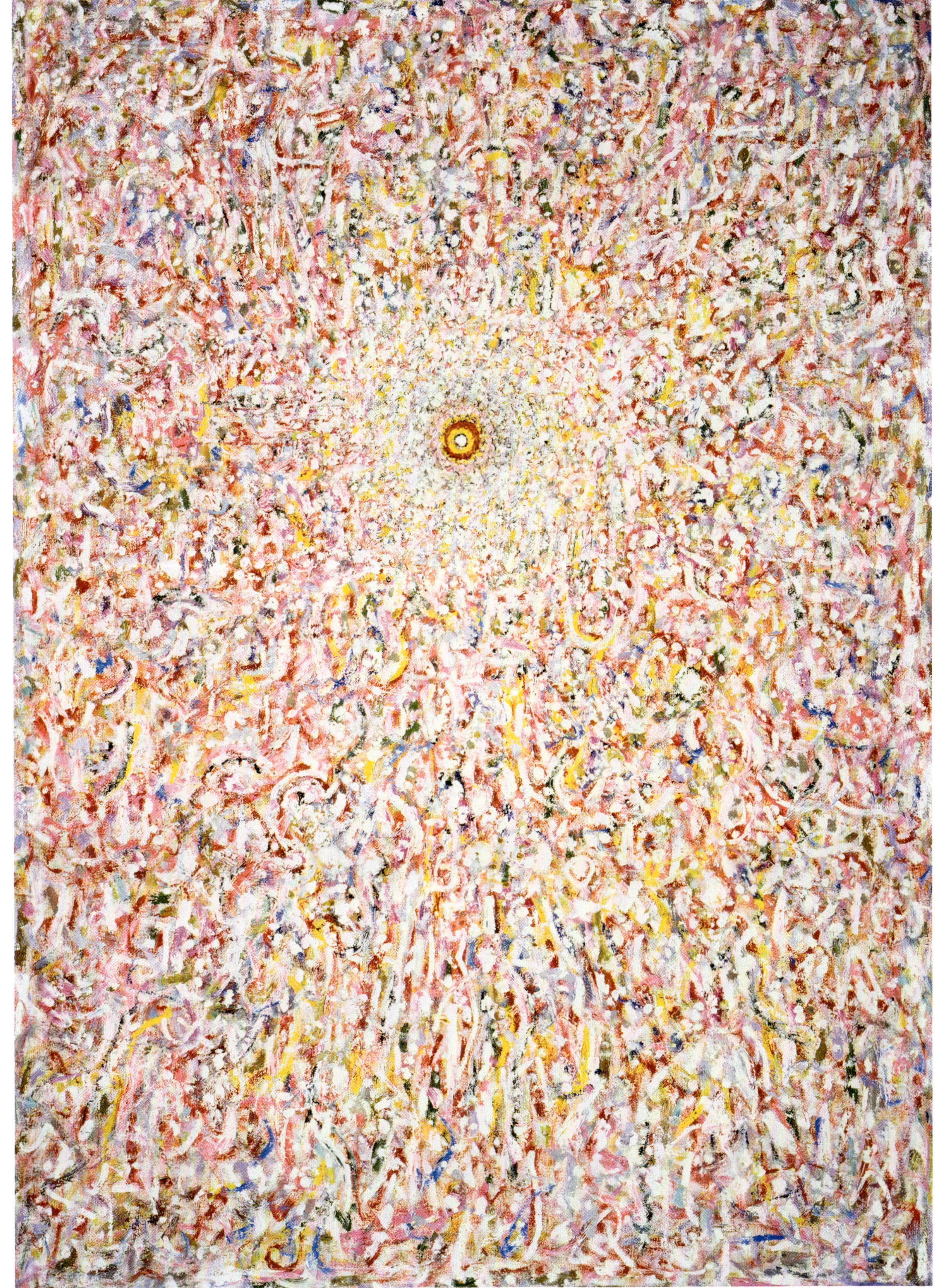

Cat. 49 *Eye of the Small Suns*, 1961–64, oil on linen, 191.1 × 142.2 cm

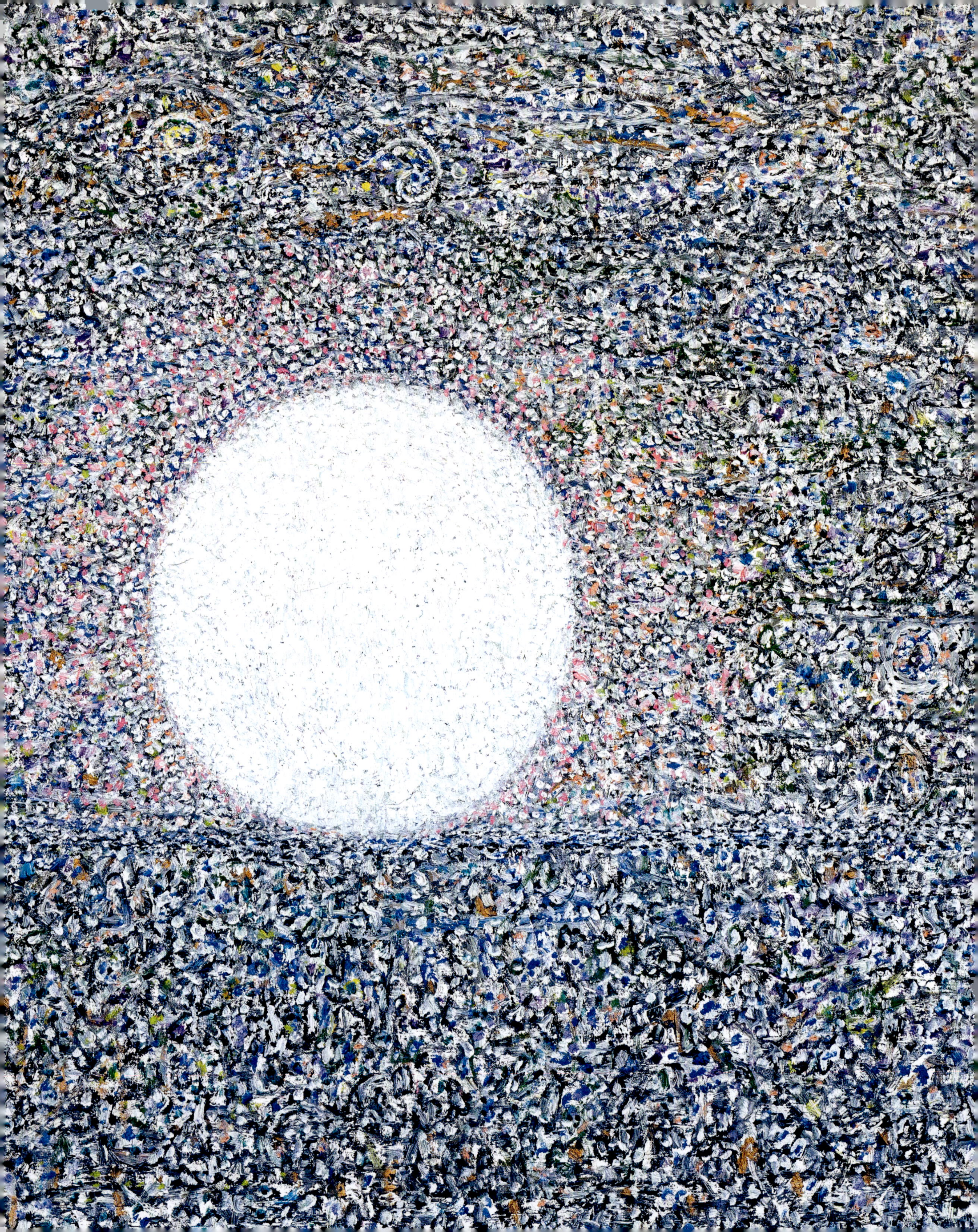

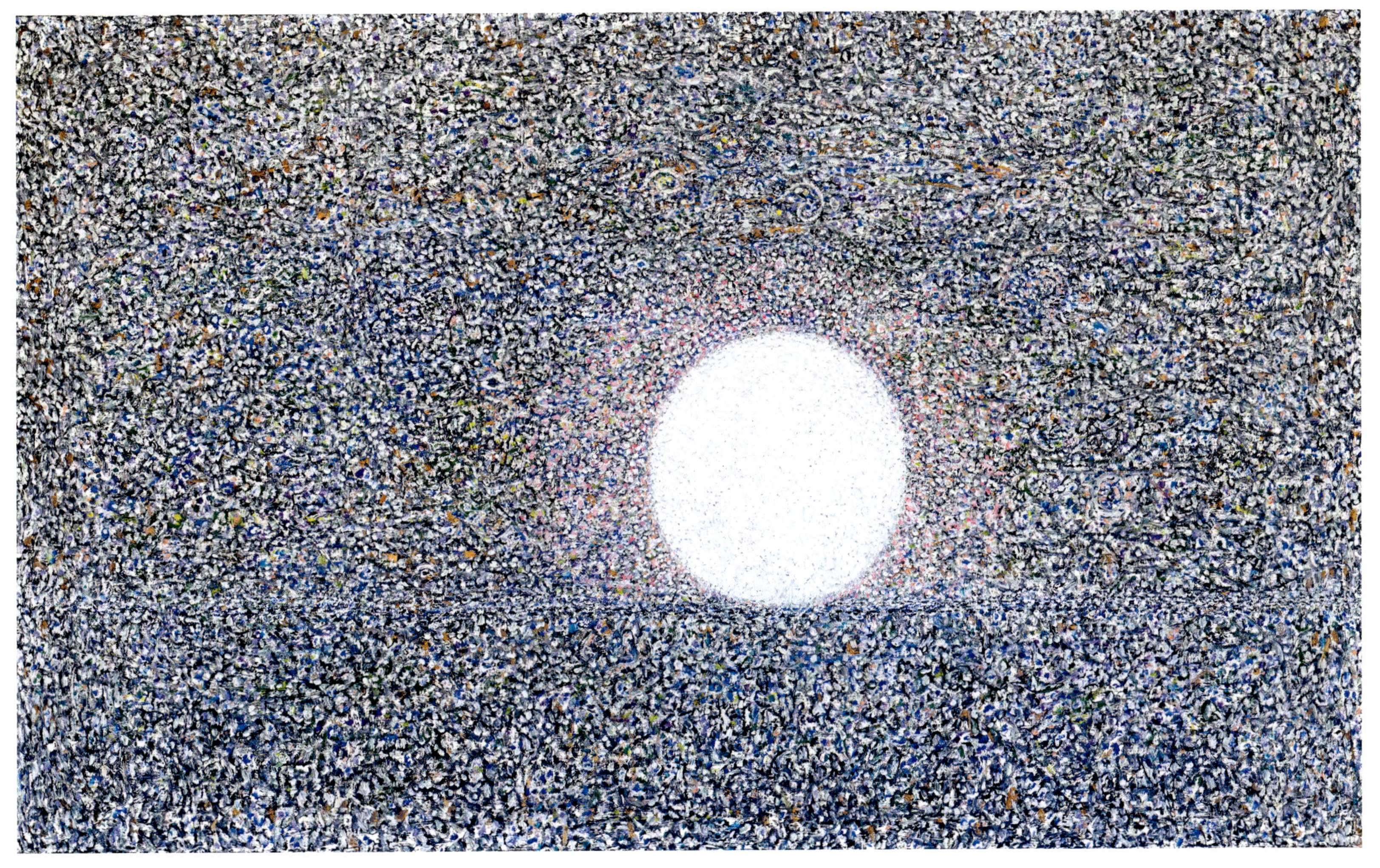

Cat. 50 *Sky Presence, Circle*, 1963, oil on canvas, 109.2 × 180.3 cm

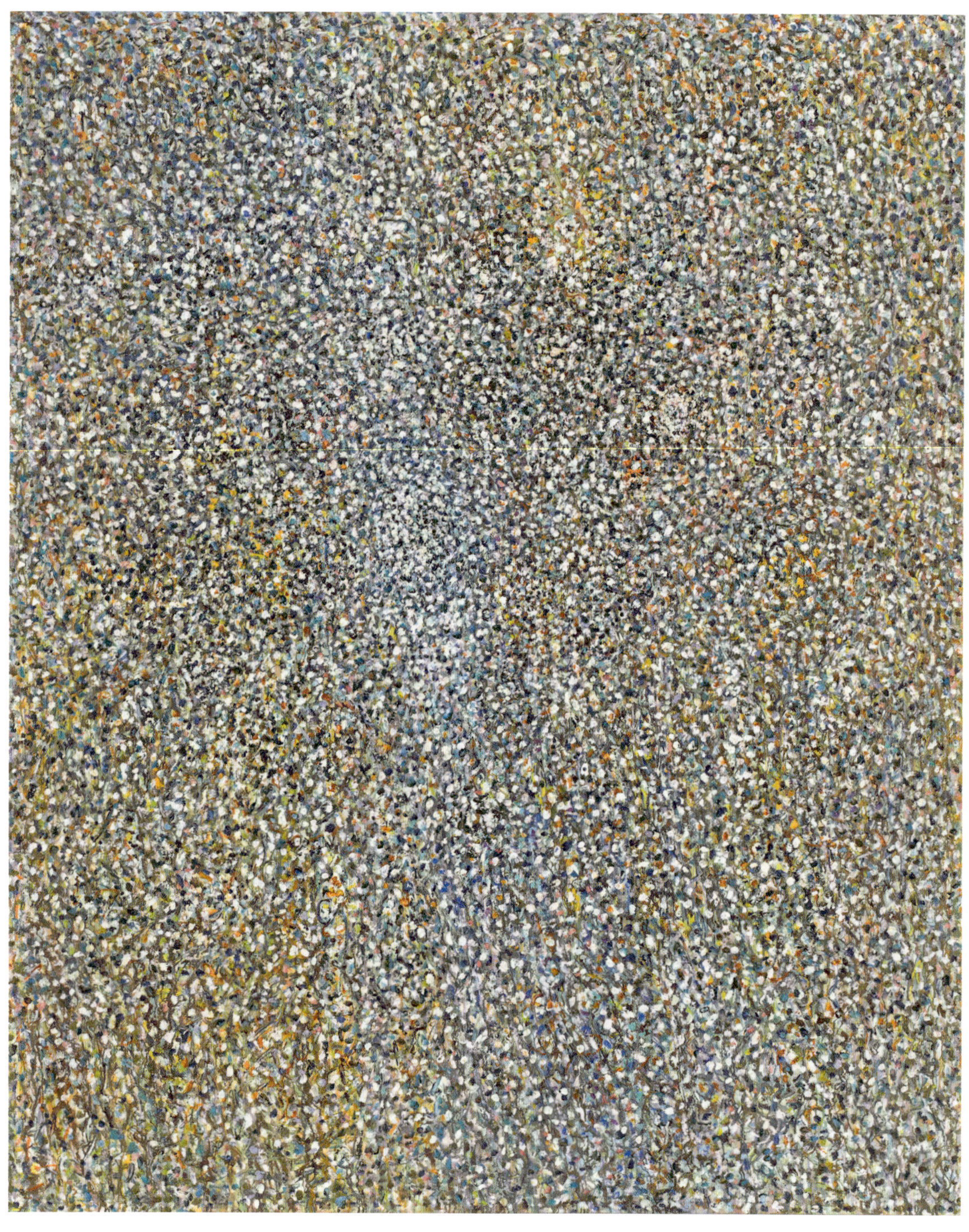

Cat. 51 *Meditation on the Drifting Stars*, 1962–63, oil on linen, 242.6 × 200.7 cm

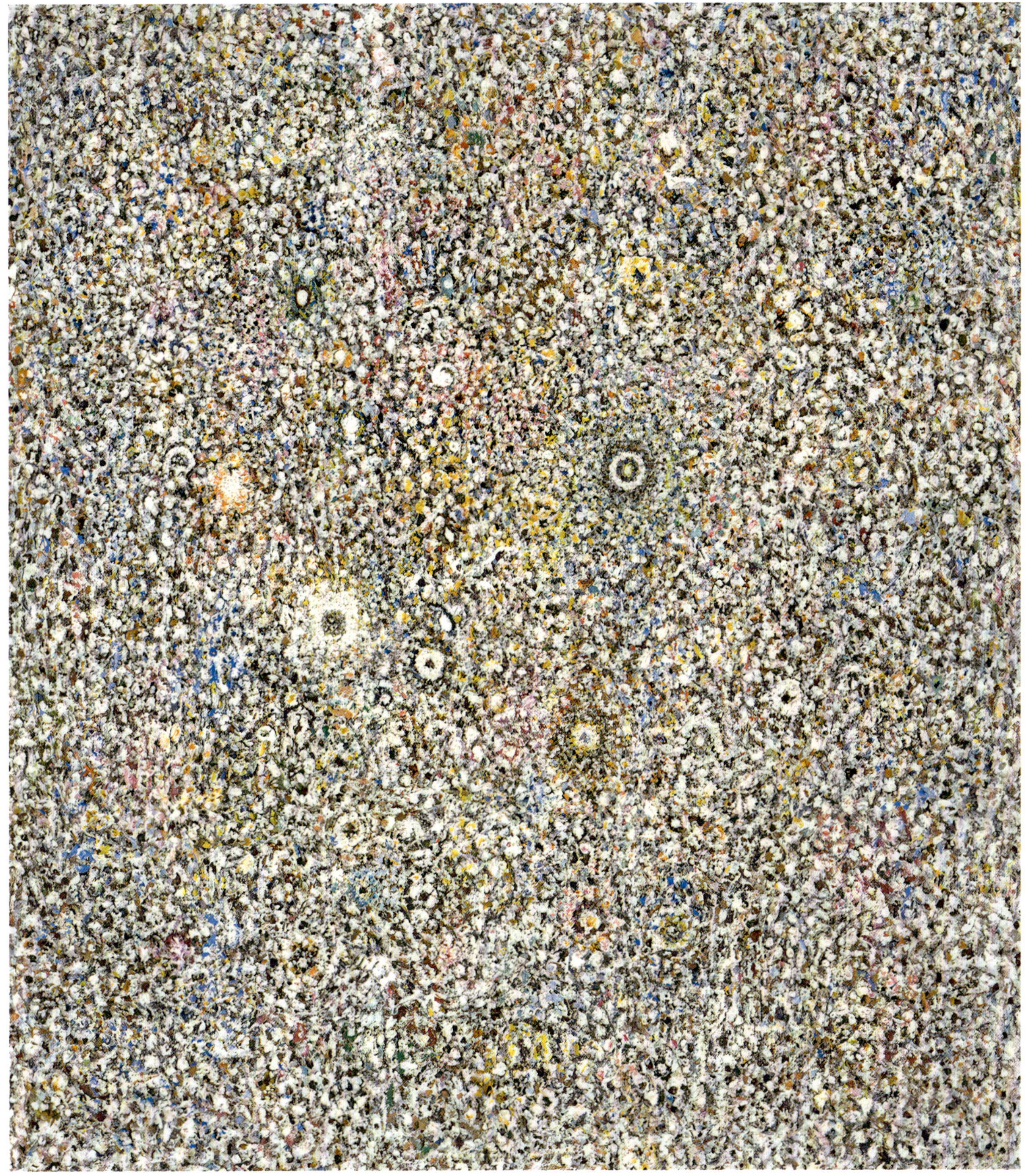

Cat. 52 *Within the Moon*, 1962–65, oil on linen, 224.2 × 203.2 cm

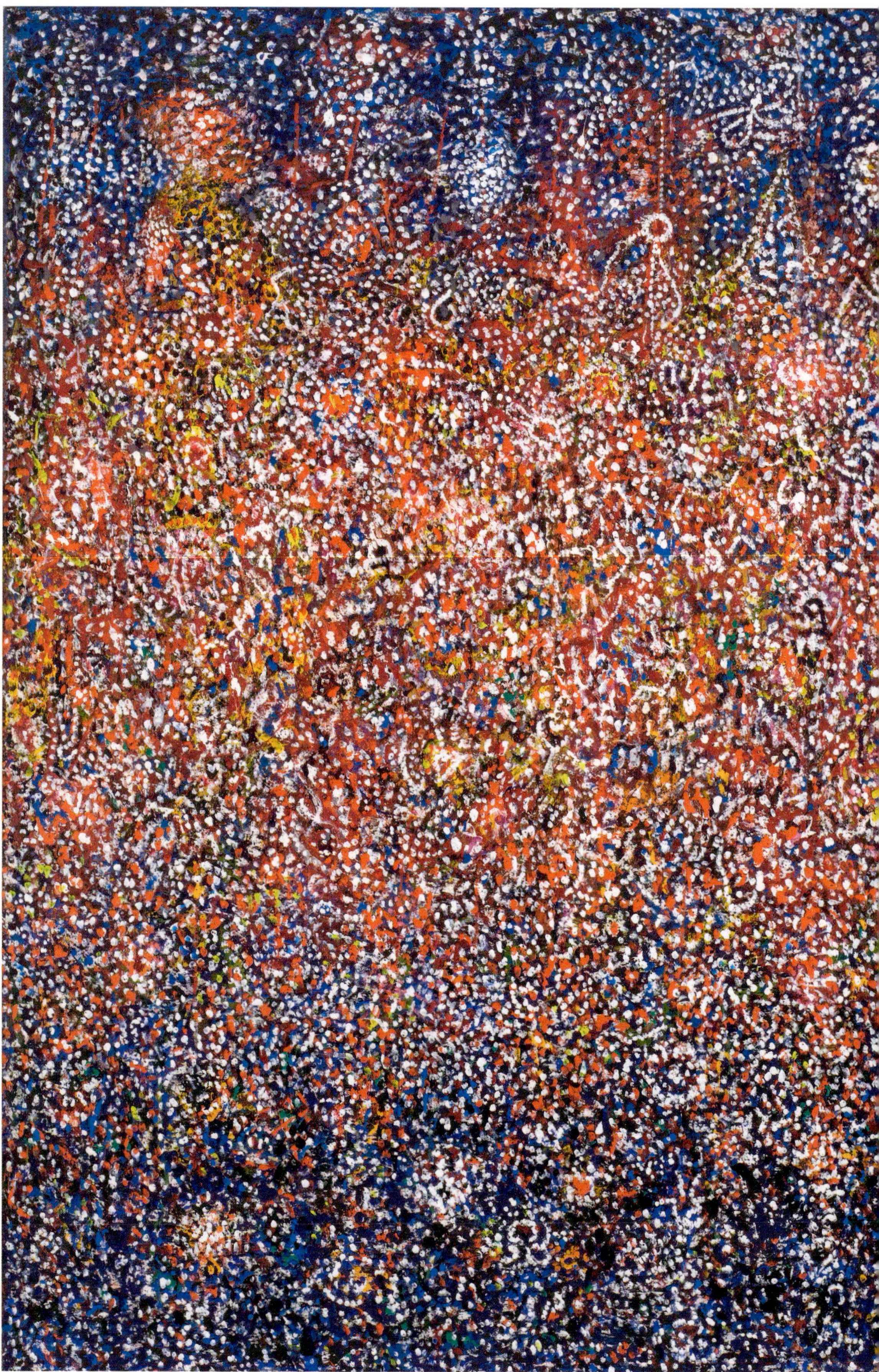

Cat. 53 *Celebration Birth*, 1975–76, acrylic on linen, 183.2 × 305.1 cm

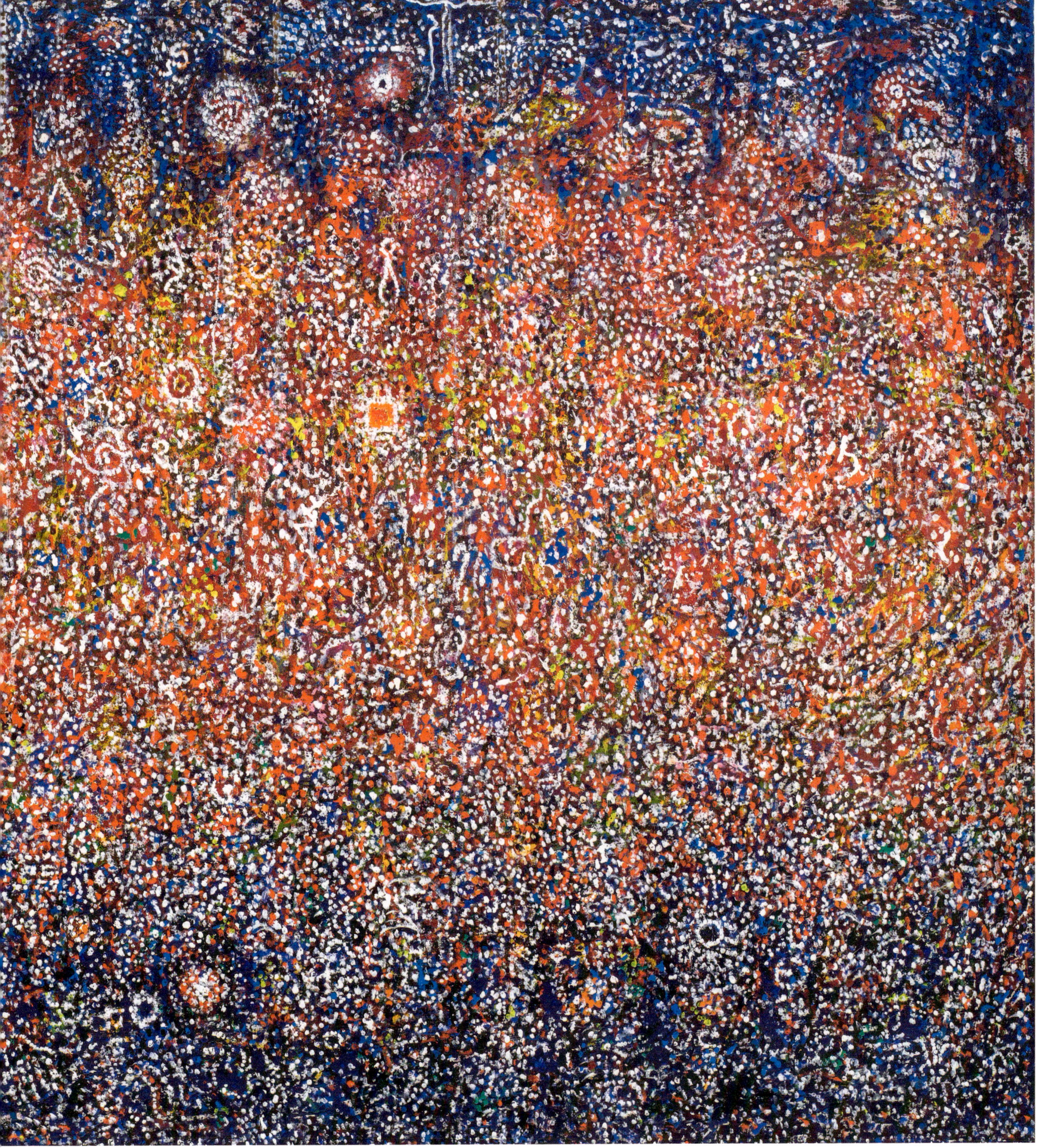

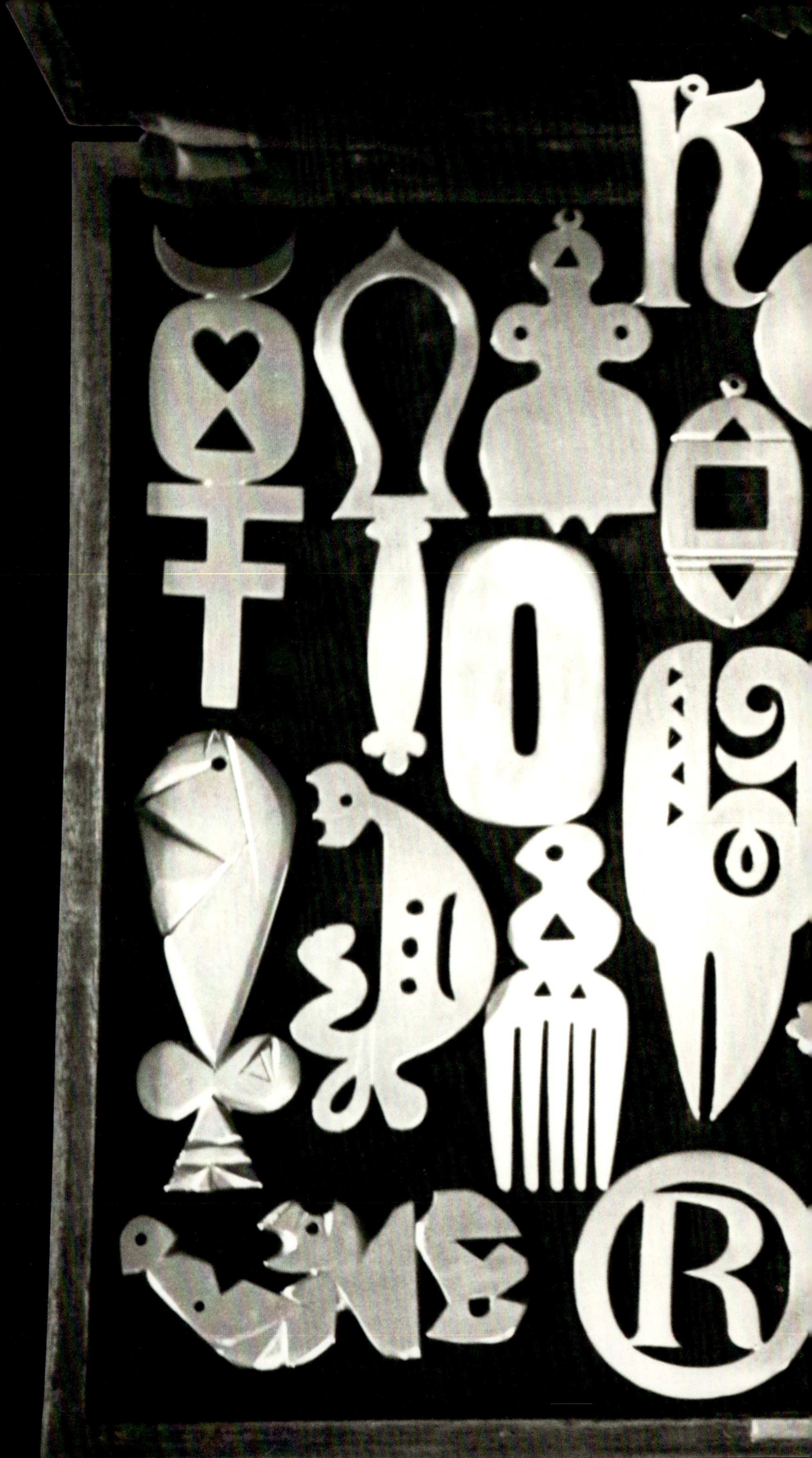

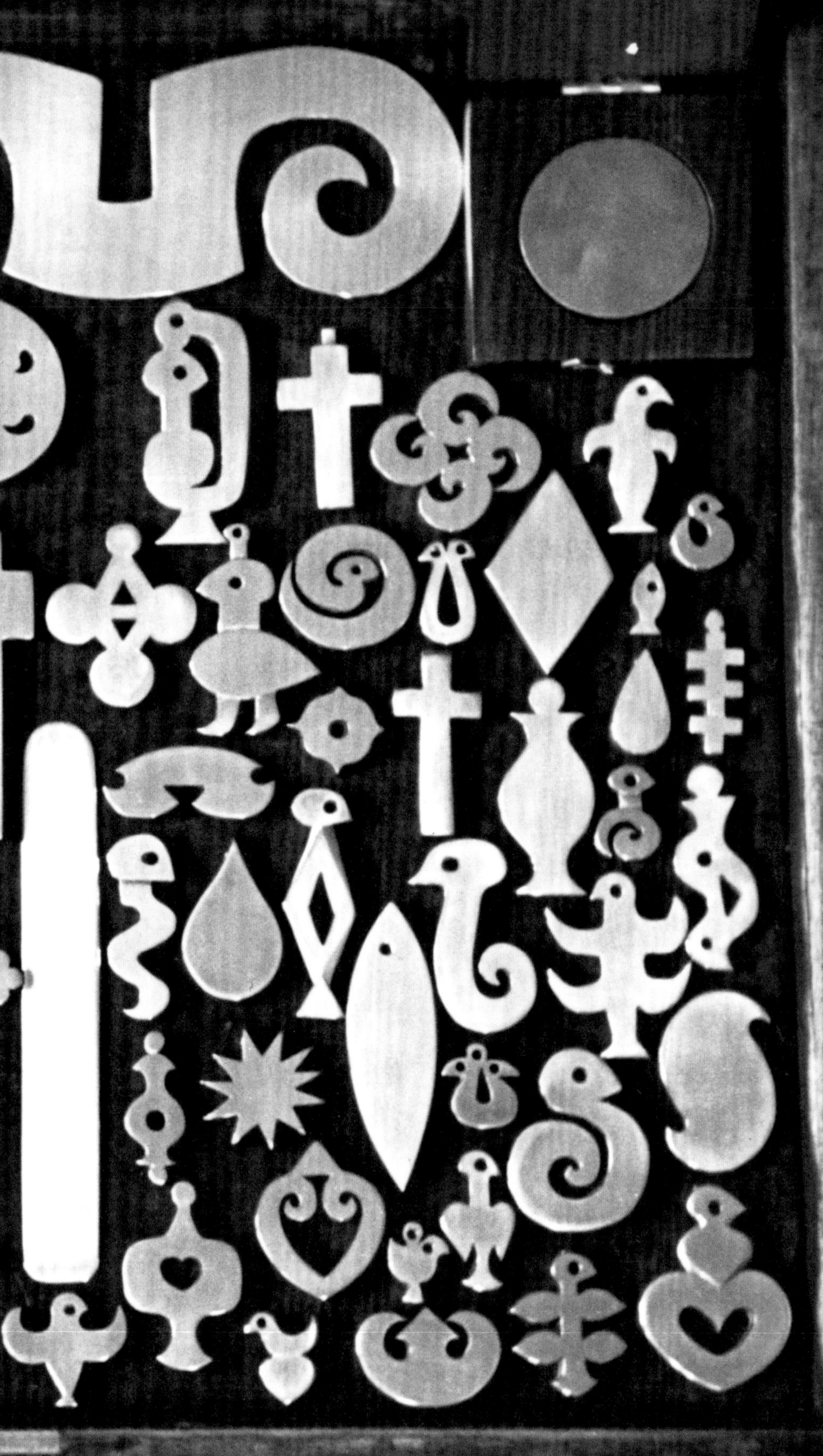

Brasses

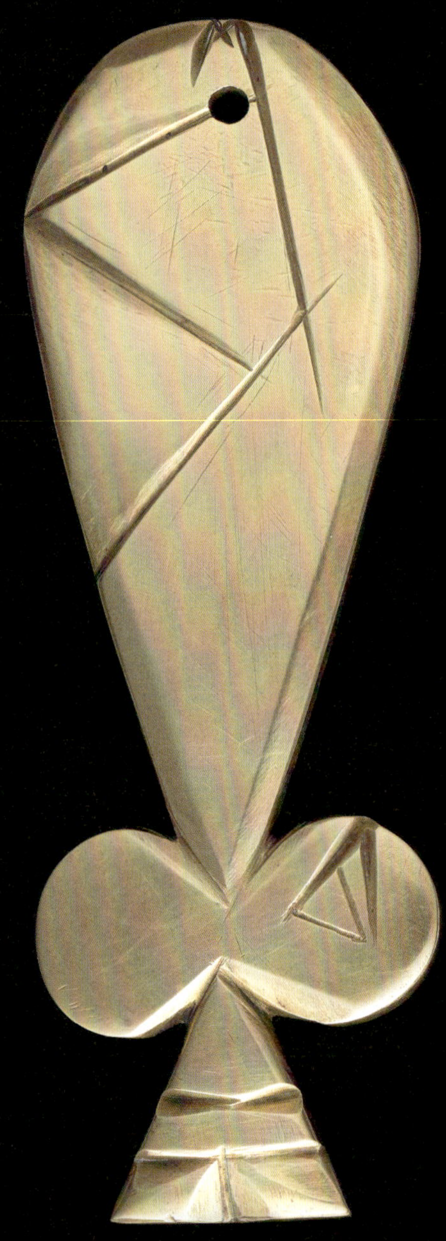

Cats. 54–96 Selected *Brasses*, ca. 1939–79, 43 hand-cut brass objects, dimensions variable (between 7 and 14 cm in height)

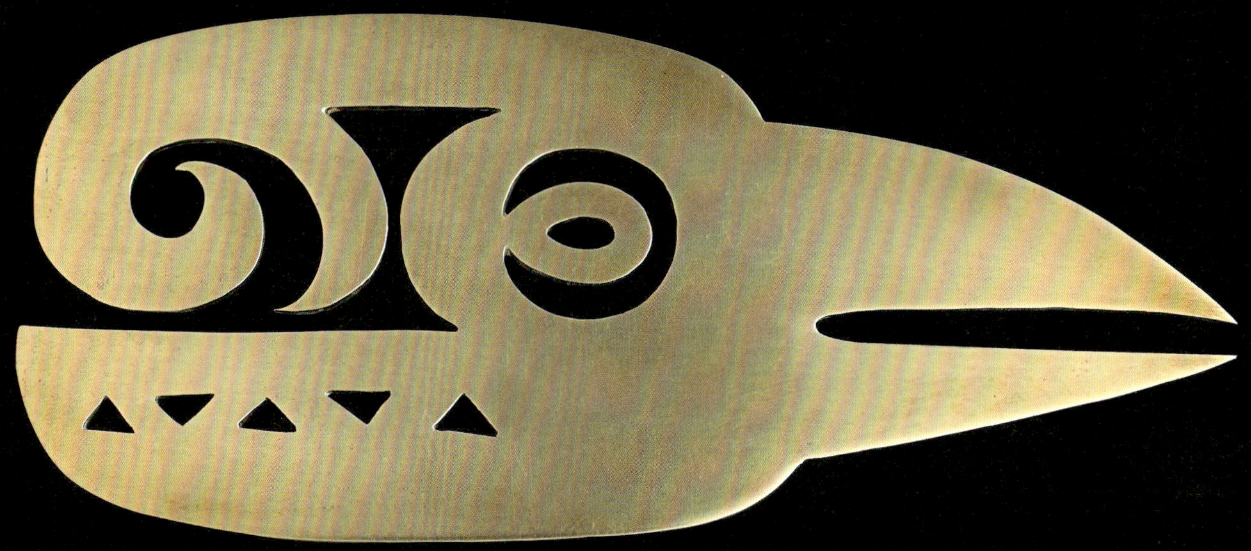

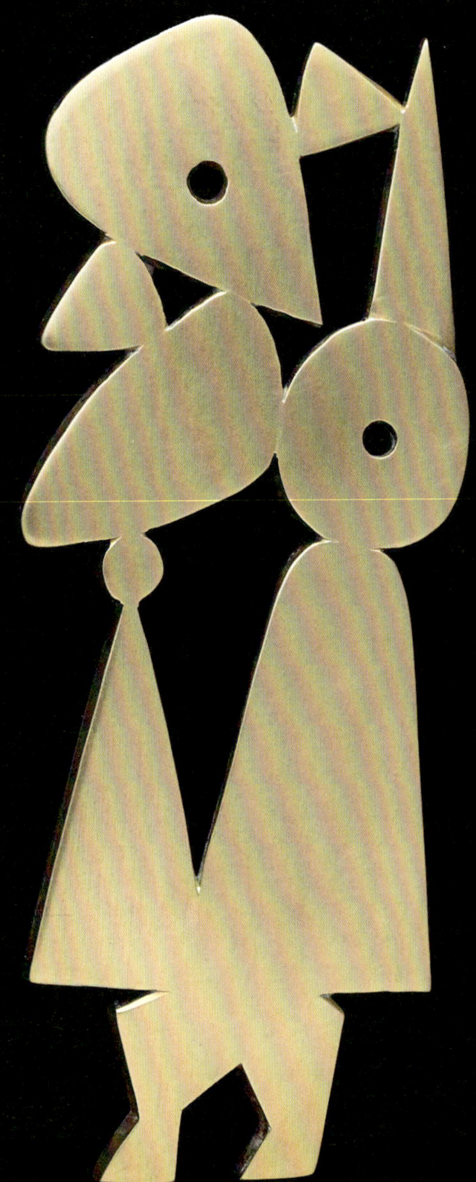

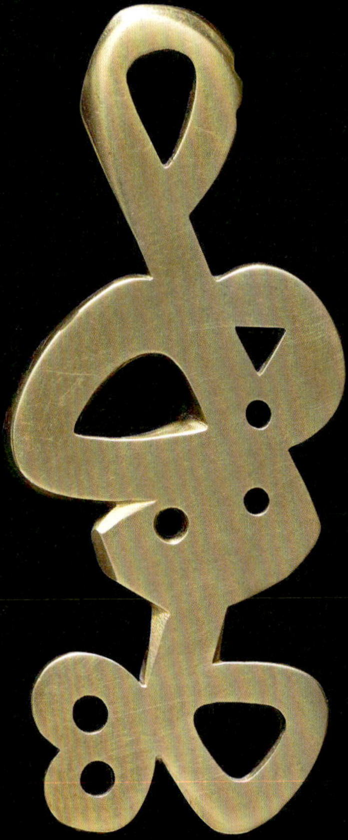

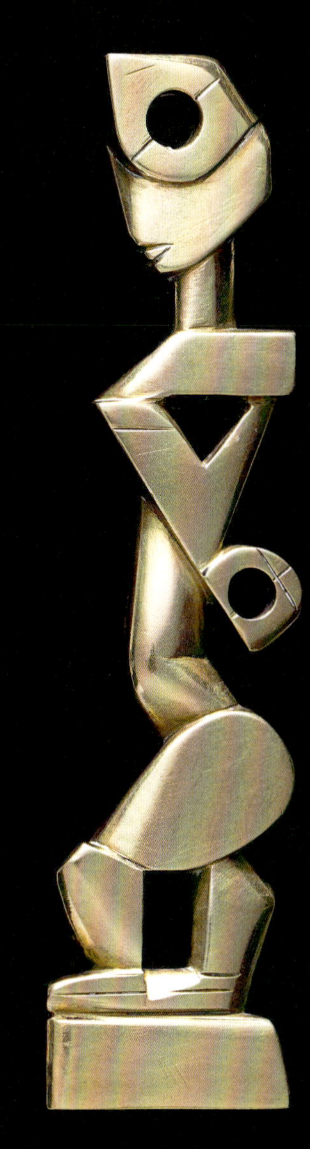

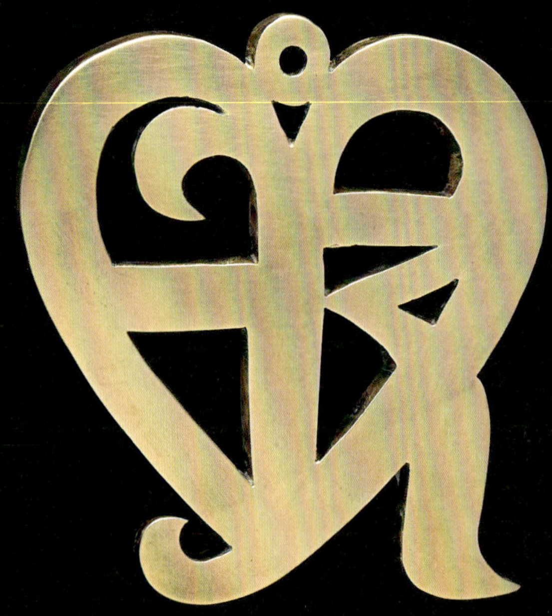

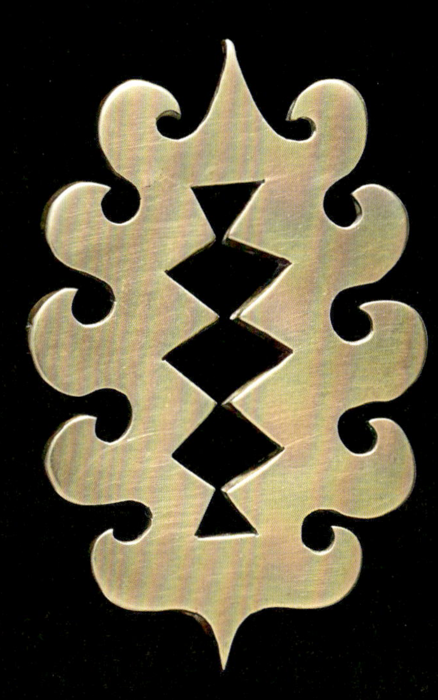

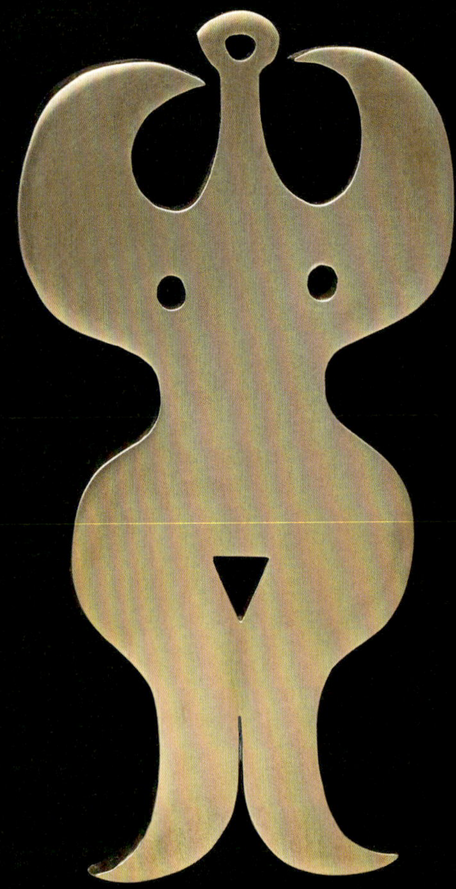

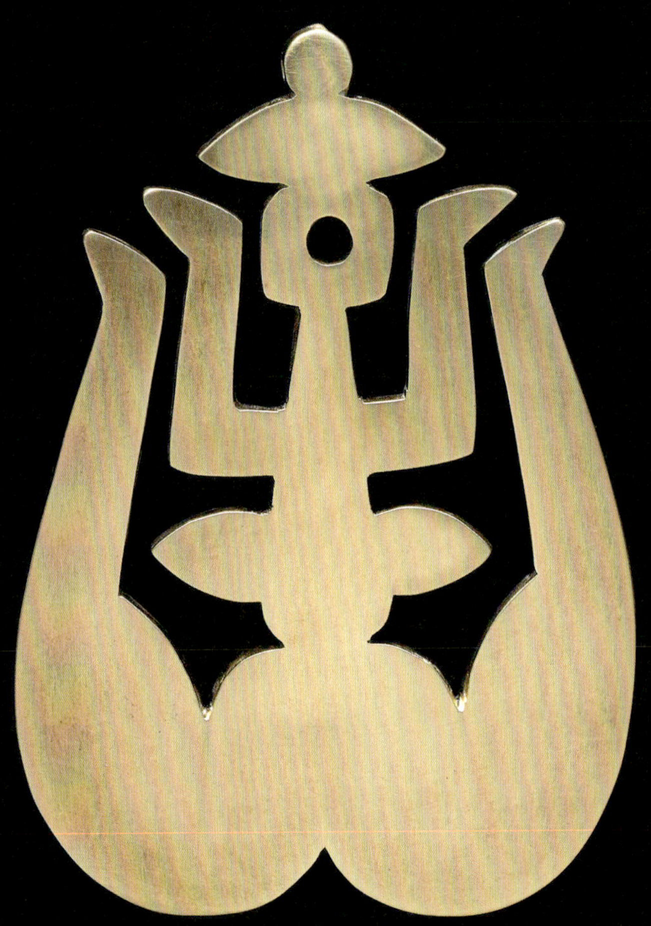

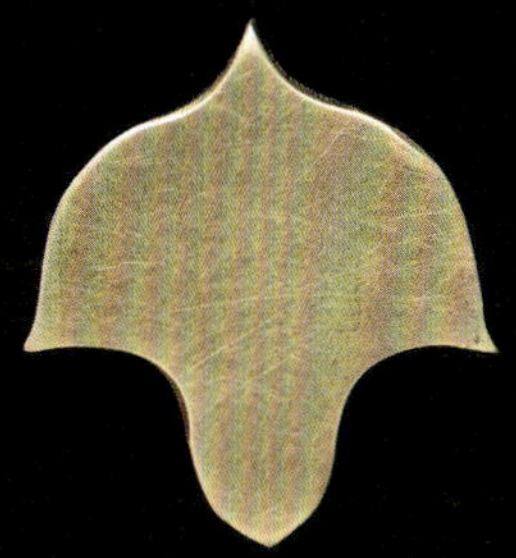

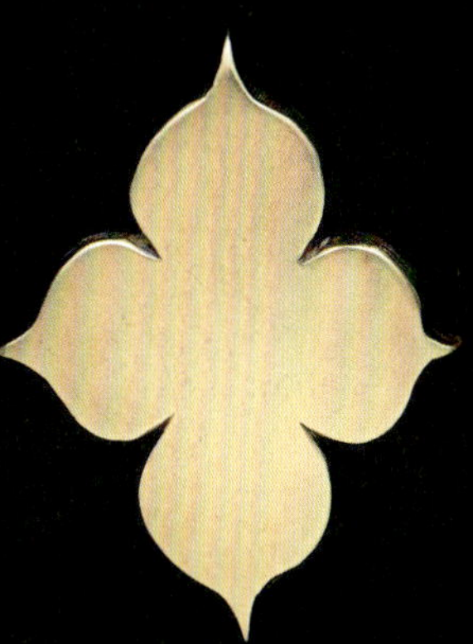

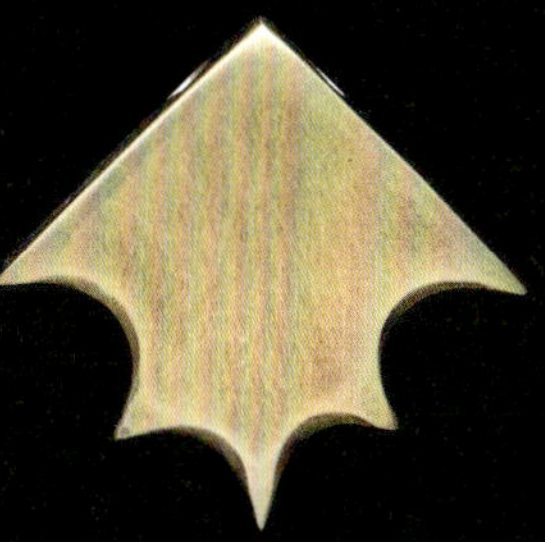

Brasses

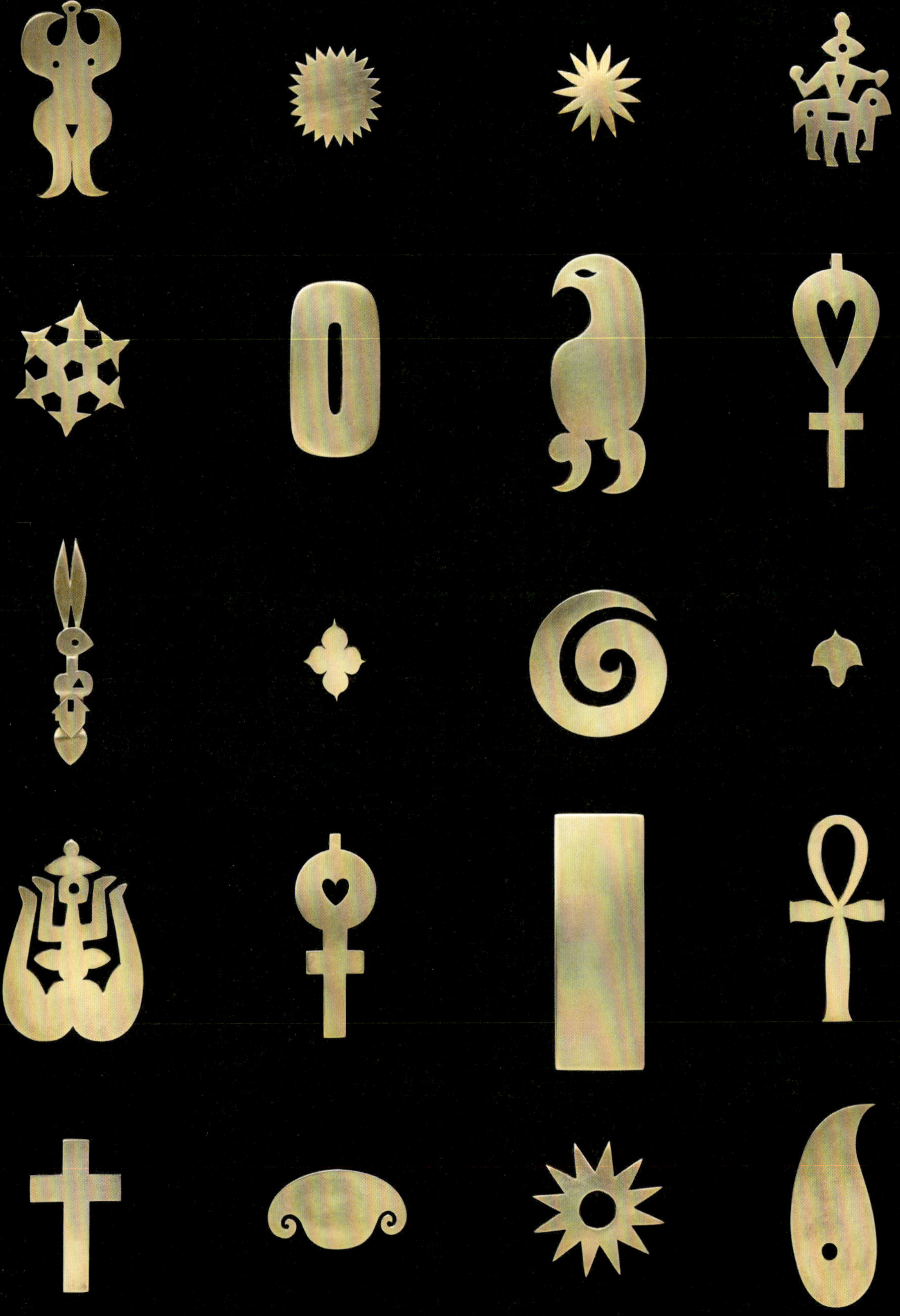

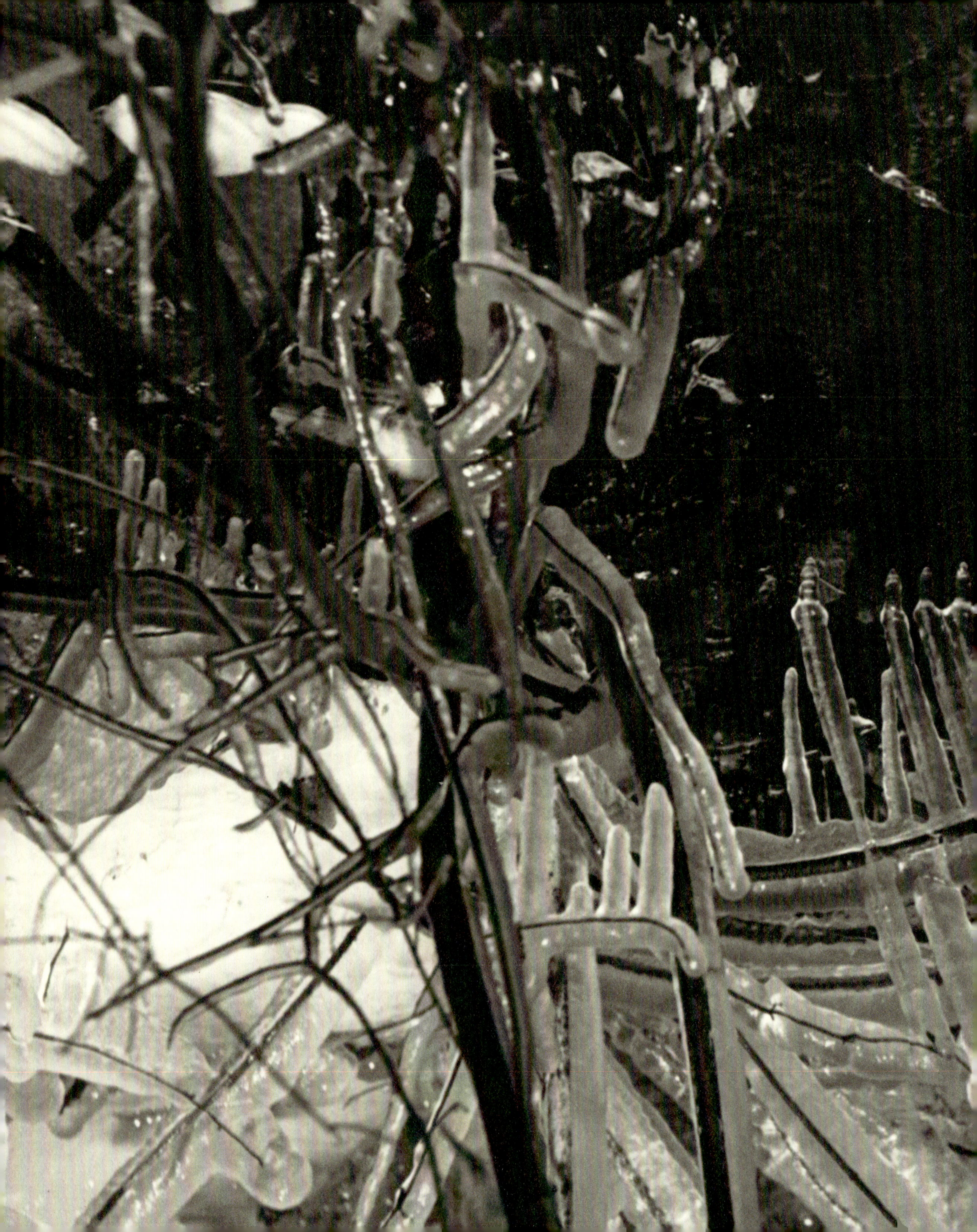

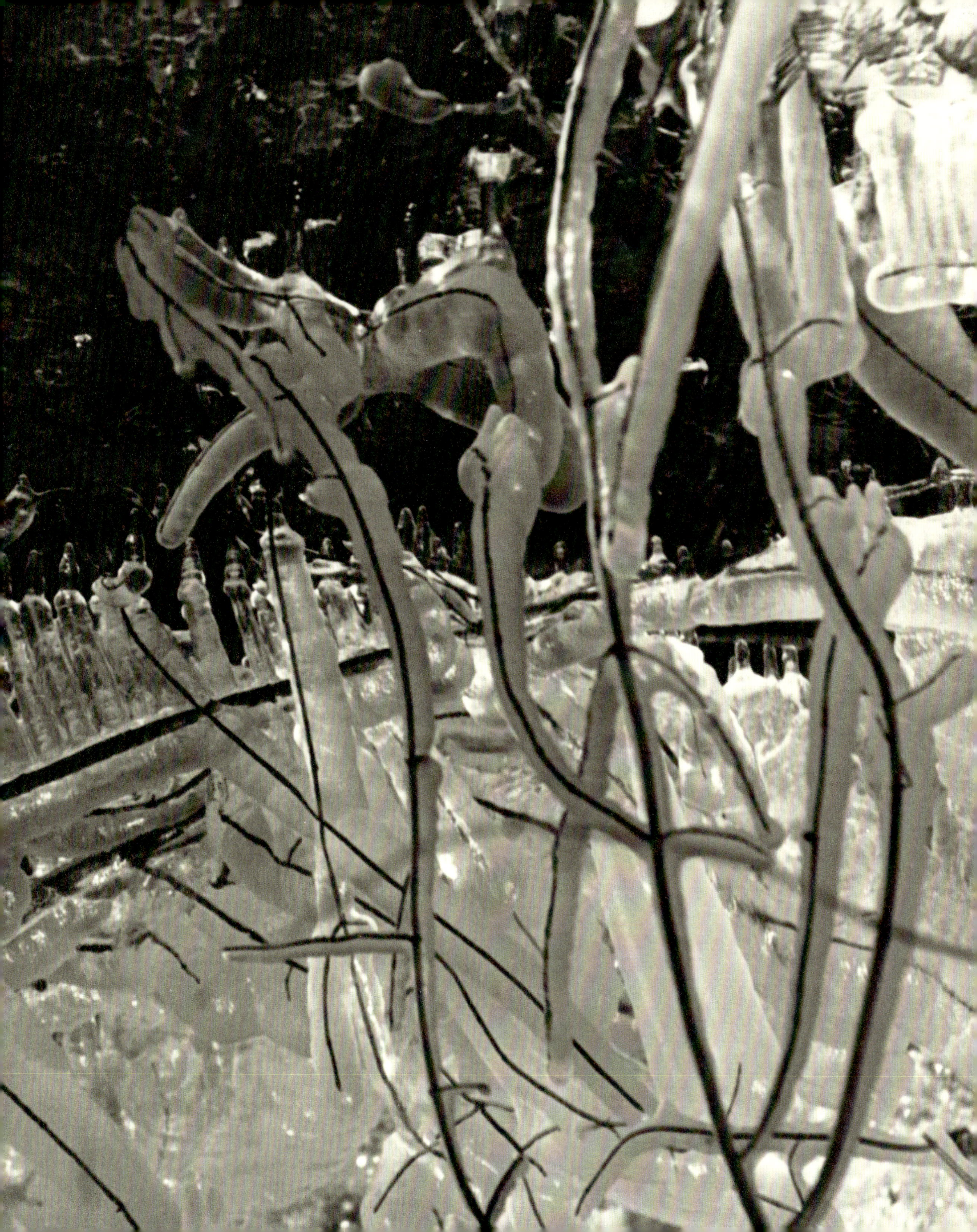

Photographs

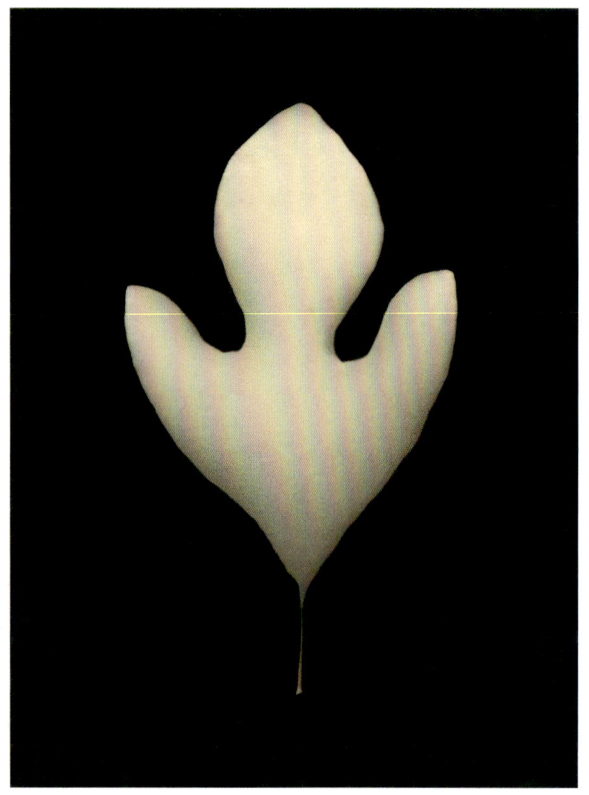

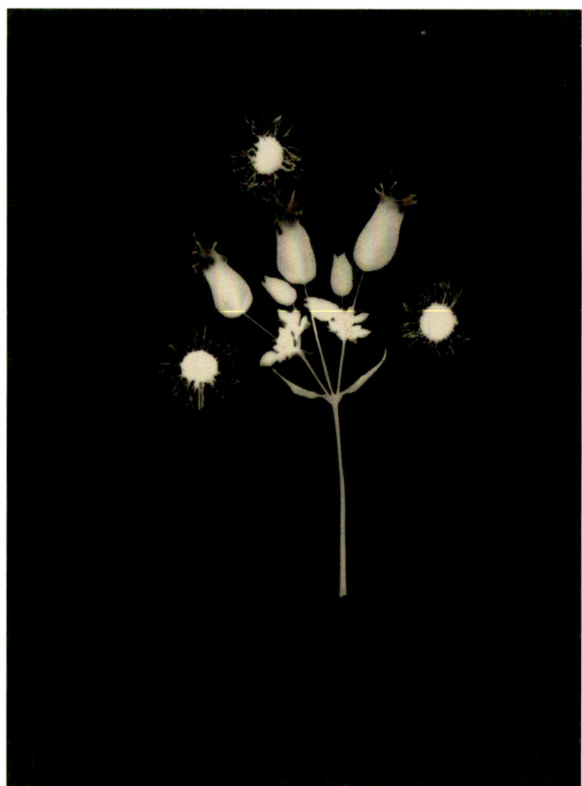

Cat. 97 *Nature Studies*, 1930s, photograms, 14 × 10.8 cm each

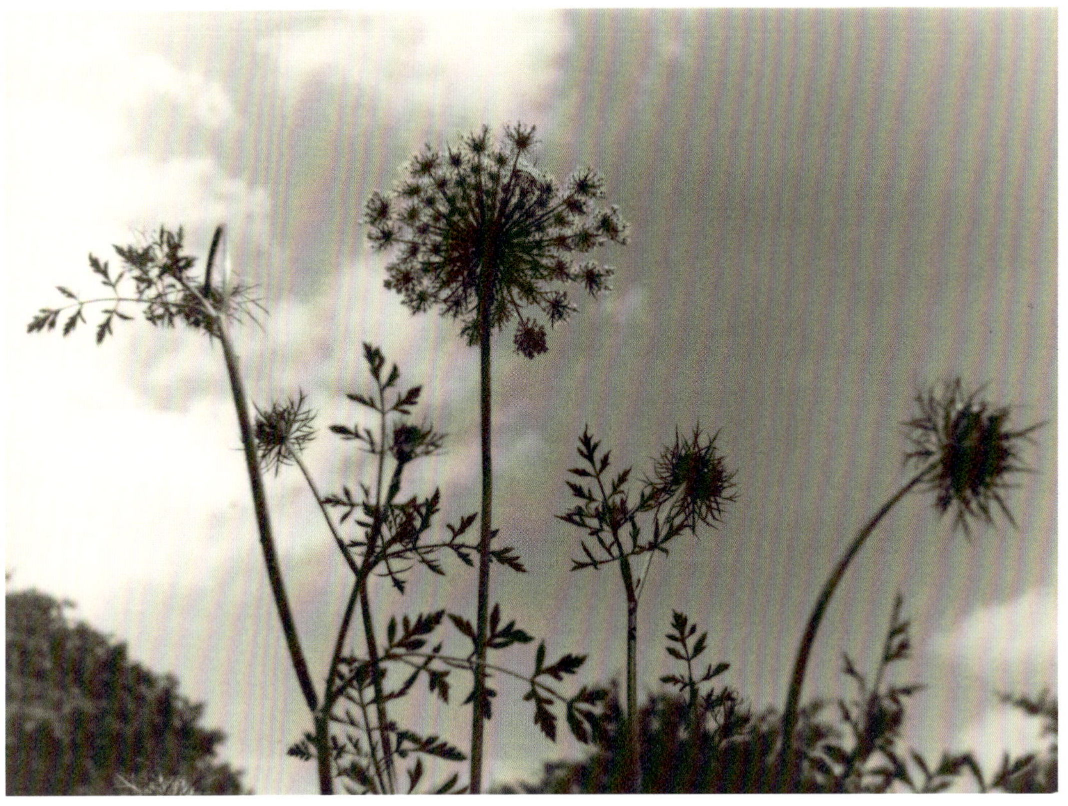

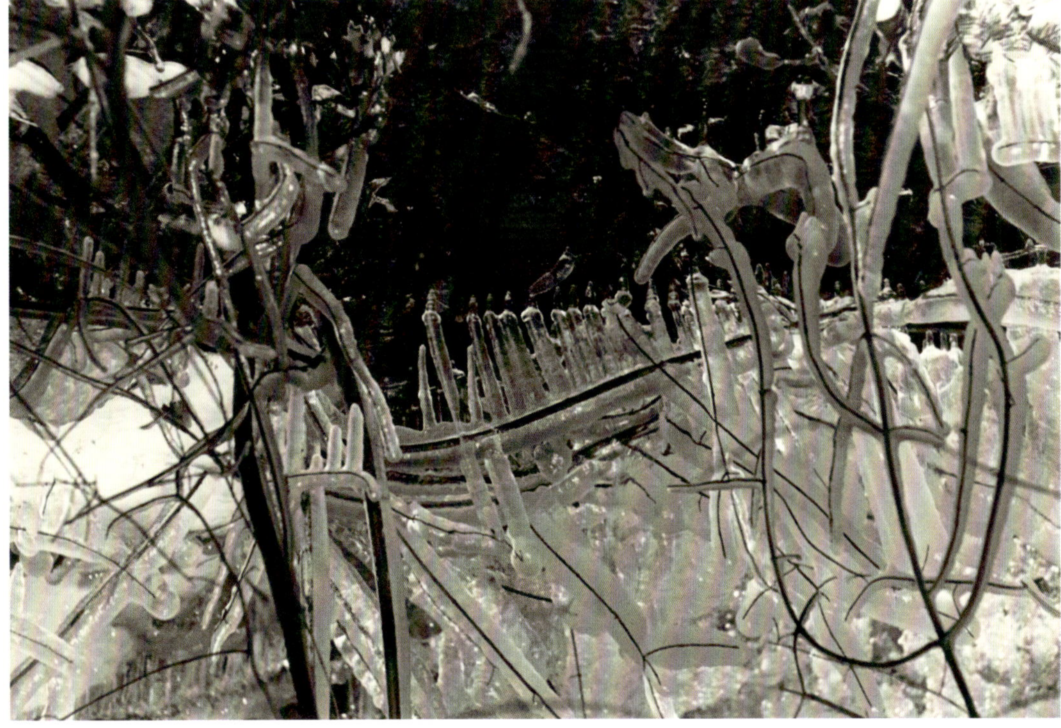

Cat. 98 *Queen Anne's Lace II*, mid-1950s, gelatin silver print, 24.4 × 33.7 cm

Cat. 99 *Ice on Branches*, mid-1950s, gelatin silver print, 21.9 × 32.7 cm

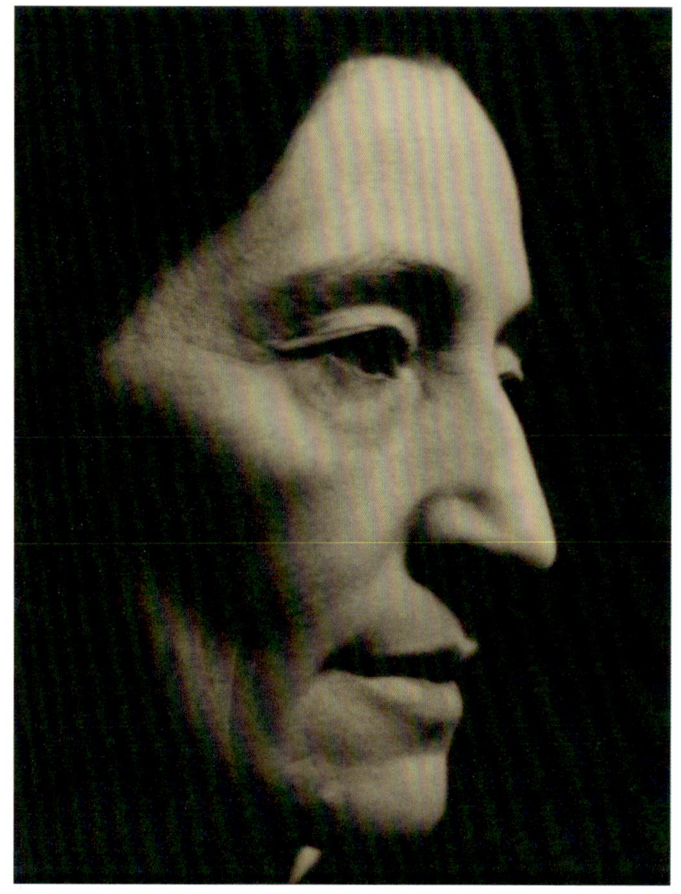

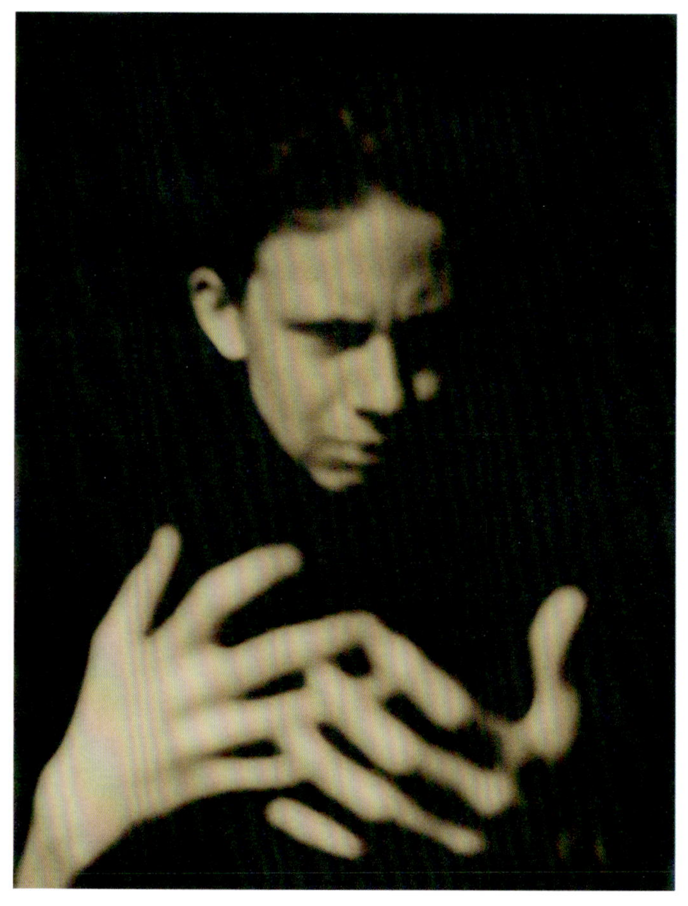

Cat. 100 *Flora Pousette-Dart*, ca. 1935, gelatin silver print, 33.7 × 27 cm

Cat. 101 *Self-Portrait*, ca. 1935, gelatin silver print, 24.4 × 18.7 cm

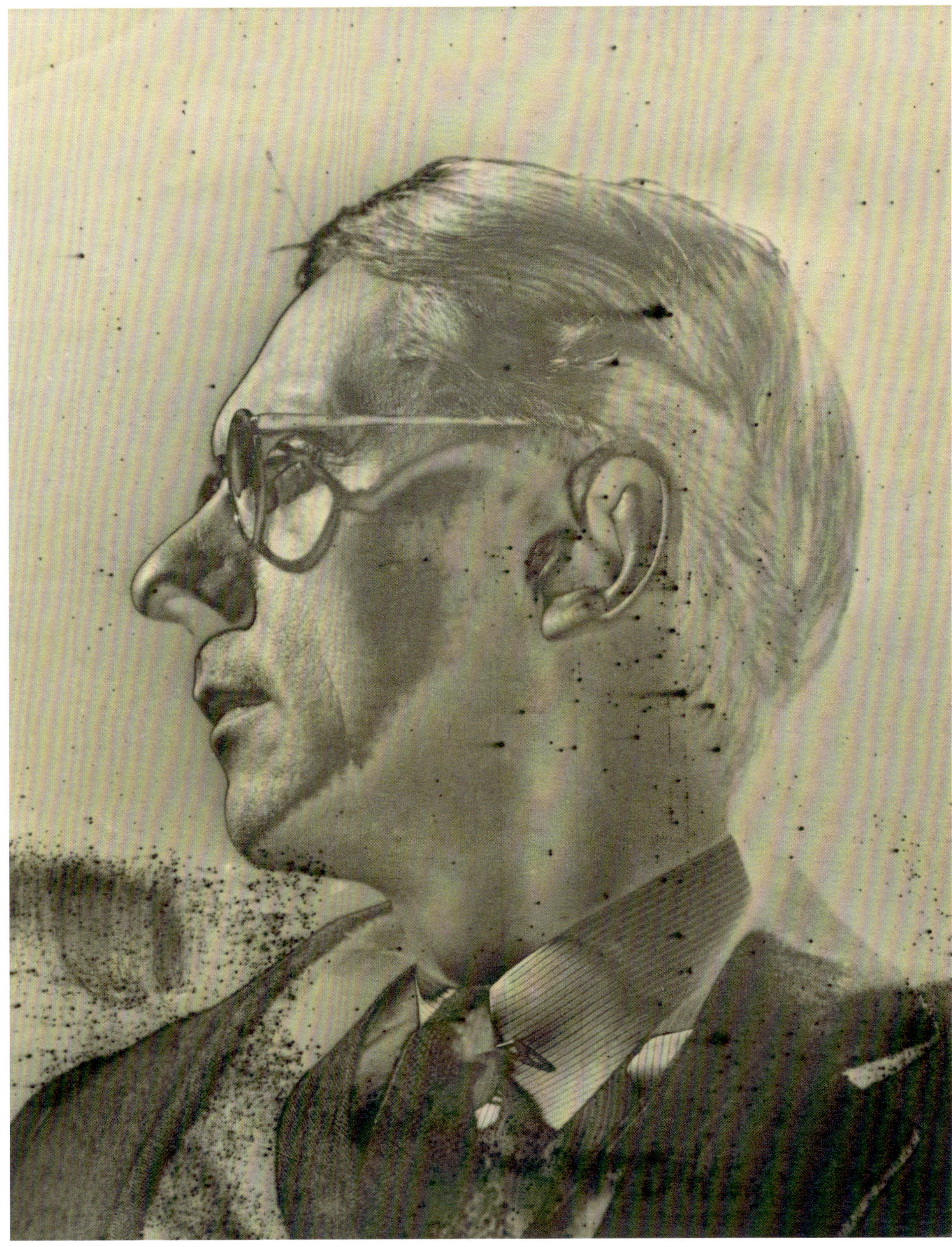

Cat. 102 *Nathaniel Pousette-Dart*, 1940s, solarized gelatin silver print, 25.4 × 20.3 cm

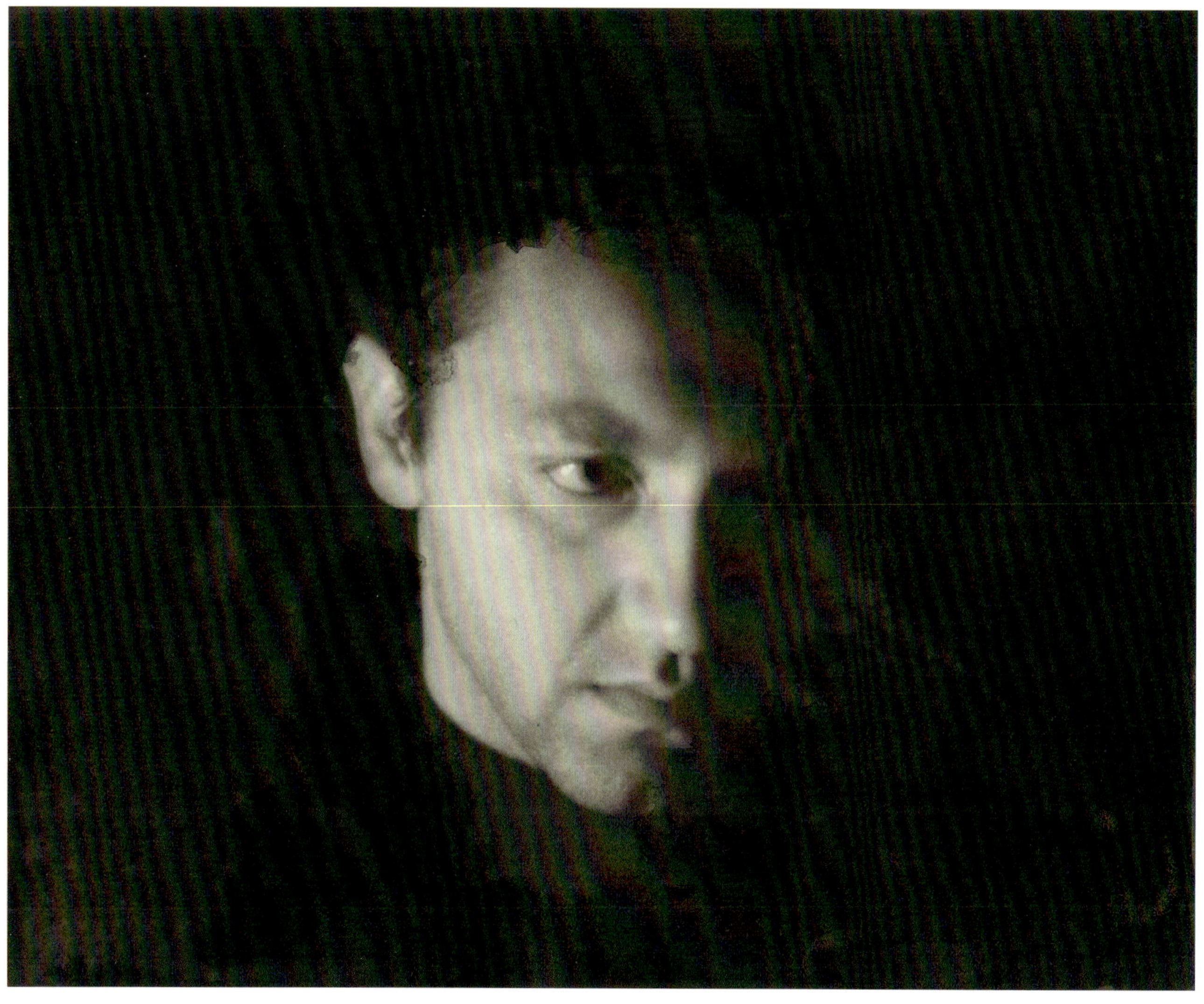

Cat. 103 *Saul Leiter*, ca. 1947, gelatin silver print with hand-applied pigment, 20 × 25.1 cm

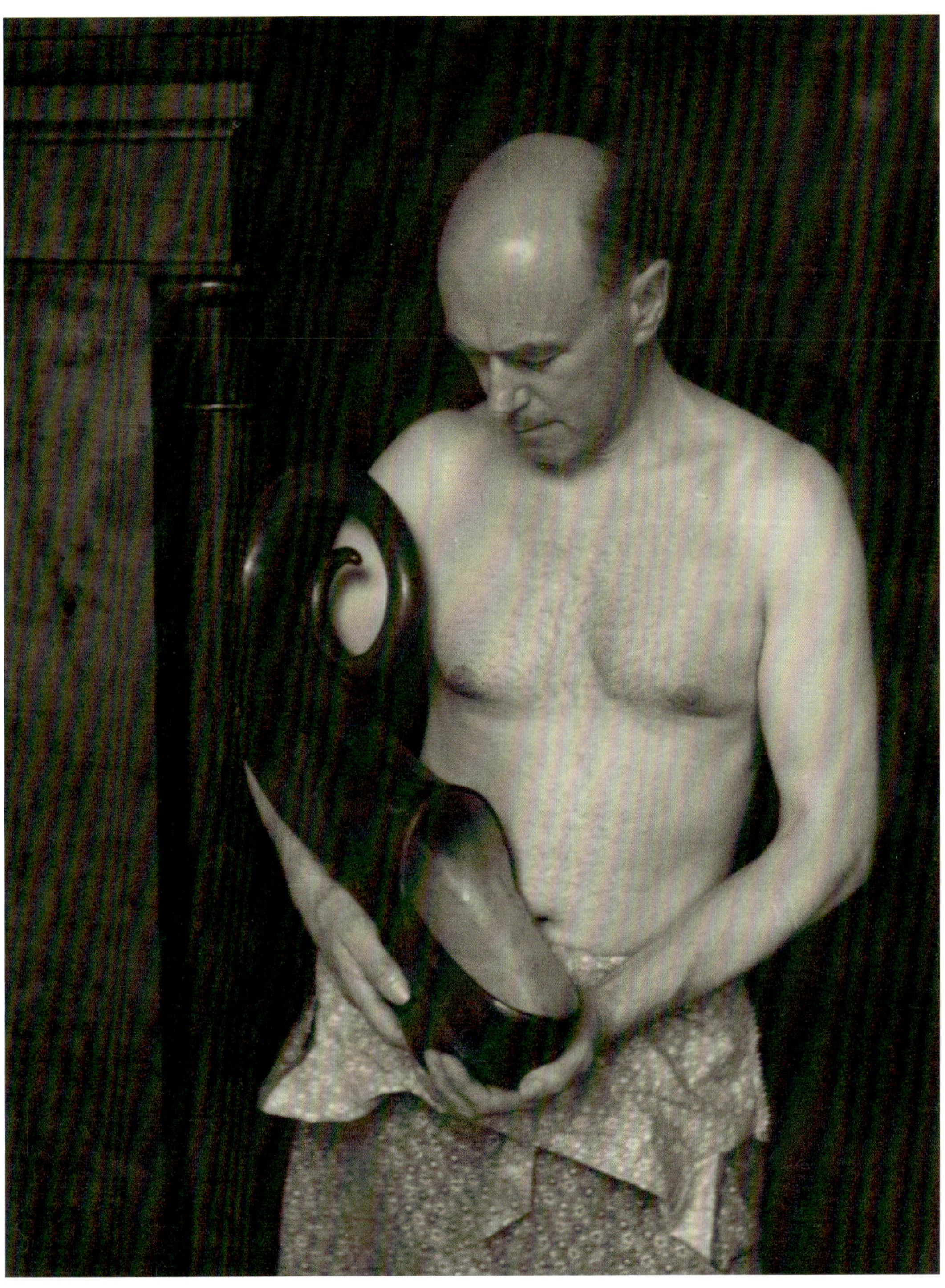

Cat. 104 *John D. Graham*, 1940, gelatin silver print, 34 × 25.7 cm

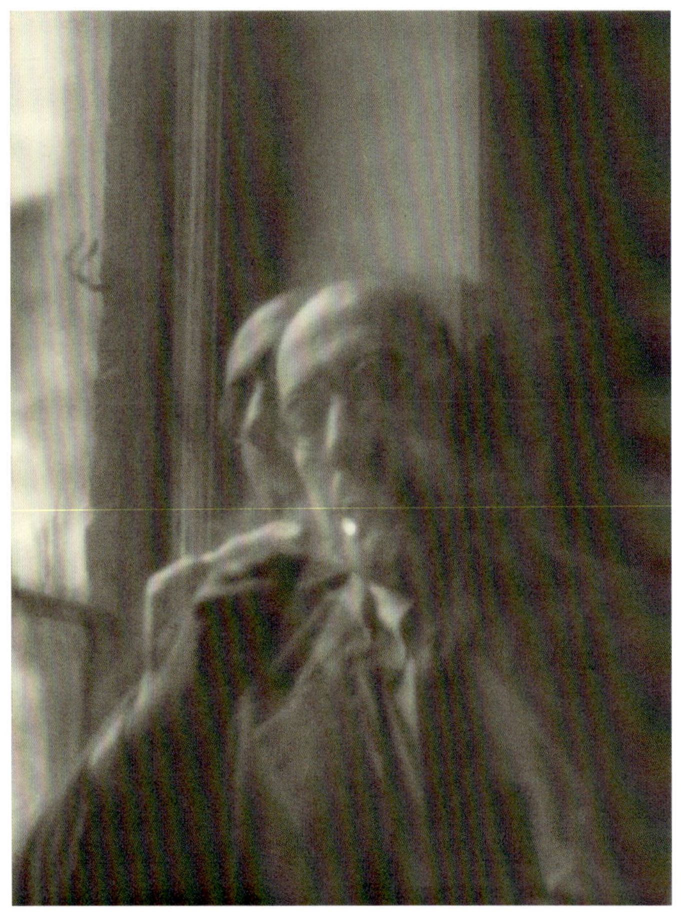

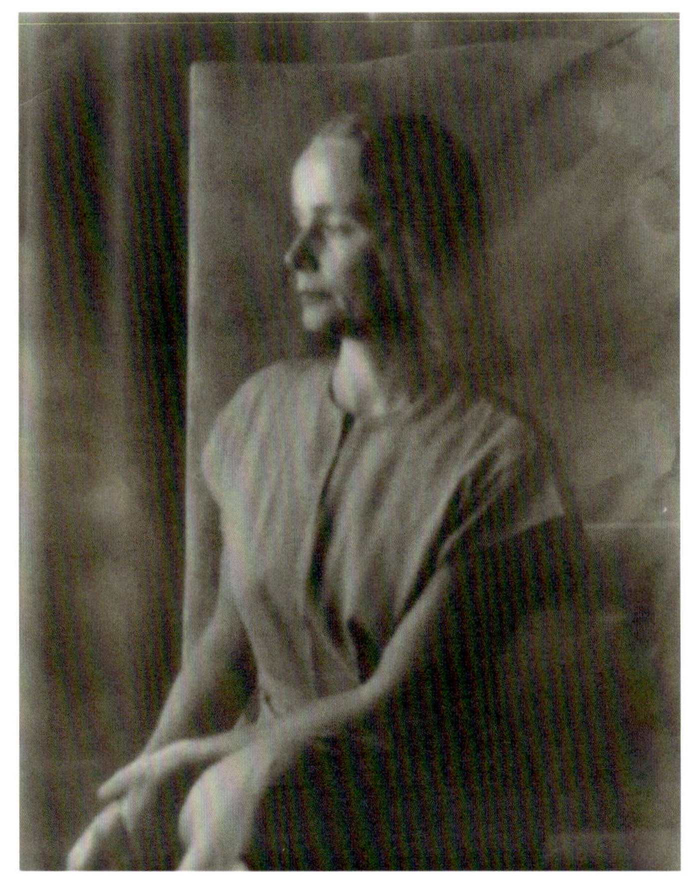

Cat. 105 *Mark Rothko*, 1948, gelatin silver print, 25.1 × 20 cm

Cat. 106 *Betty Parsons*, 1948, gelatin silver print, 32.7 × 26 cm

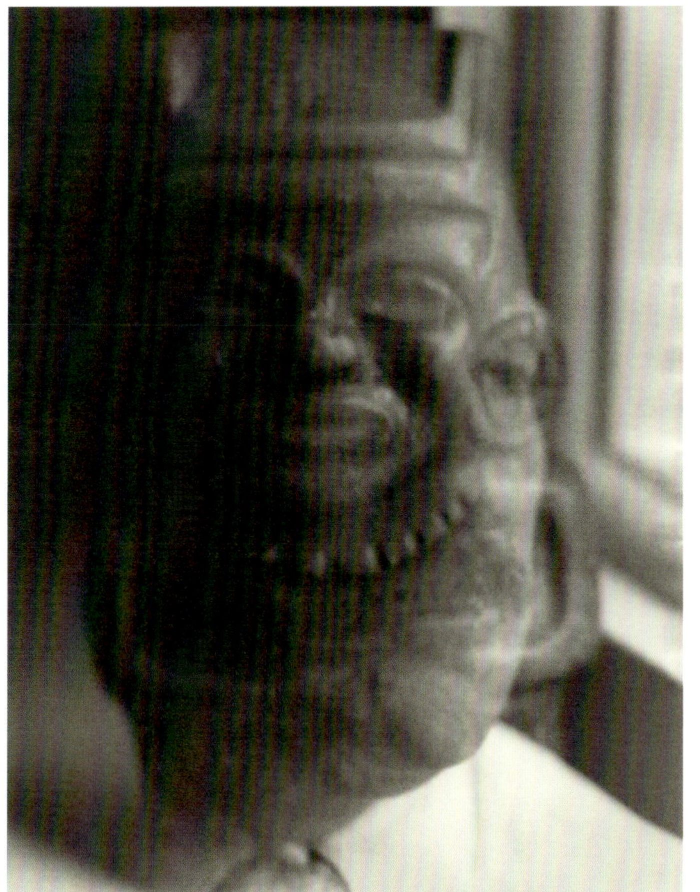

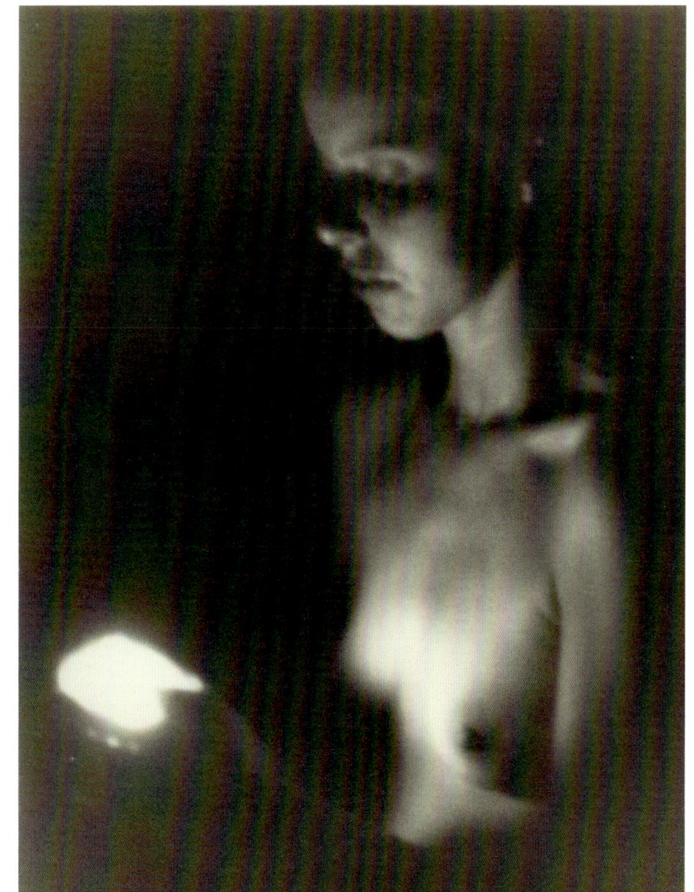

Cat. 107 *Barnett Newman*, 1948, gelatin silver print, 25.4 × 20 cm

Cat. 108 *Female Study*, ca. 1950, gelatin silver print, 25.1 × 20 cm

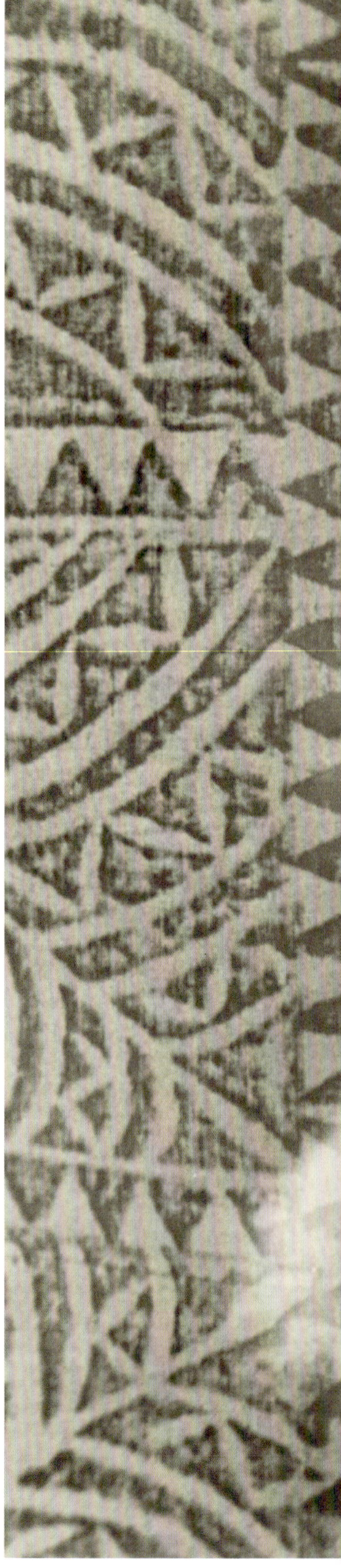

Cat. 109 *Theodoros Stamos*, 1950, gelatin silver print, 27.9 × 35.6 cm

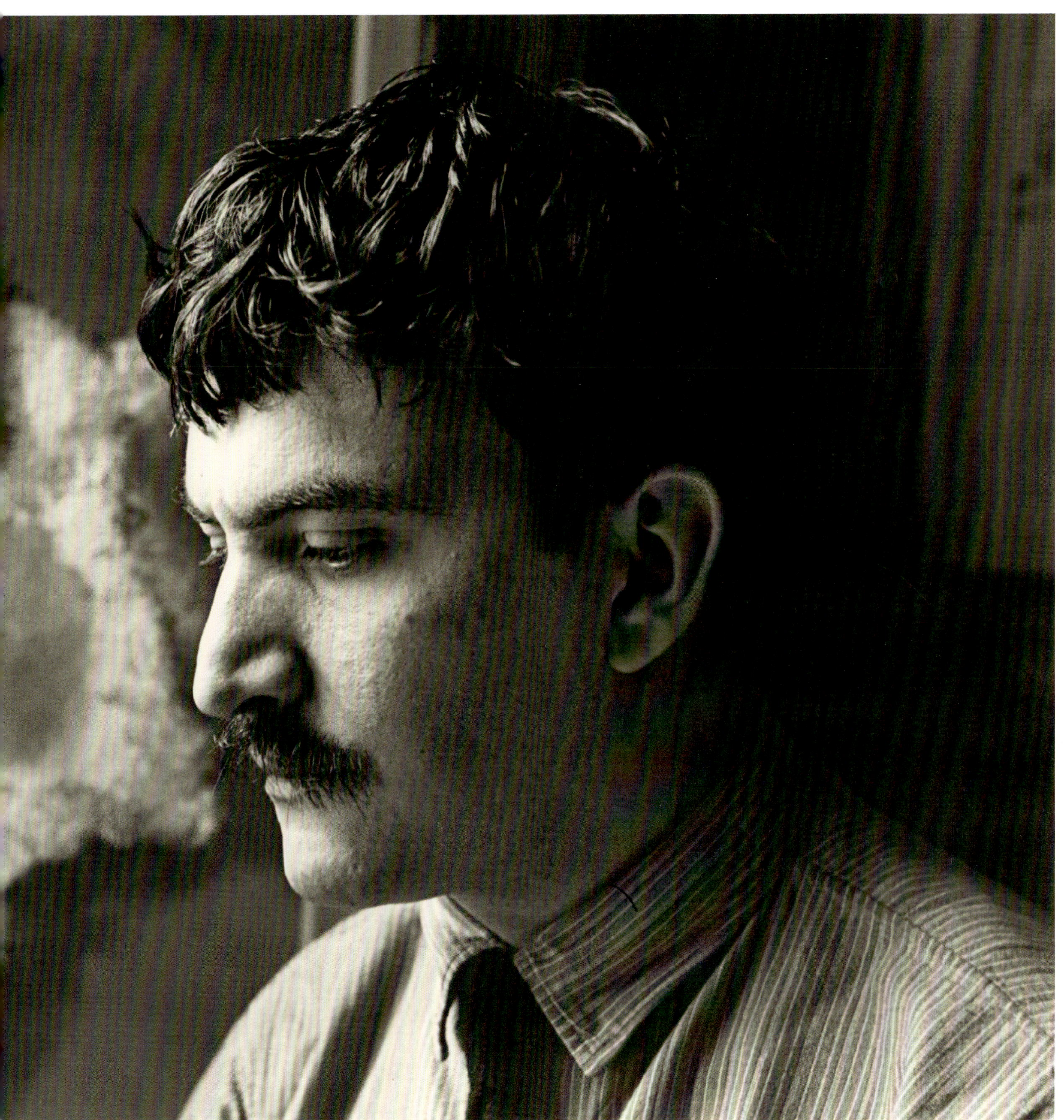

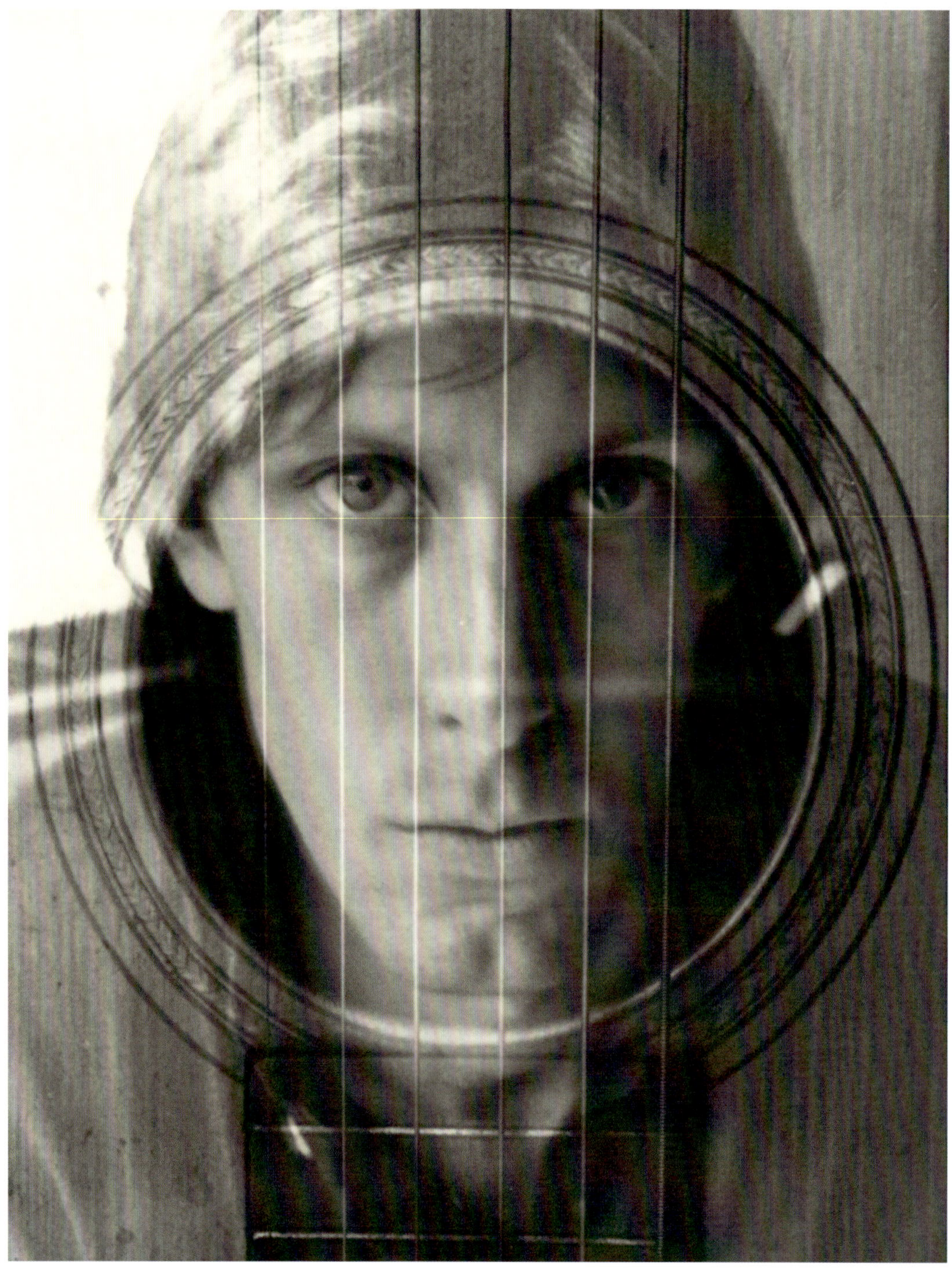

Cat. 110 *Jonathan Pousette-Dart*, 1971, gelatin silver print, 35.6 × 27.9 cm

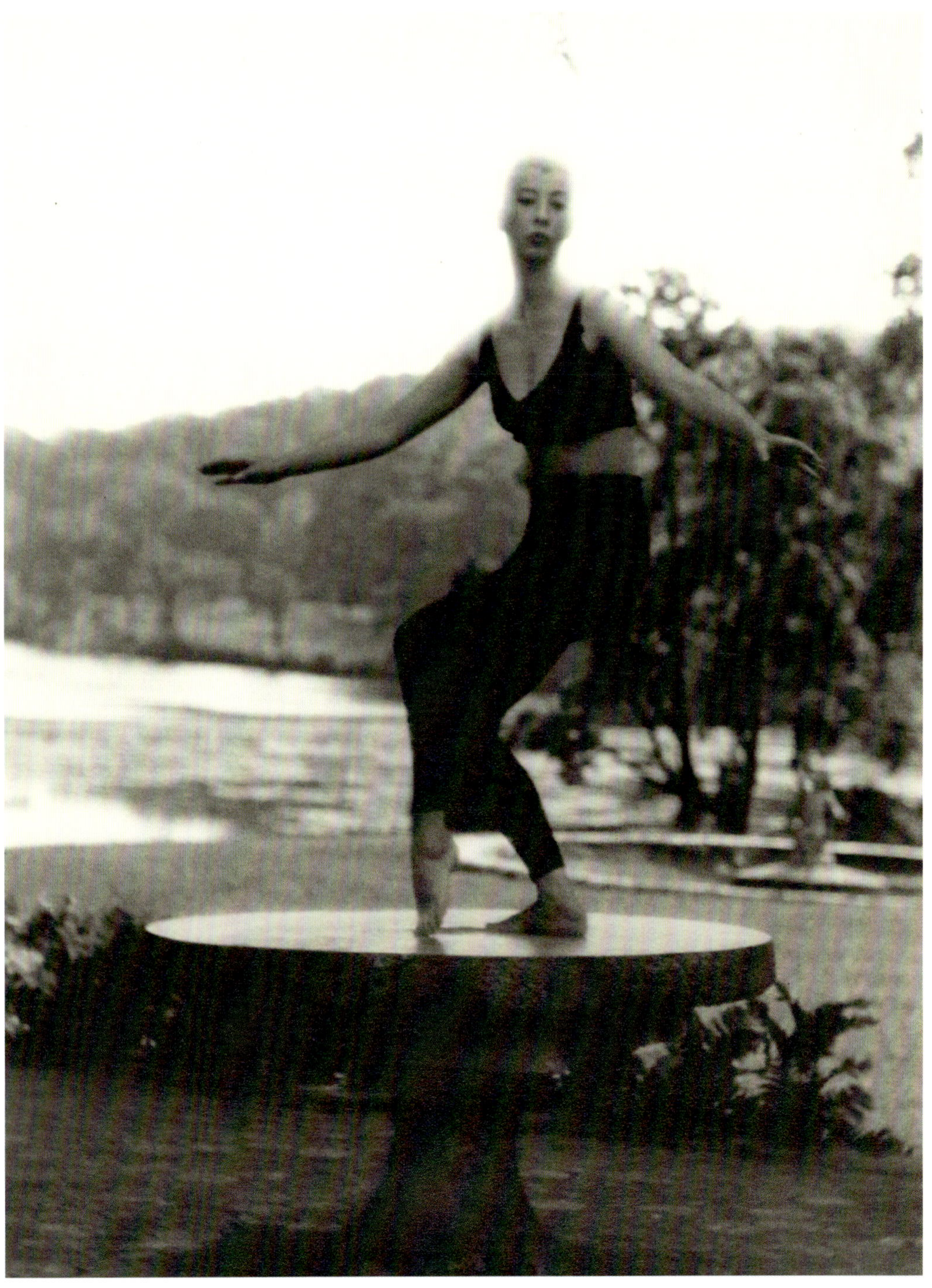

Cat. 111 *Sono Osato*, 1960s, gelatin silver print, 34.6 × 25.1 cm

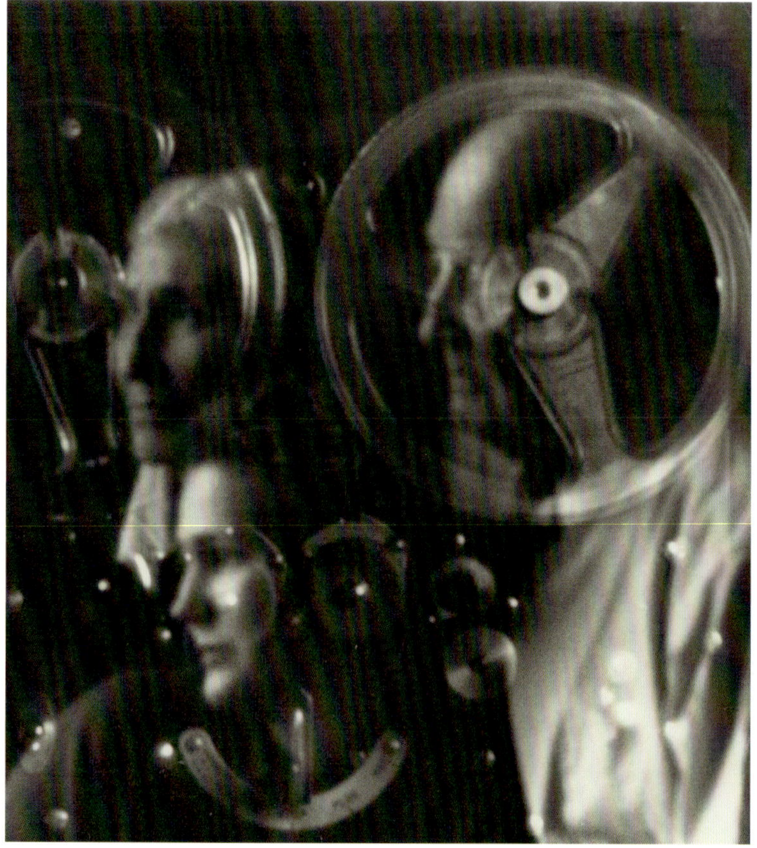

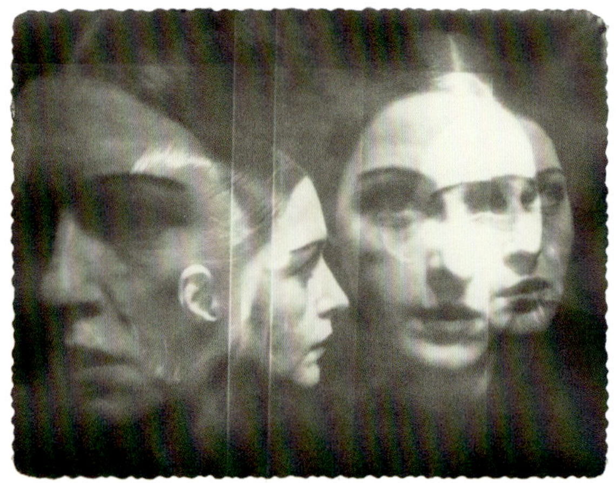

Cat. 112 *Michael West*, ca. 1946, gelatin silver print, 10.8 × 14 cm

Cat. 113 *Flaherty Family*, 1951, gelatin silver print, 25.6 × 26.4 cm

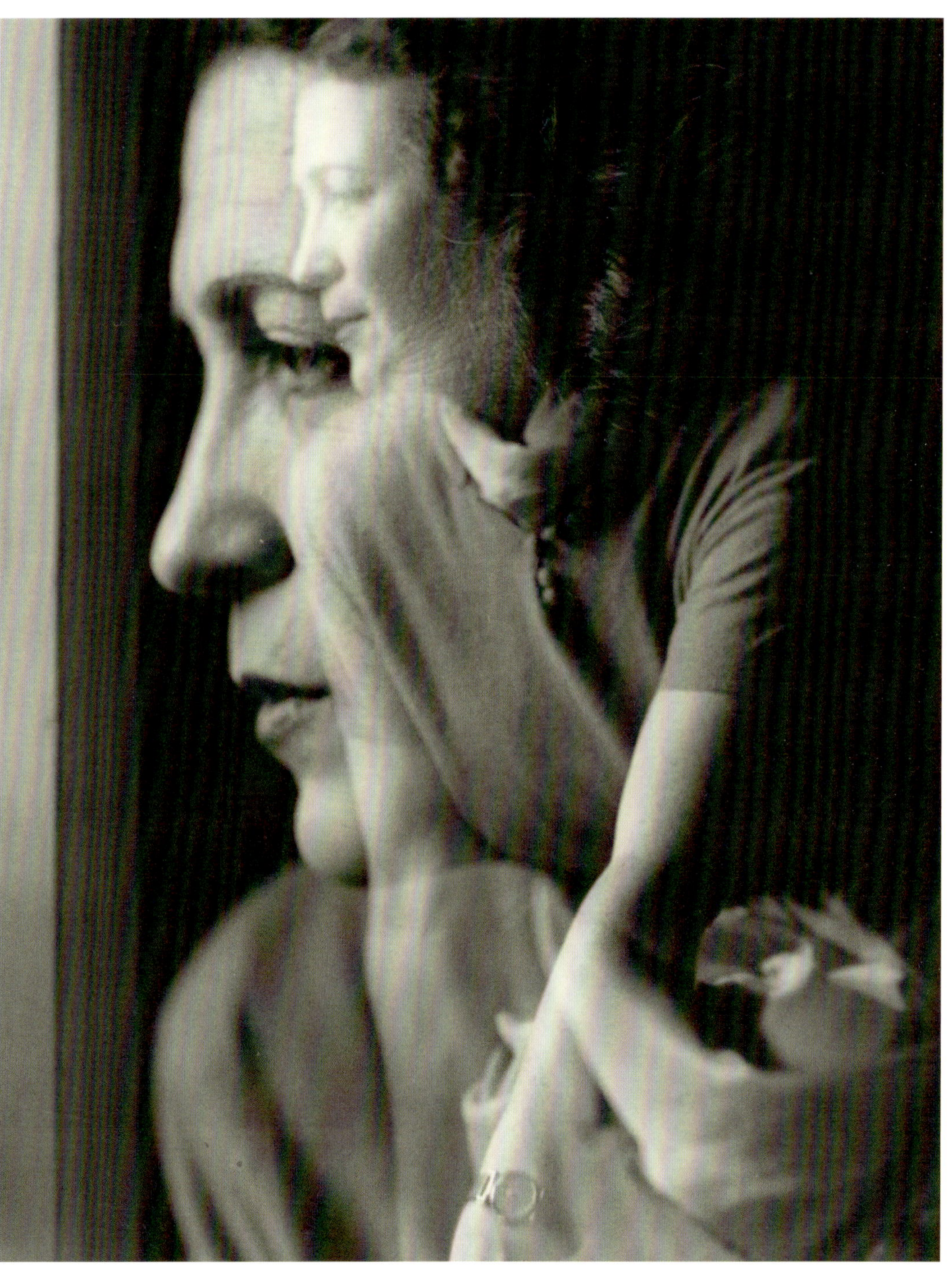

Cat. 114 *Perle Fine*, 1949, gelatin silver print, 35.2 × 27.9 cm

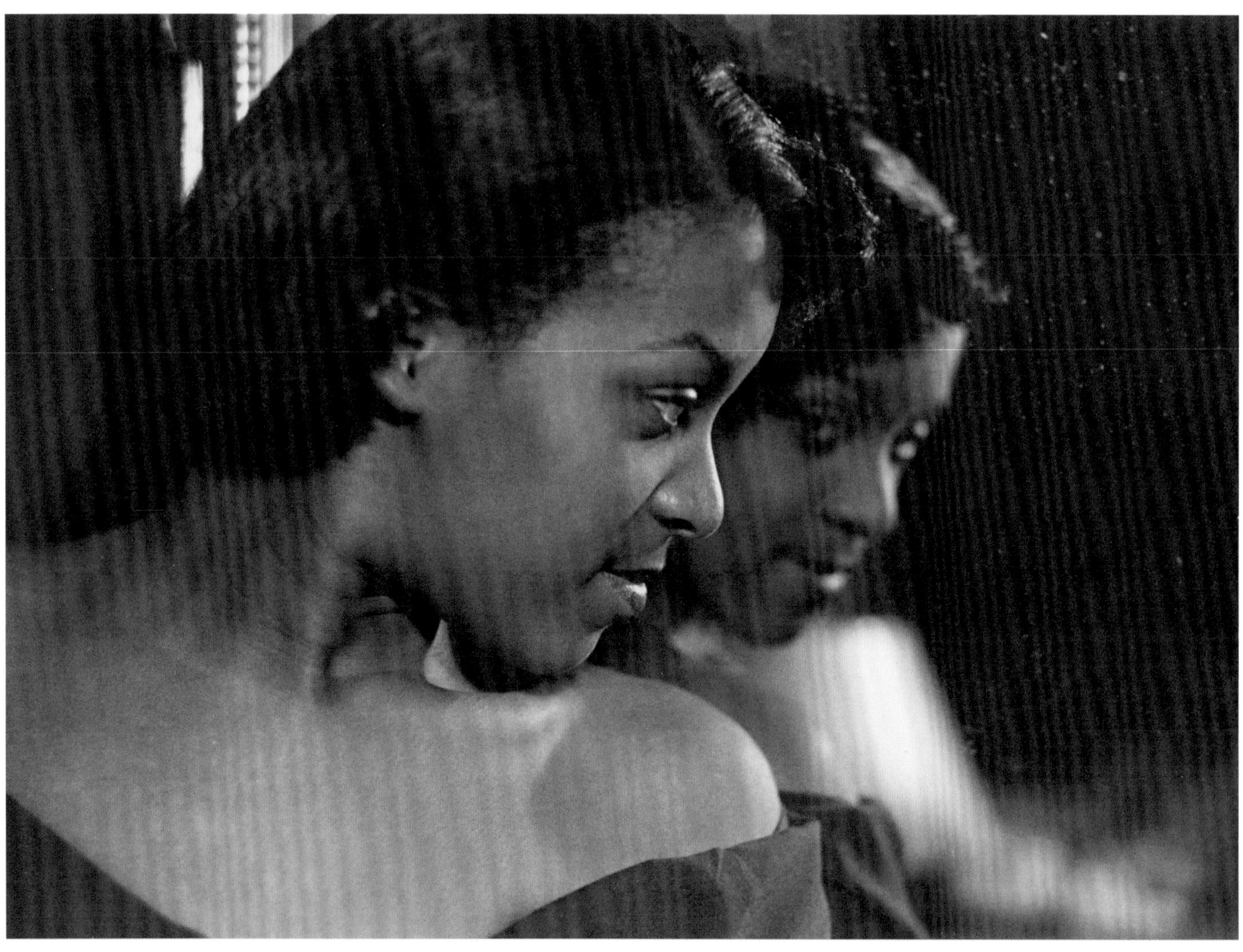

Cat. 115 *Hope Foye*, ca. 1950, gelatin silver print, 17.8 × 24.4 cm

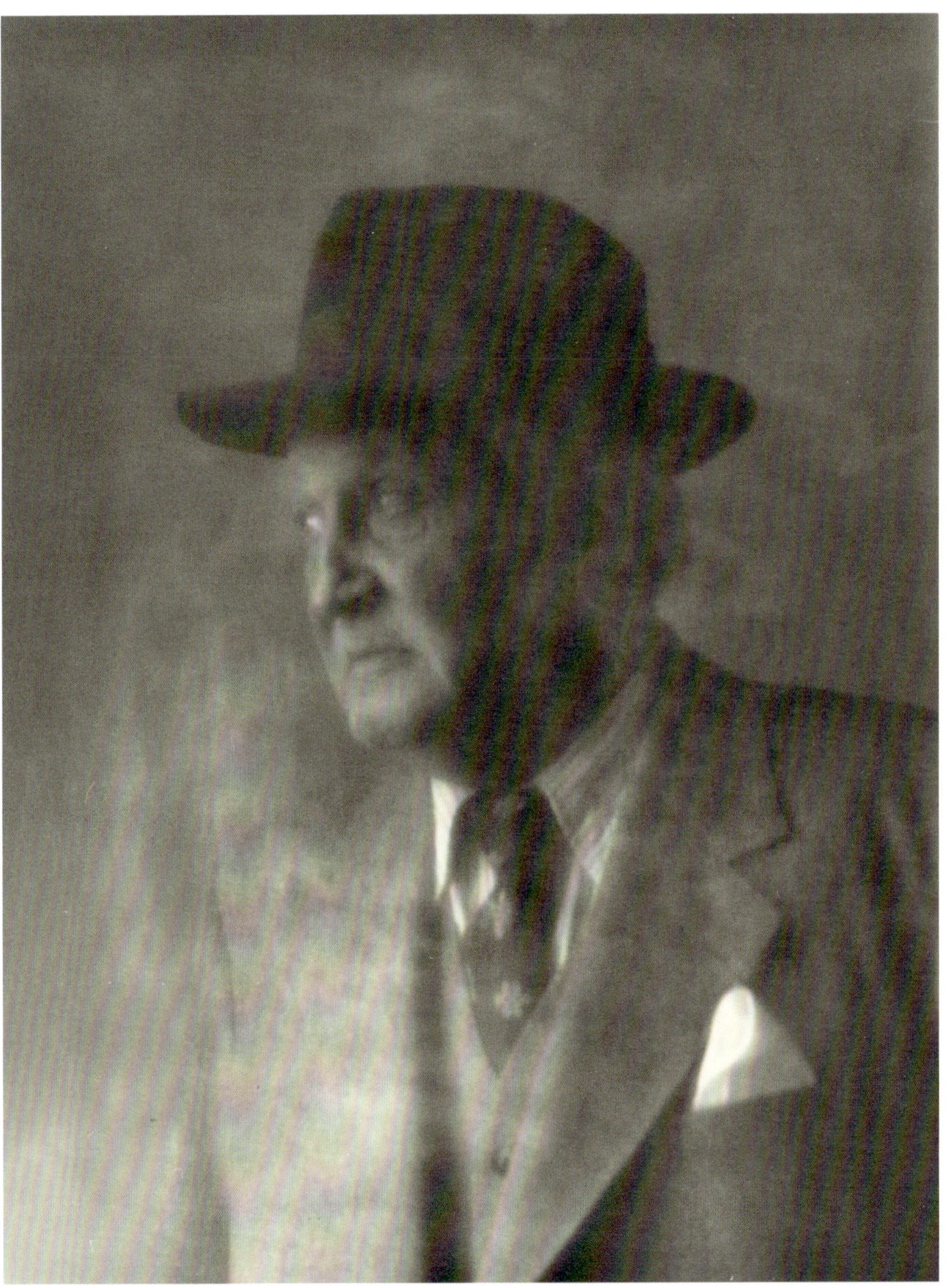

Cat. 116 *Robert J. Flaherty*, 1951, gelatin silver print, 33.7 × 26 cm

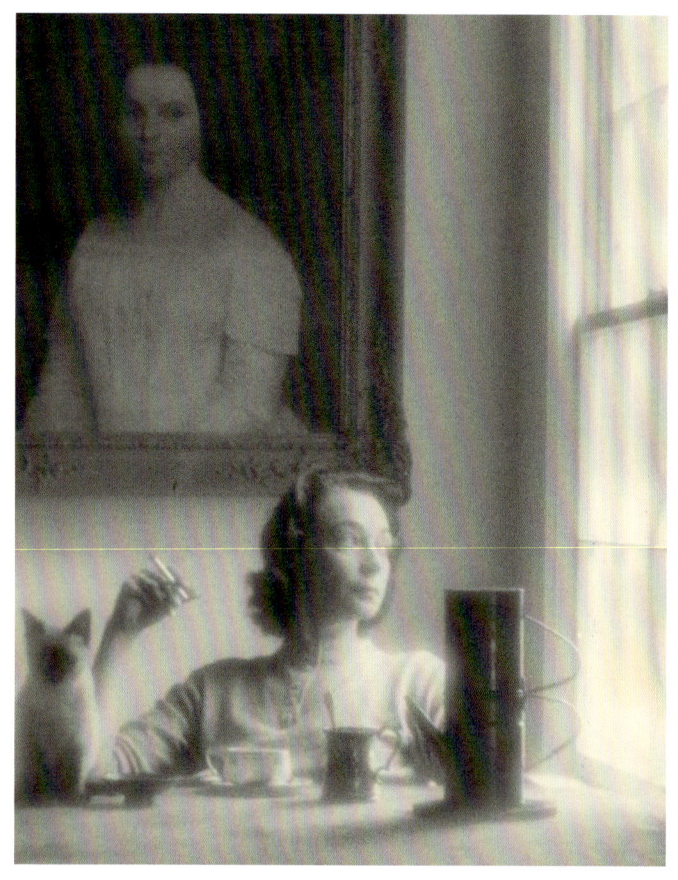

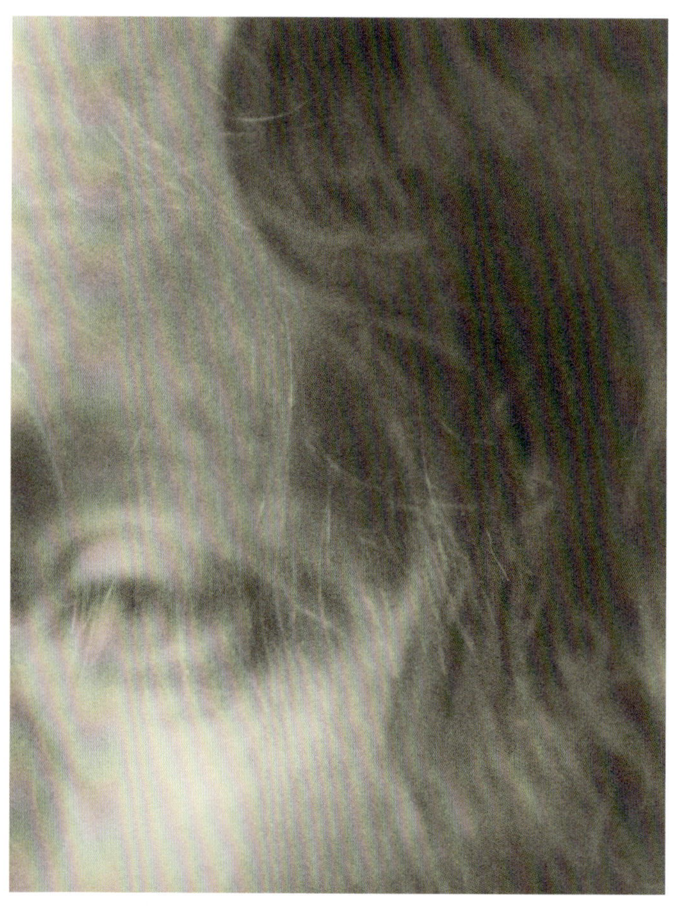

Cat. 117 *Lois Long*, ca. 1955, gelatin silver print, 35.2 × 27.9 cm

Cat. 118 *Betty Parsons's Eye*, 1948, gelatin silver print, 34.3 × 26.7 cm

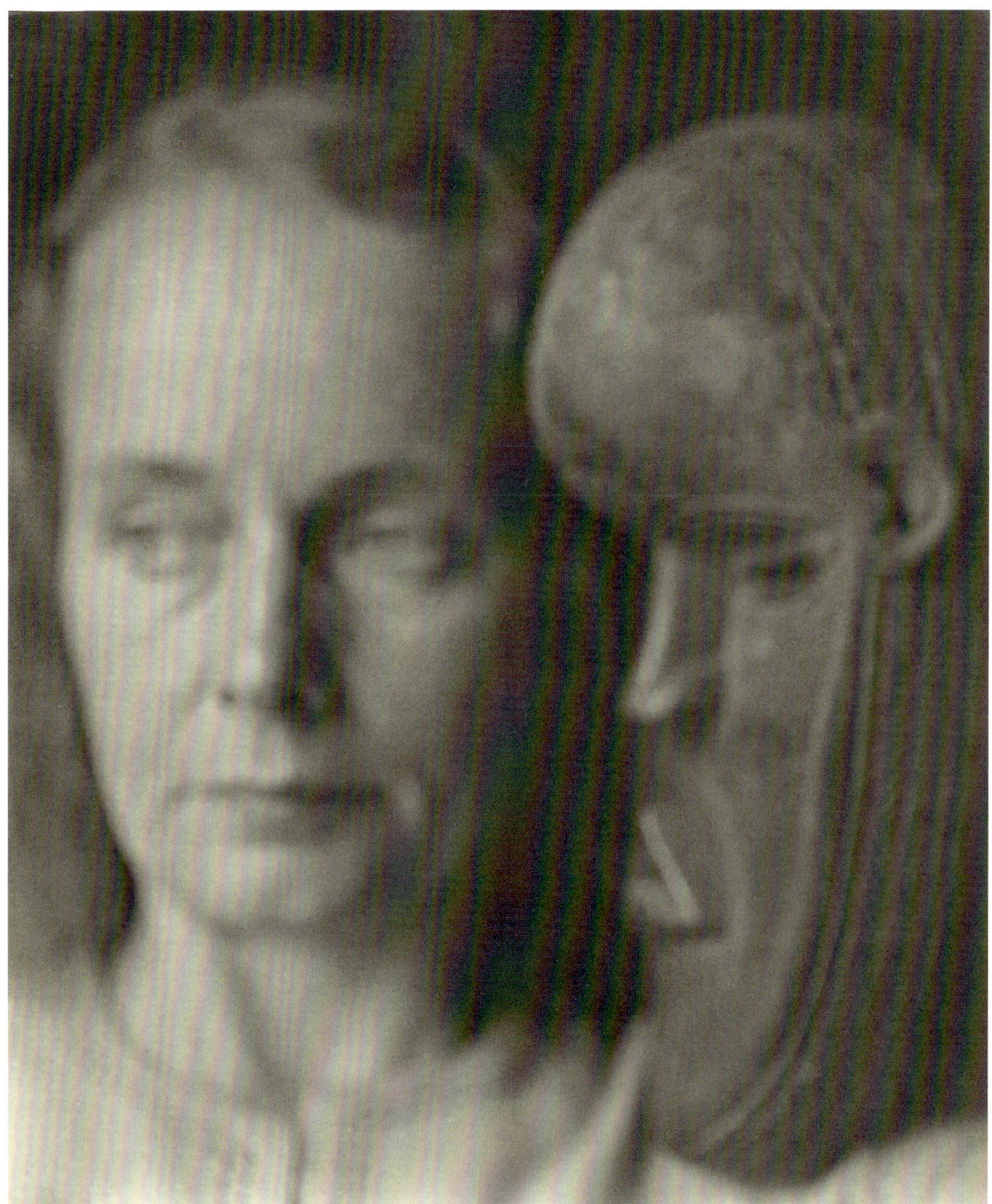

Cat. 119 *Betty Parsons with Mask*, 1948, gelatin silver print, 39.8 × 33.7 cm

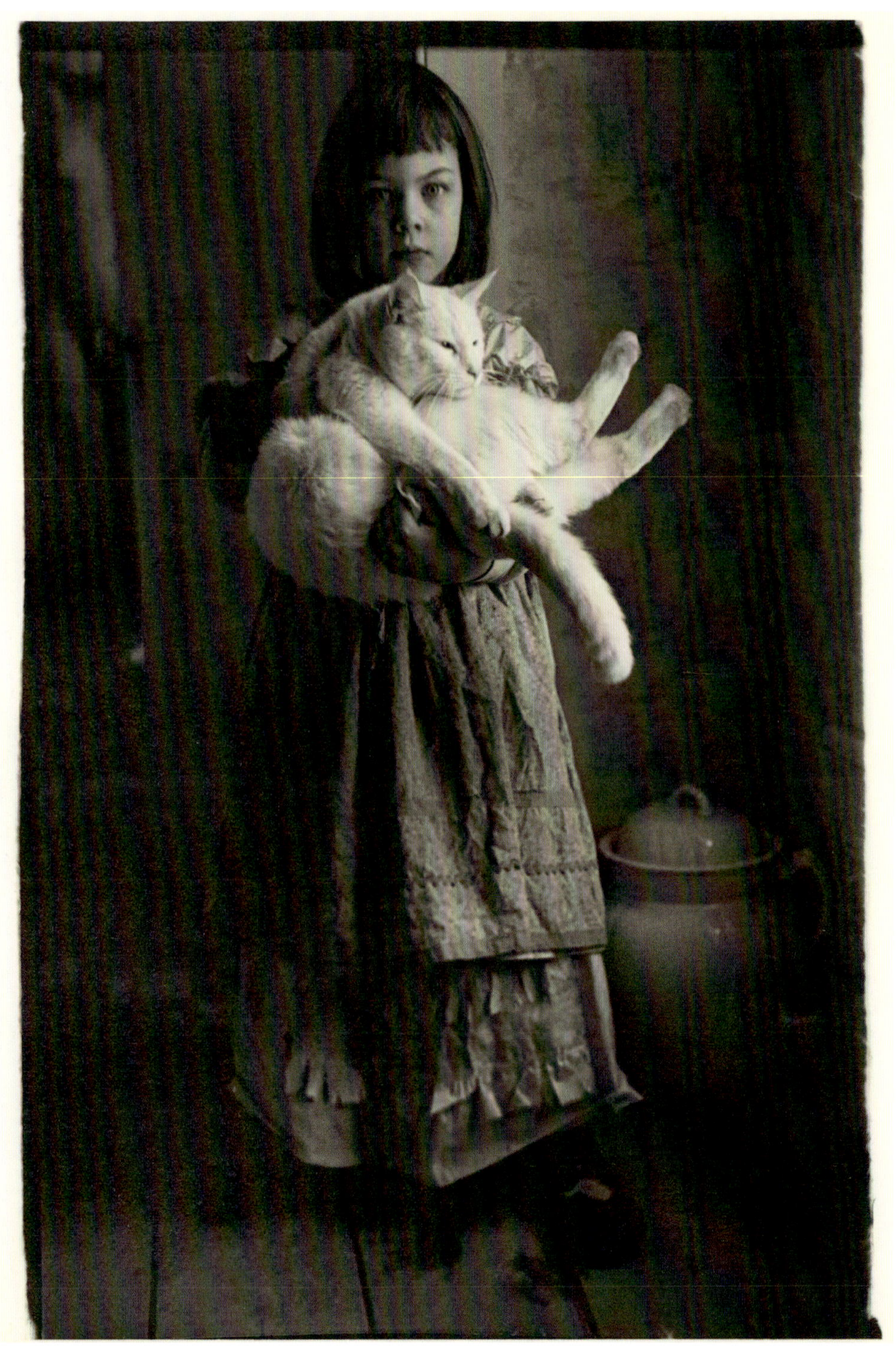

Cat. 120 *Joanna with Cat*, 1952, gelatin silver print, 35.6 × 27.9 cm

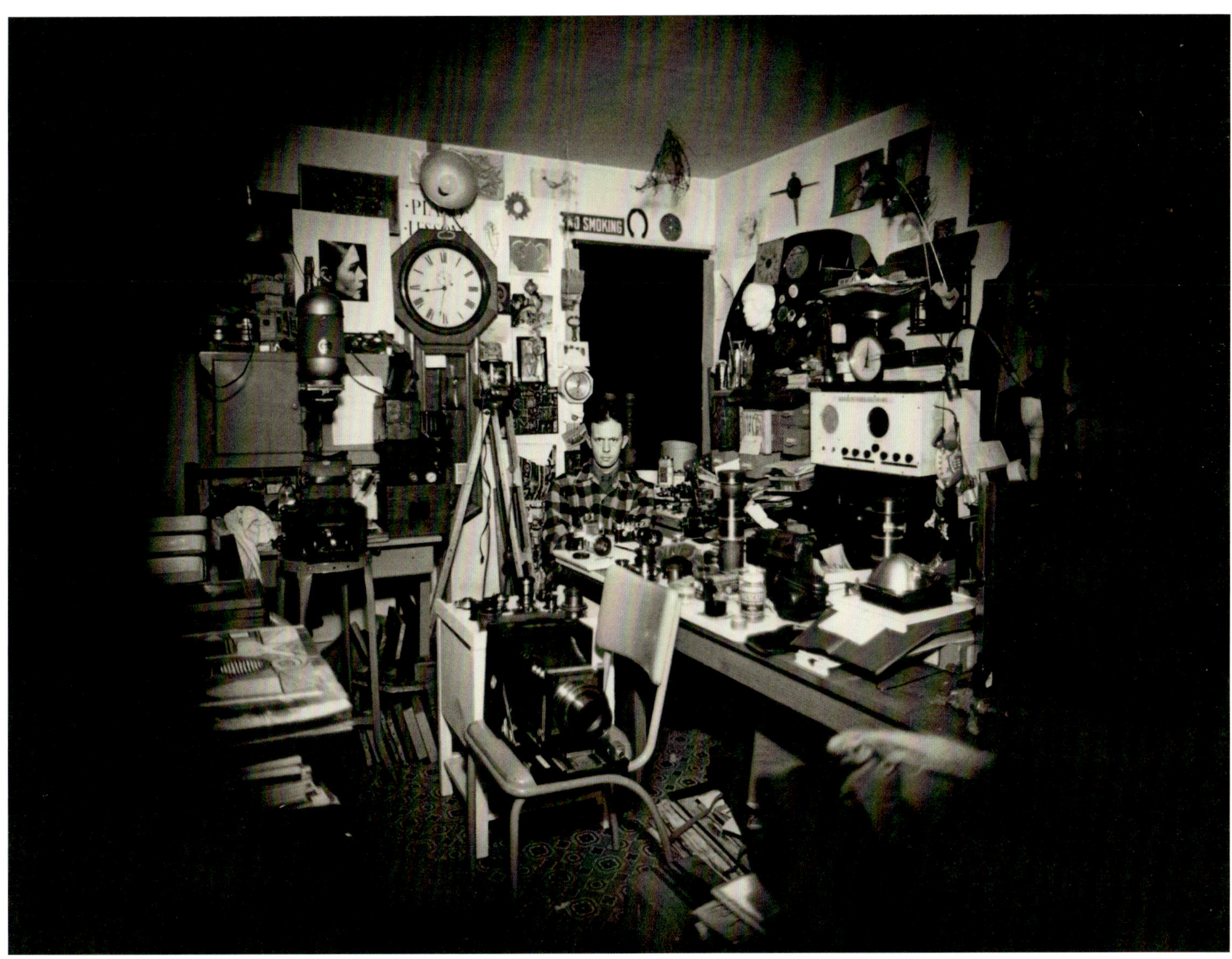

Cat. 121 *Self-Portrait in Photography Studio*, 1951, gelatin silver print, 27.9 × 35.2 cm

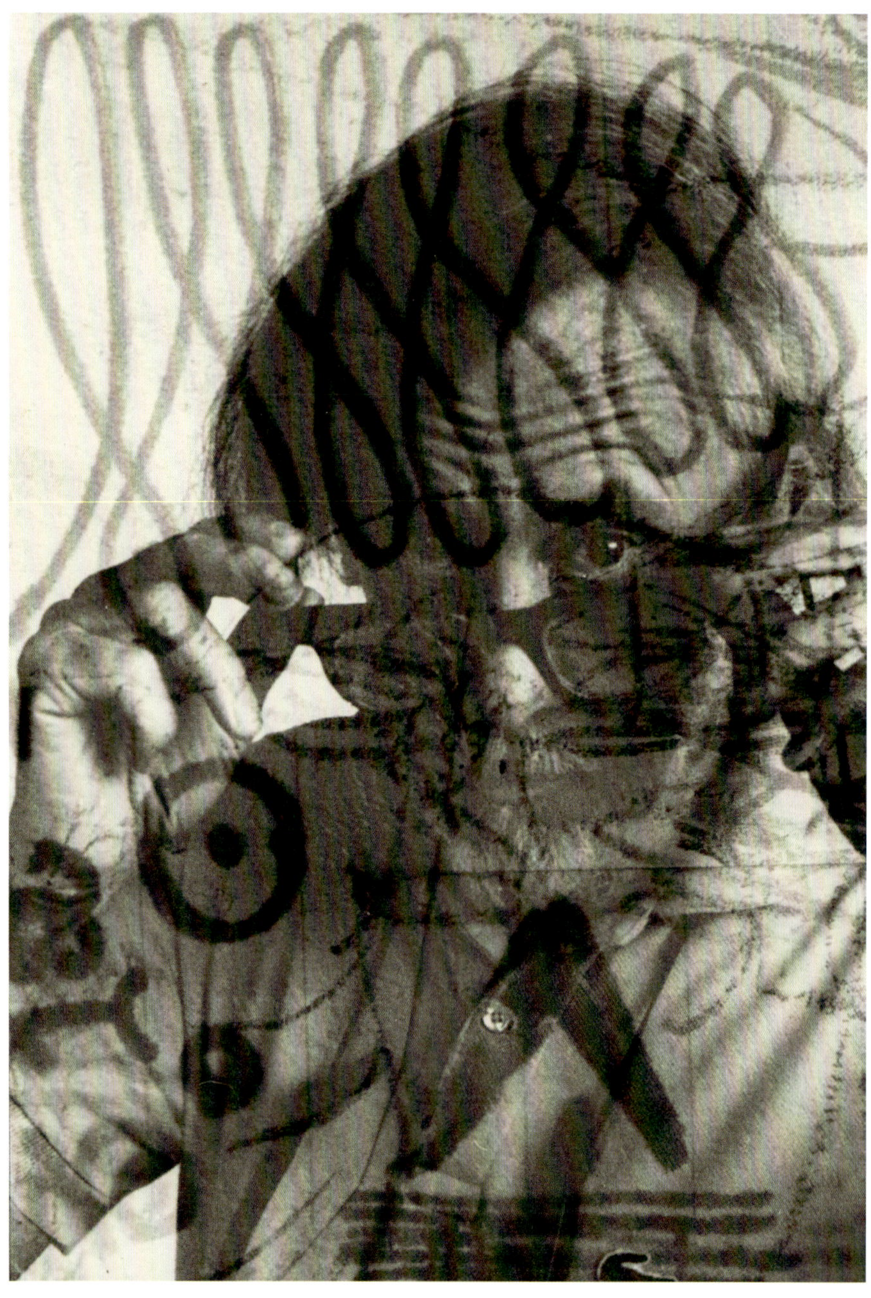

Cat. 122 *Self-Portrait*, 1985, gelatin silver print, 35.6 × 27.9 cm

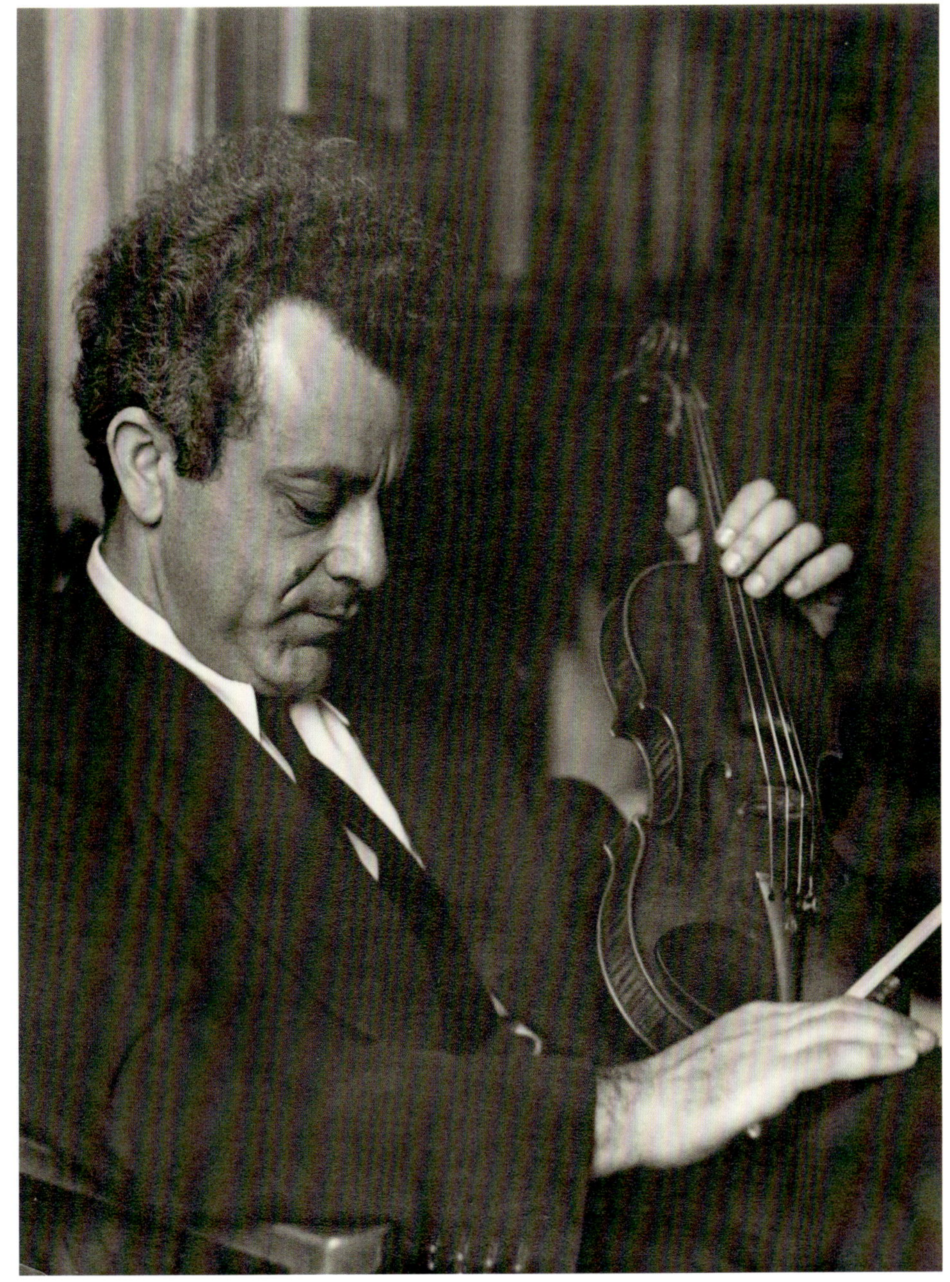

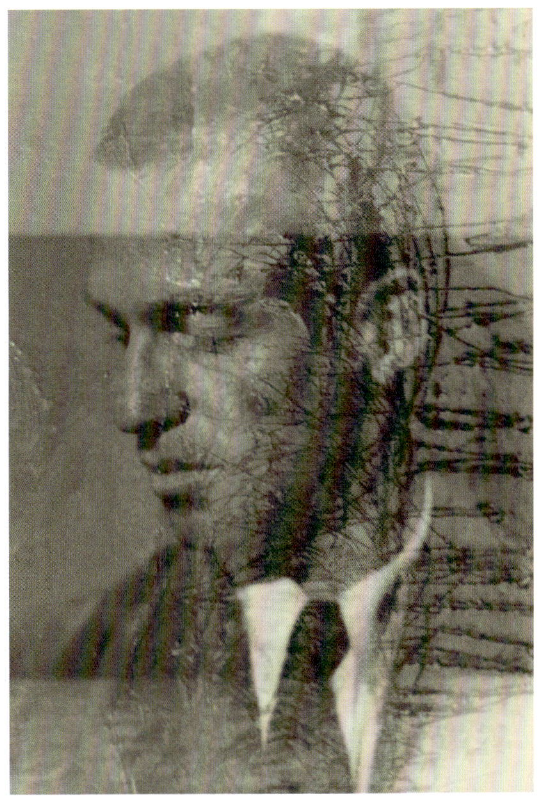

Cat. 123 *Alexander (Sasha) Schneider*, 1950, gelatin silver print, 33.7 × 26 cm

Cat. 124 *William Congdon*, ca. 1948, gelatin silver print, 23.8 × 16.5 cm

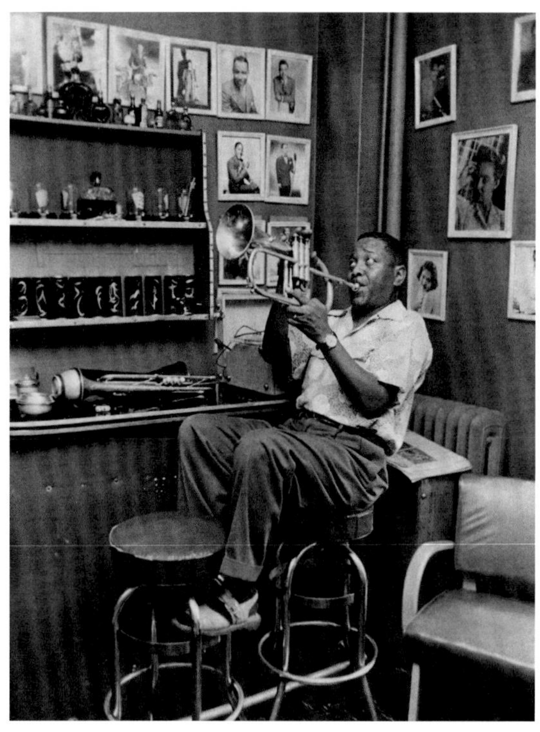

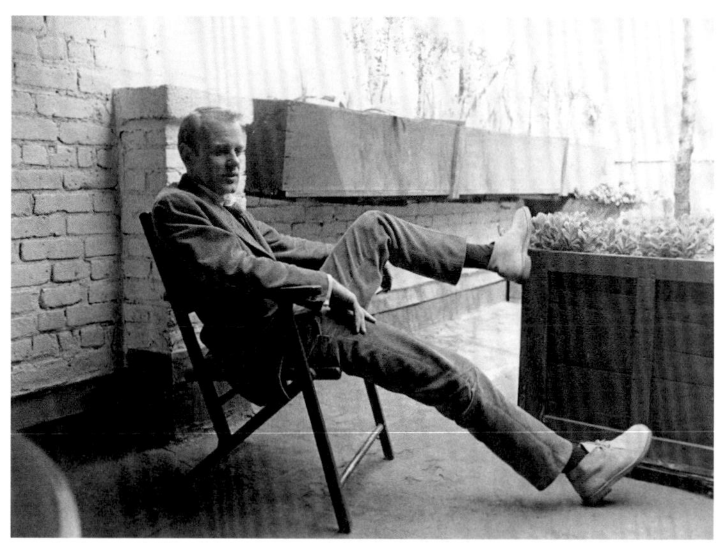

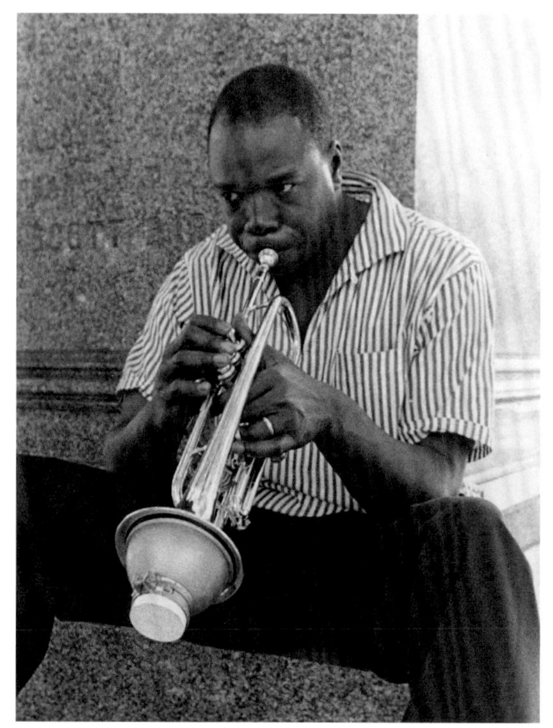

Cat. 125 *Roy Eldridge*, 1955, gelatin silver print, 35.2 × 27.9 cm

Cat. 126 *Bob Fosse*, 1955, gelatin silver print, 27.9 × 35.6 cm

Cat. 127 *Thad Jones*, 1955, gelatin silver print, 35.6 × 27.9 cm

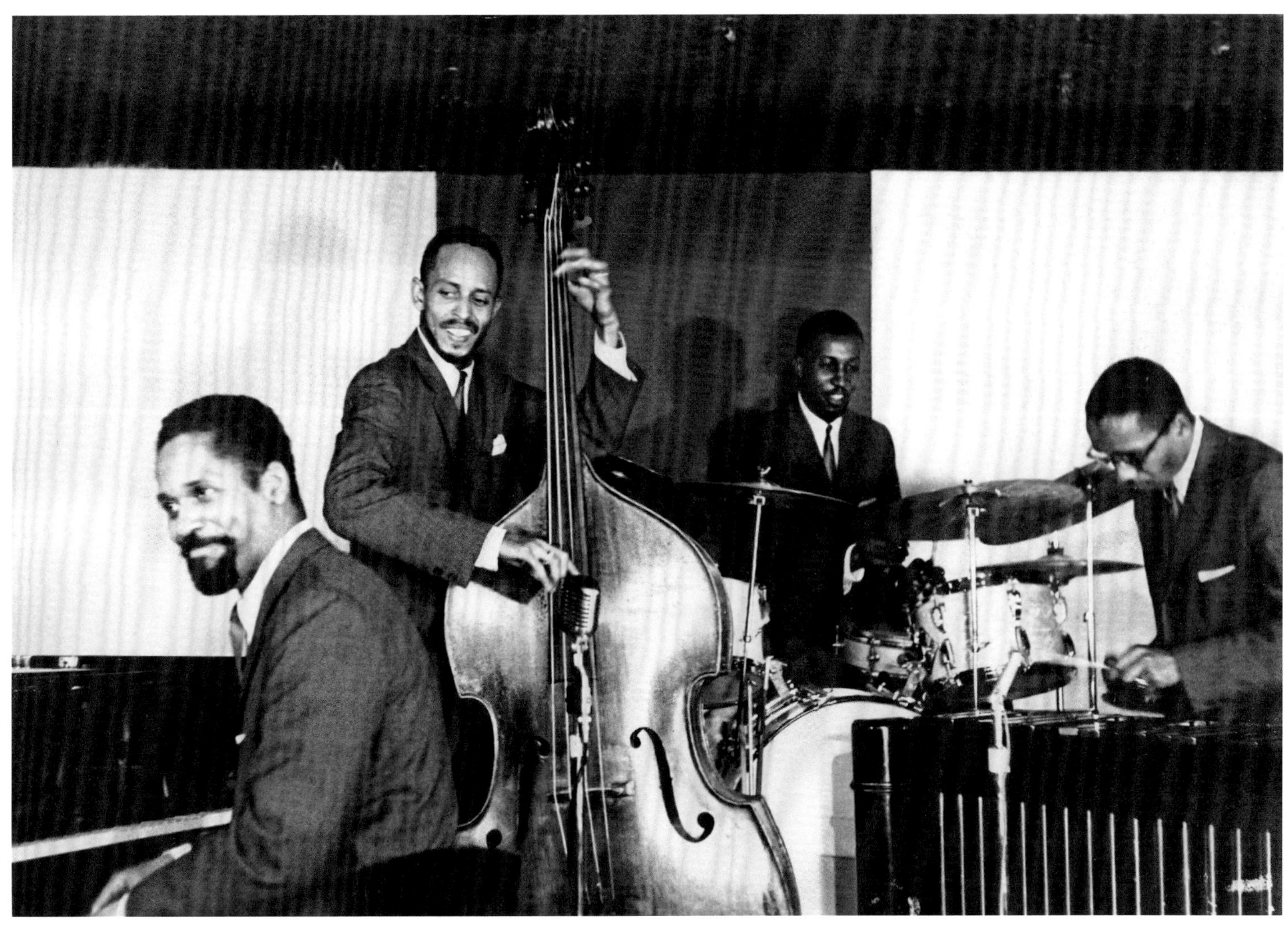

Cat. 128 *The Modern Jazz Quartet*, 1955, gelatin silver print, 27.9 × 35.2 cm

Notebooks

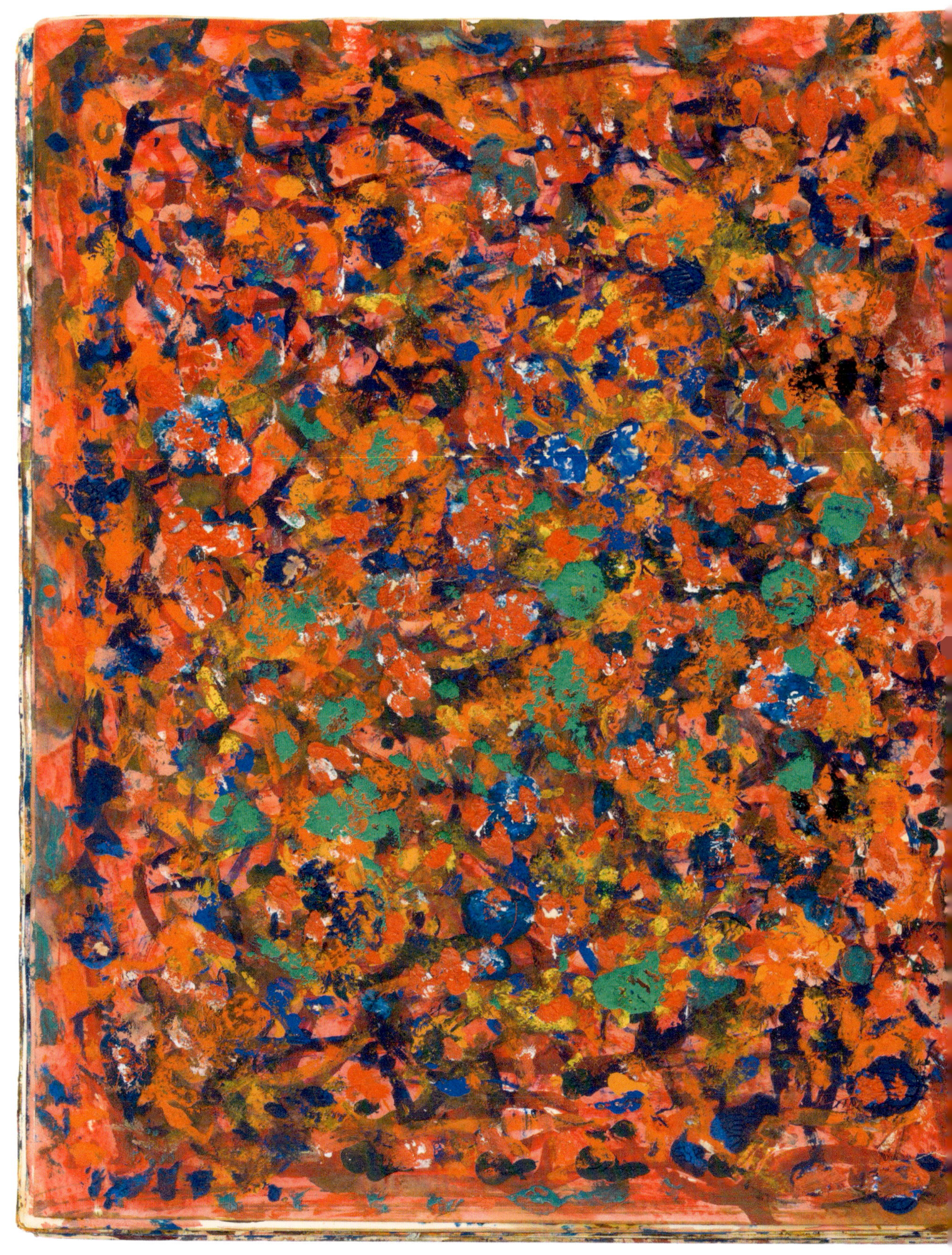

Cat. 129 *Notebook B-85*, 1970s, pp. 22-23, mixed media, 43.2 × 72.4 cm

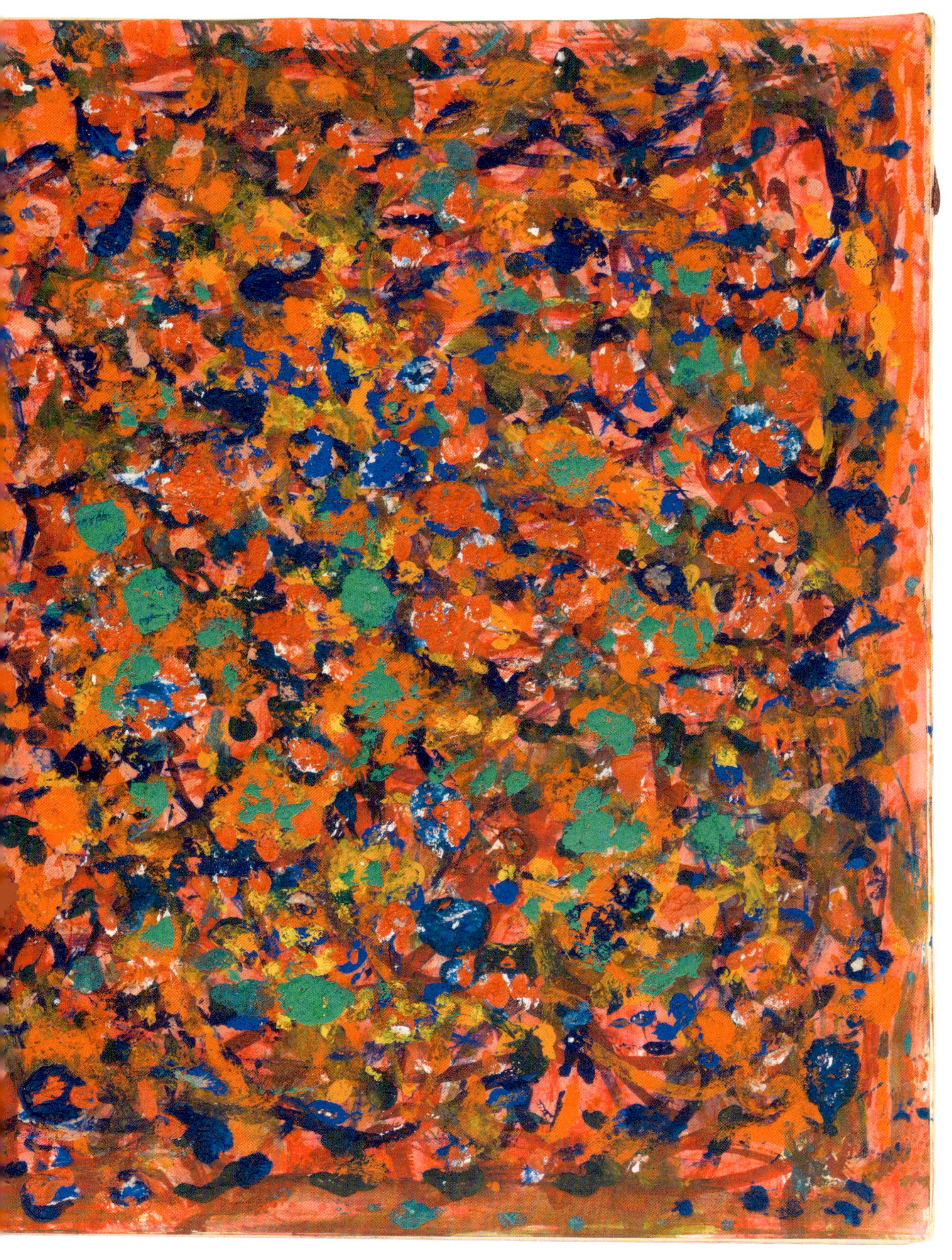

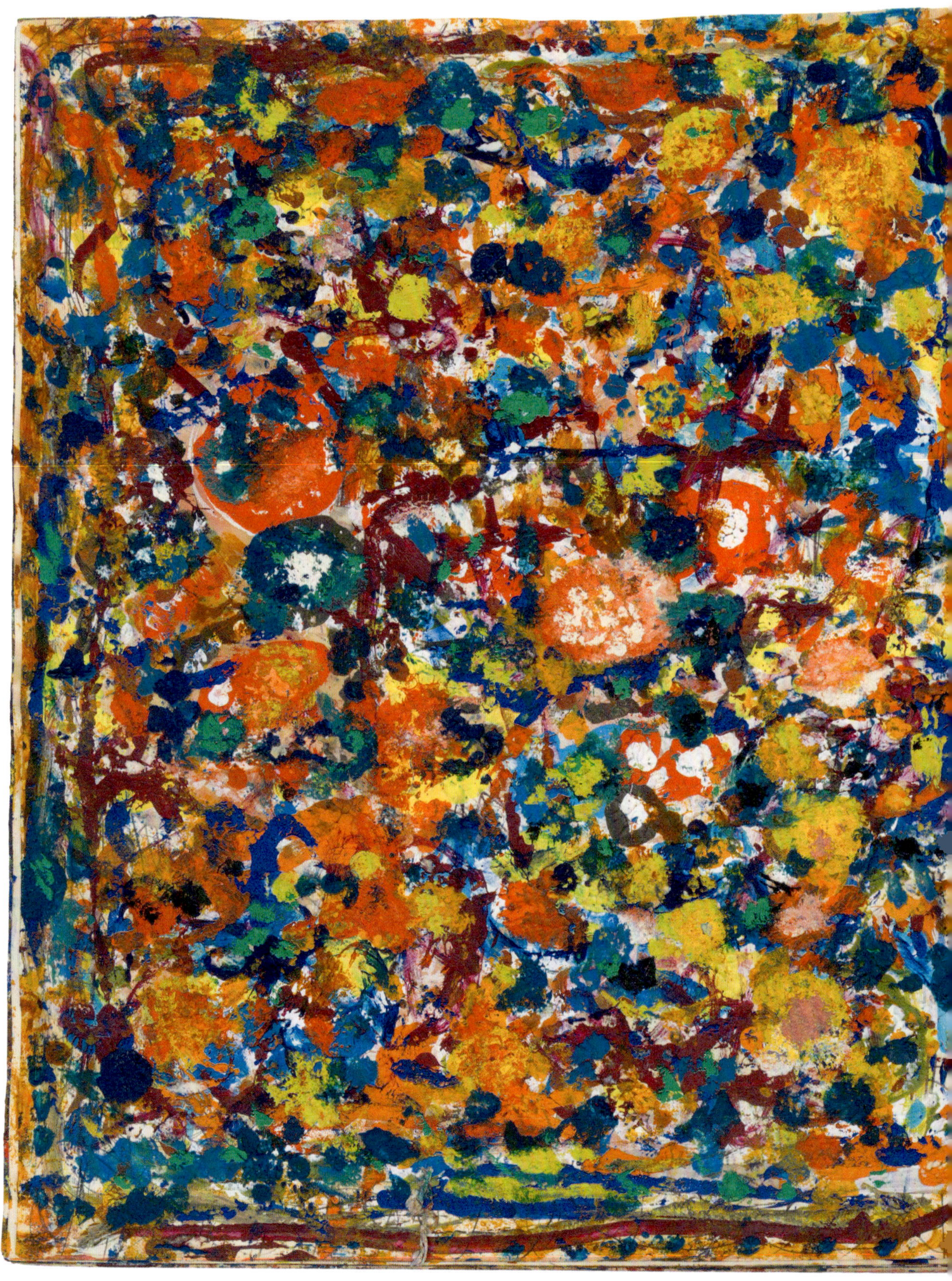

Cat. 129 *Notebook B-85*, 1970s, pp. 10-11, mixed media, 43.2 × 72.4 cm

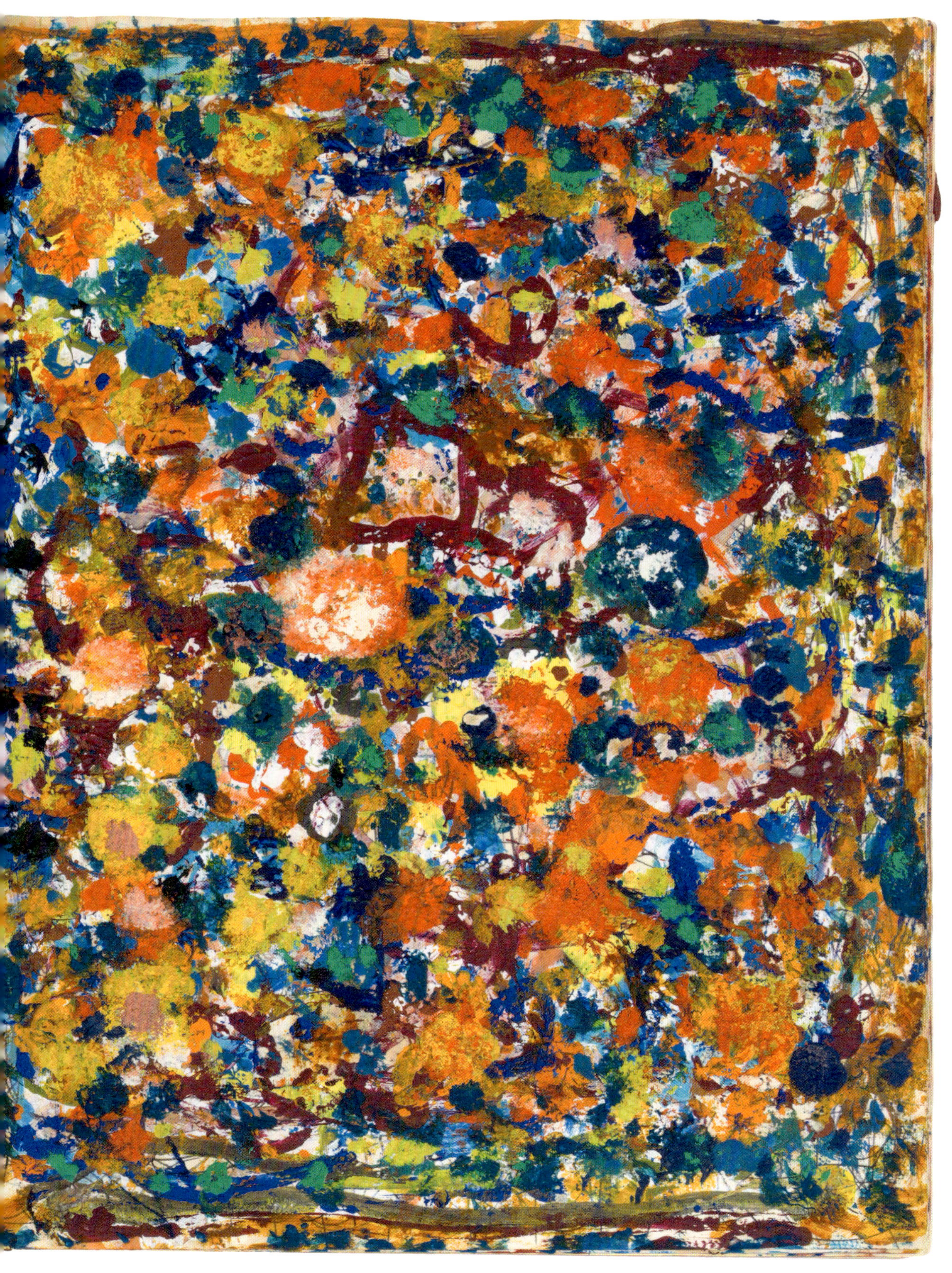

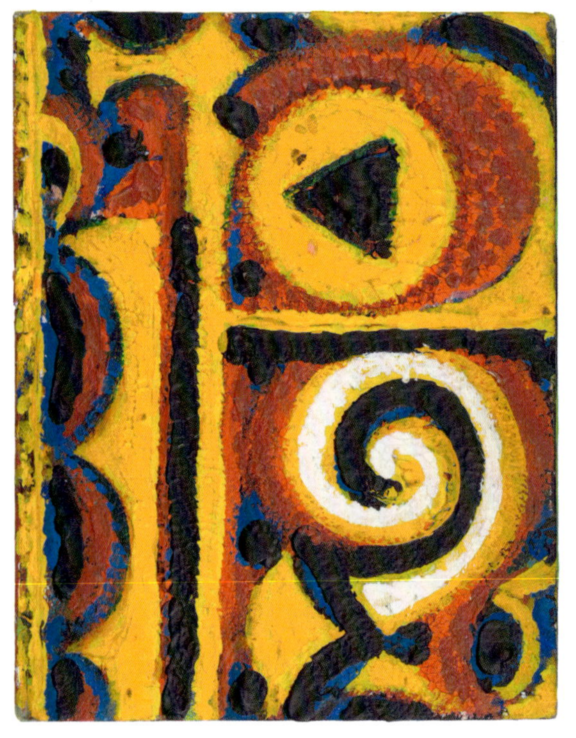

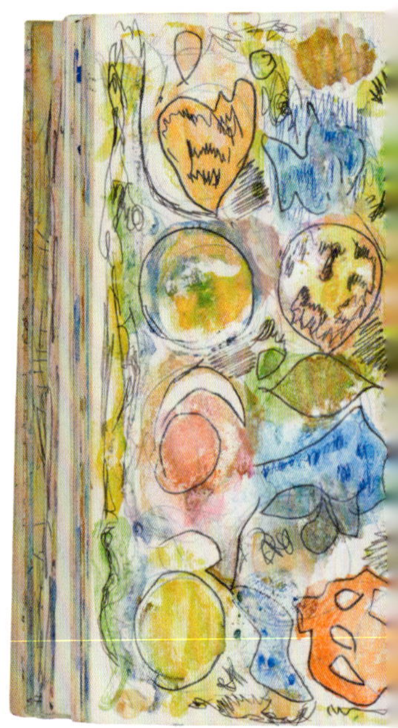

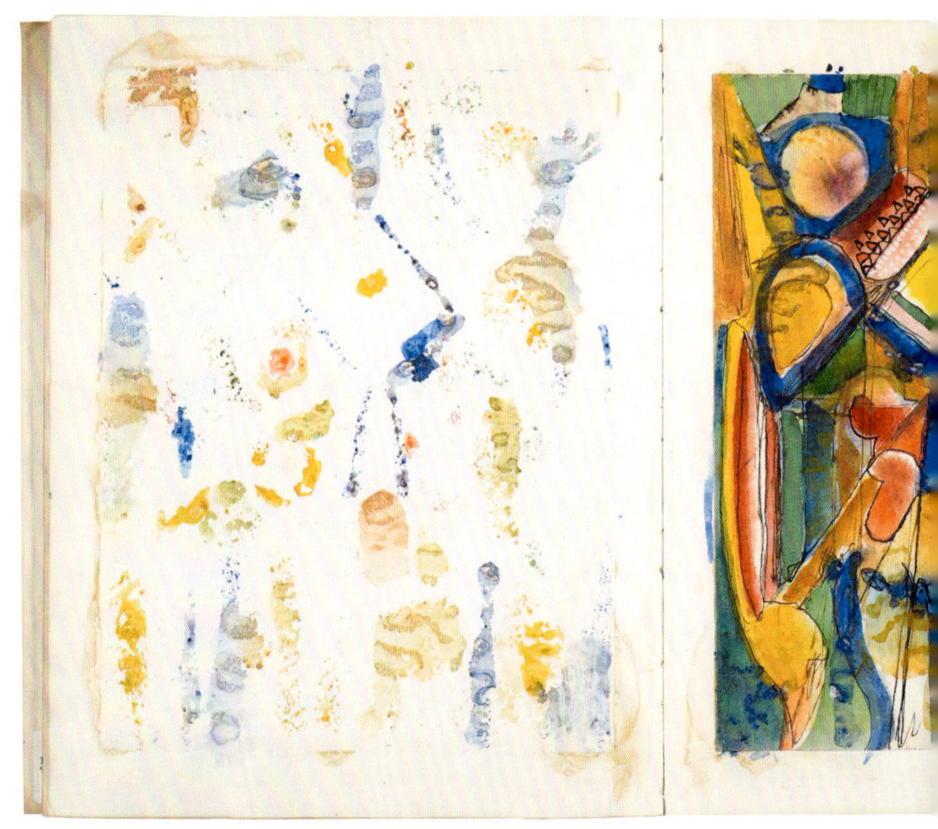

Cat. 130 *Notebook B-142*, 1970s, cover, mixed media, 27.9 × 21.6 cm

Cat. 131 *Notebook B-153*, 1970s, pp. 117–18, 93–94, mixed media, 22.2 × 28.9 cm

Cat. 132 *Notebook B-180*, 1950s, pp. 70–71, 66–67, mixed media, 34.9 × 57.2 cm

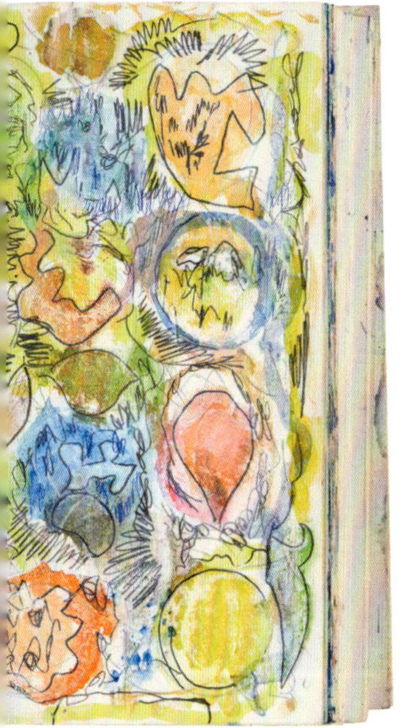

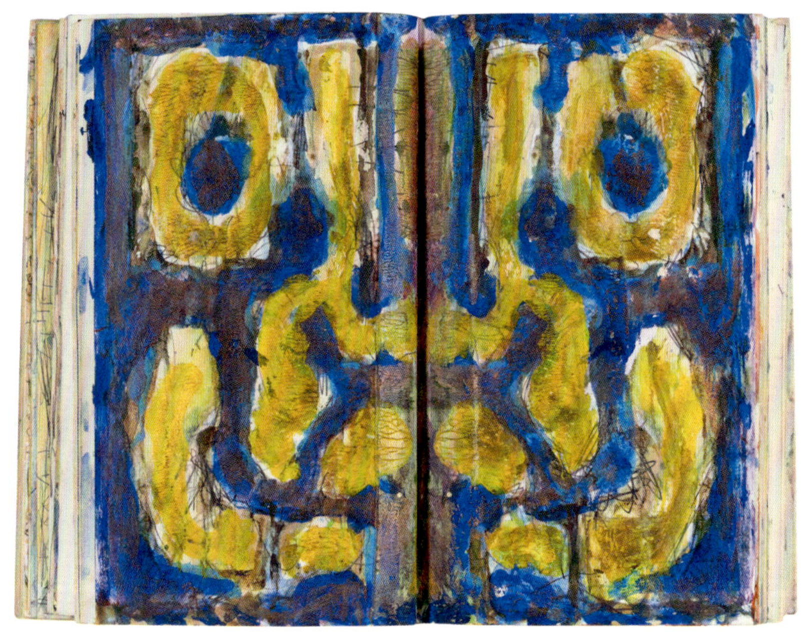

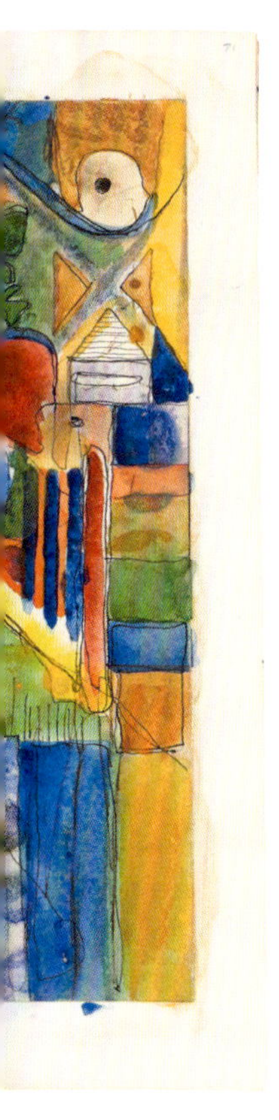

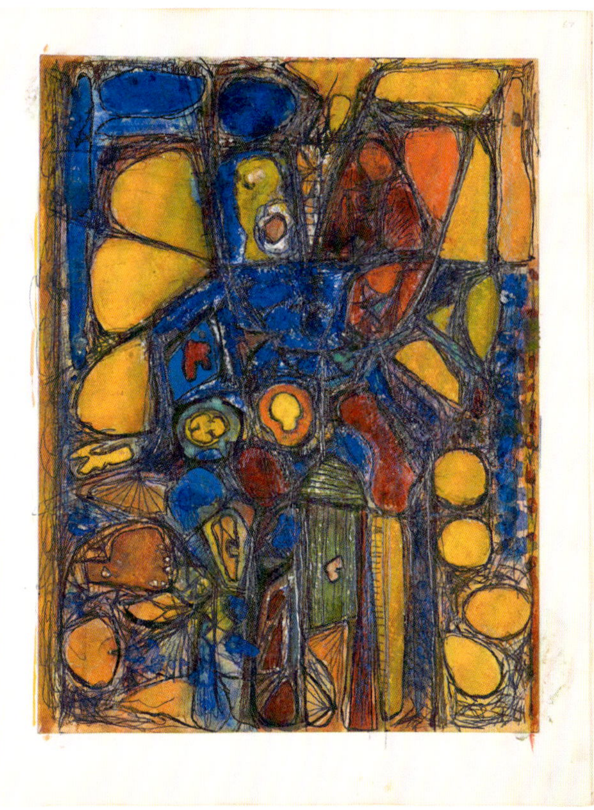

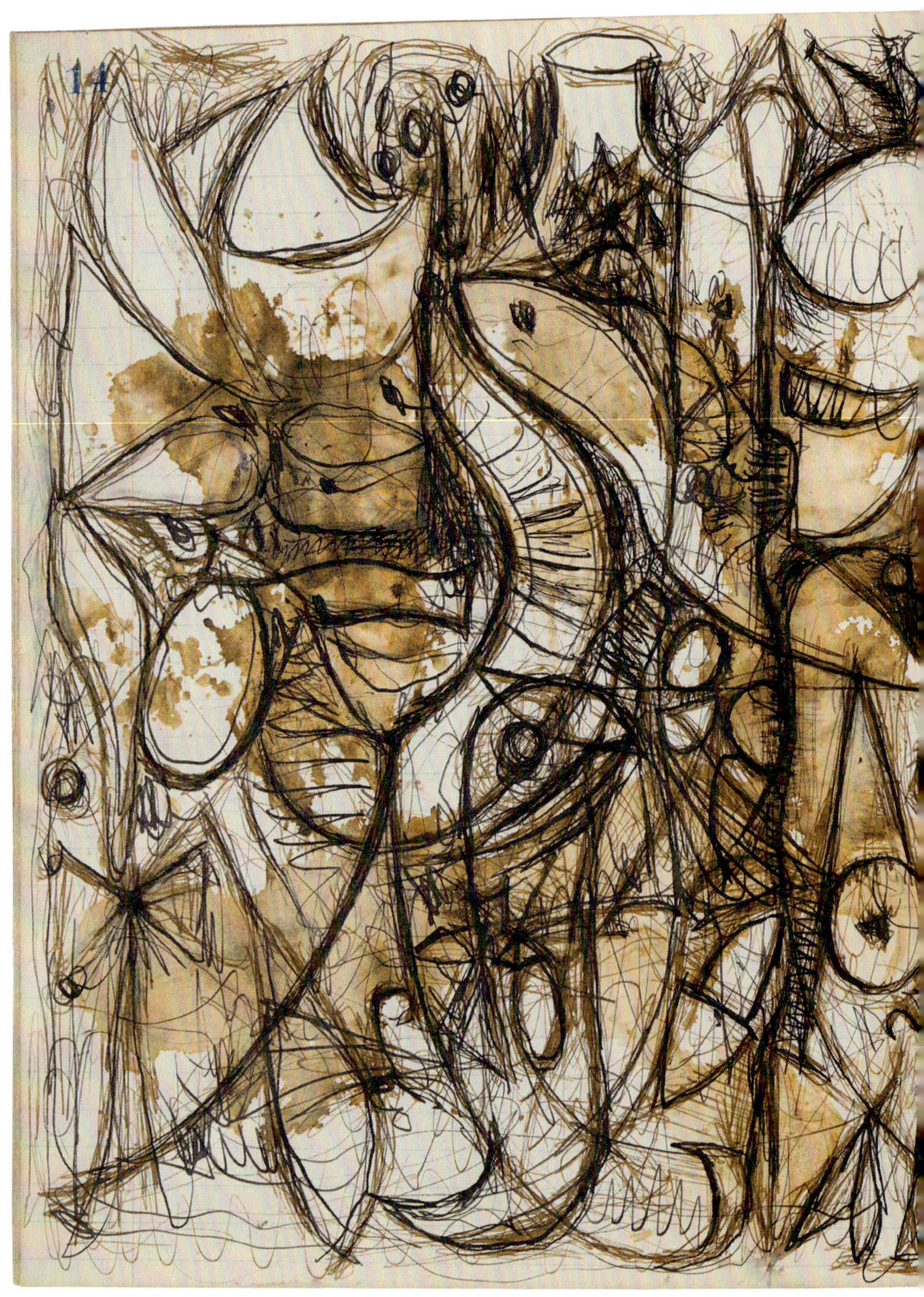

Cat. 133 *Notebook B-212*, 1940s, pp. 14–15, mixed media, 24.8 × 40.6 cm

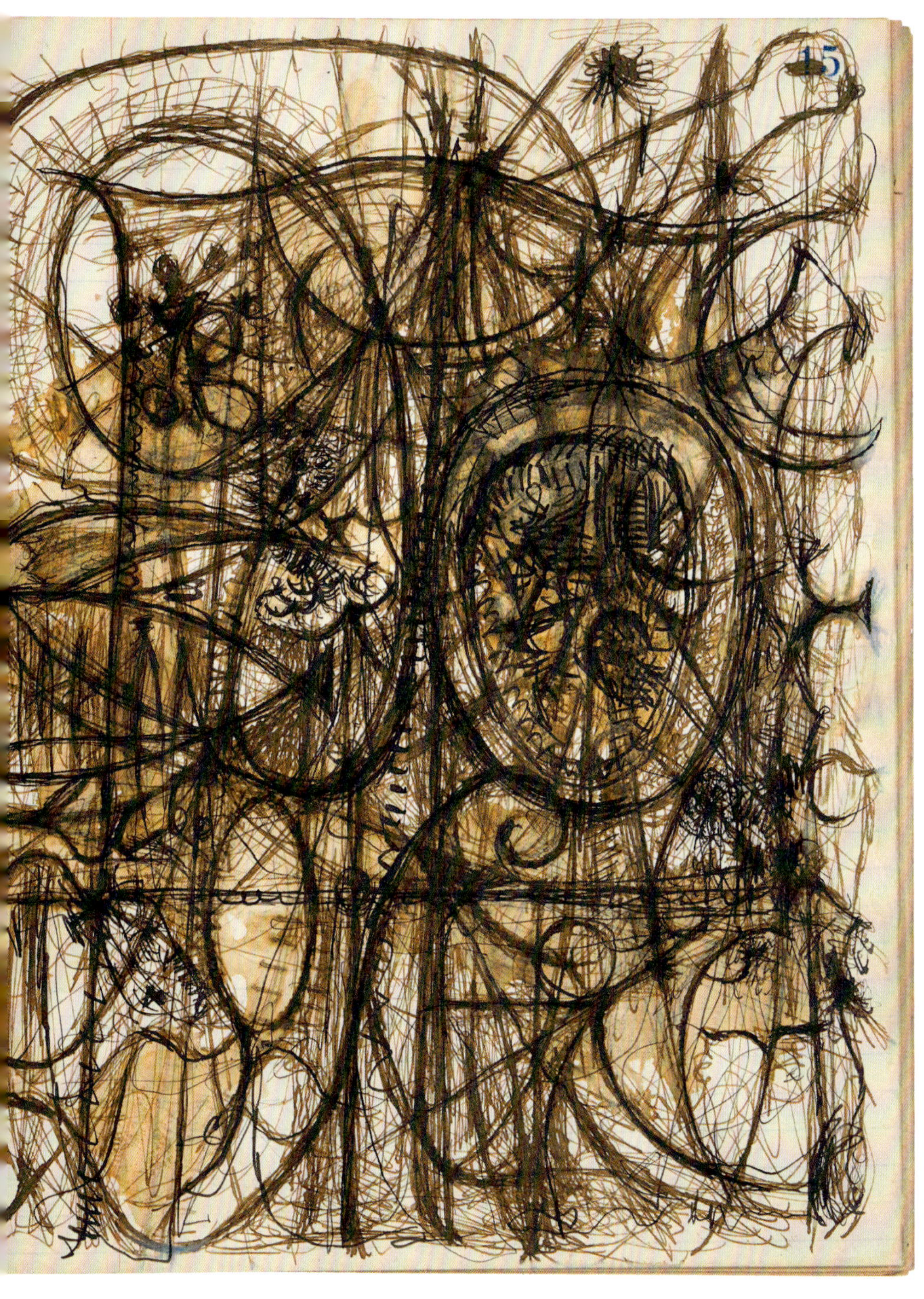
15

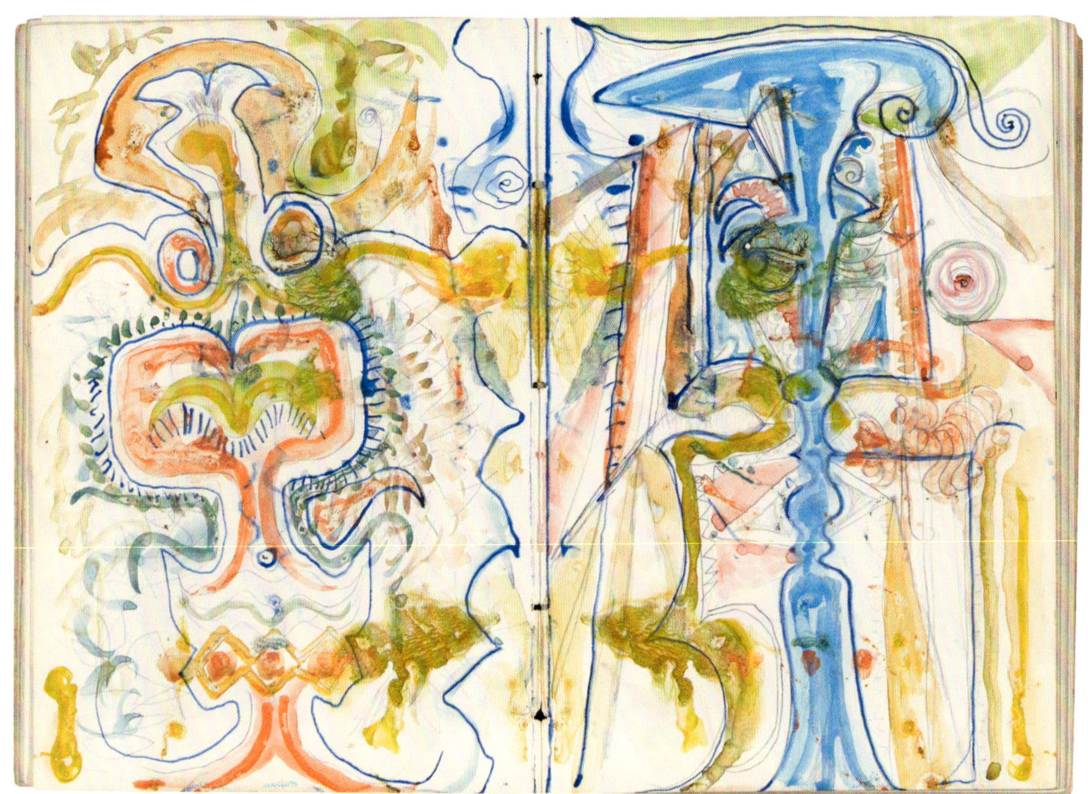

Cat. 134 *Notebook B-114*, 1940s, pp. 120–21, mixed media, 22.9 × 33 cm

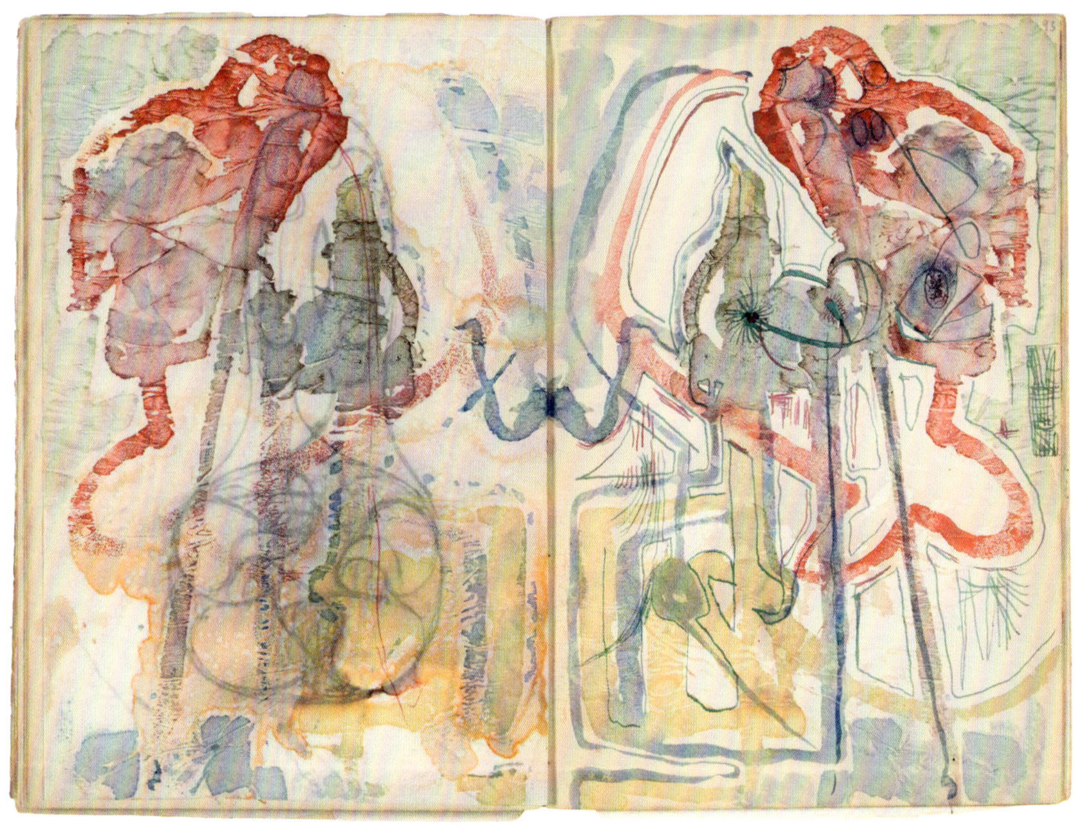

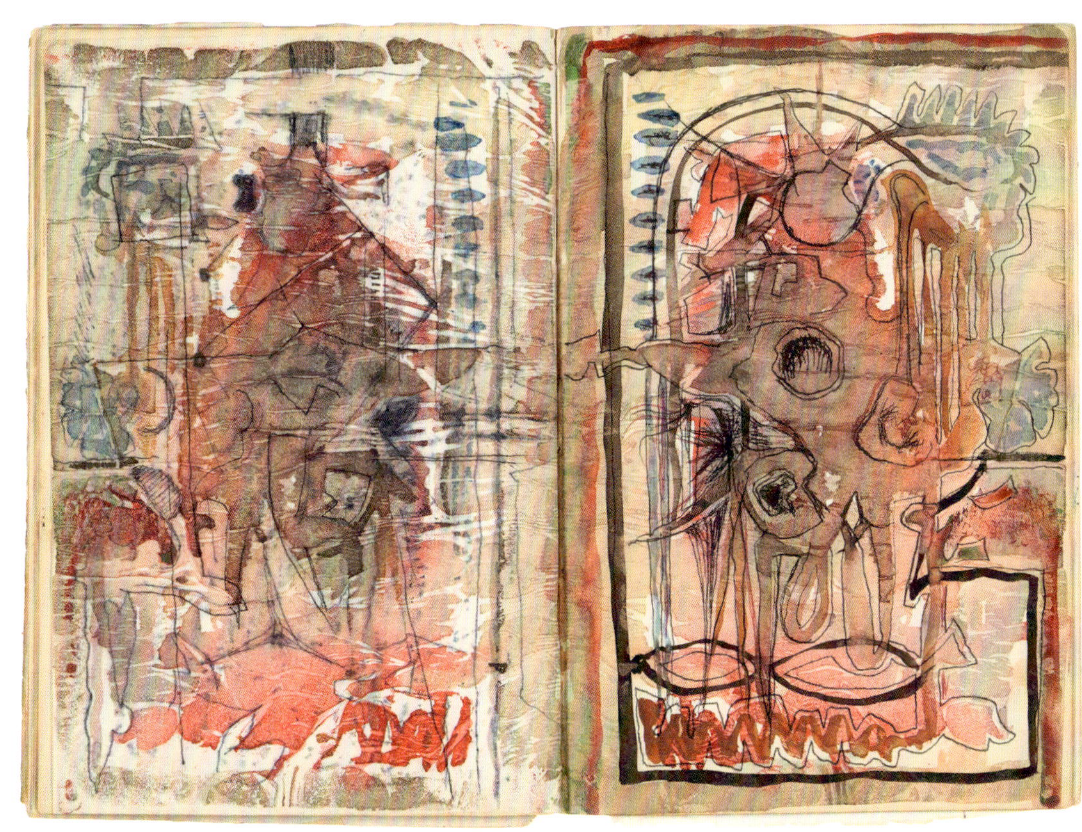

Cat. 135 *Notebook B-294*, 1940s, pp. 92–93, 96–97, mixed media, 23.5 × 33 cm

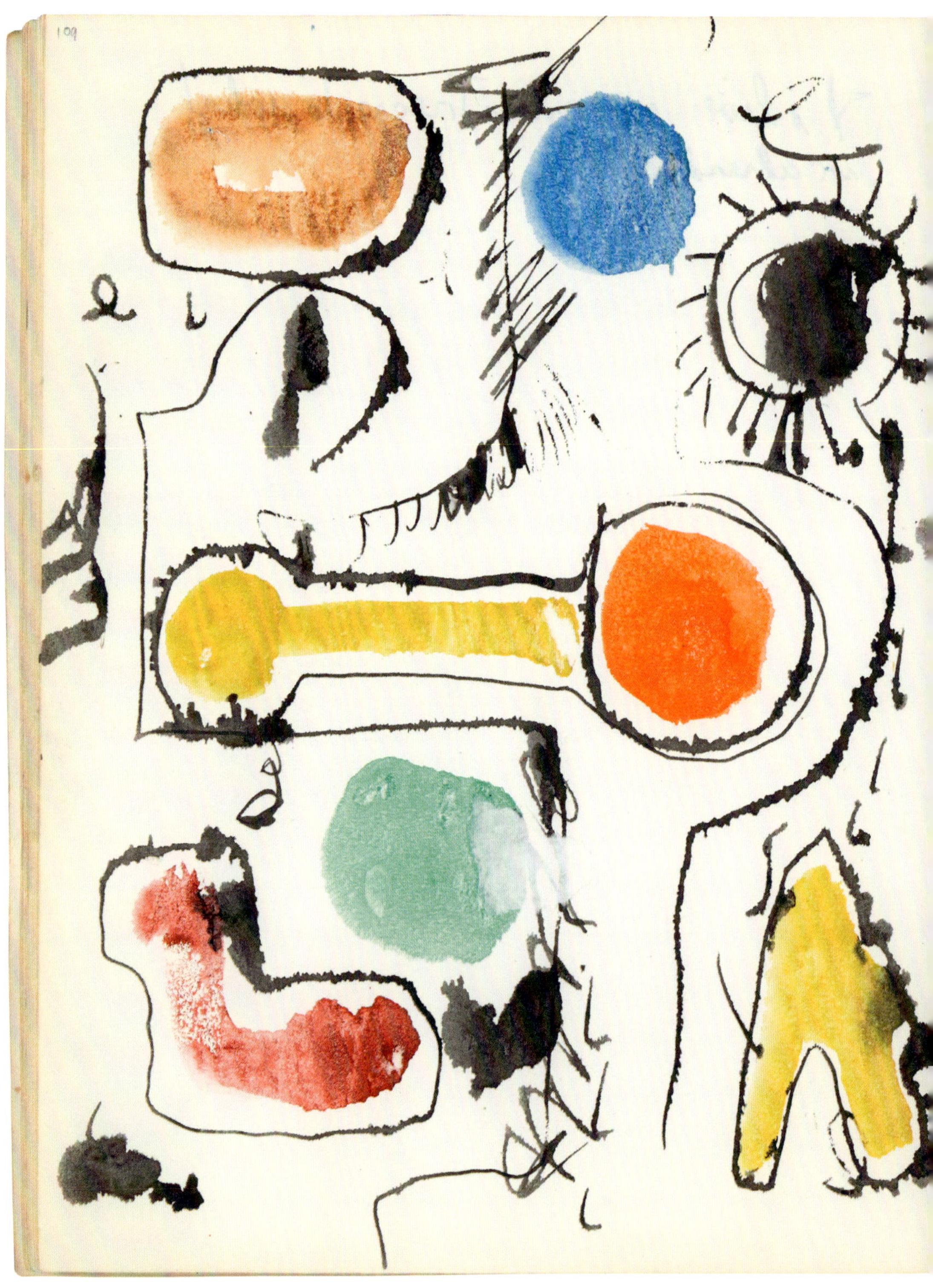

Cat. 136 *Notebook B-87,* 1950s, pp. 109–10, mixed media, 27.9 × 43.2 cm

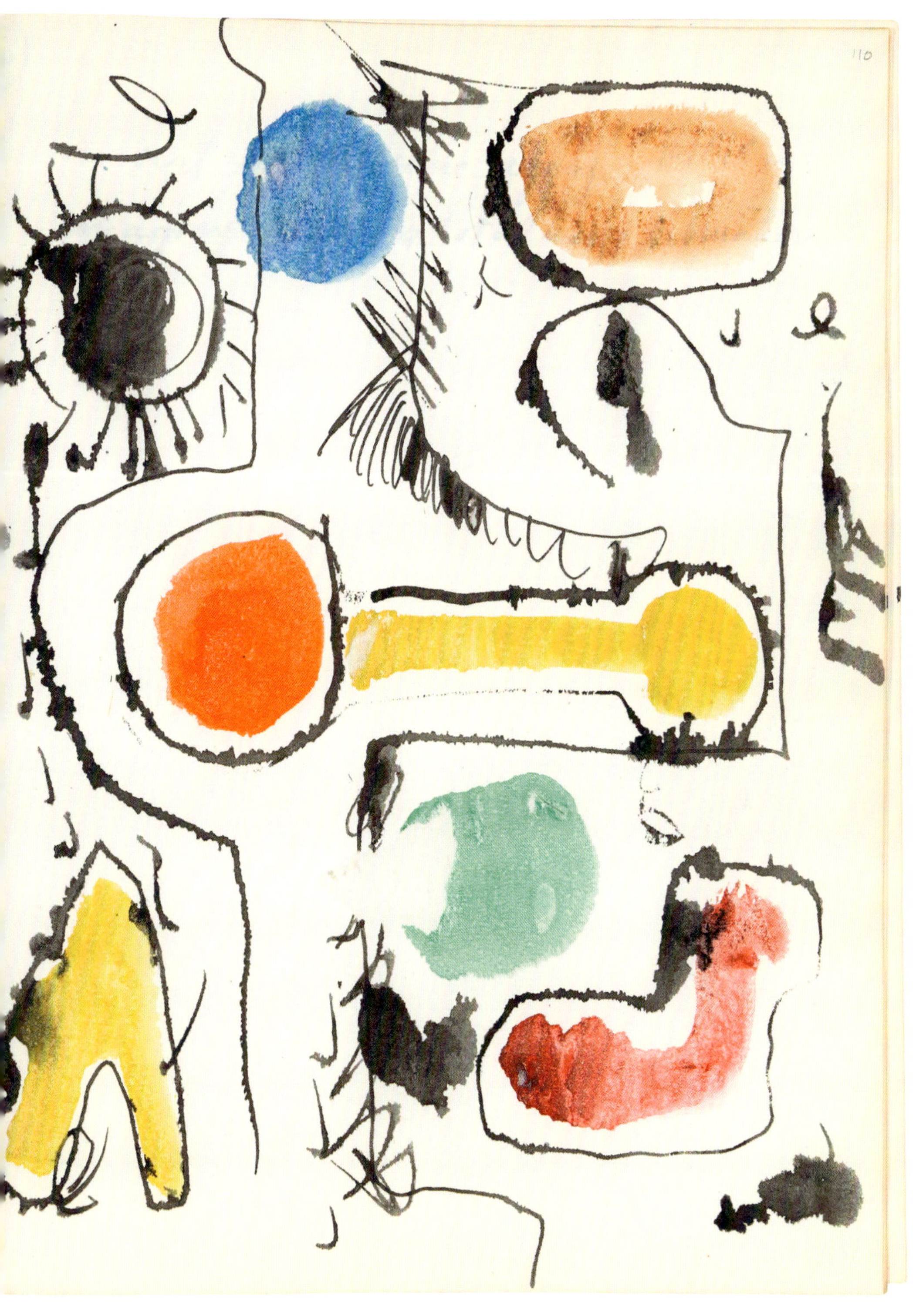

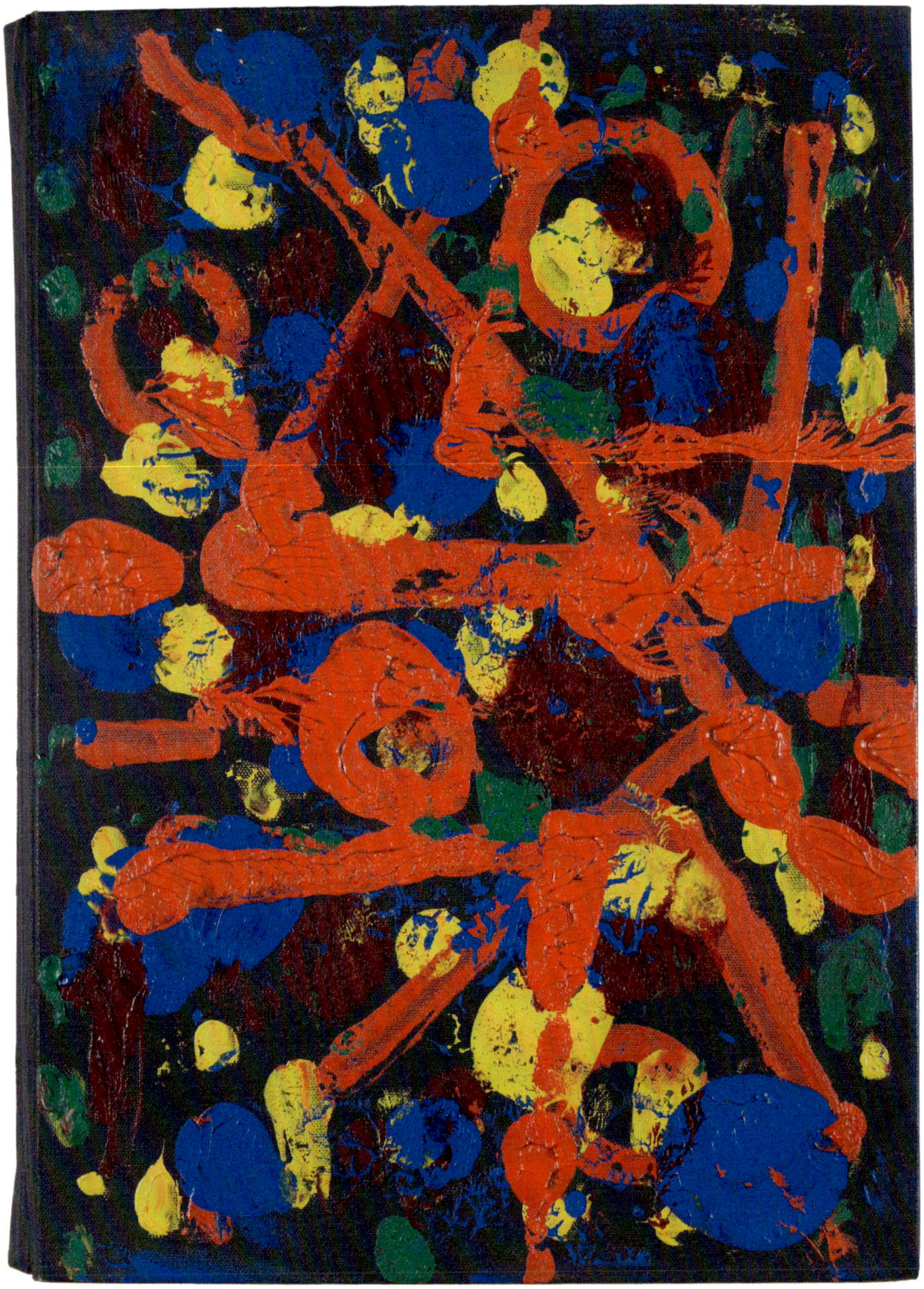

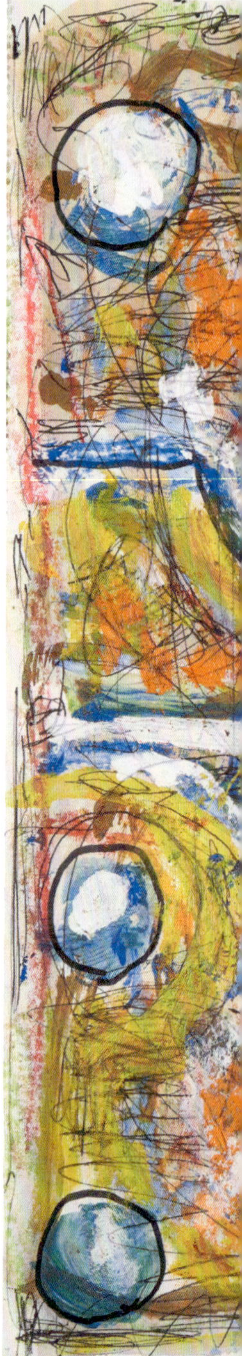

Cat. 137 *Notebook B-280*, 1990s, cover and pp. 1–2, mixed media, 31.4 × 47.6 cm

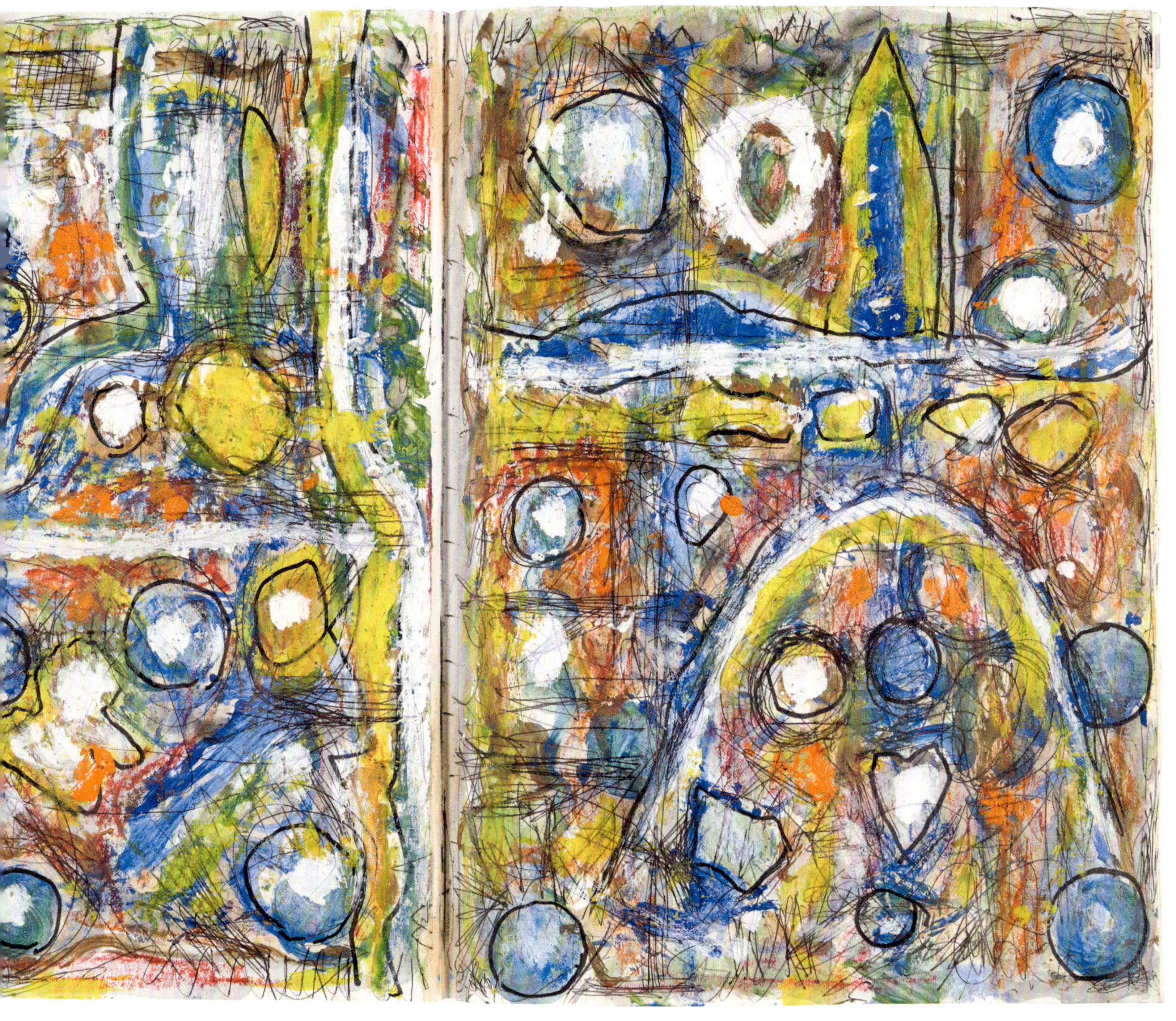

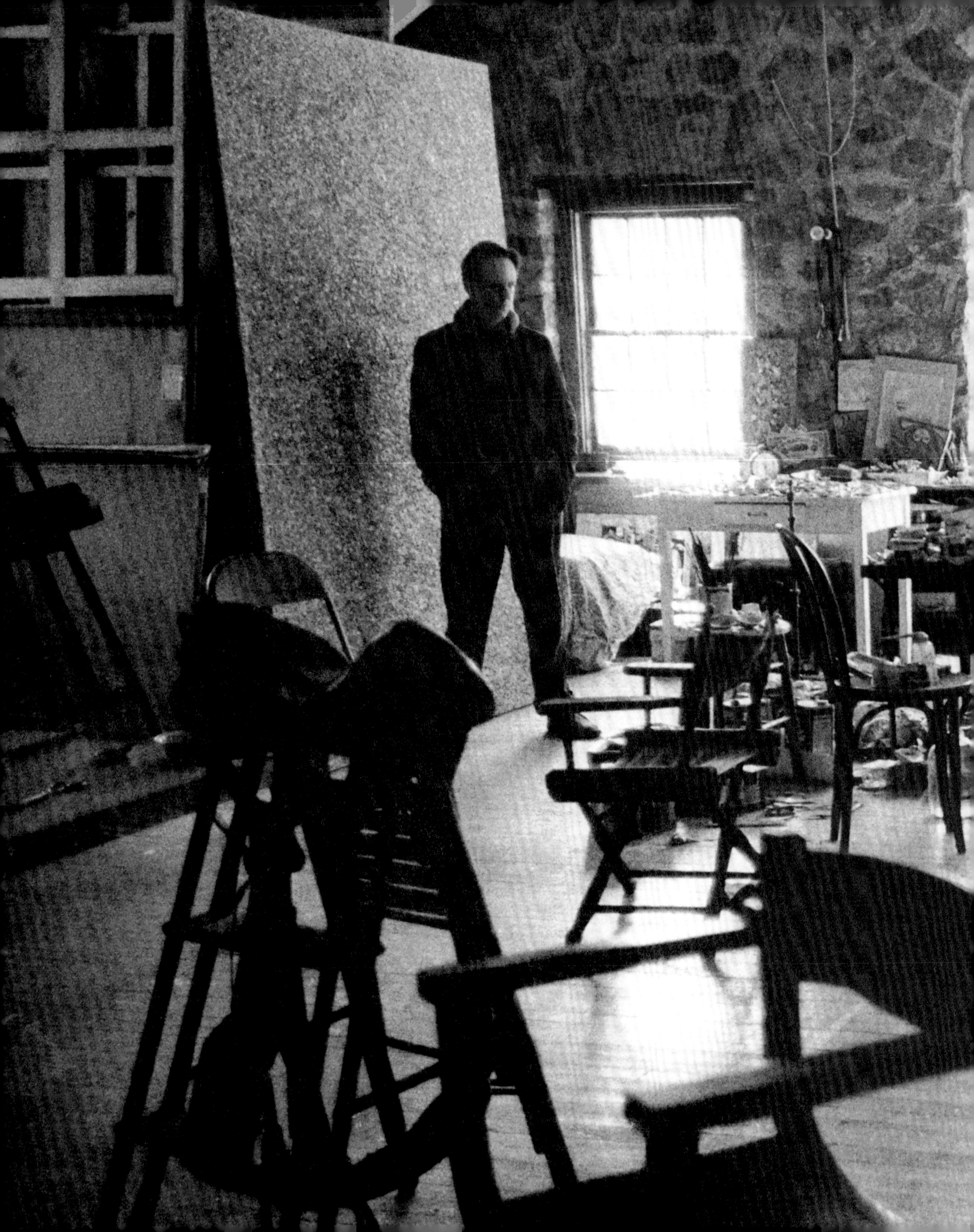

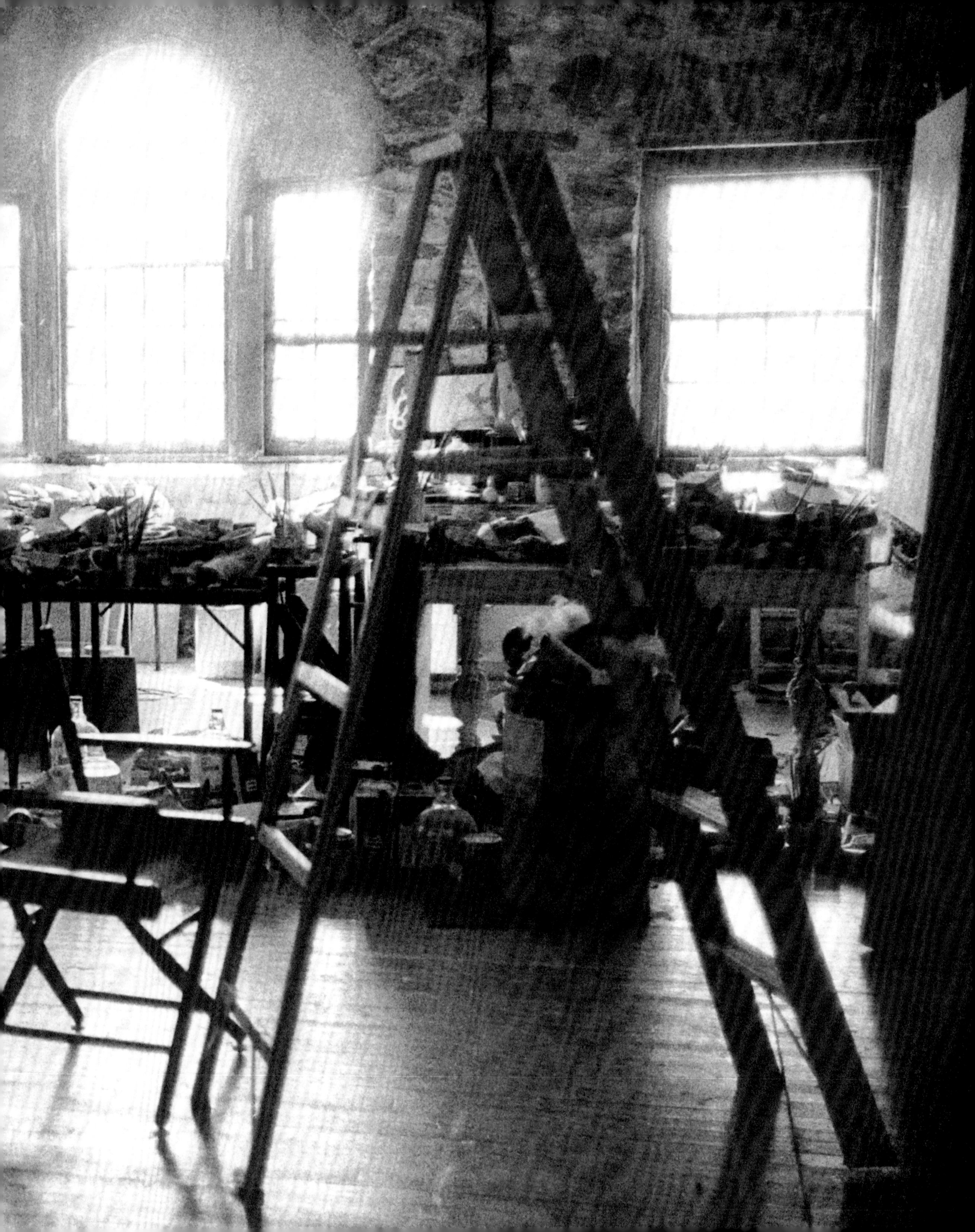

Chronology

Charles H. Duncan

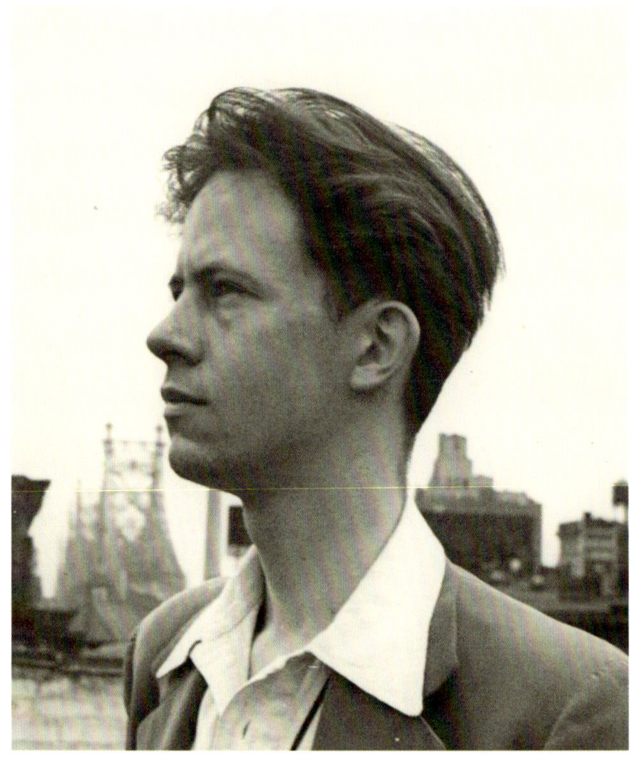

Fig. 1

Richard Pousette-Dart, early 1940s, photographer unknown

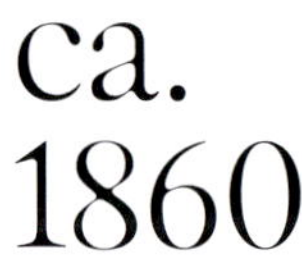

ca. 1860 Richard Pousette-Dart's paternal grandparents, Algot E. Pousette and Mathilda (née Nilson) emigrate to Minnesota from Sweden. Algot is a silversmith and painter of French Huguenot ancestry. They have three children: Nathaniel, Olga, and Charles.

1913 Richard's parents, Nathaniel Pousette (1886–1965) and Flora Louise Dart (1887–1969), are married in Saint Paul, Minnesota, combining their names in a gesture of mutual admiration. Nathaniel is trained as a fine artist at the Pennsylvania Academy of Fine Arts, and at the time of Richard's birth he is an instructor at the College of St. Catherine and the St. Paul Institute. Flora is active as a suffragette and frequently publishes poems and essays in local Minnesota newspapers on socialism, ethics, gender equality, and art discourse.

1916 Richard Warren Pousette-Dart is born on June 8 in Saint Paul, Minnesota. He has two sisters: Dora Louise is older, and Helen is younger.

1918 The Pousette-Dart family moves to Valhalla, New York. Nathaniel exhibits his paintings and watercolors in New York City. For six years he serves as an art director at the J. Walter Thompson Company and other New York advertising firms, and for the following twenty-six years he is the director and owner of his own advertising art business.

1924 Encouraged by his father, Richard begins painting at the age of eight, and by the age of ten his pencil sketches show a strong artistic talent.

1928 Nathaniel Pousette-Dart and twelve-year-old Richard are photographed drawing each other's portraits, and the father-son image appears in sixteen newspapers nationally, including *The New York Times* (see p. 13, fig. 1). In an assignment for an English class titled "What I Would Like to Be," Richard states, "I would like to be an artist and go to an art school. I would like to do oil painting. When I get old enough I would like to go abroad and study art."[1]

1931–35 Attends the Scarborough School, Scarborough-on-Hudson, New York. For a paper in a psychology course titled "Personality in Art," he discusses the power of abstract art to express universal truths: "The greater a work of art, the more abstract and impersonal it is, the more it embodies universal experience, and the fewer specific personality traits it reveals."[2] For his senior class magazine, *The Beechwood Tree*, he contributes the essay "I Have Been Called a Dreamer," his first published anti-war statement in what becomes a lifelong commitment to pacifism. Mechanically inclined, he begins building and operating ham radios (fig. 2) and becomes a member of the American Radio Relay League.

1935 Enrolls in Bard College, Annandale-on-Hudson, New York, but withdraws before the end of the first semester to pursue his own educational program as an artist. While at Bard he is employed as a telephone switchboard operator.

1936 Develops a keen interest in abstract sculpture by Gaston Lachaise, Reuben Nakian, and especially French-born British artist Henri Gaudier-Brzeska. Begins carving abstract figurative stone and wood sculptures and over the next four years executes thousands of study drawings. He begins to keep notebooks that he populates with poetry, philosophical writings, and sketches. While living with his family in Valhalla, he frequently travels to the Metropolitan Museum of Art and the American Museum of Natural History to study the iconography and styles of a wide variety of cultures.

1937 Becomes an assistant to sculptor Paul Manship, a lifelong friend of his father's, and moves to Manhattan. He assists Manship in the creation of lettering for the large-scale bronze public sculpture *Celestial Sphere*, commissioned for the grounds of the Palais des Nations, today the seat of the United Nations Office, in Geneva. Inspired by Henri Gaudier-Brzeska's practice, he begins to create small brass sculptures in biomorphic and geometric forms (cats. 54–96). These "brasses" become central to his working practice across different media and are significant in the formation of his overall visual vocabulary. He meets and becomes close friends with John D. Graham, a Russian-born artist and author of *System and Dialectics of Art*, who serves as a mentor to several of the emerging Abstract Expressionist artists. Nathaniel Pousette-Dart founds and serves as editor of the magazine *Art and Artists of Today*, and Richard Pousette-Dart's sculpture *Tennessee Marble* (1937) is featured in the November–December 1937 issue.[3] Nathaniel simultaneously founds the Art Adventure League, a correspondence school for visual arts instruction.

1938—41 Works as a secretary in the Manhattan studio of Lynn T. Morgan, an art director, painter, and printmaker who specialized in retouching black-and-white and color photographs. The appointment provides training in detailed manual manipulation of photographic prints and negatives, and the discipline of scrutinizing the enlarged granular structure of film reveals to him that "all form is made up of so many points of light and that everything has a molecular structure," a phenomenon that becomes integral to his painting technique from the 1960s onward that concentrates on the application of multitudinous dabs of pigment.[4]

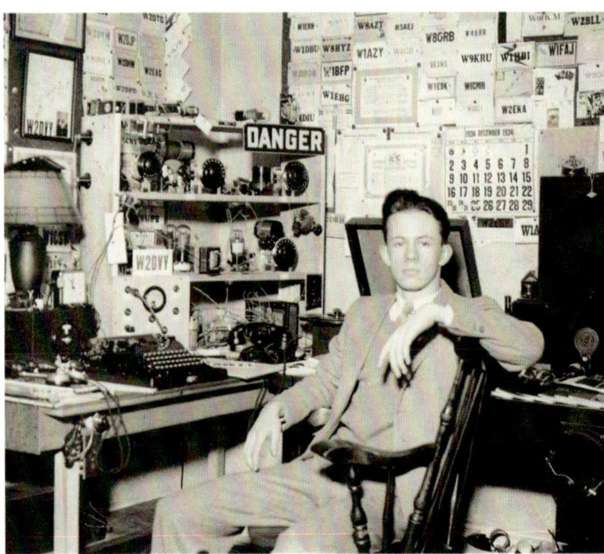

Fig. 2

Richard Pousette-Dart with radios, ca. 1935, photographer unknown

1939 Marries Blanche Grady, a dancer, model, and artist, and they live at 210 East Twenty-Second Street in Manhattan.

1940 Begins to develop a fine-art photographic practice and photographs John and Constance Graham; his mother, Flora; and close friends. In New York, he meets British historian H. S. (Jim) Ede, author of *Savage Messiah: Gaudier-Brzeska*, and the two men initiate a robust correspondence that lasts for more than forty years. Having limited resources for acquiring quality stone for direct carving, he shifts his artistic concentration to painting and drawing.

1941 First solo exhibition, primarily of abstract paintings that feature semifigurative forms defined by heavy outline, is held at the Artists' Gallery in New York. The Artists' Gallery was a nonprofit venue that afforded artists exhibition space free of charge plus income from the sale of their works, and was sponsored by Clive Bell, Meyer Schapiro, and James Johnson Sweeney. His marriage to Blanche Grady is annulled. Pousette-Dart becomes deeply engaged in anti-war activities, writing numerous pacifist tracts and attending conscientious objector gatherings at Quaker meeting houses. He registers for the draft but is relieved of miliary service due to his beliefs.

1942 Meets and marries Lydia R. Modi, a painter, and they live at 436 East Fifty-Sixth Street, New York. His painting and drawing moves confidently toward allover abstract compositions of interlocking forms and dense line. He completes *Symphony No. 1, The Transcendental* (p. 15, fig. 4), widely regarded as the first epic-scale easel painting by an Abstract Expressionist artist.

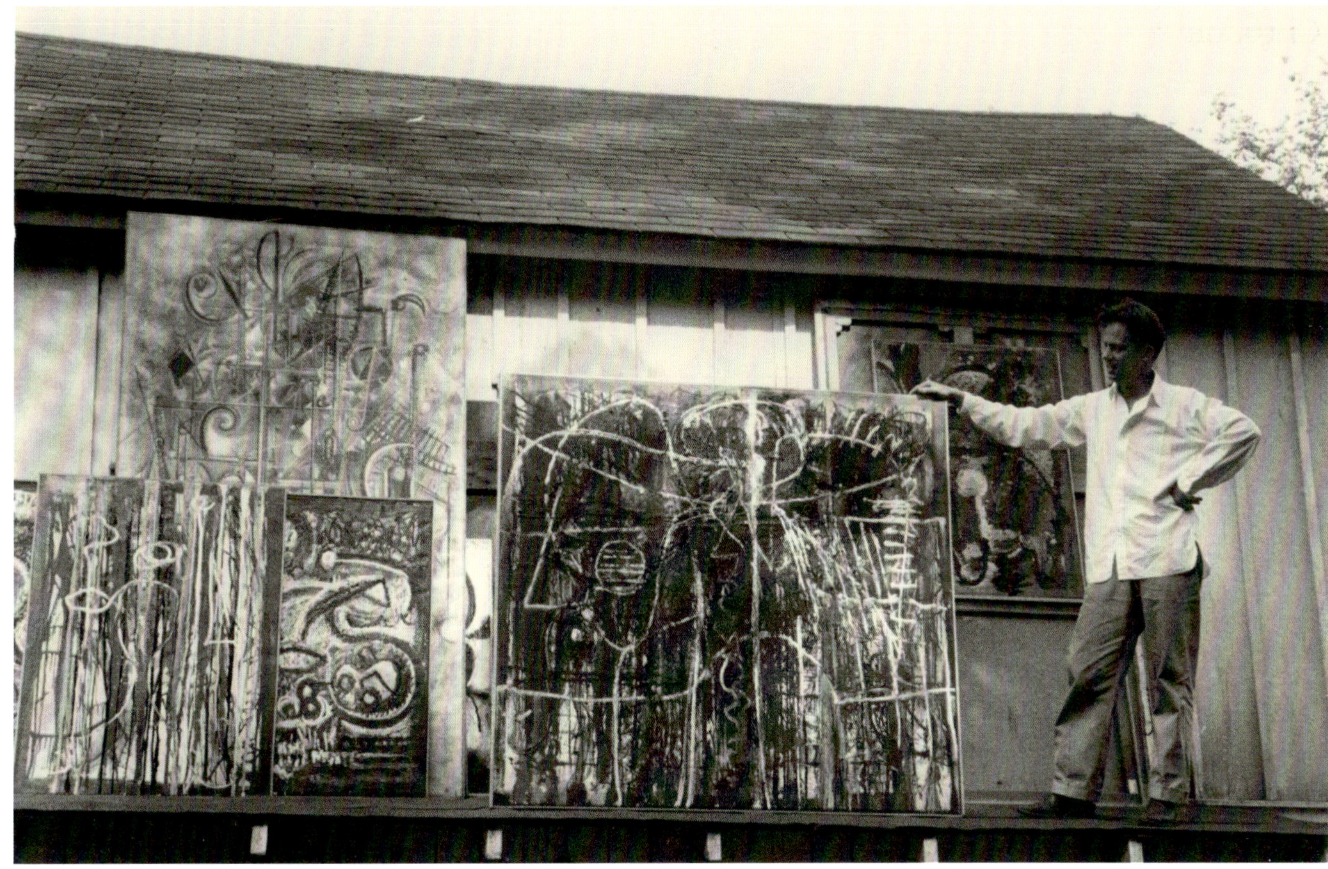

Fig. 3
Richard Pousette-Dart outside his studio, Sloatsburg, New York, 1951, photograph by Diane and Ray Witlin

1943 Begins a formal relationship with the Willard Gallery, located on 32 East Fifty-Seventh Street in New York, where he has four solo shows during the next three years. The gallery specializes in modern art and shows work by Paul Klee, Lyonel Feininger, Alexander Calder, and David Smith, among others. His first show there, in October, features brasses.

1944 Exhibits in *Spring Salon for Young Artists* at Art of This Century, a gallery founded by Peggy Guggenheim that showcased avant-garde work by New York and European artists. In October, his work is included in *Forty American Moderns* at Howard Putzel's 67 Gallery alongside paintings by Jackson Pollock, Mark Rothko, Robert Motherwell, and Hans Hofmann. This exhibition is one of the earliest group presentations of artists who will form the nucleus of the New York School. He participates in the annual exhibition at the Federation of Modern Painters and Sculptors, an organization formed to promote aesthetic values rather than political actions commonly championed by such organizations. His father, Nathaniel Pousette-Dart, is a founding member of the Federation.

1945 Exhibits in the 67 Gallery exhibition *A Problem for Critics* along with Arshile Gorky, Adolph Gottlieb, Hans Hofmann, Lee Krasner, and Mark Rothko. His solo exhibition *7 Paintings* takes place at the Willard Gallery, and his work is included in the *Autumn Salon* at Art of This Century.

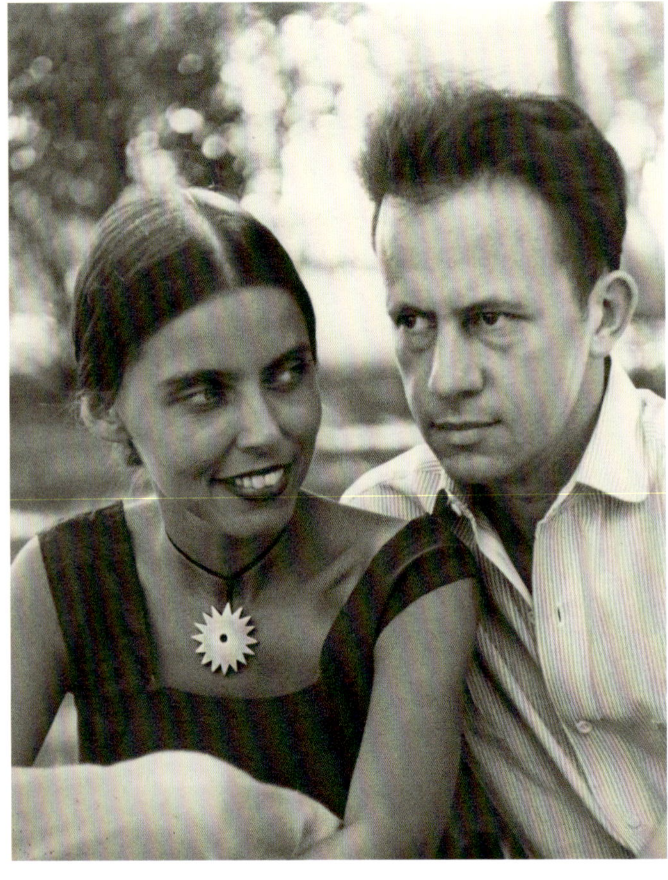

Fig. 4

Evelyn and Richard Pousette-Dart, ca. 1950s, photographer unknown

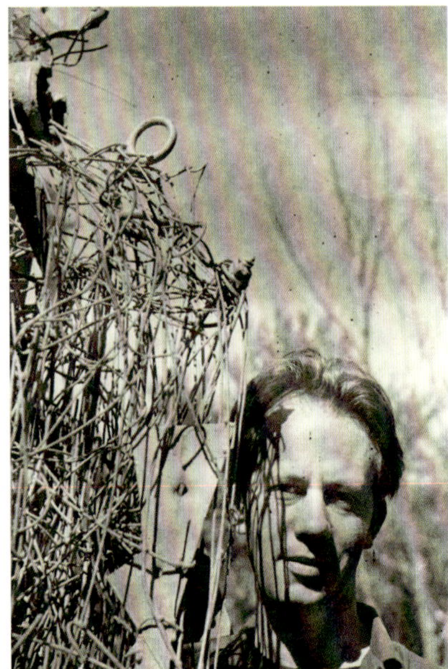

Fig. 5

Richard Pousette-Dart, self-portrait with *Apparition*, 1951

1946 His brasses are exhibited in *Modern Handmade Jewelry* at the Museum of Modern Art, New York. The solo exhibition *Richard Pousette-Dart: Paintings and Gouaches* at the Willard Gallery features the paintings *Animal Forms* (cat. 2), *Forestness* (cat. 8), and *Spirit Adagio* (cat. 4).

1947 Marriage to Lydia Modi ends in divorce. Marries Evelyn Gracey, a poet and English teacher. Their first child, Joanna, is born. His solo exhibition at Art of This Century takes place in March and includes *Crucifixion, Comprehension of the Atom* (cat. 6) and *The Center* (cat. 5). It is the first exhibition to feature *Symphony No. 1, The Transcendental*, which proved too large to exhibit at the Willard Gallery. His work is included in the *58th Annual Exhibition* at the Art Institute of Chicago and the *Annual Exhibition* at the Pennsylvania Academy of the Fine Arts. He expands his photographic practice dramatically, converting his apartment kitchen into a darkroom during the evening and experiments with avant-garde techniques, such as double exposure. Saul Leiter, who had recently moved to New York City to study painting, becomes a frequent visitor and learns the rigors of photographic practice through Pousette-Dart.

1948 Joins the Betty Parsons Gallery, which opened in 1946, one of the leading promoters of Abstract Expressionist artists, including Jackson Pollock, Mark Rothko, Ad Reinhardt, and Bradley Walker Tomlin. His exhibition *Brasses and Photographs* at Parsons is the first to feature his photographic work. He develops a friendship and strong working relationship with Parsons, staging sixteen solo shows with her through 1974. His painting *Spirit* (1946, Tel Aviv Museum of Art, Israel), which had been acquired by Peggy Guggenheim, is shown at the twenty-fourth

Venice Biennale. He is elected treasurer of the Federation of Modern Painters and Sculptors and attends occasional meetings and lectures at an informal school in Greenwich Village, New York City, called "Subjects of the Artist." This group becomes known as the Eighth Street Club and is one of the main organizations for New York School artists.

1949 The Museum of Modern Art includes his work in the exhibition *Modern American Painting: Movements and Countermovements.* He becomes a regular exhibitor in the Whitney Museum of American Art's *Annual Exhibition of Contemporary American Sculpture, Watercolors and Drawings.* His brasses are exhibited at the University Gallery at the University of Minnesota. By this time, Pousette-Dart's painting assumes a wide variety of forms, including canvases that feature diffuse, centralized abstract imagery that the artist calls Presences.

1950 *Number 11: A Presence* is purchased by the Museum of Modern Art, the first acquisition of a painting by a major museum. He participates in a three-day symposium for artists organized by Studio 35, an artist-run organization. He and other New York artists sign a letter penned by Adolph Gottlieb to protest the conservative bias toward contemporary art by the Metropolitan Museum of Art. The statement, *Open Letter to Roland L. Redmond,* dated May 20, appears on the front page of *The New York Times* on May 22. In December, the Pousette-Dart family relocates to a farmhouse on Eagle Valley Road in the rural community of Sloatsburg, New York. Here, he establishes a photography workshop and converts the second floor of the garage into a painting studio. Initially ambivalent about withdrawing from Manhattan, he comes to appreciate the setting as a refuge that affords space and quietude to concentrate on multiple artistic pursuits.

1951 *Life* magazine publishes a photo story on January 15 in response to interest created by *The New York Times* protest letter of May 1950. He is included in a group portrait by Nina Leen known as *The Irascibles* that defines the main cohort of first-generation Abstract Expressionist painters (see p. 35, fig. 1). Pousette-Dart participates in *Exhibition of American Abstractionists Loaned by the Parsons Gallery* at the School of the Museum of Fine Arts, Boston. As part of exhibition programming, he travels to Boston, where he addresses the student body through a well-defined artist's statement drawn from his notebooks. He is awarded a prestigious Guggenheim Fellowship to pursue creative painting and crafts a series of freestanding sculptures from steel wire and found objects. He participates in *9th Street: Exhibition of Paintings and Sculpture* at the 9th Street Gallery, New York, which is instrumental in establishing the critical recognition of Abstract Expressionism. *Look* magazine publishes an in-depth profile on the artist titled "Spontaneous Kaleidoscopes" and featuring his paintings, wire sculptures, and brasses.[5]

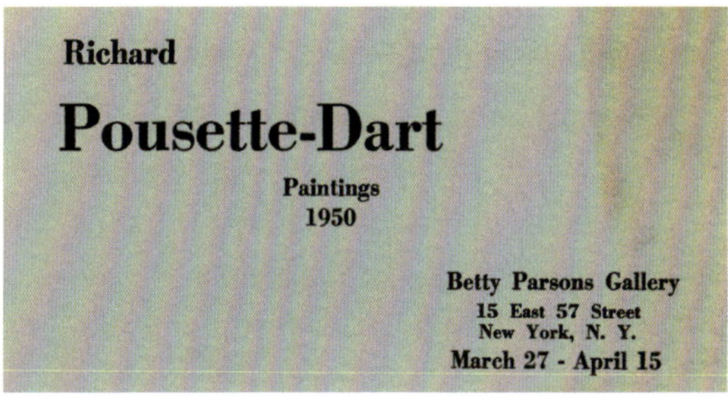

Fig. 6

Exhibition announcement, *Richard Pousette-Dart: Paintings*, Betty Parsons Gallery, 1950

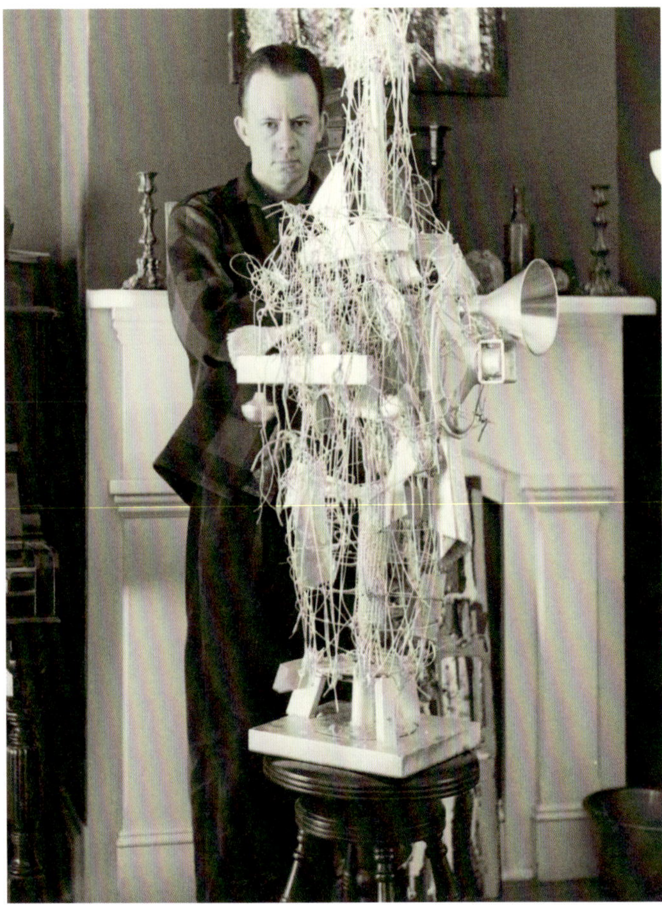

Fig. 7

Richard Pousette-Dart, self-portrait with *The Artist*, ca. 1953

1952 The sculpture *Woman with Horn* (1951, private collection) is included in the exhibition *Musical Themes* organized by the Museum of Modern Art, which travels to thirteen venues. The Union Theological Seminary, New York, organizes *An Exhibition of Contemporary Religious Art and Architecture* that includes Pousette-Dart's painting *The Magnificent* (cat. 19) as well as his drawings and brasses. There, he delivers a talk titled "What Is the Relationship Between Religion and Art?" in which he addresses the spiritual aspects of art-making: "Art is always mystical in its final meaning; it is structure which stands up by the presence and significance of its own reality. It is a thing within itself, mirroring different things to different minds, stemming from and in accord with every work of art ever created, a thing of awe and wonder and whose meaning is the measure of man's estate on earth."[6] His second child, Jonathan, is born in June.

1953 He is awarded third prize in *Photography* magazine's international picture contest for the image *Joanna with Cat* (cat. 120). *Photography* magazine publishes an extensive profile on Pousette-Dart, and his photographic work becomes sought after by publications, including *Vogue* and *Charm*.[7] The Whitney Museum of American Art acquires *The Magnificent* (cat. 19), the first of eight works by the artist to enter the museum's permanent collection.

1955 His brasses are featured in "Four Artists as Jewelers" in *Craft Horizons* magazine alongside the work of Alexander Calder.[8] Pousette-Dart continues to receive requests for photographic portraiture but accepts commissions only selectively. Among his sitters are choreographer Bob Fosse and jazz musicians Roy Eldridge and Thad Jones. *Richard Pousette-Dart: Predominantly White Paintings* opens at the Betty Parsons Gallery. This exhibition focuses on a body of work now known as White Paintings that are characterized by compositions of graphite line on variegated white grounds with occasional applications of tints of color and includes *Descending Bird Forms* (cat. 16), *White Garden, Number 3* (1950, private collection), and *Presence Number 5* (cat. 15).

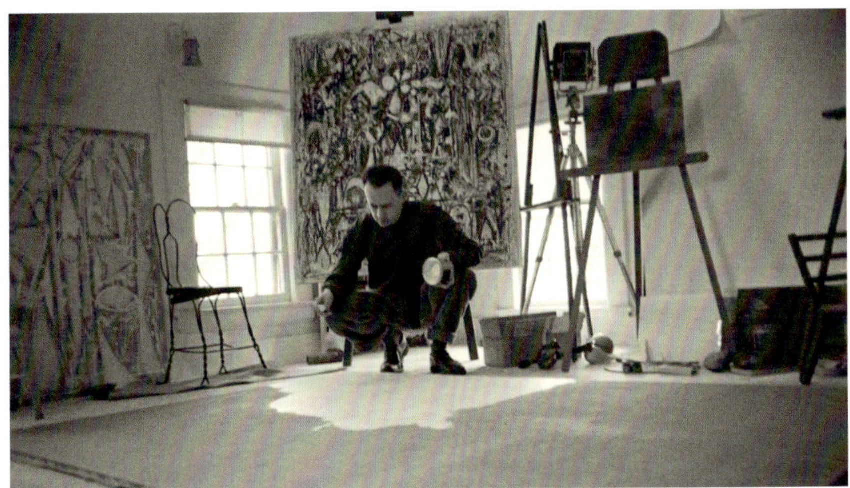

Fig. 8

Richard Pousette-Dart, self-portrait in studio, Monsey, New York, 1957

1956 The Pousette-Dart family moves to a larger home on Christmas Hill Road in Monsey, New York. Here he establishes a painting studio on the upper level of the house and uses the enclosed front porch to create large-scale paintings. He begins to paint colorful, densely painted canvases suggestive of stained-glass windows that become known as Gothic and Byzantine Paintings. He lectures at the Skowhegan School of Painting and Sculpture, Maine, speaking for the first time about his photographic practice. *Illumination Gothic* (cat. 18) is included in *The Second in a Series of Exhibitions of Painting & Sculpture: David Smith, Jackson Pollock, Mark Rothko, Richard Pousette-Dart, Alfonso Ossorio* at the Executive House, New York.

1958 He begins to offer courses in painting instruction at his home in Monsey and organizes an exhibition for thirteen of his students at the Rockland County Center for Mental Health, Monsey. His work is included in the Whitney Museum of American Art exhibition *Nature in Abstraction*.

1959 He begins a two-year faculty appointment at the New School for Social Research, New York. The description notes, "The course emphasizes individual expression and realization in painting. It strives for personal development and inner vision on the basis of each student's experience."[9] Awarded a Ford Foundation Grant and exhibits in the *Ford Foundation Jury Exhibition*. Exhibits three paintings in *Documenta II '59: Art After 1945*, in Kassel, Germany, including *Amaranth* (cat. 23). In December, he purchases a 1916 stone carriage house on Haverstraw Road in Suffern, New York, and converts the large upper story loft into a studio. He works and lives with his family at this residence until his death in 1992.

1961 Awarded the M. V. Kohnstamm Prize from the Art Institute of Chicago at the *64th Annual American Painting and Sculpture Exhibition* for the painting *Shadow of the Unknown Bird* (1955–58, Colby College Museum of Art, Waterville, Maine). Exhibits in the Museu de Arte Moderna at the sixth Bienal de São Paulo, Brazil. His solo exhibition at the Betty Parsons Gallery, *Richard Pousette-Dart: Paintings* introduces works created primarily by the application of small dabs of paint, signaling a new direction in working methods that became the artist's favored mode of painting for the remainder of his career. His work is included in the traveling exhibition *The Art of Assemblage* organized by the Museum of Modern Art, New York.

1963 The first major museum retrospective of Richard Pousette-Dart's work held at the Whitney Museum of American Art, New York, featuring forty-four paintings spanning four decades. A number of exhibited works, including *Sky Presence, Circle* (cat. 50), are based on celestial themes, and the infinite landscape is a recurring subject.

1964 Teaches graduate painting courses at the School of Visual Arts, New York.

1965 Wins second prize at the *29th Biennial of Contemporary American Painting* at the Corcoran Gallery of Art, Washington, DC. He is awarded an honorary doctorate of Humane Letters by Bard College. Eight of his paintings are included in the exhibition *New York School: The First Generation; Paintings of the 1940s and 1950s* at the Los Angeles County Museum of Art.

1966 Delivers the convocation lecture at the Minneapolis School of Art. Wins the National Council for the Arts Award for Excellence.

1967 Receives the National Endowment for the Arts Award for Individual Artists.

1968 Teaches painting at Columbia University in New York, where he also serves as guest critic.

1969 Included in the Museum of Modern Art exhibition *The New American Painting and Sculpture: The First Generation*.

1969—70 The Museum of Modern Art organizes *Richard Pousette-Dart: Presences*, curated by Lucy Lippard. The exhibition focuses on recently created works, primarily works with dense fields of color, including *Meditation on the Drifting Stars* (cat. 51) and *Within the Moon* (cat. 52). The exhibition travels to ten additional museum venues.

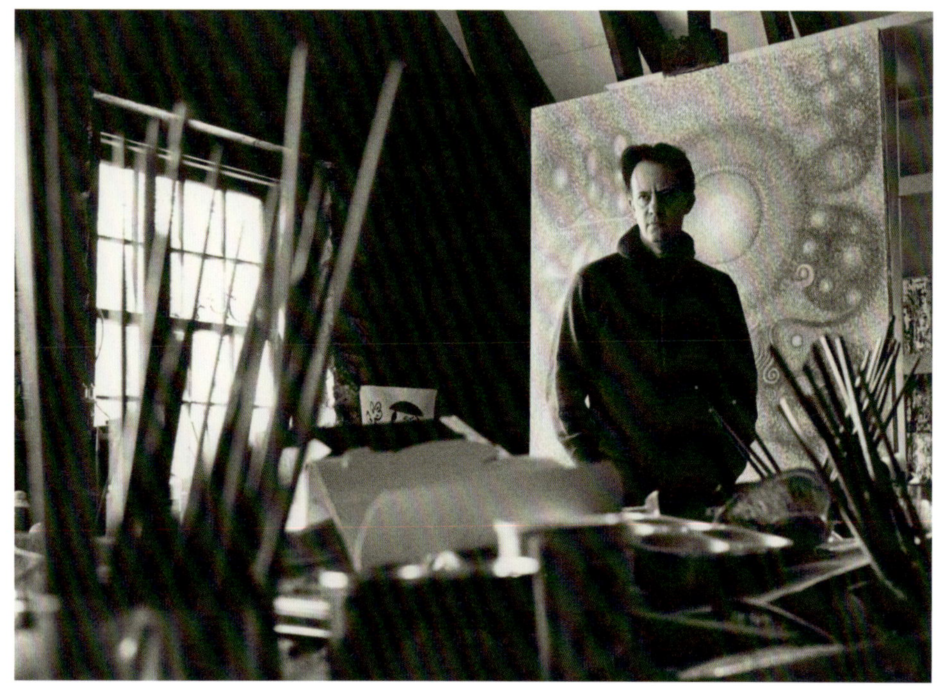

Fig. 9

Richard Pousette-Dart in his studio, Suffern, New York, 1962, photograph by Herb Breuer

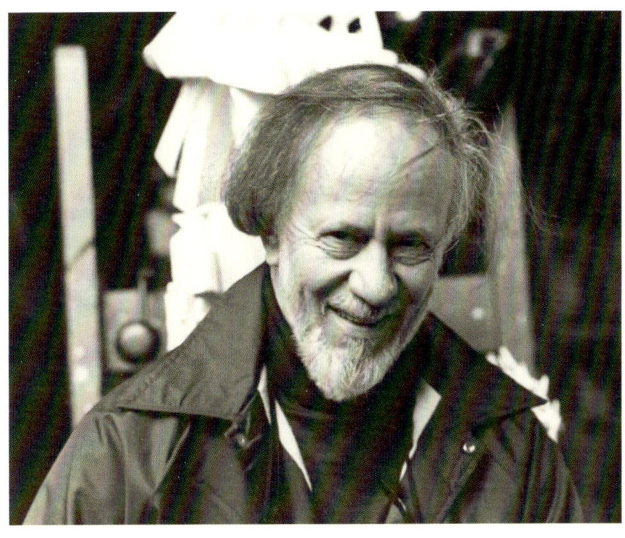

Fig. 10

Richard Pousette-Dart, 1980s, photograph by Franca Rota

1970 Begins a five-year appointment as a faculty member at Sarah Lawrence College, Bronxville, New York, where he teaches painting. At the college he works closely with the curriculum committee as it defines requirements for successful completion of a studio arts degree. He advocates that "the most important goal in any education is real, inner experience; the spark and growth of realization upon the thread of each one's own personality or being."[10] Opposed to the committee's emphasis on technical skill rather than personal development, he resigns in 1975.

1971 Travels to Europe for the first time to visit Paris, Chartres Cathedral, Rome, Florence, London, and Cambridge.

1973 Exhibits with his daughter, Joanna, at the Whitney Museum of American Art *Biennial Exhibition: Contemporary American Art*. He spends two months in Provence, France, as part of the summer program at Sarah Lawrence College. While there he concentrates on watercolors and drawings.

1974 Commissioned to create the large-scale triptych *The Healing Circles* for the North Central Bronx Hospital, New York. The Whitney Museum of American Art organizes a second major exhibition of Pousette-Dart's paintings that focuses on work from 1963 to 1974, including *Red Presence* (cat. 47) and *Hieroglyph Number 7* (cat. 42).

1975 Travels to Antibes, France, and stays near the Picasso Museum. While there he works on watercolors. The Edwin A. Ulrich Museum of Art at the Wichita State University in Kansas organizes *Richard Pousette-Dart: Paintings*. He begins to work intensively on a large body of graphite drawings on paper and canvas.

1978 He is invited to read his poetry at the Museum of Modern Art, where he presents selections from his notebooks and passages from his 1951 Boston address. He begins a series of black-and-white paintings and works on paper that are minimal in form but richly textured with dense and evocative surfaces.

1979 Participates in the symposium "Abstract Expressionism: Idea and Symbol," sponsored by the University of Virginia and including panelists such as Lee Krasner and Robert Motherwell. Working with master printer Sylvia Roth at the Rockland Foundation in Nyack, New York, he initiates an intensive program of fine-art printmaking, a medium he had first experimented with in the late 1930s. He later reworks a large number of etchings adding acrylic, gouache, and charbonnel ink to create unique and often colorful impressions.

1980 Begins teaching at the Art Students League of New York, a position he holds for the remainder of his life. There, he appreciates the freedom and nondegree orientation of the institution, which allow him to pursue his own approach to pedagogy: "I believe not really in teaching, but in creating an environment or condition or atmosphere where people can teach themselves. I love to see people discover themselves and flower in themselves, and that's what keeps me teaching."[11]

1981 Receives the first annual Distinguished Lifetime in Art Award from the Louis Comfort Tiffany Foundation. His exhibition *Presences: Black and White, 1978–80* at the Marisa del Re Gallery, New York, which includes *Square of Light* (cat. 34), is cited by Hilton Kramer in *The New York Times* as the year's best exhibition.[12]

1982 Invited by the international committee of the Venice Biennale to exhibit in the main pavilion. His work *Symphony No. 1, The Transcendental* (p. 15, fig. 4) travels to the Haus der Kunst, Munich, Germany, for the exhibition *Amerikanische Malerei: 1930–1980*.

1983 Invited to be the Milton Avery Distinguished Professor of Arts at Bard College. Included in the exhibition *Modern American Painting* at the Museum of Fine Arts, Houston. He experiments with nontraditional forms of paint and materials, expanding his decades-long interest in collage to produce heavily textured constructions that integrate found and everyday objects into painted assemblages. These works integrate materials as wide-ranging as string, metal washers, discarded paper cups, Styrofoam, and children's plastic toys, combining the practices of painting and sculpture.

1985 Represented in *Flying Tigers: Painting and Sculpture in New York, 1939–46* at the David Winton Bell Gallery, Brown University, Providence.

1986 Solo exhibition *Transcending Abstraction: Richard Pousette-Dart, Painting, 1939–1985* is held at the Museum of Art, Fort Lauderdale. Participates in *The Spiritual in Art: Abstract Painting, 1890–1985* at the Los Angeles County Museum of Art.

1987 Included in the Solomon R. Guggenheim Museum's exhibition *Peggy Guggenheim's Other Legacy*.

1989 Receives the Individual Visual Artist Award from the Arts Council of Rockland County, New York.

1990 The Indianapolis Museum of Art (now Newfields) organizes *Richard Pousette-Dart: Retrospective* that travels to the Detroit Institute of Art; the Columbus Museum of Art, Georgia; and the Phillips Gallery, Washington DC. The most extensive retrospective during his lifetime, the exhibition features 111 works of art, and he is commissioned to create the monumental bronze door *Cathedral*, based on the painting of the same title, for the museum's pavilion designed by Edward Larrabee Barnes.

1992 Richard Pousette-Dart dies on October 25, in New York City.

Fig. 11

Richard Pousette-Dart, Suffern, New York, ca. 1980, photograph by Michael Evans

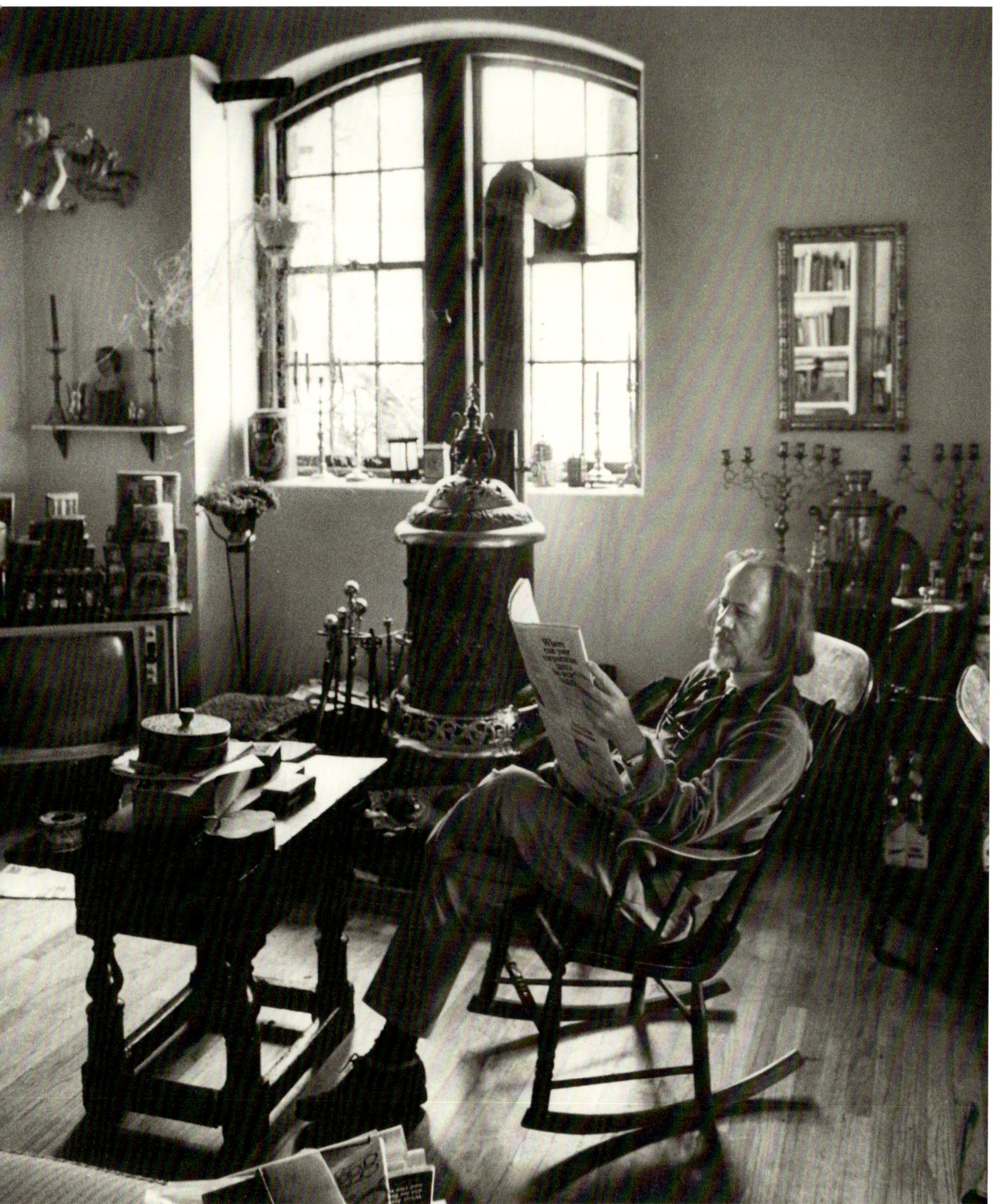

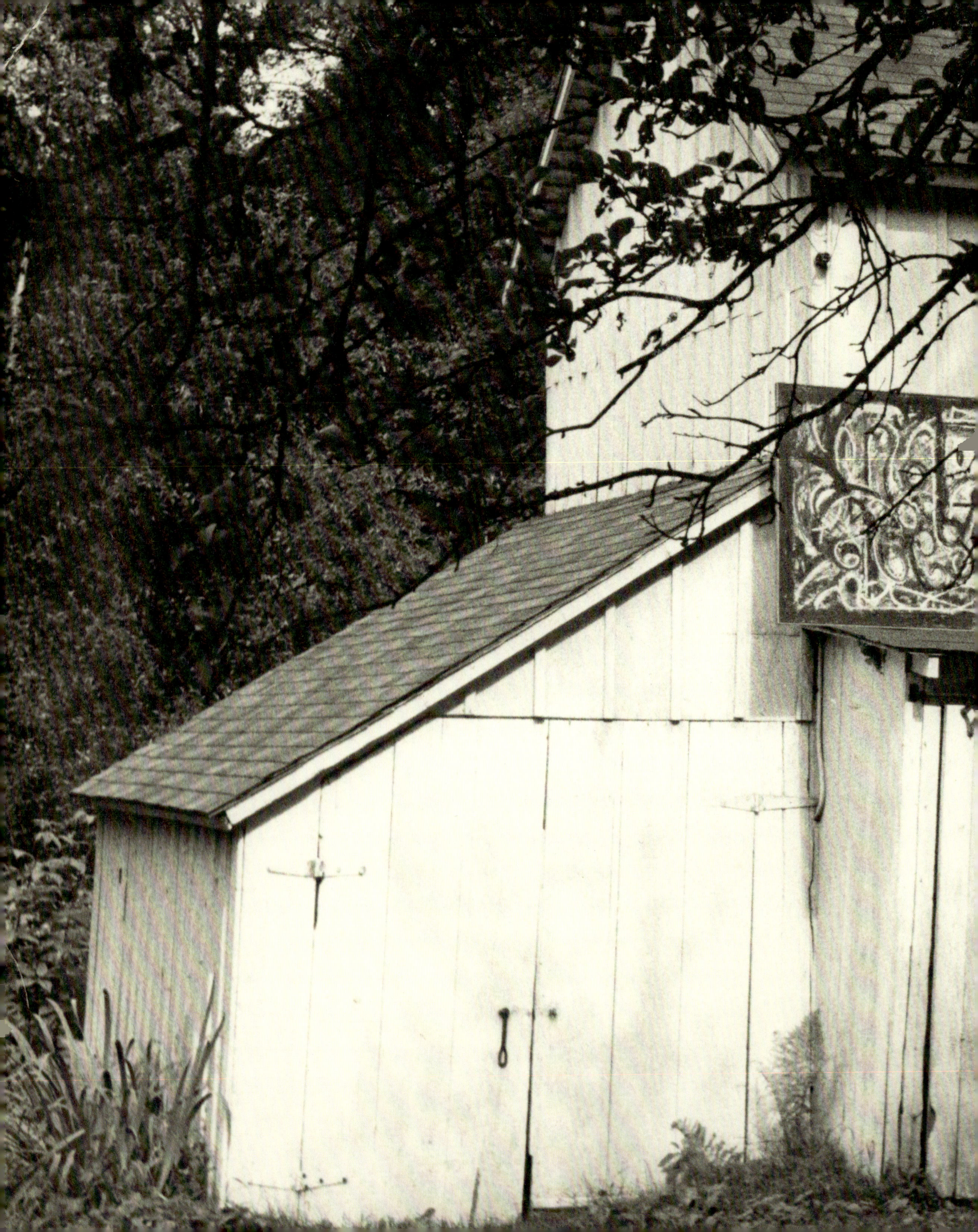

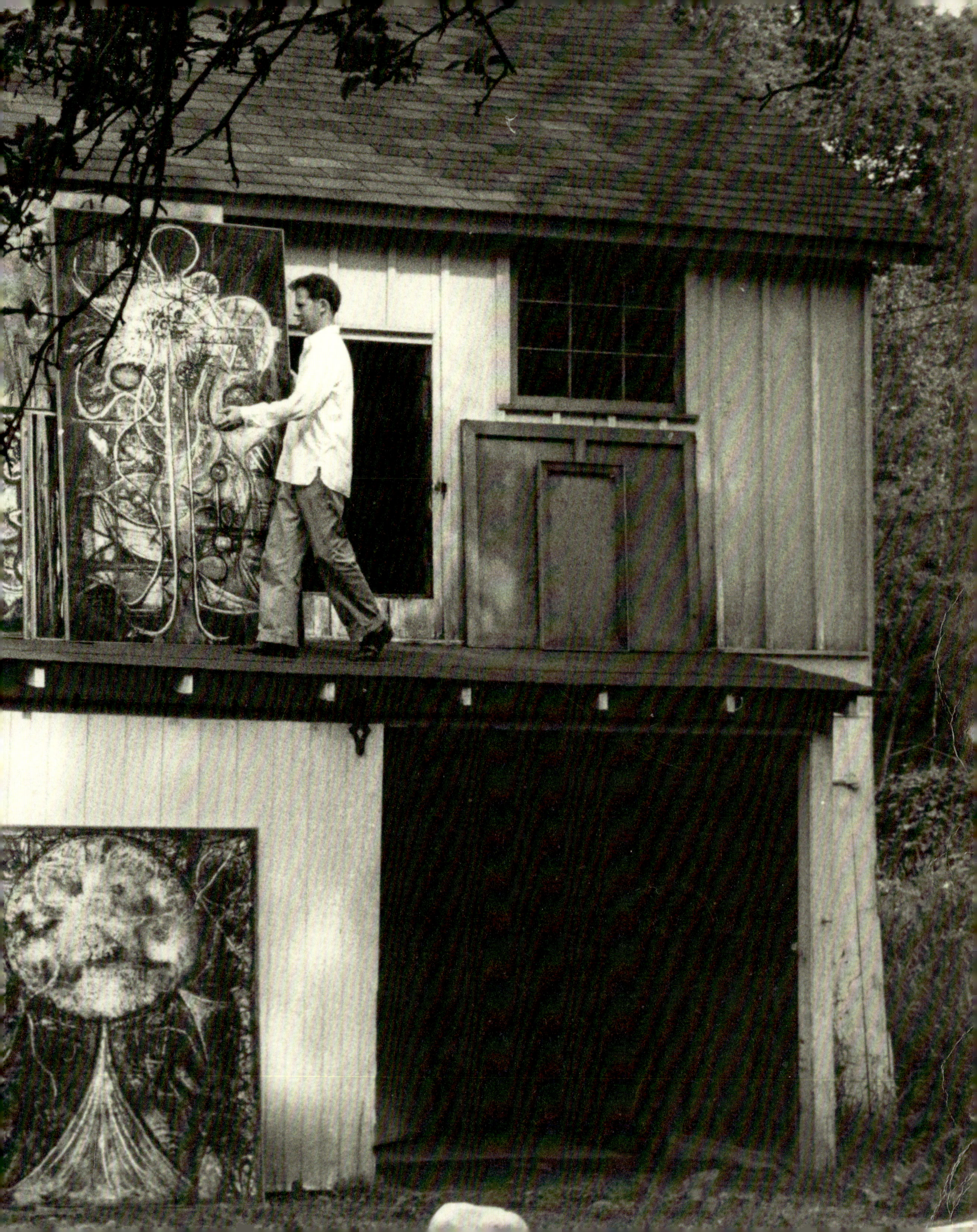

Four Texts by Richard Pousette-Dart

Charles H. Duncan

The son of a poet and art writer, Richard Pousette-Dart populated more than three hundred studio notebooks with poems, philosophical passages, practical notes, and sketches over the course of his lengthy career. His extensive paper archive similarly contains drafts of statements that explicate his philosophical, political, and artistic views. As an integral component of his visual art practice, writing allowed him to define and express the terms of his artistic vision. In several bodies of work, including a series of paintings titled *Hieroglyphs*, modes of textual expression even served as a source of visual imagery. Reproduced in this catalog are four key texts by Pousette-Dart that articulate key areas of interest.

"Plans for Work," drafted during the early 1940s, likely served as a simple template to seek funding for Pousette-Dart's developing art practice. Focusing on the brasses he had recently begun to create, the artist speaks enthusiastically about the curative power of these objects and champions a notion of wholeness that he deemed essential to the purpose of art. The desire to write a compendium titled *The Spirit of Forms* underscores the importance of both word and image within his creative process.

By his teens, Richard Pousette-Dart had fully embraced an anti-military stance. As the events of World War II unfolded in Europe, he became active within anti-war groups in New York, attending gatherings at Quaker meeting houses through which he came to assimilate Biblical cadences into the style of his writing (even though he was not interested in traditional Christian practice). "Love Is the Conqueror," from the early 1940s, presents a series of commandments that foreground the concept of "love" within the human condition, and advocates for peace through a philosophical, rather than political, outlook. Here, Pousette-Dart offers a Transcendentalist's worldview, asserting that "God is the harmonious rightness of cosmic being."

In January 1951 Richard Pousette-Dart was invited to address the student body at the School of the Museum of Fine Arts, Boston, regarding the exhibition *American Abstractionists, Loaned by the Betty Parsons Gallery*. An appeal from Joseph Gropper, organizer of the exhibition, noted, "This show of advanced abstract painters will afford an opportunity for many Bostonians to see the dynamic, original paintings which are rarely seen in this area but for small reproductions seen in magazines.

I believe an event of this type will stimulate not only the students of this school, but many of the visitors to our gallery."[1] The exhibition, which included Pousette-Dart's 1950 canvas *Quartet* (private collection), was a radical display of advanced strains of painting by New York School artists including Jackson Pollock, Theodoros Stamos, Hedda Sterne, Mark Rothko, Sonja Sekula, Calvert Coggeshall, Boris Margo, Ad Reinhardt, Bradley Walker Tomlin, and John Stephan.

Pousette-Dart's talk, delivered the same week as Nina Leen's now-iconic photograph *The Irascibles* was published in *Life* magazine (see p. 35, fig. 1), is a key statement concerning Abstract Expressionism. Keenly aware of his audience of young artists, Pousette-Dart framed his philosophies of art-making in a manner that would inform his approach to teaching during the following decades. In the talk, he chose to draw together thoughts recorded in his private studio notebooks over the years. The resulting text advocates for the transformative nature of the creative process and anchors Pousette-Dart's own orientation and methods as a painter within an expansive artistic universe guided by individual freedom. The introduction, especially, is notable for its comments on the nature and status of abstraction during this transformative moment for American art.

A year later, Pousette-Dart embraced the opportunity for his painting *The Magnificent* (cat. 19) to be included in the Union Theological Seminary's group exhibition *Contemporary Religious Art*, which ran from December 1 to 16, 1952. Invited to deliver an address as part of exhibition programming, he crafted a well-articulated statement drawn from his studio notebooks titled "What Is the Relationship Between Religion and Art?" Having become recognized by this time for the spiritual overtones of his art (frequently associated erroneously with organized religious movements), he used this address to clarify his positions, equating creative practice with religious experience, and celebrating the unique quality of art to transcend simple explanations and rationales.

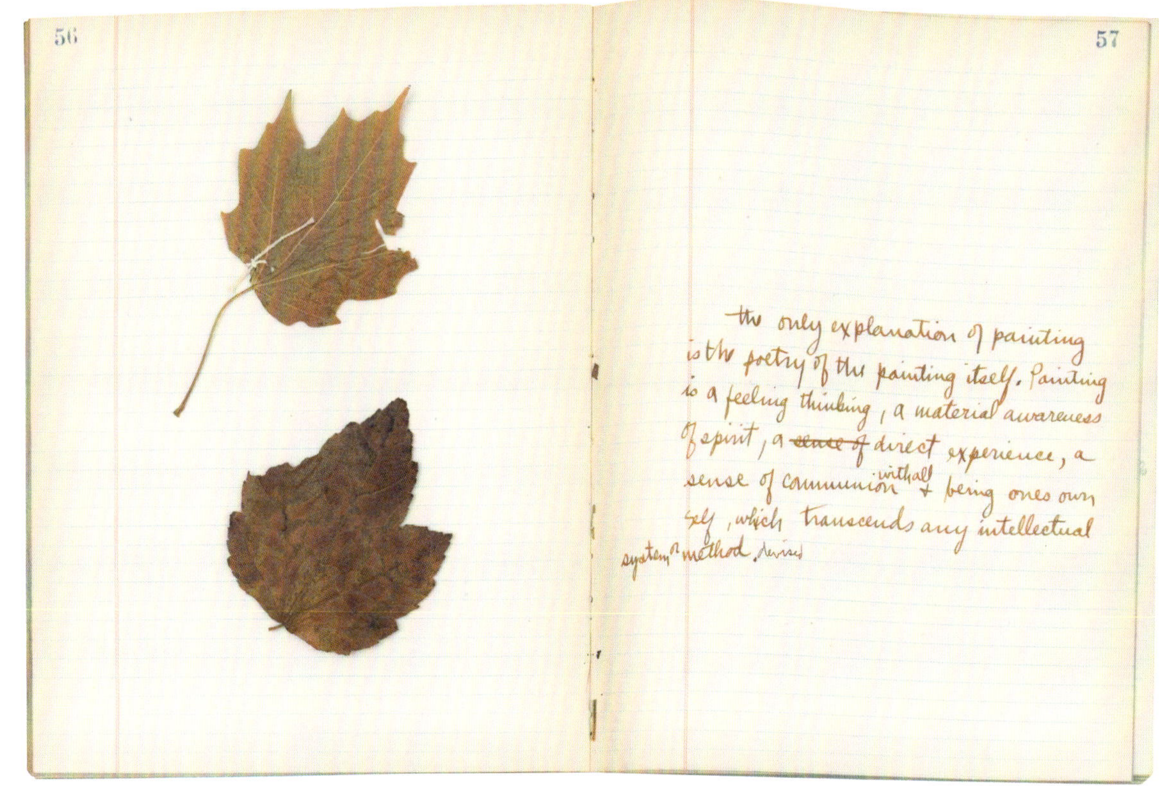

Fig. 1

Notebook B-400, 1940s, pp. 56–57, Richard Pousette-Dart Foundation

Plans for Work

Richard Pousette-Dart

To continue to evolve and perfect by hand a body of work in brass that in its form and quality is unique. I believe that these brasses hold real significant beauty for all who truly behold them. They have proved themselves in many instances to be therapeutic and inspirational.

I wish to mature many of the forms I have already found and to find many new ones. I wish to embody in them a feeling of the wholeness and harmony of life.

I wish to prepare a book to be published called *The Spirit of Forms*.

My ultimate purpose as an artist is a whole realization of myself in my work that is a happy communion with all humanity. Art for me is a craft and that craft is an art.

My work would mainly be carried on at my permanent New York studio, 436 East Fifty-Sixth Street.

Love Is the Conqueror

Richard Pousette-Dart

I am one who believes in the constructive use of energy.
Life is creative energy.
Life is love; there is no other life.
Life constructs; hate destroys.
The *means* whereby we go about forming our lives determines the *ends* at which we must soon inevitably arrive.
Peace *cannot* be won by war.
War begets war, and more war, and only war.
Militarism – war – hate and murder.
Warriors die by means of hate which their own fear evokes.
Peace is limitless love.
Love is the creator.
Love knoweth not hate.
Love is life; hate is death.
Love *cannot* be drafted nor mobilized.
Love *is* peace.
Peace is *never* military.
Love doth not bargain.
Love giveth *all* of itself away.
Love is life; life is love – deathless and without end.
True humanity is the loving brotherhood of human beings.
God is the harmonious rightness of cosmic being.
Human Rightness is the loving Goodness of compassionate Reason.
Love is the *Will to do good* which reconciles all difference unto God.

Boston
January, 1951

I come here not as a speaker but as a painter who is willing to *attempt* to clarify my own picture of art, *so-called* modern, *so-called* abstract art.

I say so-called modern art because a true work of art is eternal in its meaning, it is timeless.

I say so-called abstract, because *all* art is abstract, and all *abstract* work must *needs be* of nature because we are of nature. Art is universal in its form. It matters not to true contemporary or universal truth whether it is a painting of a face, a figure, a tree, a cube, a line, a circle, or a biormorphic structure of paint, for art work lives by the vitality of its own living significance and the integrity of its being.

I feel very *happy* that you are having the opportunity of seeing these paintings here, for I feel they are of the utmost significance in the art world today.

These paintings do not represent a trend or a movement but simply *happen* to be together in these various galleries. These artists do not wish to be labeled nor should they be, for their true relationship is extremely separate and they relate to one another only as all things do to the universe. Each is a unique personality coming to grips with universal creative problems and energy in his or her own way.

(2)

And yet with these artists as well as those in other galleries and those who have never exhibited or have exhibited in isolated places, *I believe a renaissance exists today which is felt and shared by all*. *There is the birth of a new spirit and a new significance of form*. There is a vitality and beauty in art today as penetrating and as all embracing as has ever existed.

Art lies behind the cloth of outer things, it is always deeper than appearance and must be delved for. Within or about every living work of art, or thing of beauty, or fragment of life, there is some strange inner kernel which cannot be reached with explanations, clarifications, examinations, or definitions. This kernel remains beneath, behind, beyond. It is this dimensionless particle which lives, breathes, and means. It is this living particle which makes art mystical, unknown, real, and experienceable.

Art for me is the heavens forever opening up, like assymetrical, unpredictable, spontaneous kaleidoscopes. It is magic, it is joy, it is gardens of surprise and miracle. It is energy, impulse. It is question and answer. It is transcendental reason. It is total in its spirit.

The best way to *talk* about art is to work. The best way to *study* art is to work. The best way to *think* about art is to work. Art is to *work hard* and one day it may become art and you may discover the artist that you are.

(3)

Painting is ultimately the by product of a living experience which the artist has had. Painting is a reflection of being. Painting is a window upon creative personality. It is a doorway to liberation. It is a spark from an invisible pointless central fire. Painting is a pure and rich experience. It is a quest for reality.

The order of a work is due to its harmony and integration, not to its complex number of parts *or* superficial simplicity.

Painting must have form but not necessarily in any preconceived or set known way. However, works that sustain us and endure with us do so because of the universal significance of their form. We have not learned to respect form as a thing in itself as we always have done with sound for we have been and still are under the yoke of the greek prejudice.
The authenticity of painting lies in the joy that the artist has in his own work as an end in itself.

Paintings cannot be explained, they have a life and a being and a voice of their own, they must be personally *experienced*. We must go to them and look at them, and within them find reflected our own experience, as well as inspiration for our own growth, if we care to adventure, for in truth, art is the adventure of our own growth, whether we are acting in the capacity of creating or whether we are acting in the creative capacity of appreciation.

(4)

Paintings are like people, they must be approached, won friendship with, known and loved as people are if they are to open up and reveal themselves. Paintings have being, they are mysteriously alive and to be understood, we must see them in a living way, we must approach them *without* preconceptions and with a true attitude of awe and wonder. Try to experience their inner meaning, the secret gift which each work has to give us, if we but have the humility and love to receive it.

We must learn to look past titles and labels and names and reputations. Real painting is untitled and unsigned, it is a flower of its own self, its self is its own signature and its own name. There is a need for reeducation amongst most adults to see with true feeling rather than with the intellect, for only by seeing thus can we penetrate to what really matters. Most people do not feel deeply enough to see through their own eyes, they merely recognize what their minds have catalogued and been told to remember, they need to open up their souls to the vast untouched and unknown wonders of their own feeling. I speak of feeling here as the whole intuitional sensibility.

True appreciation of paintings is a participation and a creative experience with the creator. To see paintings we must recreate them.

(5)

To know what a true artist knows, cannot be learned short of a lifetime devoted to art. There are no easy ways, methods, techniques, or short cuts. I believe anyone can create reality who perserveres and will not give up at any point, who is willing to pay the price. The price of art of any real significance is a long hard struggle with renunciations and sacrifice. But for one who perceives a glimmer of its inner total beauty, for one who realizes its wondrous meaning, there *is* no sacrifice but continuous and unending joy. The artists reward is in his own work. In truth, a reward of transcendental ecstasy. Art is a total answer.

The artist must beware of all schools, isms, creeds, or *entanglements* which would tend to make him other than himself. He must stand *alone*, free and open in all directions for exits and entrances, and yet with all freedom, he must be solid and real in the substance of his form.

I do not admire facility nor easy effects. I am an enemy of all virtuosity. I like what is sincerely won from the central core of character. The love of *doing* should find its own technique for only in this way is originality born. Imitation can be taught, but art must be inspired.

(6)

My own painting is a direct experience with my materials. I never make preliminary sketches or plans but approach my canvas directly, usually with whatever I happen to feel at the moment, however sometimes I begin with felt remembrances of form experience, impressions which built up in my mind and have remained over months or years, derived from places I have been, people, faces, figures, forms, things, little odd things I have seen, emotions I have felt; these often are for me a beginning impulse. However once the painting is begun, it seems to rise above these things, (whatever they are) and grows or evolves of its own accord, and has a creative logic of its own structure and counterpoint.
I am then as a witness to my own birth or a vigilant helper always at contact, that is, when the painting is successful, and for me a painting is always eventually successful, and this goes on, sometimes a moment, sometimes actually years, until the work becomes, is born to its own self-being, becomes a thing within itself, is inevitable.

My paintings grow as in a garden together yet in many different directions and ways. I work over and over old paintings, some of them today have twenty or thirty paintings beneath. Sometimes it seems as if I just paint one painting, from a white canvas through an experience of colors and lines and then back to white again, yet always enriched, nothing is ever lost, everything that is achieved, even though it does not appear to be present, remains, and some of my canvasses are just this, a final experience of white on white having

(7)

travelled through and through, like an area of ground wherein much dancing has occurred. Sometimes I feel my paintings exist not on canvas but in space, like musical progressions, religious in a passionate sense, *not* in any secular or representational sense.

And so with these other painters, some work primarily with washes and stains, some with trowel and knife, some with spillings and bleedings, some with pouring and splashing and some with pasting and tearing, and some primarily with mind and idea, what does it matter; each follows his own path to what most satisfies his inner need and his immagination, and all are equally valid and significant in their different meanings of provocation and purpose.

I believe in the unknown artists. I come upon their work here and there. I am *thrilled* to know that such things exist and are being done; there is so much that we do not see or hear about, and yet there are so many magical moments being created. I believe in these unknowns, I have faith in their possibilities as much as I have in the wonderful works which are already before us. There is genius among you, maybe you do not know of it, but it is there, it is evolving, growing, and at *one* moment it will spring free and affect all our lives.
There is genius in *every one of us* waiting to be born, to be awakened, and liberated.

(8)

Everyone needs to adventure to discover his own sensibility and his own form, to begin, no matter how poorly at first, to speak out of his own soul, to make a music of his own sounds, a poem of his own words, a painting of his own lines, colors and forms.

Paintings are a presence, they are best known by the spirit they leave with us after we have left them.

This little I have said, may, I hope, provoke you further to your own stimulation, belief, vitality and growth in whatever direction your personality is meant.

Typescript of the 1951 Boston speec
Richard Pousette-Dart Foundation

Address to Students at the School of the Museum of Fine Arts, Boston, January 1951

Richard Pousette-Dart

I come here not as a speaker but as a painter who is willing to *attempt* to clarify my own picture of art, *so-called* modern, *so-called* abstract art.

I say so-called modern art because a true work of art is eternal in its meaning; it is timeless.

I say so-called abstract, because *all* art is abstract, and all *abstract* work must *needs* *be* of nature because we are of nature. Art is universal in its form. It matters not to true contemporary or universal truth whether it is a painting of a face, a figure, a tree, a cube, a line, a circle, or a biomorphic structure of paint, for artwork lives by the vitality of its own living significance and the integrity of its being.

I feel very *happy* that you are having the opportunity of seeing these paintings here, for I feel they are of the utmost significance in the art world today.

These paintings do not represent a trend or a movement but simply happen to be together in these various galleries. These artists do not wish to be labeled, nor should they be, for their true relationship is extremely separate and they relate to one another only as all things do to the universe. Each is a unique personality coming to grips with universal creative problems and energy in his or her own way.

And yet with these artists as well as those in other galleries and those who have never exhibited or have exhibited in isolated places, I believe a renaissance exists today which is felt and shared by all. There is the birth of a new spirit and a new significance of form. There is a vitality and beauty in art today as penetrating and as all-embracing as has ever existed.

Art lies behind the cloth of outer things; it is always deeper than appearance and must be delved for. Within or about every living work of art, or thing of beauty, or fragment of life, there is some strange inner kernel which cannot be reached with explanations, clarifications, examinations, or definitions. This kernel remains beneath, behind, beyond. It is this dimensionless particle which lives, breathes, and means. It is this living particle which makes art mystical, unknown, real, and experienceable.

Art for me is the heavens forever opening up, like asymmetrical, unpredictable, spontaneous kaleidoscopes. It is magic; it is joy; it is gardens of surprise and miracle. It is energy, impulse. It is question and answer. It is transcendental reason. It is total in its spirit.

The best way to *talk* about art is to work. The best way to *study* art is to work. The best way to *think* about art is to work. Art is to *work hard*, and one day it may become art and you may discover the artist that you are.

Painting is ultimately the by-product of a living experience which the artist has had. Painting is a reflection of being. Painting is a window upon creative personality. It is a doorway to liberation. It is a spark from an invisible pointless central fire. Painting is a pure and rich experience. It is a quest for reality.

The order of a work is due to its harmony and integration, not to its complex number of parts *or* superficial simplicity.

Painting must have form but not necessarily in any preconceived or set, known way. However, works that sustain us and endure with us do so because of the universal significance of their form. We have not learned to respect form as a thing in itself as we always have done with sound, for we have been and still are under the yoke of the Greek prejudice.
The authenticity of painting lies in the joy that the artist has in his own work as an end in itself.

Paintings cannot be explained; they have a life and a being and a voice of their own; they must be personally *experienced*. We must go to them and look at them, and within them find reflected our own experience, as well as inspiration for our own growth, if we care to adventure, for in truth, art is the adventure of our own growth, whether we are acting in the capacity of creating or whether we are acting in the creative capacity of appreciation.

Paintings are like people; they must be approached, won friendship with, known, and loved as people if they are to open up and reveal themselves. Paintings have being; they are mysteriously alive, and to be understood we must see them in a living way. We must approach them *without* preconceptions and with a true attitude of awe and wonder. Try to experience their inner meaning, the secret gift which each work has to give us, if we but have the humility and love to receive it.

We must learn to look past titles and labels and names and reputations. Real painting is untitled and unsigned; it is a flower of its own self; its self is its own signature and its own name. There is a need for reeducation amongst most adults to see with true feeling rather than with the intellect, for only by seeing thus can we penetrate to what really matters. Most people do not feel deeply enough to see through their own eyes; they merely recognize what their minds have catalogued and been told to remember; they need to open up their souls to the vast untouched and unknown wonders of their own feeling. I speak of feeling here as the whole intuitional sensibility.

True appreciation of paintings is a participation and a creative experience with the creator. To see paintings we must recreate them.

To know what a true artist knows cannot be learned short of a lifetime devoted to art. There are no easy ways, methods, techniques, or shortcuts. I believe anyone can create reality who perseveres and will not give up at any point, who is willing to pay the price. The price of art of any real significance is a long, hard struggle with renunciations and sacrifice. But for one who perceives a glimmer of its inner total beauty, for one who realizes its wondrous meaning, there *is* no sacrifice but continuous and unending joy. The artist's reward is in his own work, in truth, a reward of transcendental ecstasy. Art is a total answer.

The artist must beware of all schools, isms, creeds, or *entanglements* which would tend to make him other than himself. He must stand *alone*, free and open in all directions for exits and entrances, and yet with all freedom, he must be solid and real in the substance of his form.

I do not admire facility nor easy effects. I am an enemy of all virtuosity. I like what is sincerely won from the central core of character. The love of *doing* should find its own technique for only in this way is originality born. Imitation can be taught, but art must be inspired.

My own painting is a direct experience with my materials. I never make preliminary sketches or plans but approach my canvas directly, usually with whatever I happen to feel at the moment; however, sometimes I begin with felt remembrances of form experience, impressions which built up in my mind and have remained over months or years, derived from places I have been, people, faces, figures, forms, things, little odd things I have seen, emotions I have felt; these often are for me a beginning impulse. However, once the painting is begun, it seems to rise above these things (whatever they are) and grows or evolves of its own accord and has a creative logic of its own structure and counterpoint.

I am then as a witness to my own birth or a vigilant helper always at contact, that is, when the painting is successful, and for me a painting is always eventually successful, and this goes on, sometimes a moment, sometimes actually years, until the work becomes, is born to its own self-being, becomes a thing within itself, is inevitable.

My paintings grow as in a garden together yet in many different directions and ways. I work over and over old paintings; some of them today have twenty or thirty paintings beneath. Sometimes it seems as if I just paint one painting, from a white canvas through an experience of colors and lines and then back to white again, yet always enriched; nothing is ever lost; everything that is achieved, even though it does not appear to be present, remains, and some of my canvasses are just this, a final experience of white on white having traveled through and through, like an area of ground wherein much dancing has occurred. Sometimes I feel my paintings exist not on canvas but in space, like musical progressions, religious in a passionate sense, *not* in any secular or representational sense.

And so with these other painters, some work primarily with washes and stains, some with trowel and knife, some with spillings and bleedings, some with pouring and splashing and some with pasting and tearing, and some primarily with mind and idea, what does it matter: each follows his own path to what most satisfies his inner need and his imagination, and all are equally valid and significant in their different meanings of provocation and purpose.

I believe in the unknown artists. I come upon their work here and there. I am *thrilled* to know that such things exist and are being done; there is so much that we do not see or hear about, and yet there are so many magical moments being created. I believe in these unknowns; I have faith in their possibilities as much as I have in the wonderful works which are already before us. There is genius among you; maybe you do not know of it, but it is there; it is evolving, growing, and at *one* moment it will spring free and affect all our lives.
There is genius in *every one of us* waiting to be born, to be awakened and liberated.

Everyone needs to adventure to discover his own sensibility and his own form, to begin, no matter how poorly at first, to speak out of his own soul, to make a music of his own sounds, a poem of his own words, a painting of his lines, colors, and forms.

Paintings are a presence; they are best known by the spirit they leave with us after we have left them.

This little I have said may, I hope, provoke you further to your own stimulation, belief, vitality, and growth in whatever direction your personality is meant.

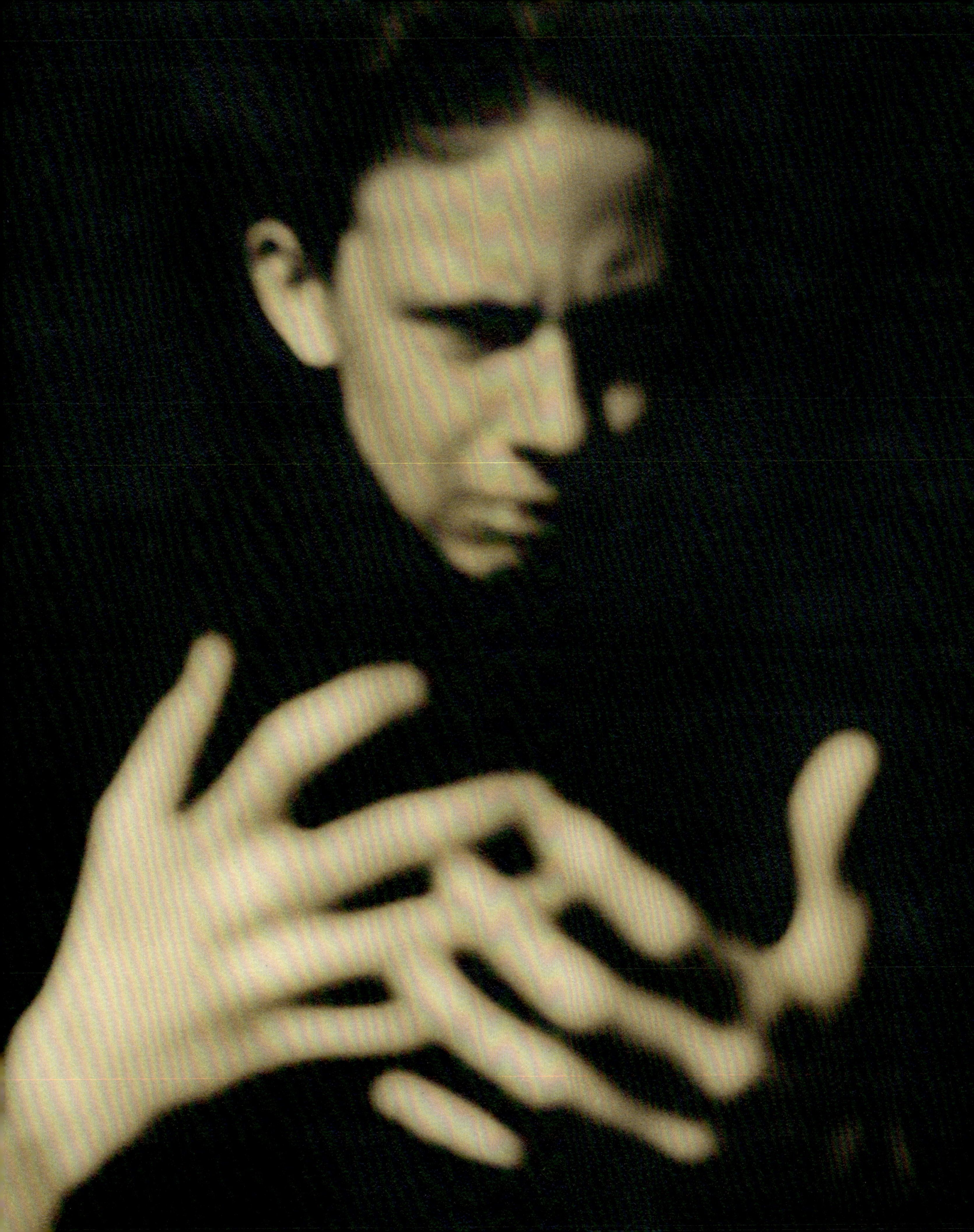

Talk Given at the Union Theological Seminary, New York, December 2, 1952

What Is the Relationship Between Religion and Art?

Richard Pousette-Dart

I am excited and impressed by this show. I feel it is pertinent and timely; it seems sensitively chosen, extremely well hung, presented with feeling, and as a whole to be decided direction and purpose.

I consented to speak on this controversial subject because it is above all meaningful to me. I tried to write a speech, but after much writing I decided simply to read several fragments from my notebooks.

My definition of religion amounts to art, and my definition of art amounts to religion. I don't believe you can have one significantly without the other. Art and religion are the inseparable structure and living adventure of the creative.

By the creative I mean the most penetrating, bursting through the particular to the universal, from the one thing to all things, from time to the eternal spirit. Religion is what dynamically realizes all within itself; it sees not in parts but in wholes. It is what passionately loves and emanates a feeling of aspiration and inspiration. It is what is directly in contact with the ultimate or absolute and gives us bridge to the unknown within ourselves. Solid of form and free of spirit, it is timeless within the eternal present.

Every work is potentially religious but only becomes realized in itself and meaningful when it sufficiently burns its way through into its own reality. It is this quality of penetration or intensity which I call religious in an art sense and art in a religious sense. I believe in doing it yourself, and no intellectual premise can suffice to attain religion or art apart from the deep and actual coming to grips with one's own work or one's own soul.

Art is always mystical in its final meaning; it is structure which stands up by the presence and significance of its own reality. It is a thing within itself, mirroring different things to different minds, stemming from and in accord with every work ever created, a thing of awe and wonder and whose meaning is the measure of man's estate on earth.

Art is not a matter of perfect technique; it is life of the soul. It is my belief that ultimate reality can only be achieved by a passionate burning devotion to one's work.

Participation is the only explanation of art. Only another work of art clarifies or explains a work of art, and the only critic who tells no lies is the one whose criticism is the creation of his own work.

It does not matter how an artist works, whether he uses circles of squares or flowers or people, whether he works thick or thin, large or small, with metal, plaster, stone, or wood, tightly delicate filigree or bold and sparse and spacious, and whether he suggests with subtle shade or knifelike edge; it is the inner life of the work which breathes and truly means.

The artist is the only moral man because he alone overcomes fear and has the courage to create his own soul and to live by means of the light of it.

I do not consider that a religious theme or subject ever makes for a true religious work of art. Only an inner reality achieved through a lifelong devotion of love can make for a work of art.

Religious art for our time is, as it is in any time, the purest to itself, turning and returning us to our own beings.

I feel that what I write and read here is always a besideness, and I return as always back to the painting or work of art itself which is the only explanation of religion in art.

↖ p. 12
Richard Pousette-Dart: The Abstract Transcendentalist
– Charles H. Duncan

1
Richard Pousette-Dart, untitled, Boston address (January 1951), Richard Pousette-Dart Papers, 1918–2015, bulk 1930s–1992, Richard Pousette-Dart Foundation. The full text is reprinted in this catalog on pages 205–11.

2
John Keats, "Ode on a Grecian Urn," in *Ode on a Grecian Urn, The Eve of St. Agnes, and Other Poems*, Boston 1901, 14.

3
First published in 1841, *Self-Reliance* advocates for individualism and encourages readers to trust and follow their own instincts and intuition rather than blindly adhere to the will of others. Emerson draws supporting examples from major historical figures ranging from Aristotle to Napoleon Bonaparte to show how their success and genius came from originality and innovation, instead of conformity.

4
Lowery Stokes Sims provides an overview of major critical assessments in "Richard Pousette-Dart and Abstract Expressionism: Critical Perspectives," in Cambridge 2018, 16–23.

5
An unpublished letter from Richard Pousette-Dart to Flora Pousette-Dart (January 5, 1939), states, "I have just finished reading all of Emerson's essays again and I must say I have never read anything better. There is passage upon passage of perfection. His philosophy is so sound sometimes it is infuriating." Flora Pousette-Dart papers, 1895–1975, Richard Pousette-Dart Foundation.

6
The image, with varying captions, was widely published by East Coast newspapers in September 1928.

7
Richard Pousette-Dart, "My Life in Brief" (September 4, 1937), Richard Pousette-Dart papers, bulk 1930s–1992, Richard Pousette-Dart Foundation.

8
While Richard Pousette-Dart possessed a deep familiarity with Vorticist sculpture and Nathaniel Pousette-Dart referenced Gaudier in *Art and Artists of Today* in 1937, it is improbable that either had the opportunity to encounter actual works by the artist in New York City apart from Gaudier's *Birds Erect*, sold from the John Quinn Collection in 1927, and a collection of minor sketches that were exhibited in 1935. The most likely visual source was H. S. Ede's annotated and illustrated compilation of Gaudier's correspondence, *Savage Messiah*, published in several editions during the 1930s.

9
See Clive Bell, *Art*, London 1914. Bell postulated that for an object to be deemed a work of art it required potential to provoke aesthetic emotion in its viewer, a quality he termed "significant form." Bell argued that aesthetic emotion arises from certain combinations of color and line, not from the subject matter of works of art.

10
Three of Dubuffet's paintings were included in the exhibition *Paintings from Paris* at the Pierre Matisse Gallery, New York, May 1946. Pousette-Dart's library contains an original catalog for this exhibition.

11
"Gorky has taken a turn for the better – from Picasso through Miro – Kandinsky and Matta. Gottlieb and Rothko are doing some interesting stuff – also Pousette-Dart." Letter from Jackson Pollock to Louis Bunce (June 2, 1946), Louis Bunce papers, 1890s–1983, Archives of American Art, Smithsonian Institution, Washington, DC.

12
Henry McBride, "In the Abstract," in *New York Herald Tribune* (January 21, 1945).

13
See Lucy Kent, "Kindred Spirits: The Spiritual Alliance of Richard Pousette-Dart and Jim Ede," in Cambridge 2018, 121–30, here 121.

14
See, for instance, Mikhail Sergeev, *The Crucifixion in Painting: From the Middle Ages to Post-Modernism*, Boston 2023.

15
Richard Pousette-Dart, quoted in David Porter, *Personal Statement: Painting Prophecy 1950*, exh. brochure, Gallery Press, Washington, DC, 1945.

16
Undated statement, Richard Pousette-Dart papers, 1918–2015, bulk 1930s–1992, Richard Pousette-Dart Foundation. Additionally, at the Union Theological Seminary in 1952, Pousette-Dart addressed the spiritual nature of his work via the question "What is the relationship between religion and art?" and offered the response, "Art is always mystical in its final meaning, it is structure which stands up by the presence and significance of its own reality. It is a thing within itself, mirroring different

things to different minds, stemming from and in accord with every work of art ever created, a thing of awe and wonder and whose meaning is the measure of man's estate on earth." Richard Pousette-Dart papers. The full text is reprinted in this catalog on pages 213–15.

17
Rosalind Browne, "The Modern and the Ancient," in *New York Star* (November 19, 1948), Pleasure Section, 8.

18
Ralph Waldo Emerson, *Ralph Waldo Emerson Essays and Lectures*, New York 1983, 10.

19
Richard Pousette-Dart, interview by Richard Kaplan 1989, VHS video, Richard Pousette-Dart Foundation.

20
Martica Sawin, "The Pleasure of Non-Associative Seeing," in *Richard Pousette-Dart: Painting/Light/Space*, exh. brochure, Bowdoin College Museum of Art, Brunswick, ME, 2018, 7; https://media.pousette-dartfoundation.org/pdf/Pousette-Dart-Bowdoin-2018.pdf (accessed on December 5, 2024).

21
Richard Pousette-Dart, quoted in Utica 2014, 13.

22
Pousette-Dart 1951 (see note 1).

23
Pousette-Dart, quoted in Higgins 1987, 112.

24
Richard Pousette-Dart, Notebook B-270, Richard Pousette-Dart Foundation.

25
Joachim Homann, "Pousette-Dart as Mentor and Maverick," in Brunswick 2018 (see note 20), 11.

26
Richard Pousette-Dart, interview by Richard Kaplan 1989, VHS video, Richard Pousette-Dart Foundation.

27
This has been worded in various iterations; see, for example, *Richard Pousette-Dart: The Healing Circles*, dir. Laurie Marshall, 2016, https://vimeo.com/user60954230 (accessed on December 17, 2024), 7:15.

28
Pousette-Dart 1951 (see note 1).

↖ p. 22
"A Garden of Forms": The Art of Richard Pousette-Dart
– Megan Kincaid

1
In unpublished correspondence, Charles Duncan has noted, for instance, that Pousette-Dart's forms can often be discovered in the legs of furniture or lamps collected by both him and his wife, Evelyn, and inherited from his parents, who also avidly collected antiques. Similarly, I also observe the resemblance between vertical lines that end in curling capitals and the ornamental patterns on wrought iron gates typical to New York City, which the artist photographed.

2
Adolph Gottlieb and Mark Rothko promulgated this generational phrase, "tragic and timeless," in "Statement," in *New York Times* (June 13, 1943).

3
See, for instance, a brief discussion of Clive Bell's concept of "significant form" in Joanne Kuebler, "Concerning Richard Pousette-Dart," in Indianapolis 1990, 26.

4
Pousette-Dart's culturally enriching childhood included access to aesthetic and philosophical discourses from a young age. By the time he entered the New York School, he was among the youngest but also the most assured of its practitioners.

5
Richard Pousette-Dart, Notebook B-280, 1990s, 74, Richard Pousette-Dart Foundation.

6
Robert Storr, "No Joy in Mudville: Greenberg's Modernism Then and New," in *Modern Art and Popular Culture: Readings in High & Low*, exh. cat., Museum of Modern Art, New York 1990, 165.

7
Pousette-Dart 1938.

8
Richard Pousette-Dart, interview with Albert Perret, ca. 1974, 22, Richard Pousette-Dart papers, 1918–2015, bulk 1930s–1992, Richard Pousette-Dart Foundation.

9
Lippard 1975, 53.

10
Pousette-Dart ca. 1974 (see note 8), 22.

11
Richard Pousette-Dart, Notebook B-97, 116, Richard Pousette-Dart Foundation.

12
This series, debuted at the Betty Parsons Gallery in 1955, continued periodically throughout the 1980s.

13
Christopher Rothko imparted this interpretation in a recent audio guide produced for the Museum of Modern Art, New York; https://www.moma.org/audio/playlist/297/28 (accessed on December 10, 2024).

14
David Anfam, "Section II: Murals, War, Action and Energy," in Anfam, *Jackson Pollock's Mural: Energy Made Visible*, London 2015, 55.

15
Letter to Richard W. Dart from the Federal Communications Commission Engineering Department, June 3, 1936. Richard Pousette-Dart papers, 1918–2015, bulk 1930s–1992, Richard Pousette-Dart Foundation.

16
I sincerely thank Charles Duncan for sharing his sharp observations about the

circuitry systems and step-by-step manuals that Pousette-Dart used to assemble appliances and kept among his possessions until his death.

17
Pousette-Dart ca. 1974 (see note 8), 31.

18
Kuebler 1990 (see note 3), 35.

19
Richard Pousette-Dart, Notebook B-280, 1990s, 203, Richard Pousette-Dart Foundation.

20
Richard Pousette-Dart, untitled statement, notebook, 1938, loose-leaf page, Richard Pousette-Dart papers, 1918–2015, bulk 1930s–1992, Richard Pousette-Dart Foundation.

21
D. Kenneth Winebrenner, *Jewelry Making: A Guide to Creative Contemporary Work in Jewelry*, Scranton, PA, 1953, 54, 155.

22
A list of prices for individual brasses can be found in a studio notebook titled "Brasses." Richard Pousette-Dart papers, 1918–2015, bulk 1930s–1992, Richard Pousette-Dart Foundation.

23
In one of the artist's studio notebooks, he even listed the various "entrances & exits" he pictorialized: "walls touchstones mirrors windows doorways." Notebook B-280, 1990s, 215, Richard Pousette-Dart Foundation.

24
Flora Pousette-Dart, preface to *I Saw Time Open*, New York 1947, 7.

25
Letter from Richard Pousette-Dart to Flora Pousette-Dart (August 2, 1940), Flora Pousette-Dart papers, 1895–1975, Richard Pousette-Dart Foundation.

↖ **p. 34**
Richard Pousette-Dart: The Conscientious Creator
– Beatriz Cordero Martín

1
Richard Pousette-Dart, untitled Boston address (January 1951), Richard Pousette-Dart Papers, 1918–2015, bulk 1930s–1992, Richard Pousette-Dart Foundation. The full text is reprinted in this catalog on pages 205-11.

2
"Art has to do with who we are," he would often say. See "Richard Pousette-Dart Interviewed by Avis Berman," New York City, 1986, typescript, 36, Richard Pousette-Dart Foundation.

3
Richard Pousette-Dart, talk at the symposium "Abstract Expressionism: Idea and Symbol," University of Virginia, 1979, typescript, Richard Pousette-Dart Foundation.

4
"18 Painters Boycott Metropolitan; Charge 'Hostility to Advanced Art,'" in *New York Times* (May 22, 1950), 1 and 15; and "The Irascible Eighteen," in *New York Herald Tribune* (May 23, 1950).

5
"Irascible Group of Advanced Artists Led Fight Against Show," *Life* 30,3 (January 15, 1951), 34.

6
Bradford R. Collins, "The Irascibles, *Life* Magazine, and the Story of Modern Art," in Madrid 2020, 46–75, here 49.

7
The exhibition included Jackson Pollock, Ad Reinhardt, Mark Rothko, Theodoros Stamos, and Hedda Sterne, all of whom had signed the letter, as well as other artists such as Joseph Albers.

8
Pousette-Dart 1951 (see note 1), 1.

9
For instance, concurrently with the exhibition at the Boston Museum of Fine Arts (January 12–30, 1951), and also significantly in a venue outside New York City, "Seventeen Modern American Painters" at the Frank Perls Gallery in Beverly Hills (January 11 – February 7, 1951) showed William Baziotes, de Kooning, Adolph Gottlieb, Hans Hofmann, Robert Motherwell, Pollock, Pousette-Dart, Reinhardt, Rothko, Stamos, Sterne, Clyfford Still, Mark Tobey, and Bradley Walker Tomlin (all of them painters who had signed the protest letter in 1950), together with Lee Gatch, Morris Graves, and Roberto Matta. In parallel, a comprehensive project at the Museum of Modern Art in New York, *Abstract Painting and Sculpture in America* (January 23–March 25, 1951), exhibited twelve of the eighteen Irascibles. Even five years before the Irascibles controversy, Pousette-Dart was included in *Personal Statement: Painting Prophecy, 1950*, an exhibition at the David Porter Gallery in Washington, DC (February 1945) that included the works of Baziotes, Motherwell, Pollock, Rothko, Gottlieb, de Kooning, Tomlin, Pousette-Dart, Louise Bourgeois, and Jimmy Ernst, all of them future members of the "Irascibles" group. (Bourgeois would be one of the ten sculptors to sign the protest letter to Roland L. Redmond five years later).

10
Their collaboration began in 1948, and she also showed Newman, Pollock, Rothko, and Still.

11
Pousette-Dart had his first solo exhibition at Art of This Century in 1947. Baziotes, Gottlieb, Motherwell, Pollock, Reinhardt, and Stamos would also work with Peggy Guggenheim.

12
As explained by Irving Sandler, "The Irascible Eighteen," in *The Irascibles*, exh. cat., CDS Gallery, New York 1988, unpaginated.

13
Interview with Richard Kaplan, June 7, 1990, video, reel 2, Richard Pousette-Dart Foundation.

14
See Lowery Stokes Sims, "Pousette-Dart and Abstract Expressionism: Critical Perspectives," in Venice 2007, 24–35.

15
In a conversation with Irving Sandler, Motherwell explained, "I think my generation is the most tragic that has ever existed. American painting is really after a sense of the tragic... If [it] is really tragic, then it may be great. If not then it is of no consequence." Sandler adds that "The compelling evocation of the tragic mood in the work of Pollock, Still, de Kooning, Rothko, and Newman was responsible for their growing recognition," while "The he-man stance of the Abstract Expressionism (much as it was shot through with anxiety) may have prompted them to enlarge their canvases and to shun decoration and elegance. It also led, if inadvertently, to the marginalization of the lyrical paintings of male first-generation Abstract Expressionists." See Irving Sandler, *Abstract Expressionism and the American Experience: A Reevaluation*, Lenox, MA, and New York 2009, 30, 222.

16
According to Peter Plagens, Pousette-Dart "was a spiritual optimist" as opposed to most Abstract Expressionists, who were "agnostic pessimists." See Peter Plagens, "Richard Pousette-Dart: Metropolitan Museum of Art," in *Artforum International* 36,7 (March 1998), 94. Ken Johnson labeled Pousette-Dart a Symbolist rather than an expressionist because "his art was driven less by darkness and conflict than by light, harmony and spiritual optimism." See Ken Johnson, "Driven by Light and Dark," in *New York Times* (November 4, 1997), E3.

17
Art therapist Christine Randolph studied with Richard Pousette-Dart at Sarah Lawrence College between 1971 and 1972. See *Richard Pousette-Dart: The Healing Circles*, dir. Laurie Marshall, 2016, https://vimeo.com/user60954230 (accessed on January 28, 2025).

18
"The authenticity of painting lies in the joy that the artist has in his own work as an end in itself." See Pousette-Dart 1951 (see note 1), p. 3.

19
Pousette-Dart's notebooks have notations such as "the passionate love of beauty which goes on forever" or "divine is the beauty held within craftmanship." See Notebook B-1, 1930s, Richard Pousette-Dart Foundation.

20
David Anfam has noted that it was Pousette-Dart's "religious mysticism which separated him from the mainstream." See David Anfam, *Abstract Expressionism*, London 1990, 86.

21
Richard Pousette-Dart, notebook entry, 1939, quoted in Indianapolis 1990, 11.

22
Favoring risk-taking attitudes that went beyond the canvas, such as alcohol abuse, were habits associated with the normative masculinity at the time, and his refraining from such behavior set Pousette-Dart aside from most of his peers. As noted by W. Jackson Rushing III, "Pousette-Dart: 'Forever is Now,'" in *Art on Paper* (March–April 2002), 53.

23
"I was very much–as is well known–I was a loner. I was not–I didn't move in the groups, with the other artists." See Berman 1986 (see note 2), 52.

24
Kaplan 1990 (see note 13).

25
This "leads to war as surely as does manufacture of munitions as a private, profit-making business." Richard Pousette-Dart, "I Have Been Called a Dreamer," in *The Beechwood Tree* 17,1 (February 1935), 7–10, here 7.

26
Ibid., 8–9. He defended these ideas all his life, stating in 1986 "it is shocking what sheep most people are. We tell them to go off to war, and they go off to war." See Berman 1986 (see note 2), 33.

27
Pousette-Dart started teaching in 1950 at the New School for Social Research. He also taught at Sarah Lawrence, Columbia University, the Art Students League, and Bard College. Christopher Wool and Ai Weiwei are among the artists who received Pousette-Dart's guidance.

28
There are a couple of versions of this letter in the archives dated July 17 and July 23, 1941. Richard Pousette-Dart papers, 1918–2015, bulk 1930s–1992, Richard Pousette-Dart Foundation.

29
Letter from Richard Pousette-Dart to Sidney Clark, Chief Clerk, Local Board 40 (August 6, 1941), Richard Pousette-Dart papers, 1918–2015, bulk 1930s–1992, Richard Pousette-Dart Foundation. The Archives

of the Pousette-Dart Foundation keep numerous letters, some of which include poems and small drawings.

30
Between 1959 and 1972, the period during which the United States was involved in the Vietnam War, and for the first time in American history there were more registrants claiming conscientious objection status than joining the army. In the 1960s several Abstract Expressionists joined anti-war organizations, including Motherwell, Reinhardt, and Rothko, who were among those who participated in the Writers and Artists Protest. However, Pousette-Dart's commitment to pacificism was unparalleled among his fellow artists.

31
Literature on the subject reveals that conscientious objection was not yet fully regulated during World War II and the law was inconsistently applied by the local authorities. According to Sibley and Jacob, about 50,000 men in the United States were conferred status as conscientious objectors during World War II, half of whom were taken to the Army to perform some kind of noncombatant work, and 14,000 were considered unfit for combat due to medical reasons. According to the Selective Training and Service Act of 1940, the other 12,000 were classified 4-E or eligible to do works for the benefit of the country (from planting trees or canning foods to testing experimental drugs). The first Civilian Public Service camp opened in May 1941, before the United States was at war. See Mulford Q. Sibley and Philip E. Jacob, *Conscription of Conscience: The American State and the Conscientious Objector, 1940–1947*, Ithaca, NY, 1953, 83, 487. According to a blog on the website of the Center on Conscience and War, 75,000 men filed for CO status during World War II (see "The Heritage of American Objectors: Conscience Since Colonial Times," February 15, 1992, https://centeronconscience.org/heritage-american-objectors/ [accessed on January 28, 2025]). The Committee for Amnesty estimates that over 6,000 objectors to war and conscription were imprisoned during World War II. Over 4,000 of them were held in federal prisons even after the war was over.

32
Together with Thoreau, other significant references for pacificism in American literature before the Vietnam War were Stephen Crane's novel *The Red Badge of Courage* (1895) and Mark Twain's satirical prose poem *The War Prayer*, left unpublished at the time of its author's death in 1910 due to fear of it being considered sacrilegious. *Peace with Honor* (1934) by British writer A. A. Milne analyzed reasons to resist war from the perspective of a World War I veteran, and it had a certain repercussion in the US. Although not necessarily anti-war works, John Dos Passos's *Three Soldiers* (1921) and Ernest Hemingway's *A Farewell to Arms* (1929) soon became classic examples of novels that offered a realistic view of World War I.

33
Pousette-Dart was in touch with many organizations such as the War Resisters League, United Pacifist Committee, Committee for Amnesty, Break-with-Conscription Committee, National Council Against Conscription, and the National Council to Repeal the Draft. He joined the Committee to Defend America by Waging Peace and regularly received publications such as the *Conscientious Objector*, *Fellowship*, *World Peace Car Bulletin*, *World Brotherhood Mobilization*, *Amnesty Bulletin*, and *The Absolutist* (official organ of the Absolutist War Objectors Association). He was also part of the Committee for Amnesty, with whom writers and activists such as John Dos Passos, A. Philip Randolph, Joseph Schlossberg, and Dwight Macdonald were also involved. Macdonald was a speaker in protests against conscription (1947), and his series of articles in *Politics* on the responsibility of intellectuals inspired Noam Chomsky's famous essay of the same title, published on February 23, 1967, in *The New York Review of Books*.

34
"Painting is a reflection of being." See Pousette-Dart 1951 (see note 1), 3. "Art has to do with who we are," he would often say. See Berman 1986 (see note 2), 36.

35
Berman 1986 (see note 2), 36.

36
Pousette-Dart 1951 (see note 1), p. 2.

↖ p. 42
Through the Artist's Lens: Richard Pousette-Dart as a Photographer
– Charles H. Duncan

1
Unpublished letter from Richard Pousette-Dart to Philip Verre, curatorial coordinator at the Solomon R. Guggenheim Museum (September 1, 1979), Richard Pousette-Dart Papers, 1918–2015, bulk 1930s–1992, Richard Pousette-Dart Foundation.

2
Variations of photograms appeared as early as the nineteenth century. It is highly likely that Pousette-Dart

was familiar with Man Ray's photograms, called rayographs, that became well-known in New York through the monograph *Man Ray: Photographs 1920–1934 Paris*, Hartford 1934.

3
Lynn T. Morgan's photographic studio, located on West Forty-Seventh Street in Manhattan, specialized in retouching black-and-white and color photographs. Pousette-Dart was employed there for several years, approximately between 1938 and 1941.

4
Nathaniel Pousette-Dart, "A Tact That Should Be a Bible: A Review of John D. Graham's Book Systems and Dialectics of Art," in *Art and Artist of Today* 1,3 (September–October 1937), 14, 16.

5
Letter from John Graham to Richard Pousette-Dart (May 17, 1939), Richard Pousette-Dart Papers, 1918–2015, bulk 1930s-1992, Richard Pousette-Dart Foundation.

6
Evelyn Pousette-Dart in an interview with Charles H. Duncan, New York City, 2011.

7
Richard Pousette-Dart, Notebook B-318, Richard Pousette-Dart Papers, 1918–2015, bulk 1930s–1992, Richard Pousette-Dart Foundation.

8
Letter, Corinne Michelle West to Richard Pousette-Dart (February 1945), Richard Pousette-Dart Papers, 1918–2015, bulk 1930s–1992, Richard Pousette-Dart Foundation.

9
Judith Higgins, "To the Point of Vision: A Profile of Richard Pousette-Dart," in Fort Lauderdale 1986, 13–24, here 20.

10
Edna Bennett, "Pousette-Dart, *Photography*'s 1953 Picture Contest Uncovers a Modern Painter with a Gadgeteer's Yen for Cameras," in *Photography* (January 1954), 44–49, 212, here 49.

↖ **p. 186**
Chronology
– Charles H. Duncan

1
April 26, 1928, Richard Pousette-Dart papers, 1918–2015, bulk 1930s–1992, Richard Pousette-Dart Foundation.

2
Indianapolis 1990, 15.

3
Jermund 1937, 13.

4
Richard Pousette-Dart, quoted in Utica 2014, 13.

5
"Spontaneous Kaleidoscopes," *Look* 15,21 (October 9, 1951), 96–98.

6
Undated manuscript, Richard Pousette-Dart papers, 1918–2015, bulk 1930s–1992, Richard Pousette-Dart Foundation.

7
Edna Bennett, "Pousette-Dart: PHOTOGRAPHY'S 1953 Picture Contest Uncovers a Modern Painter with a Gadgeteer's Yen for Cameras," *Photography* 34,1 (January 1954), 44–49, here 112.

8
Gage 1955, 14, 16.

9
New School Bulletin 16,19 (January 5, 1959), 110.

10
Undated draft document "To the Curriculum Committee," Richard Pousette-Dart papers, 1918–2015, bulk 1930s–1992, Richard Pousette-Dart Foundation.

11
Richard Pousette-Dart, interview by Richard Kaplan 1989, VHS video, Richard Pousette-Dart Foundation.

12
Hilton Kramer, "Art View: A Year of Treasures, Revisions and Trends," in *New York Times* (December 27, 1981), D27.

↖ **p. 200**
Four Texts by Richard Pousette-Dart
– Charles H. Duncan

1
Letter to Richard Pousette-Dart from Joseph Groper (January 5, 1951), Richard Pousette-Dart papers, 1918–2015, bulk 1930s–1992, Richard Pousette-Dart Foundation.

Cat. 1
Beneath the Sea, 1939
Oil and ink on parchment
59.7 × 59.7 cm
RICHARD POUSETTE-DART FOUNDATION

Cat. 2
Animal Forms, 1939–43
Oil on linen
97.8 × 106.7 cm
RICHARD POUSETTE-DART FOUNDATION

Cat. 3
Undulation, 1941–42
Oil and sand on linen
121.9 × 238.8 cm
PRIVATE COLLECTION

Cat. 4
Spirit Adagio, 1943
Oil on linen
124.5 × 109.2 cm
PRIVATE COLLECTION

Cat. 5
The Center, 1943
Oil on linen
141 × 121 cm
PRIVATE COLLECTION

Cat. 6
Crucifixion, Comprehension of the Atom, 1944
Oil on linen
197.2 × 124.8 cm
PRIVATE COLLECTION

Cat. 7
Eagle's Nest, 1946
Oil on linen
91.8 × 101.3 cm
RICHARD POUSETTE-DART FOUNDATION

Cat. 8
Forestness, 1946
Oil and sand on linen
109.2 × 130.8 cm
RICHARD POUSETTE-DART FOUNDATION, COURTESY OF PACE GALLERY

Cat. 9
Blue Transition / Convolutions of Music, 1942–43
Ink and gouache on paper
57.8 × 79.4 cm
RICHARD POUSETTE-DART FOUNDATION

Cat. 10
Partitions of Unity, 1940s
Ink and gouache on paper
57.8 × 79.7 cm
RICHARD POUSETTE-DART ESTATE

Cat. 11
Icarus, 1951
Oil on linen
105.4 × 183.5 cm
PRIVATE COLLECTION

Cat. 12
Creature of Clouds, 1951
Steel wire and sheet metal, painted gray
125.7 × 71.1 × 35.6 cm
RICHARD POUSETTE-DART ESTATE

Cat. 13
Chavade, 1951
Oil and pencil on canvas
135.6 × 245 cm
MUSEUM OF MODERN ART, NEW YORK, PHILIP JOHNSON FUND, INV. 503.1969

Cat. 14
White Etude, 1952
Oil and graphite on linen
125.7 × 93.3 cm
COLLECTION OF LAURA ARRILLAGA-ANDREESSEN AND MARC ANDREESSEN

Cat. 15
Presence Number 5, 1950–54
Oil and graphite on linen
164.5 × 135.5 cm
PRIVATE COLLECTION

Cat. 16
Descending Bird Forms, 1950–51
Oil and graphite on panel
121.9 × 243.8 cm
PRIVATE COLLECTION, COURTESY AMERICAN CONTEMPORARY ART GALLERY, MUNICH

Cat. 17
Arc of the Bird, 1951
Steel wire and objets trouvés, painted orange
124.5 × 58.4 × 35.6 cm
RICHARD POUSETTE-DART ESTATE

Cat. 18
Illumination Gothic, 1955
Oil on canvas
182.9 × 135.9 cm
PRIVATE COLLECTION

Cat. 19
The Magnificent, 1950–51
Oil on canvas
219.2 × 111.8 cm
WHITNEY MUSEUM OF AMERICAN ART, NEW YORK, GIFT OF MRS. ETHEL K. SCHWABACHER, INV. 53.43

Cat. 20
Illumination Vertical, 1958
Oil on linen
199.4 × 123.2 cm
PRIVATE COLLECTION

Cat. 21
Window Number 4, 1948–50
Oil on linen
134.6 × 111.8 cm
PRIVATE COLLECTION

Cat. 22
Window, Cathedral, 1941–42
Oil on linen
133.7 × 92.7 cm
PRIVATE COLLECTION

Cat. 23
Amaranth, 1958
Oil on canvas
192.6 × 164.5 cm
BROOKLYN MUSEUM, NEW YORK, GIFT OF DR. AND MRS. ARTHUR E. KAHN, INV. 87.239

Cat. 24
Pillars of Odysseus, 1949
Oil enamel and collage on canvas
203.2 × 88.9 cm
PRIVATE COLLECTION

Cat. 25
Naples Fugue, 1982
Acrylic on canvas
138 × 183 cm
PRIVATE COLLECTION

Cat. 26
Fountains of Penelope,
1960–62
Oil on linen
189.2 × 144.1 cm
PRIVATE COLLECTION

Cat. 27
Gothic #2, 1951–52
Oil on linen
152.4 × 127 cm
PRIVATE COLLECTION

Cat. 28
Apparition, 1951
Steel wire and objets trouvés
223.5 × 55.9 × 53.3 cm
RICHARD POUSETTE-DART FOUNDATION

Cat. 29
Black and White Fugue,
1979–80
Acrylic on canvas
108 × 217.2 cm
RICHARD POUSETTE-DART FOUNDATION

Cat. 30
Black and White Arch #1,
1978–80
Acrylic on linen
248.9 × 127 cm
RICHARD POUSETTE-DART ESTATE

Cat. 31
Black and White Arch #2,
1978–80
Acrylic on linen
248.9 × 127 cm
RICHARD POUSETTE-DART ESTATE

Cat. 32
Wall of Signs, 1979–80
Acrylic on linen
Four panels:
each 213 × 128 cm
PRIVATE COLLECTION

Cat. 33
Spiral of Darkness,
1979–80
Acrylic on linen
182.9 × 137.2 cm
RICHARD POUSETTE-DART FOUNDATION

Cat. 34
The Square of Light,
1979–80
Oil on linen
228.6 × 228.6 cm
RICHARD POUSETTE-DART ESTATE

Cat. 35
Circles, One Spiral, 1978
Acrylic on paper
76.8 × 57.8 cm
RICHARD POUSETTE-DART FOUNDATION

Cat. 36
Carmine, 1977–82
Acrylic on paper
57.5 × 76.2 cm
RICHARD POUSETTE-DART FOUNDATION

Cat. 37
Always the Center, 1978
Acrylic on paper
56.5 × 76.8 cm
RICHARD POUSETTE-DART FOUNDATION

Cat. 38
Micro Black, 1978
Acrylic on paper
57.8 × 76.8 cm
RICHARD POUSETTE-DART FOUNDATION

Cat. 39
Inscribed Landscape, 1979
Acrylic on paper
77.5 × 57.2 cm
RICHARD POUSETTE-DART ESTATE

Cat. 40
Four Quarter Harmony, 1982
Acrylic on paper
57.2 × 76.2 cm
RICHARD POUSETTE-DART ESTATE

Cat. 41
Lost in the Beginning of Infinity, 1991
Acrylic on linen
Diameter: 182.9 cm
PRIVATE COLLECTION, COURTESY AMERICAN CONTEMPORARY ART GALLERY, MUNICH

Cat. 42
Hieroglyph Number 7,
1968–69
Oil on linen
193 × 129.5 cm
RICHARD POUSETTE-DART FOUNDATION

Cat. 43
Presence Number 3, Black, 1969
Oil on linen
203.2 × 203.2 cm
RICHARD POUSETTE-DART ESTATE

Cat. 44
Imploding Black, 1985–86
Acrylic on linen
182.9 × 182.9 cm
RICHARD POUSETTE-DART ESTATE, PACE GALLERY

Cat. 45
Byzantine Cathedral I, II, III, 1988–90
Acrylic on linen
Triptych: each panel 183 × 183 cm
RICHARD POUSETTE-DART ESTATE

Cat. 46
Radiance Number 8 (Imploding Red Light), 1973–74
Acrylic on linen
228.6 × 228.6 cm
RICHARD POUSETTE-DART ESTATE

Cat. 47
Red Presence, 1960
Oil on linen
188 × 142.9 cm
PRIVATE COLLECTION, COURTESY AMERICAN CONTEMPORARY ART GALLERY, MUNICH

Cat. 48
From the Flaming Suns,
1960–64
Oil on linen
133 × 243.8 cm
PRIVATE COLLECTION

Cat. 49
Eye of the Small Suns, 1961–64
Oil on linen
191.1 × 142.2 cm
RICHARD POUSETTE-DART ESTATE

Cat. 50
Sky Presence, Circle, 1963
Oil on canvas
109.2 × 180.3 cm
PRIVATE COLLECTION, COURTESY AMERICAN CONTEMPORARY ART GALLERY, MUNICH

Cat. 51
Meditation on the Drifting Stars,
1962–63
Oil on linen
242.6 × 200.7 cm
RICHARD POUSETTE-DART ESTATE

Cat. 52
Within the Moon, 1962–65
Oil on linen
224.2 × 203.2
PRIVATE COLLECTION

Cat. 53
Celebration Birth, 1975–76
Acrylic on linen
183.2 × 305.1 cm
PRIVATE COLLECTION

Cat. 54–96
Selected *Brasses*, ca. 1939–79
43 hand-cut brass objects
Dimensions variable (between 7 and 14 cm in height)
RICHARD POUSETTE-DART ESTATE

Cat. 97
Nature Studies, 1930s
Photograms
14 × 10.8 cm each
RICHARD POUSETTE-DART FOUNDATION

Cat. 98
Queen Anne's Lace II, mid-1950s
Gelatin silver print
24.4 × 33.7 cm
RICHARD POUSETTE-DART FOUNDATION

Cat. 99
Ice on Branches, mid-1950s
Gelatin silver print
21.9 × 32.7 cm
RICHARD POUSETTE-DART FOUNDATION

Cat. 100
Flora Pousette-Dart, ca. 1935
Gelatin silver print
33.7 × 27 cm
RICHARD POUSETTE-DART FOUNDATION

Cat. 101
Self-Portrait, ca. 1935
Gelatin silver print
24.4 × 18.7 cm
RICHARD POUSETTE-DART FOUNDATION

Cat. 102
Nathaniel Pousette-Dart, 1940s
Solarized gelatin silver print
25.4 × 20.3 cm
RICHARD POUSETTE-DART FOUNDATION

Cat. 103
Saul Leiter, ca. 1947
Gelatin silver print with hand-applied pigment
20 × 25.1 cm
RICHARD POUSETTE-DART FOUNDATION

Cat. 104
John D. Graham, 1940
Gelatin silver print
34 × 25.7 cm
RICHARD POUSETTE-DART FOUNDATION

Cat. 105
Mark Rothko, 1948
Gelatin silver print
25.1 × 20 cm
RICHARD POUSETTE-DART FOUNDATION

Cat. 106
Betty Parsons, 1948
Gelatin silver print
32.7 × 26 cm
RICHARD POUSETTE-DART FOUNDATION

Cat. 107
Barnett Newman, 1948
Gelatin silver print
25.4 × 20 cm
RICHARD POUSETTE-DART FOUNDATION

Cat. 108
Female Study, ca. 1950
Gelatin silver print
25.1 × 20 cm
RICHARD POUSETTE-DART FOUNDATION

Cat. 109
Theodoros Stamos, 1950
Gelatin silver print
27.9 × 35.6 cm
RICHARD POUSETTE-DART FOUNDATION

Cat. 110
Jonathan Pousette-Dart, 1971
Gelatin silver print
35.6 × 27.9 cm
RICHARD POUSETTE-DART FOUNDATION

Cat. 111
Sono Osato, 1960s
Gelatin silver print
34.6 × 25.1 cm
RICHARD POUSETTE-DART FOUNDATION

Cat. 112
Michael West, ca. 1946
Gelatin silver print
10.8 × 14 cm
RICHARD POUSETTE-DART FOUNDATION

Cat. 113
Flaherty Family, 1951
Gelatin silver print
25.6 × 26.4 cm
RICHARD POUSETTE-DART FOUNDATION

Cat. 114
Perle Fine, 1949
Gelatin silver print
35.2 × 27.9 cm
RICHARD POUSETTE-DART FOUNDATION

Cat. 115
Hope Foye, ca. 1950
Gelatin silver print
17.8 × 24.4 cm
RICHARD POUSETTE-DART FOUNDATION

Cat. 116
Robert J. Flaherty, 1951
Gelatin silver print
33.7 × 26 cm
RICHARD POUSETTE-DART FOUNDATION

Cat. 117
Lois Long, ca. 1955
Gelatin silver print
35.2 × 27.9 cm
RICHARD POUSETTE-DART FOUNDATION

Cat. 118
Betty Parsons's Eye, 1948
Gelatin silver print
34.3 × 26.7 cm
RICHARD POUSETTE-DART FOUNDATION

Cat. 119
Betty Parsons with Mask, 1948
Gelatin silver print
39.8 × 33.7 cm
RICHARD POUSETTE-DART FOUNDATION

Cat. 120
Joanna with Cat, 1952
Gelatin silver print
35.6 × 27.9 cm
RICHARD POUSETTE-DART FOUNDATION

Cat. 121
Self-Portrait in Photography Studio, 1951
Gelatin silver print
27.9 × 35.2 cm
RICHARD POUSETTE-DART FOUNDATION

Cat. 122
Self-Portrait, 1985
Gelatin silver print
35.6 × 27.9 cm
RICHARD POUSETTE-DART FOUNDATION

Cat. 123
Alexander (Sasha) Schneider, 1950
Gelatin silver print
33.7 × 26 cm
RICHARD POUSETTE-DART FOUNDATION

Cat. 124
William Congdon, ca. 1948
Gelatin silver print
23.8 × 16.5 cm
RICHARD POUSETTE-DART FOUNDATION

Cat. 125
Roy Eldridge, 1955
Gelatin silver print
35.2 × 27.9 cm
RICHARD POUSETTE-DART FOUNDATION

Cat. 126
Bob Fosse, 1955
Gelatin silver print
27.9 × 35.6 cm
RICHARD POUSETTE-DART FOUNDATION

Cat. 127
Thad Jones, 1955
Gelatin silver print
35.6 × 27.9 cm
RICHARD POUSETTE-DART FOUNDATION

Cat. 128
The Modern Jazz Quartet, 1955
Gelatin silver print
27.9 × 35.2 cm
RICHARD POUSETTE-DART FOUNDATION

Cat. 129
Notebook B-85, 1970s
Mixed media
43.2 × 72.4 cm
RICHARD POUSETTE-DART FOUNDATION

Cat. 130
Notebook B-142, 1970s
Mixed media
Cover: 29.7 × 21.6 cm
RICHARD POUSETTE-DART FOUNDATION

Cat. 131
Notebook B-153, 1970s
Mixed media
22.2 × 28.9 cm
RICHARD POUSETTE-DART FOUNDATION

Cat. 132
Notebook B-180, 1950s
Mixed media
34.9 × 57.2 cm
RICHARD POUSETTE-DART FOUNDATION

Cat. 133
Notebook B-212, 1940s
Mixed media
24.8 × 40.6 cm
RICHARD POUSETTE-DART FOUNDATION

Cat. 134
Notebook B-114, 1940s
Mixed media
22.9 × 33 cm
RICHARD POUSETTE-DART FOUNDATION

Cat. 135
Notebook B-294, 1940s
Mixed media
23.5 × 33 cm
RICHARD POUSETTE-DART FOUNDATION

Cat. 136
Notebook B-87, 1950s
Mixed media
27.9 × 43.2 cm
RICHARD POUSETTE-DART FOUNDATION

Cat. 137
Notebook B-280, 1990s
Mixed media
31.4 × 47.6 cm
RICHARD POUSETTE-DART FOUNDATION

Balken 2005
Debra Bricker Balken, *Abstract Expressionism*, London 2005.

Baro 1982
Gene Baro, "New York Letter: Richard Pousette-Dart," in *Art International* 25,3–4 (March–April 1982), 104.

Bogart 1995
Michele H. Bogart, *Artists, Advertising, and the Borders of Art*, Chicago 1995.

Buffalo 1952
Expressionism in American Painting, exh. cat., Albright Art Gallery, Buffalo 1952.

Cambridge 2018
Richard Pousette-Dart: Beginnings; A Young Abstract Expressionist in New York, exh. cat., Kettle's Yard, Cambridge 2018.

Campbell 1963
Lawrence Campbell, "Pousette-Dart: Circles and Cycles," in *ARTnews* 62,3 (May 1963), 42–45, 56–57.

Chicago 2004
Presence: Paintings and Works on Paper by Richard Pousette-Dart, exh. cat., Valerie Carberry Gallery, Chicago 2004.

Cohane 1982
Rosemary Cohane, "Abstract Sources of an Abstract Expressionist Style: Richard Pousette-Dart," master's thesis, Tufts University, Boston 1982.

Fort Lauderdale 1986
Transcending Abstraction: Richard Pousette-Dart; Paintings 1939–1985, exh. cat., Museum of Art, Fort Lauderdale 1986.

Frankfurt am Main 2001
The Living Edge: Richard Pousette-Dart (1916–1992); Arbeiten auf Papier/Works on Paper, exh. cat., Schirn Kunsthalle, Frankfurt am Main 2001.

Friedman 1978
B. H. Friedman, "'The Irascibles': A Split Second in Art History," in *Arts Magazine* 53,1 (September 1978), 96–102.

Gage 1955
Otis Gage, "Four Artists as Jewelers," in *Craft Horizons* 15,3 (May–June 1955), 14, 16.

Glaude 1996
Marissa Quin Glaude, "Richard Pousette-Dart: Culminating Concepts of Spirituality," master's thesis, George Washington University, Washington, DC, 1996.

Higgins 1987
Judith Higgins, "Pousette-Dart's Windows into the Unknowing," in *ARTnews* 86,1 (January 1987), 108–16.

Hunter/Kuebler 2005
Sam Hunter and Joanne Kuebler, eds., *Richard Pousette-Dart: The New York School and Beyond*, Milan and New York 2005.

Indianapolis 1990
Richard Pousette-Dart, exh. cat., Indianapolis Museum of Art, 1990.

Ithaca 1978
Abstract Expressionism: The Formative Years, exh. cat., Herbert F. Johnson Museum of Art, Ithaca 1978.

Jermund 1937
T. N. Jermund, "Pure Sculpture," in *Art and Artists of Today* 1,4 (November–December 1937), 13.

Kaiserslautern 1997
Malerei des amerikanischen abstrakten Expressionismus: Jackson Pollock, Robert Motherwell, Adolph Gottlieb, Richard Pousette-Dart, exh. cat., Pfalzgalerie Kaiserslautern, 1997.

Kaiserslautern 2013
Richard Pousette-Dart: The Circle—Vom Kreis zum Kosmos, exh. cat., Museum Pfalzgalerie Kaiserslautern, 2013.

Karmel 2020
Pepe Karmel, *Abstract Art: A Global History*, London and New York 2020.

Kimmelman 1992a
Michael Kimmelman, "Richard Pousette-Dart, Abstract Expressionist," in *Baltimore Sun* (October 28, 1992), 10B.

Kimmelman 1992b
Michael Kimmelman, "Richard Pousette-Dart, 76, Dies: An Early Abstract Expressionist," in *New York Times* (October 27, 1992), B8.

Kramer 1991
Hilton Kramer, "The Critic's Eye: 'Five Decades of Richard Pousette-Dart,'" in *MD* 35,1 (mid-January 1991), 12–14, 19.

Kramer 2006
Hilton Kramer, *The Triumph of Modernism: The Art World, 1987–2005*, Chicago 2006.

Kroll 1961
Jack Kroll, "Richard Pousette-Dart: Transcendental Expressionist," in *ARTnews* 60,2 (April 1961), 32–35, 56.

Levin 1980
Gail Levin, "Richard Pousette-Dart's Emergence as an Abstract Expressionist," in *Arts Magazine* 54,7 (March 1980), 125–29.

Lippard 1975
Lucy Lippard, "Richard Pousette-Dart: Toward an Invisible Center," in *Artforum International* 13,5 (January 1975), 51–53.

London 2016
Abstract Expressionism, exh. cat., Royal Academy, London 2016.

Los Angeles 1965
New York School: The First Generation; Paintings of the 1940s and 1950s, exh. cat., Los Angeles County Museum of Art, 1965.

Los Angeles 1987
The Spiritual in Art: Abstract Painting, 1890–1985, exh. cat., Los Angeles County Museum of Art, 1987.

Madrid 2020
The Irascibles: Painters Against the Museum, New York, 1950, exh. cat., Fundación Juan March, Madrid 2020.

Mezei 1978
Arpad Mezei, "New York Report: Richard Pousette-Dart; A Visit in His Studio," in *Onion* (October 1978), 6.

Nadelman 2012
Cynthia Nadelman, "Richard Pousette-Dart," in *ARTnews* 111,2 (February 2012), 104.

New Brunswick 1989
Abstract Expressionism: Other Dimensions; An Introduction to Small Scale Painterly Abstraction in America, 1940–1965, exh. cat., Jane Voorhees Zimmerli Art Museum, New Brunswick, NJ, 1989.

Newport Beach 1986
The Interpretive Link: Abstract Surrealism into Abstract Expressionism; Works on Paper, 1938–1948, exh. cat., Newport Harbor Art Museum, Newport Beach, CA, 1986.

New York 1952
An Exhibition of Contemporary Religious Art and Architecture, exhibition brochure, Union Theological Seminary, Religious Art Committee of the Student Body, New York 1952.

New York 1953
An Exhibition of Contemporary Religious Art, exhibition brochure, Church of the Ascension, New York 1953.

New York 1961
American Abstract Expressionists and Imagists, exh. cat., Solomon R. Guggenheim Foundation, New York 1961.

New York 1963
Richard Pousette-Dart, exh. cat., Whitney Museum of American Art, New York 1963.

New York 1974
Richard Pousette-Dart, exh. cat., Whitney Museum of American Art, New York 1974.

New York 1988
The Irascibles, exhibition brochure, CDS Gallery, New York 1988.

New York 1990
Richard Pousette-Dart: White Paintings, 1950–1959, exh. cat., Marisa del Re Gallery, New York 1990.

New York 1991
Richard Pousette-Dart: Recent Paintings, exh. cat., ACA Galleries, New York 1991.

New York 1995
From Omaha to Abstract Expressionism: American Artists Respond to World War II, exh. cat., Sidney Mishkin Gallery, Baruch College, New York 1995.

New York 1996a
Richard Pousette-Dart: Paintings from the 40's and 50's, exh. cat., Knoedler, New York 1996.

New York 1996b
Richard Pousette-Dart (1916–1992): Photographs, exh. cat., Zabriskie Gallery, New York 1996.

New York 1997
Richard Pousette-Dart (1916–1992), exh. cat., Metropolitan Museum of Art, New York 1997.

New York 1998
Richard Pousette-Dart: The Studio Within, exhibition brochure, Whitney Museum of American Art, New York 1998.

New York 2000
Richard Pousette-Dart: Painting to Paper, Black to White, exh. cat., Knoedler, New York 2000.

New York 2003
Richard Pousette-Dart: Mythic Heads and Forms; Paintings and Drawings from 1935 to 1942, exh. cat., Knoedler, New York 2003.

New York 2005
Richard Pousette-Dart, Presences: The Imploding of Color, exh. cat., Knoedler, New York 2005.

New York 2008
Richard Pousette-Dart: Drawing Form Is a Verb, exh. cat., Knoedler, New York 2008.

New York 2011
Richard Pousette-Dart: East River Studio, exh. cat., Luhring Augustine, New York, 2011.

New York 2014
Richard Pousette-Dart's Luminous Geometry, exh. cat., Pace Gallery, New York 2014.

New York 2015
Richard Pousette-Dart: 1930s, exh. cat., Drawing Center, New York 2015.

New York 2016
Richard Pousette-Dart: The Centennial, exh. cat., Pace Gallery, New York 2016.

New York 2019
Richard Pousette-Dart: Works, 1940–1992, exh. cat., Pace Gallery, New York 2019.

New York 2023
Richard Pousette-Dart, 1950s: Spirit and Substance, exh. cat., Pace Gallery, New York 2023.

Partridge 1993
Deborah Partridge, "In Memory of Richard Pousette-Dart, 1916–1992," in *Arts Happenings* 18, 1 (January–February 1993), 2.

Philadelphia 2014
Full Circle: Works on Paper by Richard Pousette-Dart, exh. cat., Philadelphia Museum of Art, 2014.

Polcari 1991
Stephen Polcari, *Abstract Expressionism and the Modern Experience*, New York 1991.

Polcari 1998
Stephen Polcari, *The Portal: Pousette-Dart*, New York 1998.

Potsdam 2022
The Shape of Freedom: International Abstraction after 1945, exh. cat., Museum Barberini, Potsdam 2022.

Pousette-Dart 1938
Richard Pousette-Dart, "Vortex," in *Art and Artists of Today* 1,5 (February–March 1938), 12.

Providence 1985
Flying Tigers: Painting and Sculpture in New York, 1939–1946, exh. cat., Bell Gallery, Brown University, Providence 1985.

Rhodes 1994
Colin Rhodes, *Primitivism and Modern Art*, London and New York 1994.

Richard 1992
Paul Richard, "The Solitary Visions of Richard Pousette-Dart," in *Washington Post* (February 9, 1992), G1, G9.

Ridgefield 1985
A Second Talent: Painters and Sculptors Who Are Also Photographers, exh. cat., Aldrich Museum of Contemporary Art, Ridgefield, CT, 1985.

Rose 1991
Barbara Rose, "Richard Pousette-Dart: Expression in Paint," in *Journal of Art* 4,3 (March 1991), 50–52.

Rushing 1991
W. Jackson Rushing III, "Richard Pousette-Dart's Spirit-Object," in *Art Journal* 50,2 (Summer 1991), 72–75.

Rushing 1995
W. Jackson Rushing III, *Native American Art and the New York Avant-Garde: A History of Cultural Primitivism*, Austin 1995.

Rushing 2002
W. Jackson Rushing III, "Richard Pousette-Dart: 'Forever Is Now,'" in *Art on Paper* 6,4 (March–April 2002), 52–57.

San Francisco 2006
Transparent Reflections: Richard Pousette-Dart; Works on Paper, 1940–1992, exh. cat., Fine Arts Museums of San Francisco, 2006.

Sawin 1958
Martica Sawin, "Richard Pousette-Dart," in *Arts Magazine* 32,7 (April 1958), 58.

Sawin 1974
Martica Sawin, "Transcending Shape: Richard Pousette-Dart," in *Arts Magazine* 49,3 (November 1974), front cover, 58–60.

Sawin 1995
Martica Sawin, *Surrealism in Exile and the Beginning of the New York School*, Cambridge, MA, and London 1995.

Smith 1991
Maresca Smith, "Richard Pousette-Dart: Pioneering New York School Artist Strives to Express the Spiritual Nature of the Universe," in *Sunstorm Arts Magazine* (Ronkonkoma, NY) 16,4 (October 1991), 3, 16–17.

Utica 2014
Absence/Presence: Richard Pousette-Dart as Photographer, exh. cat., Munson-Williams-Proctor Arts Institute, Utica, NY, 2014.

Venice 2007
Richard Pousette-Dart, exh. cat., Peggy Guggenheim Collection, Venice 2007.

Washington 2010
Pousette-Dart: Predominantly White Paintings, exh. cat., Phillips Collection, Washington, DC, 2010.

Worcester 2001
The Stamp of Impulse: Abstract Expressionist Prints, exh. cat., Worcester Art Museum 2001.

This catalog is published on occasion of the exhibition

POETRY OF LIGHT
RICHARD POUSETTE-DART

Museum Frieder Burda,
Baden-Baden

May 17 to September 14, 2025

Curators
Charles Duncan and
Daniel Zamani

Project Manager
Judith Irrgang

An exhibition of the Museum Frieder Burda, Baden-Baden, in collaboration with the Richard Pousette-Dart Foundation

Executive Board, Stiftung Frieder Burda
Elke Burda
Dominic Kamp
Florian Trott
Daniel Zamani

Advisory Board, Stiftung Frieder Burda
Elke Burda
Klaus-Albrecht Gerstenmaier
Dominic Kamp
Bert Antonius Kaufmann
Christine Macel
Florian Schulte
Gražina Subelytė

MUSEUM FRIEDER BURDA

Managing Director
Florian Trott

Artistic Director
Daniel Zamani

Assistant to the Directors
Saskia Kohler

Head of the Frieder Burda Collection
Judith Irrgang

Research Associate for Exhibitions
Christiane Righetti

Head of Press and Public Relations / Communications
Daniela Sistermanns

Head of Digital Communications
Sophie Mattheus

Head of Finance and Accounting
Jürgen Aßmus

Finance and Administration
Corinna Loedel

Visitor Services / Administrative Assistant
Iris Haedecke

Facility Management and Exhibition Installation
Benedikt Doll,
Josef Merkel, Arnd Merkle,
and Ralph Vollmer

Art Workshop
Kathrin Dorfner

Concept Store
Jens Hofmann, Gertrud Geibel, and Anette Zenner

Ticket Desk
Reiner Schwarz, Susanne Dinse, Diana Snounou, and Barbara Wierzbicki

Cleaning Service
Sabine Huck

CATALOG

Editors for the Stiftung Frieder Burda
Charles Duncan and Daniel Zamani

Editing
Daniel Zamani

Catalog Design
tonique, Frankfurt am Main
Alexander Horn
Lukas Schmidt
Charlotte Singer-Fischer

Essays
Charles Duncan,
Beatriz Cordero Martín,
and Megan Kincaid

Copyediting
Tas Skorupa

Project Management, Hirmer Publishers
Jutta Allekotte

Production, Hirmer Publishers
Hannes Halder

Prepress and Repro
Reproline Genceller, Munich

Fonts
Exposure, 205TF
Gaisyr, Dinamo Typefaces

Paper
Arctic Volume, 150 g/m²

Printing and Binding
Appl Druck GmbH, Wemding

Printed in Germany

Bibliographic information published by the Deutsche Nationalbibliothek

The Deutsche Nationalbibliothek lists this publication in the Deutsche Nationalbibliografie; detailed bibliographic data is available on the Internet at https://www.dnb.de.

© 2025 Museum Frieder Burda, Baden-Baden; Hirmer Verlag GmbH, Munich; and the authors

All internet sources cited (or external links) were current at the time this catalog went to press. The publisher and editors have no influence on subsequent changes. Any liability is therefore excluded.

All rights reserved. No part of this book may be reproduced or transmitted in any form or by any means, electronic or mechanical, including photocopy, recording, or any other information storage and retrieval system, or otherwise without written permission from the publishers. The automated analysis of individual or multiple digital or digitized works for the purpose of obtaining information, in particular about patterns, trends, and correlations, is prohibited (German Copyright Act § 44b: Text and Data Mining).

ISBN 978-3-7774-4522-9
(English edition)

ISBN 978-3-7774-4519-9
(German edition)

Hirmer Publishers (Hirmer Verlag GmbH)

Managing Director
Kerstin Ludolph

Bayerstrasse 57–59
80335 Munich
Germany

www.hirmerpublishers.com
www.hirmerpublishers.co.uk

Image Credits

© for all works by Richard Pousette-Dart: Richard Pousette-Dart Estate/VG Bild-Kunst, Bonn 2025; Kate Rothko-Prizel and Christopher Rothko/VG Bild-Kunst, Bonn 2025: p. 25, fig. 3; Life Picture Collection/Shutterstock: p. 35, fig. 1. © Photo: Digital image, Museum of Modern Art, New York/Scala, Florence: cat. 13; p. 25, fig. 3; Photo: Benjamin Antony Monn, Munich: cats. 16, 41, 47, 50.

Cover image
Cat. 46 (detail)

Black-and-white photographs
Frontispiece: Richard Pousette-Dart in his studio in Monsey, New York, ca. 1957–58, photograph by Arthur Shriftman; pp. 124–25: Selection of Brasses, ca. 1940s, photograph by Richard Pousette-Dart; pp. 184–85: Richard Pousette-Dart in his studio in Suffern, New York, 1963, photograph by Herb Breuer; pp. 198–99: Richard Pousette-Dart at his studio, Sloatsburg, New York, 1951, photograph by Diane and Ray Witlin.

Image details
Image details from works shown in the exhibition and illustrated full-page in the sequence of plates have been used on the following pages: p. 4 (cat. 46), p. 9 (cat. 46), pp. 10–11 (cat. 53), pp. 20–21 (cat. 41), pp. 32–33 (cat. 44), pp. 40–41 (cat. 45), pp. 50–51 (cat. 48), p. 62 (cat. 7), p. 79 (cat. 18), p. 82 (cat. 20), p. 87 (cat. 23), p. 88 (cat. 24), p. 111 (cat. 44), p. 118 (cat. 50), pp. 138–39 (cat. 99), pp. 166–67 (cat. 43), p. 212 (cat. 101), and p. 229 (cat. 42)

Every effort has been made to trace the copyright holders and to obtain permission to reproduce material. Please contact us with enquiries or any information relating to images or copyright holders.

The assertion of claims according to §60h UrhG for the reproduction of pictures of the exhibitions/existing works has been carried out by VG Bild-Kunst.

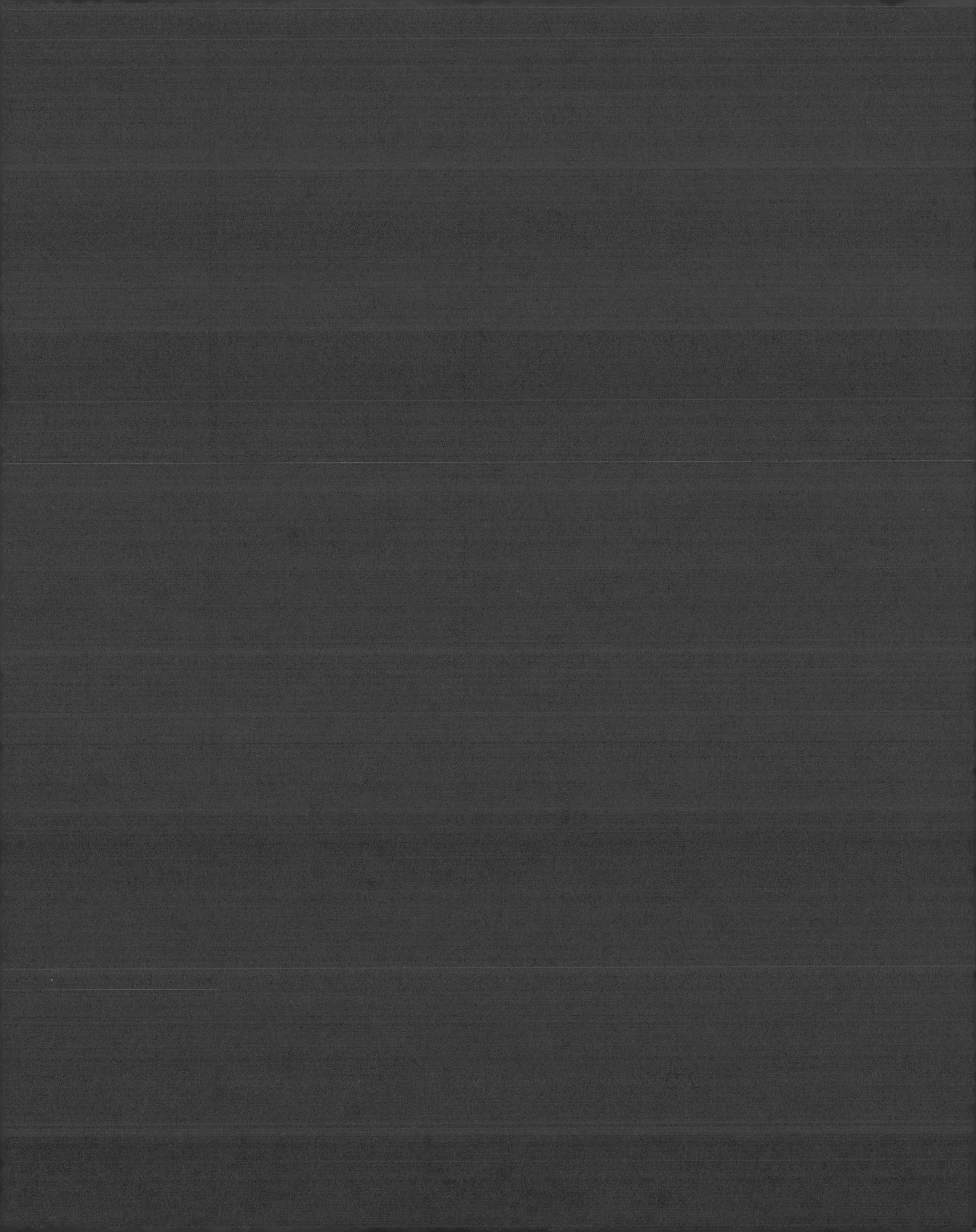